D1646814

THOMAS ROTHERHAM

WITHDRAWN FROM
Thomas Rotherham
College
Learning Resources

ONE WEEK LOAN

FINES: 10P PER DAY IF OVERDUE

Thomas Rotherham College

008914

INFORMATION AT YOUR FINGERTIPS

*Up-to-date and comprehensive, Pitman
Dictionaries are indispensable reference
books, providing clear, crisp explanations
of specialist terminologies in an
easy-to-use format.*

Dictionary of Advertising
Dictionary of Banking
Dictionary of Business Studies
Dictionary of Economics and Commerce
Dictionary of Insurance
Dictionary of Law
Dictionary of Purchasing Supply Management

WITHDRAWN FROM
Thomas Rotherham
College
Learning Resources

DICTIONARY OF PERSONNEL AND HUMAN RESOURCES MANAGEMENT

R BENNETT

Pitman

Pitman Publishing

128 Long Acre, London WC2E 9AN

A Division of Longman Group UK Limited

First published in 1992

© Longman Group UK Limited 1992

British Library Cataloguing in Publication Data

A CIP catalogue record for this book can be obtained from the British Library

ISBN 0 273 03877 X

All rights reserved; no part of this publication may be
reproduced, stored in a retrieval system, or transmitted in any
form or by any means, electronic, mechanical, photocopying,
recording, or otherwise without either the prior written
permission of the Publishers or a licence permitting restricted
copying issued by the Copyright Licensing Agency, 90 Tottenham
Court Road, London W1P 9HE. This book may not be lent, resold,
hired out or otherwise disposed of by way of trade in any form
of binding or cover other than that in which it is published,
without the prior consent of the Publishers.

Typeset, printed and bound in Great Britain

PREFACE

Personnel and human resources management are diverse and extensive subjects which require a familiarity with a wide range of technical terms. This dictionary is intended to help both the student and the practitioner to understand the language of personnel and human resources management, and to assist readers to increase their knowledge of the human resources field. Entries cover the practical and utilitarian aspects of the personnel function (laws and regulations, methods, systems, procedures and techniques), plus broader topics concerned with organisational behaviour, human resources planning, strategy and control. Certain general management terms likely to be encountered by personnel managers in their day-to-day work have also been included.

My thanks are due to Rosalind Bailey, who word-processed the entire manuscript, and to Pitman Publishing for rapidly and efficiently expediting the production of the book. Cross-references are denoted by (qv) and small capitals within and at the ends of entries.

LEARNING RESOURCE CENTRE
THOMAS ROTHERHAM COLLEGE
MOORGATE ROAD
ROTHERHAM S60 2BE
TEL. 0709 828606

A

AAT. *See* ASSOCIATION OF ACCOUNTING TECHNICIANS.

abatement formula. A formula applied in a company pension scheme in order to relate benefits payable under the scheme to ex-employees' state pensions. The effect of an abatement formula is to reduce monthly company pension benefits whenever state benefits increase by significantly more than the current rate of inflation.

ABC analysis (Pareto analysis). The classification of items (stock, for example) into three categories according to their frequency of use or monetary value. A typical result is that around 20 per cent of items account for about 80 per cent of value or use.

ABC model. *See* ANTECEDENTS, BEHAVIOUR, CONSEQUENCES MODEL.

abient behaviour. Actions taken by a person in attempts to minimise his or her exposure to a certain stimulus. *See* ADIENT BEHAVIOUR.

Abilene paradox. The anomalous situation that occurs when a group decision is made without any of the individuals taking the decision actually being committed to it. Each person mistakenly thinks that others want the decision to be taken and hence do not wish to interfere with what they perceive other people want.

abreaction. The discharge of emotions resulting from a previously repressed experience.

ABS. *See* ASSOCIATION OF BROADCASTING STAFFS.

absence without leave. Technically, a refusal to work and as such grounds for fair dismissal. Examples are arriving late for work, leaving early, taking excessively long lunch breaks, absenteeism, returning late from holiday, etc. Occasional absences do *not* justify dismissal. If absenteeism is persistent then formal warnings must be issued prior to dismissing the employee.

absenteeism. Frequent unauthorised absence from work. 'Involuntary absenteeism' means absences from work caused by reasons entirely beyond the worker's control, e.g. transport strikes, bad weather closing down the railway system, etc.

absolute efficiency. Another term for TECHNICAL EFFICIENCY.

ACAS. *See* ADVISORY, CONCILIATION AND ARBITRATION SERVICE.

ACAS Code on Disciplinary and other Procedures in Employment. A Code of Practice (qv) (first issued in 1977 and periodically updated) outlining model procedures for (i) the stages leading up to the dismissal of a worker, (ii) actions short of dismissal (qv), (iii) appeals following dismissal, (iv) dealing with absenteeism, (v) assisting sick or injured workers and (vi) other employment matters requiring tact and discretion.

ACCA. The title under which the Chartered Association of Certified Accountants (a leading UK professional accountancy body) continues to operate. It is the acronym for 'Association of Certified and Corporate Accountants', the name of the organisation before it received its Royal Charter in 1987. On receipt of the Royal Charter the ACCA decided to continue to be known by its old name, which was firmly embedded in the public mind. Members are statutorily entitled to audit the books of limited companies.

access course. A gateway to higher education for students (particularly mature students) who do not possess conventional academic or vocational qualifications. Access courses are designed to equip students with the academic competencies needed to cope with advanced educational programmes.

access time. The period it takes to obtain information from a computerised information storage system.

Access to Medical Reports Act 1988. A statute requiring employers to obtain the consent of prospective or existing employees prior to their being ordered to take medical examinations to assess their fitness for work. Individuals must be given free access to the results of such examinations, and they possess the legal right to have incorrect information removed or amended.

access to premises, legal requirements. Rules contained in the Factories Act 1961 (qv), regarding safety standards for the entrances into and exits from the place of work. The Act states that all gangways, floors, steps and passages must be soundly constructed, properly maintained, and (so far is reasonably practicable) kept free of obstructions and slippery substances.

accident book. A permanent record of the details of industrial injuries caused by workplace accidents. Factories and certain other types of undertaking are legally required to maintain an accident book. See REPORTING OF INJURIES, ETC., REGULATIONS 1985.

Accident Prevention Advisory Unit. An office of the Health and Safety Executive (qv) concerned with the analysis of national accident statistics. Additionally the unit audits the health and safety standards of large UK organisations, offering help and guidance where appropriate.

accident proneness. The proposition that certain individuals possess innate personal characteristics which increase their propensity to have accidents. Hence, people exhibiting these characteristics will naturally experience more accidents than the average for the workforce as a whole.

accident reports. See REPORTING OF INJURIES, ETC., REGULATIONS 1985.

accidents, domino theory of. The idea that accidents typically occur following a series of predictable independent stages, usually involving (i) an unsafe environment, (ii) individual fault and (iii) a dangerous act.

accidents, situational theory of. The hypothesis that accidents normally result from failures in working systems rather than from individual behaviour or accident proneness (qv).

accomplishment record inventory. A document requiring job holders to specify the major accomplishments of their work, using a critical incidents (qv) approach. Results are used in the behaviour expectation scale (qv) method of performance appraisal.

accord and satisfaction. A legal term which means that all the parties to a contract (a contract of employment for instance) agree to a change in its terms and conditions.

accountability. The requirement that a person justify his or her actions to other people, e.g. to supervisors, a board of directors or to shareholders.

accountants, EC Directive on the training of. A 1989 European Community Directive designed to enable an accountant who qualifies in one EC country to practice in others without having to requalify. See HIGHER EDUCATION DIPLOMA.

accounting. The systematic recording, analysis and appraisal of financial data.

accreditation of prior learning (APL). Evaluative processes leading to the award to trainees of credits towards the completion of a vocational training course, each credit being based on what trainees already know. It involves (i) the division of courses into small units in order to permit the advance testing of trainees' abilities within each constituent part, (ii) counselling, and (iii) the systematic assembly of evidence about trainees' past activities and achievements.

accreditation of union officials. The system whereby an employing firm formally recognises certain workers (usually shop stewards (qv)) as representatives of their trade unions in relation to particular groups of employees. 'Credentials' are then issued which set out the accredited representatives' rights and duties. Thereafter supervisors and other managers are obliged to communicate and negotiate with these individuals on matters covered by the accreditation agreement – which will also specify their entitlements to paid time off for union duties, details of each representative's constituency, etc. A typical agreement will include clauses stating that the representative promises to abide by the rules of the union, will not initiate unofficial industrial action (qv), will be elected by secret ballot, adhere to agreed negotiating procedures, and so on.

Accredited Training Centre (ATC). *See* TRAINER TRAINING.

accretion learning. Learning (qv) of unrelated items of information through repeatedly creating mental associations between them.

accrual rate. In an occupational pension scheme, the fraction of earnings for each year of a worker's service with an employing organisation that forms the basis of the superannuated person's pension entitlement, e.g. one sixtieth of final salary for each year of pensionable service (giving an employee with 20 years' service a retirement pension of one third of his or her final wage).

accrued rights premium (ARP). An extra amount that has to be paid into SERPS (qv) by an employee whose private occupational pension scheme ceases to be contracted out from the state system and who will not be entitled to receive a guaranteed minimum pension (qv) in any other way. *See* CONTRACTED OUT OCCUPATIONAL PENSION SCHEME.

acculturation. Conditioning a member of an outgroup (qv) for incorporation into an ingroup (qv). Acculturation may be voluntary or imposed.

achieved status. *See* ASCRIBED STATUS.

achievement motive. Motivation (qv) derived from a person's compulsion to attain a self-imposed and internalised standard of excellence. *See* INTERNALISATION.

achievement (attainment) tests. Selection tests intended to reveal whether job applicants actually possess certain skills. Typing and driving tests are examples. Such tests do not seek to evaluate the whole person; just a small sub-set of his or her abilities.

acquiescence problem. The tendency of job applicants to answer questions asked in psychometric tests (qv) according to the responses which they assume best fit in with job requirements. *See* BARNUM EFFECT.

acquired rights of employees. Statutory rights to redundancy (qv) and maternity pay (qv), the right not to be unfairly dismissed (qv), and other employee rights acquired by workers under various employment laws in consequence of their having accumulated certain periods of continuous employment (qv), as specified in the relevant Acts of Parliament.

acquisitive society. A society in which individuals are motivated to acquire possessions and/or to accumulate wealth. *See* WORK ETHIC.

acquisitive vandalism. According to S. Cohen, vandalism (qv) associated with theft (qv). Damage to property is inflicted as a corollary to unlawful gain. Cohen distinguishes four other types of vandalism: tactical vandalism, e.g. sabotaging a production line in order to have a day off work; vindictive vandalism involving the destruction of property in revenge for a personal grievance; malicious vandalism resulting from feelings of personal failure, boredom, frustration or despair; and 'play' vandalism, which represents little more than 'messing around'.

acquittance. A written discharge of a contract, debt or other legal obligation.

across the board negotiations. Collective bargaining (qv) intended to result in all the employees of a firm or industry receiving the same proportionate pay increase, hence perpetuating existing wage differentials (qv).

action centred leadership. *See* ADAIR, JOHN.

Action for Cities Programme. A government scheme introduced in 1988 to help reduce long term unemployment in inner city areas. It co-ordinates the activities of relevant government departments and agencies and channels resources towards the training and employment of disadvantaged inner city residents.

action learning. A training technique designed to develop employees' abilities through requiring them to (i) collect and evaluate data relating to a real life problem, (ii) devise appropriate measures for dealing with the problem and (iii) select and implement a solution and analyse its effect.

action research model. An approach to organisational development (qv) that focuses on group involvement in the identification of problems; the collection and analysis of data; and in the diagnosis, planning, implementation and continuous re-evaluation of results.

Action Resource Centre. A body formed to promote the non-cash support of charitable work by UK companies, especially through their seconding staff to help improve the management of charitable organisations.

action short of dismissal. A disciplinary penalty other than dismissal. Examples are demotion, denial of promotions or pay increases, loss of increments, refusal of requests for time off, etc. Such actions are lawful under the Employment Act 1982 (qv), provided they do not discriminate unfairly with respect to race, sex, marital status or involvement with or refusal to join a trade union. Victims of unfair actions short of dismissal may seek compensation not only from employers, but also from fellow workers who pressurised the employer into taking the unfair action.

activities analysis. According to Peter Drucker, a useful means for determining the best form of organisational structure within an enterprise. It seeks to identify the key activities of the firm, i.e. what it actually does, rather than what it does in theory. See DECISION ANALYSIS; RELATIONS ANALYSIS.

activity chart. A diagram illustrating the sequential breakdown of a work process over time.

activity drive. The need felt by some people to be constantly on the go and to engage in activities. Activity drive arguably provides a primary motivator for the acquisition of skills and competencies by certain individuals.

activity rate. The percentage of people in a certain category (male, female, members of a particular ethnic group, people aged between 24 and 35 years, etc.) who are economically active, i.e. either in a job or seeking employment.

activity sampling. A technique of work measurement (qv) involving the recording of many successive observations of the time taken by operatives to complete a certain task.

activity theory. The proposition that work is crucially important for an individual's emotional and physical well-being. The theory predicts, therefore, that retirement from work is naturally and inevitably detrimental to the health of the retiring person – unless he or she can find alternative interests requiring the same amounts of activity. See DISENGAGEMENT THEORY.

Actors' Equity Association, British. A trade union (qv) which recruits persons who exercise professional skill in the provision of entertainment, e.g. as artists, choreographers, producers or stage managers.

ACTT. See ASSOCIATION OF CINEMATOGRAPH, TELEVISION AND ALLIED TECHNICIANS.

actuarial certificate. A document issued by the Occupational Pensions Board (qv) to a contracted out occupational pension scheme (qv) in order to attest the scheme's solvency.

actuarial selection methods. Employee selection based on objective, statistical analyses of data about candidates. See CLINICAL SELECTION OF EMPLOYEES.

acuity. A perceptual ability involving the capacities to scan environments comprehensively and quickly and to be able to identify possible problems.

ACVT. The European Commission's Advisory Committee for Vocational Training.

Adair, John. A UK management theorist who asserts that effective leadership requires the simultaneous satisfaction of three sets of interdependent needs: task needs relating to the work being completed; group needs associated with morale and team spirit; and the individual needs of members of the group.

adaptability. A worker's ability to adapt to changes in working methods and environments *between* jobs, as opposed to 'versatility', i.e. the capacity to handle a variety of tasks *within* a job.

adaptation. Behavioural responses to changes in physical and social environments. It can occur unconsciously, or consciously via deliberate attempts to conform or succeed.

adaptive control system. A self-regulating control (qv) system wherein objectives automatically change as circumstances alter.

adaptive expectations hypothesis. The proposition that individuals adjust their responses to rising prices (including their wage bargaining behaviour) gradually, so that future expectations of the rate of inflation (qv) are simply extrapolations of past experience. This differs from the 'rational expectations' view, which asserts that workers' predictions of future inflation incorporate their anticipations of the national economic policies they expect to be implemented in government attempts to combat high rates of inflation.

Adaptive Planning and Control Sequence (APACS). A planning model with eight main steps: statement of objectives; SWOT and PEST analysis (qv); specification of activities necessary to achieve objectives; evaluation of the consequences of alternative actions; prediction of the results of selected options; issue of instructions; assessment of actual outcomes and, if necessary, the modification of the plan.

adaptive testing. See COMPUTER BASED TRAINING.

added value incentive scheme. A group bonus arrangement that links individual employee remuneration to the increase in value added to production by an entire organisation, above a predetermined norm. Added value is sales revenue less the costs of materials and services purchased from outside the organisation.

added years. A means for increasing the retirement benefits of a member of an occupational pension scheme. The individual pays additional voluntary contributions during each month of employment in order to build up the notional number of years of service upon which his or her retirement pension is to be calculated.

additional award. Extra compensation paid to a sacked worker for unfair dismissal (qv) when the employing organisation refuses to comply with an order of an industrial tribunal (qv) for the reinstatement (qv) or re-engagement (qv) of the employee.

additional voluntary contributions (AVCs). Extra payments into an occupational pension scheme over and above a member's normal contributions in order to obtain increased benefits. See FREESTANDING AVC.

ad-hocracy. A term sometimes used to describe managements that adopt short time horizons, are reluctant to plan and tend only to respond to urgent problems. Management focuses its attention on individual projects rather than the progress of the enterprise as a whole.

adient behaviour. Actions intended to increase a person's exposure to a stimulus. See ABIENT BEHAVIOUR.

adjudication. Peaceful resolution of disputes via authoritative decisions imposed on both parties by an impartial outsider.

adjudication order. A Court order declaring a person bankrupt (qv), thus enabling the person's financial affairs to be placed in the hands of a trustee (qv) and for his or her assets to be liquidated in order to settle amounts owed to creditors.

administration. The establishment, implementation and co-ordination of activities, policies and procedures for achieving the goals of an organisation.

Administration Order. A Court order through which a Court supervises the financial affairs of a debtor or insolvent company until its financial situation improves. As long as an Administration Order remains in effect, individual creditors cannot enforce individual claims against the debtor person or company without the express permission of the Court.

administrative law. The body of law which regulates the executive functions of government and provides remedies for individuals damaged by unlawful administrative actions.

administrative management school. A term sometimes used to describe the classical approach (qv) to management, particularly the work of Mary Parker Follett (qv) and Henri Fayol (qv).

administrative science theory. A classical approach (qv) to management which seeks to formulate general principles of administration (qv) that are equally applicable to firms, the public sector and non-profit organisations.

adrenalin secretion. A consequence of stress (qv) which increases the heart beat and causes physiological changes in the stomach, muscles and the nervous system.

ADST. See APPROVED DEFERRED SHARE TRUST.

advance against wages. A prepayment of part of an employee's weekly or monthly wages. Advances are sometimes made to workers who have just started jobs, or in consequence of unforeseen financial emergencies.

advanced factories. A term used to describe factory premises built by the government in underdeveloped areas and then let out to firms at extremely low rents and free of local authority business rates.

advanced manufacturing technology (AMT). A term used to describe technically sophisticated production methods such as cadcam (qv), robotics (qv), materials requirements planning (qv), optimised production technology (qv), etc.

advertisements for jobs, rules on unfair discrimination. Provisions of the Sex Discrimination Act 1975 (qv) which make it unlawful to publish or cause to be published any job advertisement intended to violate the Act. Hence, use of terms such as 'waitress' or 'salesman' are forbidden unless they specifically refer to jobs excluded from the statute. Internal job advertisements within companies are also covered by the legislation. Responsibility for preventing unfairly discriminatory job advertisements lies with the Equal Opportunities Commission (qv), which may apply for Court injunctions (qv) restraining publication. Aggrieved individuals must approach the EOC in the first instance; they cannot personally approach the Courts. See GENUINE OCCUPATIONAL QUALIFICATION.

Advisory Committee on Equal Opportunities. A specialist European Community body comprising representatives of the national statutory bodies responsible for promoting equal employment opportunities for women in EC member nations (the UK Equal Opportunities Commission for instance).

Advisory Committee on Training in Nursing. See NURSES PRACTISING IN THE EUROPEAN COMMUNITY.

Advisory, Conciliation and Arbitration Service (ACAS). A government agency which (i) attempts to conciliate between parties in industrial disputes (qv) and to resolve informally cases of alleged unfair dismissal and (ii) publishes codes of practice (qv) on employment matters. All applications to industrial tribunals (qv) are automatically referred to ACAS, which tries to achieve out of Court settlements. ACAS possesses a 'work research unit' which provides employers and employee representatives with information and advice on job design (qv), work or-

ganisation, ergonomics (qv), stress (qv) and motivation (qv). Also, ACAS maintains lists of arbitrators qualified to mediate in various types of dispute.

advisory role of the personnel manager. Aspects of the personnel manager's role (qv) which involve the personnel manager proffering expert counsel to line managers (qv) on personnel matters such as job evaluation (qv), the regrading of employees, industrial relations (qv), and so on. The personnel manager suggests certain courses of action, but leaves final decisions to line executives. See SERVICE ROLE OF THE PERSONNEL MANAGER.

AEEU. See AMALGAMATED ENGINEERING AND ELECTRICAL UNION.

AEU. See AMALGAMATED ENGINEERING UNION.

AFE. The acronym for advanced further education, i.e. high level courses undertaken in colleges that are not universities or polytechnics.

affect. A general term for emotion or feeling.

affect structure. Patterns of interpersonal attraction that determine the nature and frequency of associations among members of a group. These depend on the needs and resources of group members, individual personalities, the alternatives available and the demands of the situation.

affective reaction. A form of psychotic behaviour (qv) characterised by excessively emotional outbursts of elation or despondency.

affidavit. A written declaration made on oath, normally before a notary public (qv).

affiliated companies. Businesses owned by the same holding company (qv).

affiliation need. Feelings of constantly wanting to be with and/or to form close relationships with other people.

affirmative action programmes. United States federal and local government purchasing policies under which a supplying firm's continuing access to public sector contracts is made conditional on the supplier achieving certain prespecified equal opportunity targets, e.g. to increase ethnic minority representation in the workforce by 20 per cent within the next 18 months.

after sensation. The continuation of a sensual experience following the removal of the original stimulus that initiated the experience, e.g. continuing to see something after it is no longer there. After sensations have many ergonomic (qv) implications.

AGCAS. The acronym for the Association of Graduate Careers Advisory Services.

agency labour. Workers sent to jobs by an employment agency (qv). Whether the workers are employees of the agency or of the agency's client depends on who controls them and the degree of supervision involved.

agent. An individual or an organisation undertaking assignments on a client's behalf, but who then 'drops out' of resulting contracts with third parties. Contracts arranged by an agent are binding on the principal. However, the agent is not liable if the principal defaults.

aggregate planning. Determination of future plant and equipment (qv) utilisation in a situation where total capacity is fixed. It requires the scheduling of plant maintenance to coincide with slack periods, preplanning the hiring and laying off of casual workers, assessing overtime requirements and smoothing out production through occasionally producing for stock.

aggression, instrumental. In a negotiation (qv), aggression displayed not because a person is genuinely angry, but as a means for achieving an end.

aggressive behaviour. Actions intended to cause injury to persons or damage to objects. *See* CRIMINAL DAMAGE; INTRA-PUNITIVE AGGRESSION.

ageism. Unfair discrimination based on a person's age. At the time of writing ageism is not illegal in the UK.

agitation. Attempting to forment feelings of discontent with existing conditions among a group of workers.

agricultural wage board. The equivalent of a wages council (qv) but for farm employees.

AH test. *See* ALICE HEIM TEST.

Aids and Employment (DOE booklet). A Department of Employment publication advising employers on model procedures for dealing with employees with AIDS. It seeks to avoid unfair discrimination against AIDS sufferers through recommending that (i) victims shall not be required to disclose the fact that they have the virus (unless there exist genuine risks of infecting other workers) and (ii) employees with AIDS or who are HIV positive shall not be treated differently to anyone else suffering a serious illness. The dismissal of AIDS carriers in consequence of other workers refusing to work with them will normally represent unfair dismissal (qv), unless there is a demonstrable risk of spreading infection (e.g. if the employee works with blood products).

alarm reaction. Stress (qv) induced activation of the endocrine system following recognition of a stressor (qv). The body prepares for 'fight or flight'.

alcoholic employees, Joint Code of Practice concerning. A code of practice (qv) jointly issued in 1981 by the UK Department of Employment, the Health and Safety Executive (qv) and the DHSS recommending that alcoholism be regarded as a health rather than a disciplinary problem, and suggesting procedures for dealing with alcoholic employees.

algorithm. A set of standard rules and procedures for solving a certain type of problem.

Alice Heim test (AH test). An intelligence test which attempts to avoid ambiguity in the interpretation of test subjects' responses through asking respondents a high proportion of non-verbal questions (e.g. predicting the next number in a series, or identifying relationships between symbols). Verbal questions involve the arrangement of words in order, not the interpretation of sentences.

alienation. The estrangement of an employee from his or her work causing the person to feel that work is not a relevant or important part of life.

alienation, normative. Rejection of or feelings of uncertainty concerning the norms (qv) and values of a group to which a person belongs.

all in wage rate. An hourly or weekly rate of pay that includes all elements of the wage package (bonuses, fringe benefits, etc.). *See* CONSOLIDATION.

allocative efficiency. An economics term describing the most efficient allocation of scarce resources among competing wants. *See* X-INEFFICIENCY; TECHNICAL EFFICIENCY.

Alpha test. One of the earliest intelligence tests (qv). It was used to assess recruits to the US Army during the First World War.

alter ego. According to the psychologist Carl Gustav Jung (qv), a person's 'other self' – typically the repressed and repudiated part of his or her psyche.

alternance. A term coined by the European Commission to describe the establishment within training programmes of effective links between off-job training and work experience (as in a sandwich course (qv) for instance).

alternate standards. In work study (qv), a variety of alternative standard times (qv) for completing the same job, each standard time depending on the technique of production adopted (e.g. capital intensive (qv) rather than labour intensive (qv) methods).

alternating shift system. A shift work pattern whereby employees have to work a certain number of day shifts on consecutive days followed by a predetermined number of night shifts on consecutive nights.

alternative employment. A job offered by an employer to a redundant worker in circumstances where the capacity or place in which the employee is to work differs wholly or partly from that previously specified in the worker's contract of employment (qv). In determining whether an alternative job is 'suitable' for the worker, a Court will examine the type of work done and its pay, the status attached to the position, overtime opportunities, shift work, fringe benefits, travelling time, and other relevant factors.

ALVEY project. A government scheme through which the government would meet half the costs of information technology research projects in certain fields, especially those involving IKB systems (qv) and the human–machine interface (qv). Funding for ALVEY projects was effectively terminated in 1991.

Amalgamated Engineering and Electrical Union (AEEU). Britain's largest trade union (qv) formed in 1992 through the merger of the AEU (qv) and the EETPU (qv).

Amalgamated Engineering Union (AEU). One of the largest trade unions (qv) in Britain, active among engineering, foundry and construction workers. In 1992 the AEU merged with the EETPU to form the Amalgamated Engineering and Electrical Union (qv). *See* AUEW.

Amalgamated Union of Engineering Workers (AUEW). The 1971 amalgamation of several unions in the engineering industry. It had manual and white collar sections (the latter being known as the Technical, Administrative and Supervisory Section [TASS]). In 1984 the AUEW split into two separate and independent organisations: the AEU and the MSF (formerly TASS).

ambiversion. The phenomenon of an individual oscillating between introversion and extroversion in his or her personality (qv).

AMT. *See* ADVANCED MANUFACTURING TECHNOLOGY.

analogue model. A model of a system constructed to represent its properties, behaviour or methods of functioning.

analogous test (work sample test). A selection test which attempts to replicate key aspects of the job that the successful applicant will have to perform. Examples are typing tests for secretaries or driving tests for goods delivery workers. *See* ANALYTICAL TESTS.

analytical estimating. A work measurement (qv) technique whereby the times necessary to complete the elements of a job at a predefined level of competence are estimated partly from a combination of direct observation, personal knowledge and experience of the job, and partly from synthesis (qv).

analytical job evaluation. Methods for job evaluation (qv) that seek to quantify and evaluate all the constituent elements of a job. *See* POINTS SYSTEM.

analytical tests. Selection tests which attempt to measure job applicants' fundamental characteristics, e.g. intelligence, personality, sociability, etc. *See* ANALOGOUS TESTS.

androcentrism. Use of masculine traits as criteria for evaluating the worth of individuals (in performance appraisal (qv), for example).

annualised hours agreement. An arrangement under which an employee agrees to work a certain number of hours per year, with that person's precise start and finishing times being subject to individual negotiation and depending on his or her personal circumstances. Management retains the right to impose longer working hours during busy periods and shorter hours when business is slack.

annuity. A series of equal payments made at fixed intervals (e.g. monthly or annually) in consequence of an earlier lump sum investment. For example, a person can purchase today an annuity which gives him or her an annual fixed income for the rest of his or her life. The annuitant will profit if he or she lives for many years following the investment.

annuity, contingent. An annuity (qv) that comes into effect only if a certain event occurs, e.g. the death of a specified person.

annuity, retirement. A means for financing a retirement pension whereby the recipient purchases an annuity for a lump sum on the day of his or her retirement. Thereafter the annuitant receives an annual pension for the remainder of his or her life. Typically the purchase of the annuity is financed by the proceeds of a maturing endowment assurance policy included in the person's occupational pension scheme. See GUARANTEED ANNUITY OPTION.

anomie. The absence of norms (qv) and common values within a group.

Antecedents, Behaviour, Consequences (ABC) model. A technique for analysing and modifying behaviour which seeks to identify the conditions leading to certain types of behaviour, and provides a framework for investigating the consequences of various alternative responses to external events.

ante-natal appointments, right of attendance. The statutory right of a pregnant employee to paid time off work to attend 'reasonable' numbers of antenatal appointments, regardless of how long the woman has been employed by the organisation. An employer is entitled to demand a doctor's note confirming the woman is pregnant, plus evidence that appointments have actually been made.

anthropology. The study of physical and cultural differences among peoples and societies, especially where institutions and social relationships are concerned.

anthropometry. Measurement of human physical characteristics. See ERGONOMICS.

anticipatory breach. The situation that arises when one of the parties to a contract of employment (qv) informs the other of his or her intention to take unlawful action. An example would be an employer's announcement that an employee's wages are to be halved. The threatened party may immediately withdraw from the contract (by claiming constructive dismissal (qv) for instance) and does not have to wait for the breach actually to occur.

anticipatory coping. A stress (qv) management method involving the identification of the situations and activities that an individual finds exceptionally taxing and then deliberately avoiding these.

anticipatory socialisation. The phenomenon of people acquiring new attitudes and behaviour deemed congruous with roles they have not yet assumed. Examples are workers about to be promoted into management who, on hearing they are to be upgraded, immediately adopt managerial perspectives, or young people accepted for a full time course at a polytechnic, university or other college of higher education who begin to act as if they were students, even before starting their studies.

anti-conformists. Individuals who automatically and deliberately behave in a manner directly antithetical to group norms (qv).

anxiety. A consequence of long term stress (qv). It comes in two forms: 'objective' anxiety caused by external events; and 'neurotic' anxiety that arises internally within the person. Anxiety prevents the individual being able to relax and causes feelings of irritability and unease with surroundings.

any difference rule. A legal principle relating to unfair dismissal (qv) cases. It states that if the administrative procedures followed prior to a dismissal were somehow defective (e.g. through failure to issue written warnings, not giving the worker sufficient time to improve, etc.), then provided the non-occurrence of the administrative error would have made no difference to the eventual outcome, the commission of the administrative error is not *of itself* sufficient to render the dismissal unfair.

APACS. *See* ADAPTIVE PLANNING AND CONTROL SEQUENCE.

APEX (Association of Professional, Executive, Clerical and Computer Staff). *See* GENERAL, MUNICIPAL AND BOILERMAKERS UNION.

APL. *See* ACCREDITATION OF PRIOR LEARNING.

apopathetic behaviour. Actions not directed towards other people but which, nevertheless, are influenced by the presence of other individuals.

applicant to an Industrial Tribunal. The person initiating a Tribunal action. Normally the applicant speaks second (after the employer) at a Tribunal hearing, although in sex and race discrimination cases it is normal for the applicant to speak first. *See* RESPONDENT; PROCEDURE IN INDUSTRIAL TRIBUNALS.

applications software. Computer packages that perform particular functions, e.g. word processing, spreadsheet (qv) formulations or the manipulation of databases (qv).

applied psychology. Attempts to relate academic psychology (qv) to practical affairs, e.g. to ergonomics (qv), counselling (qv), negotiation (qv) or industrial relations (qv).

apprentices, rules of dismissal. Special requirements that apply to the sacking of apprentices who, because they are legally considered to be trainees rather than 'employees', can only be dismissed if their conduct makes it impossible for the employing firm to carry out its instructional obligations. Apprentices, moreover, are legally entitled to have their work regularly appraised and to receive proper advice, teaching and supervision.

apprenticeship. A form of on-job training, possibly lasting several years, for young people aspiring to become craft workers (qv). Apprentices are normally paid lower than average wages during their apprenticeships.

Approved All-Employee Savings Related Share Option Scheme. An employee share ownership system in which the employee is given the option to buy shares in his or her employing company in five or seven years' time, at a fixed predetermined price. The money needed to purchase the shares is deducted from the employee's monthly salary and invested in interest earning savings accounts. After five or seven years the employee decides whether to exercise the option, depending on the market price of the shares at that time. If the option is not taken up the employee receives the accrued interest on his or her accumulated deposits plus repayment of the principal. Unlike an Approved Deferred Share Trust (qv) scheme, the company receives no tax benefits.

Approved Deferred Share Trust (ADST). An employee share ownership arrangement whereby the employing company pays part of its profits directly into a trust (qv) which then buys shares in the firm. These shares are distributed to full time employees with at least five years' service. The company is exempt from corporation tax on the sum donated and employees pay no income tax on the value of the shares they receive, provided the shares are held for at least five years. Approval for these tax exemptions must be obtained from the Inland Revenue.

Approved Discretionary Share Option Scheme. A share ownership scheme for senior managers, who acquire options to purchase shares in their employing company in three to ten years' time at a fixed predetermined price. Often, the purchase of the shares is financed by low interest loans from the firm.

aptitude. A person's potential for acquiring a particular ability or skill.

aptitude tests. Selection tests intended to assess candidates' promise, trainability and potential ability to undertake duties at future times (rather than testing previously acquired competencies).

arbitration. Resolution of disputes via the appointment of independent referees who hear and adjudicate cases. Parties promise in advance to abide by the arbitrator's decision. Each side nominates potential arbitrators, and a mutually acceptable name is chosen.

Arbitration Act 1975. The statute which established ACAS (qv).

arbitration, unilateral. A decision by a party to an industrial dispute (qv) to approach an independent third party unilaterally and request a ruling on the disputed issue, regardless of the feelings of the other side.

Area Manpower Boards. Regional bodies established in 1983 by the Manpower Services Commission (qv) to advise on the implementation of MSC training initiatives at the local level. They were especially concerned with the introduction of the Youth Training Scheme (qv), informing local employers and unions of the availability of YTS labour, and monitoring the effectiveness of YTS programmes.

Argyris, Chris. A management theorist noted for his analysis of the causes of employee's feelings of failure, inadequacy and frustration within organisations. Argyis argued that apathy, indifference and alienation were common among workers in large enterprises; while resistance to change, unwillingness to take risks and unthinking conformity to the status quo characterised many managements. He suggested that open relations between management and labour, and employee involvement in managerial decision making could solve most of these problems.

ARP. *See* ACCRUED RIGHTS PREMIUM.

Article 119 of the Treaty of Rome. A clause in the Treaty which set up the European Common Market explicitly demanding 'the application of the principle that men and women should receive equal pay for equal work'.

Articles of association. A document setting out the rules and conditions governing internal relations (e.g. shareholders' voting rights, election of directors, conduct of company meetings, transfer of shares) between the directors and shareholders of a limited company.

Articles 117 and 118 of the Treaty of Rome. Clauses in the Treaty of Rome (qv) that require the European Community to improve employees' working conditions. It also compels member states to harmonise their employment law, health and safety regulations and rights of association of workers, and to co-operate in matters relating to basic and advanced vocational training.

artificer. A skilled craftworker.

Asbestos (Licensing) Regulations 1963. Legislation requiring employers or the self employed to obtain a Health and Safety Executive (qv) licence prior to working with asbestos insulation or coating materials, unless the people involved will spend less than one hour exposed to such materials in any period of seven consecutive days *and* total exposure is less than two hours.

Asbestosis, need to maintain medical records. The rule contained in the Control of Asbestos at Work Regulations 1987 (qv) that firms employing workers exposed to asbestos must keep health records on these workers for at least 30 years. Any worker experiencing contact with asbestos above a legally specified danger level is entitled to a medical check-up at the employer's expense every two years for the rest of his or her life.

ascribed status. A position in an organisation that a person assumes automatically, as of right. The status is attained involuntarily and is not open to competition from others. This contrasts with 'achieved status' which is earned by an individual in open competition with fellow group members.

ASLEF. *See* ASSOCIATED SOCIETY OF LOCOMOTIVE ENGINEERS AND FIREFIGHTERS.

ASLIB. See ASSOCIATION OF SPECIAL LIBRARIES AND INFORMATION BUREAUX.

aspiration level. The personal objectives an individual would like to achieve given his or her past experience, knowledge of opportunities, and comparisons made with reference groups (qv).

assembly lines. Production systems involving the physical movement of work in progress (e.g. by conveyor belt) from one workstation to the next. They are normally characterised by the division of labour (qv) and, increasingly, the use of robotics (qv).

assertiveness training. Courses that seek to assist employees develop their abilities to exercise initiative, translate ideas into action, present themselves convincingly and generally maximise their creative potentials. Assertiveness training aims to convince individuals that they possess certain personal rights, e.g. to express themselves forcefully and to have other people listen and take seriously what they have to say.

assessment. The process of measuring and evaluating a person's attributes, based on information about his or her performance. *See* FORMATIVE ASSESSMENT; SUMMATIVE ASSESSMENT; DIAGNOSTIC ASSESSMENT; CRITERION REFERENCING; NORM BASED REFERENCING.

assessment centre. A place where job applicants' behaviour and performance in job-related tasks and activities can be conveniently evaluated. Typically the centre is an hotel or an industry training organisation. Examples of exercises completed at such centres include leaderless group discussion (qv), in-tray exercises (qv), role-playing (qv) and business games (qv). Candidates are brought together for an appropriate period (usually two or three days) and are tested and observed by a panel of assessors.

assessment map. A diagram showing how, where and when a trainee has been assessed and the results obtained from assessments.

assessment of work-based learning. Assessment (qv) of occupational competencies derived from the employee's own workplace learning, plus structured on-job and off-job training.

asset stripping. The acquisition of a business in order to shut it down and sell off its land, buildings, plant and equipment, etc. rather than to run the enterprise as a going concern.

assignment. The transfer of legal rights or obligations from one person to another.

assignment, deed of. A document which transfers rights or property from one person to another.

associated employer. According to the Employment Protection (Consolidation) Act 1978 (qv) any two limited companies where one is a company controlled (directly or indirectly) by the other, or where both are companies controlled by a third party. *See* HOLDING COMPANY.

Associated Society of Locomotive Engineers and Firefighters (ASLEF). A leading UK trade union (qv) active in the railway industry.

Association Agreements. Negotiated deals between the European Community and Turkey, Morocco, Tunisia, Algeria and Yugoslavia granting immigrant workers from these countries certain rights relating to their employment in EC states.

Association of Accounting Technicians (AAT). A UK professional body established and supervised by the four major accountancy institutions (ACCA, CIMA, CIPFA and ICAEW) to provide a means whereby students without formal qualifications may obtain recognised accountancy qualifications. Students who pass the final AAT examinations may progress to the higher level qualifications offered by the main accountancy bodies.

Association of Broadcasting Staffs (ABS). A UK trade union (qv) active in the radio and television broadcasting industry. The other major union in this field is the Association of Cinematograph, Television and Allied Technicians (qv).

Association of Cinematograph, Television and Allied Technicians (ACTT). A trade union (qv) active in the technical side of film production. It is a craft union (qv), recruiting such people as directors, producers, camera operators, animators, sound maintenance workers, etc.

Association of First Division Civil Servants (FDA). A trade union (qv) representing the highest grades in the UK civil service, including HM inspectors of schools, and lawyers in the Crown Prosecution Service.

Association of Professional, Executive, Clerical and Computing Staff (APEX). A UK trade union (qv) active among white collar workers (qv). It works in conjunction with the General, Municipal and Boilermakers Union (qv).

Association of Scientific, Technical and Managerial Staffs (ASTMS). A UK trade union (qv) that recruits white collar workers (qv), especially those at the technician and junior management level.

Association of Special Libraries and Information Bureaux (ASLIB). An organisation formed to promote the use of specialist libraries and commercial databases (qv) in industry and commerce.

ASTMS. *See* ASSOCIATION OF SCIENTIFIC, TECHNICAL AND MANAGERIAL STAFFS.

ATC. *See* TRAINER TRAINING.

attachment of earnings order. A Court order against an individual compelling his or her employer to pay that person's wages direct to the Court (for distribution to creditors or to settle a fine) and not to the worker.

attainment test. See ACHIEVEMENT TEST.

attendance allowance. State benefit payable to severely disabled people who require large amounts of attention and supervision. Claims for the allowance may be registered once a person has received frequent daily or nightly care for a continuous six-month period (unless the individual is terminally ill, in which case the qualifying period is disregarded).

attendance bonus. A special payment for turning up for work on a certain number of consecutive occasions or for punctual time keeping over a pre-specified period.

attested document. A verified copy of an original document, examined by at least two persons and certified by them as a true copy. A declaration to this effect is written on the copy and signed by the two confirmatories.

attitude. A long term inclination to perceive, interpret and evaluate events and issues in a certain manner.

attitude discrepant behaviour. The situation that arises when an employee behaves in a manner opposite to his or her attitudes in order to achieve an objective or to make a good impression.

attitude scale. A collection of short and unambiguous statements of attitudes or opinions with which a test subject is required to agree or disagree.

attitudes, information processing theory of. A theory of attitude (qv) formation which asserts that a person's long term memory stores information in such a way as to create biases and frames of reference (qv) that influence the manner in which freshly received information is processed and interpreted by the short term memory.

attribution. How individuals explain their own behaviour or that of other people. See STEREOTYPING; HALO EFFECT.

attribution error. A wrongful assumption that the behaviour problems of other individuals are caused by their personalities and not by their environmental situations.

attrition of salary costs. The situation that occurs when a firm's total salary bill falls significantly over a year, even though all employees have received inflation and/or merit wage increases. This results from staff resignations (especially of senior high paid staff) followed by lengthy delays (during which no-one is drawing a salary in respect of the vacant positions) before their replacement. Note, moreover, that the costs of secretarial and other support may be reduced significantly while the jobs remain open.

au pairs, rule on the employment status of. The decision by the DHSS that au pairs are *not* gainfully employed and hence not liable to tax or Class 1 National Insurance (qv) contributions.

auditors, rules on the dismissal of. Special laws whereby the auditors of a limited company may only be dismissed by the firm's shareholders, not its directors. If directors attempt to remove an auditor then the latter is legally entitled to circularise shareholders with his or her version of events, at the expense of the employing company.

AUEW. See AMALGAMATED UNION OF ENGINEERING WORKERS.

Austrian School. An influential group of economists who in the early 1900s argued that free competition between large organisations will automatically lead to technical progress and to the new product development necessary for constantly rising living standards. The name derives from the presence within the school of several leading Austrian economic theorists.

authority. The right to control, usually evidenced by a formal position in a firm's managerial hierarchy. See ORGANISATION CHART; POWER.

authority structure. The formal pattern of authority (qv) relations within an organisational hierarchy, involving positions on organisation charts (qv), spans of control (qv), etc.

autistic behaviour. Behaviour that is largely governed by subjective needs, emotions and wishes.

autocratic leadership. A leadership style (qv) that emphasises the close supervision of subordinates and the issue of precise and detailed instructions to subordinates. See DICTATORIAL LEADERSHIP, PATERNALISTIC LEADERSHIP.

automatically unfair dismissals. Sackings prohibited by law. Industrial Tribunals (qv) will always rule in favour of the dismissed worker in these cases, which concern (i) employees sacked for joining or refusing to join an independent trade union (qv), (ii) dismissals for becoming involved in lawful union activity, (iii) a woman being sacked simply because she is pregnant and (iv) dismissals when a business changes hands (unless significant technical, economic or organisational changes warranting the sackings simultaneously occur).

automation, fixed and flexible. Assembly and/or processing via predetermined sequences of mechanical operations that cannot be altered by virtue of the nature of the equipment used (fixed automation); or processing or assembly using equipment that allows for changes in the order and character of operations, thus enabling the periodic variation of output (flexible automation).

autonomation. A Japanese approach to production management whereby machinery is self-monitoring and itself signals the need for attention when problems arise. This minimises the need for human operators to oversee production processes.

autonomic nervous system. That part of the human nervous system which controls the internal body organs such as the stomach, intestines, heart, kidneys and urinary bladder. It is so named because the individual normally has little control over its activities.

autonomous bargaining. Settlement of pay and employment conditions via negotiations between management and individual workers with minimal interference from trade unions (qv) or employers' associations (qv).

autonomous imagery. Mental imagery which the individual cannot control in terms of its content, occurrence or termination. This contrasts with 'controlled imagery' which may be adjusted as the individual wishes.

autonomous work groups. Teams of workers that are given self-contained tasks and the authority to implement team decisions. Each group member is trained to be able to undertake all jobs performed within the group, so that frequent job rotation is possible.

autonomy. An employee's ability to exercise self-determination and to work in an independent manner unfettered by close supervision or bureaucratic control.

autonomy of learning. The extent to which trainees have control over their own learning, e.g. through choosing various modes of instruction or the sequence in which topics are learned.

Autumn statement. An economic forecast published by HM Treasury intended to predict economic conditions over the next 12–15 months.

AVCs *See* ADDITIONAL VOLUNTARY CONTRIBUTIONS.

average outgoing quality. The average proportion of defective units of output leaving a firm after initial inspection and quality sampling. *See* ZERO DEFECTS QUALITY CONTROL.

average salary retirement pension scheme. An occupational pension system in which a worker's final pension depends on his or her average income over the entire period of membership of the scheme, rather than on the worker's salary immediately or shortly preceding retirement.

average weekly earnings. For the purpose of calculating benefits under UK employment legislation, the summation of all earnings over the eight weeks prior to and including the worker's last pay day, divided by eight.

avoidance learning. Learning (qv) what to do in order to avoid an unpleasant event ('active' avoidance learning), or learning what not to do to avoid an unpleasant event ('passive' avoidance learning).

axiological crisis. A crisis that threatens a group's entire value system.

B

Babbage, Charles. An early nineteenth century mathematician who analysed the human skills needed for operatives to undertake the (then) latest techniques of factory production. He also invented a mechanical computer and devised methods for reducing the amount of training required by factory workers. Babbage was an important precursor of scientific management (qv).

BACIE. See BRITISH ASSOCIATION FOR COMMERCIAL AND INDUSTRIAL EDUCATION.

backshift. The late afternoon/early evening shift (usually between 2.00 and 10.00 pm) in a three-shift system.

backing store. That part of a computerised information system which holds information for reference rather than for immediate execution of commands.

bailment. The delivery of goods in trust (qv) by one person (the bailor) to another (the bailee) under a contract whereby the goods will be returned when the purpose for which they were bailed has been fulfilled.

balance sheet. A statement of a business's fixed and current assets and long and short term liabilities on a given date.

balancing time. Work undertaken to make up a certain number of hours in a flexitime (qv) arrangement that requires a set minimum number of hours to be worked each week (or other period).

balloting, Code of Practice on. A Code of Practice (qv) issued under the 1988 Employment Act (qv) to guide trade unions (qv) on how they should ballot their members. The Code recommends that postal ballots be used wherever practicable, that individuals be able to express their views, and that ballots be conducted 'democratically' in all respects.

balloting prior to a strike, rules concerning. Requirements of the Trade Union Act 1984 (qv) and the Employment Act 1988 (qv) that (i) every worker likely to be asked to participate in an industrial action (qv) be given the opportunity to vote on whether it should take place, (ii) initial authorisation of the action occur within four weeks of the ballot being held and (iii) ballot papers ask as a separate question whether the voter wishes to take part in action short of a strike as an alternative to stopping work. Ballots must be secret but need not be postal, must ask simple yes/no answers, and invite only those union members likely to be called upon to strike to take part in the ballot. At least a 51 per cent majority is needed before the resulting strike is immune from civil liability. The 1988 Act demands that voting papers carry the words: 'if you take part in a strike or other industrial action you may be in breach of your contract of employment'. See BALLOTING, CODE OF PRACTICE ON.

ballots. See TRADE UNION BALLOTS; ELECTIONS FOR UNION OFFICERS; STRIKE BALLOTS; POLITICAL FUNDS.

banded day work. A variation on measured day work (qv) whereby management establishes a series of bands for performance and pay. Workers whose output is within a certain range receive a predetermined flat rate (qv) wage. Other wage rates are paid for performance levels in other bands. The aim is the simplification of bonus payments.

bandwidth. Upper and lower limits on the total numbers of hours to be worked each day in a flexitime (qv) system.

Banking, Insurance and Finance Union (BIFU). A trade union (qv) representing all grades of worker in banks, insurance companies, finance houses and building societies.

bankrupt. A private person or sole trader declared insolvent by a County Court. The financial affairs of a bankrupt are placed in the hands of a trustee (qv), who sells off the bankrupt's assets and collects monies owing to that person in order to raise money for distribution to creditors. For a limited company the equivalent to bankruptcy is known as company 'liquidation'.

Barber judgment. A name given to the decision of the European Court in a test case in May 1990 concerning equal pay for men and women. The Court ruled that 'equal pay' extends to equal pensions rights.

bargaining depth. See BARGAINING STRUCTURE.

bargaining structure. The key dimensions of collective bargaining (qv) procedures and agreements, comprising: (i) bargaining 'scope', i.e. the range of issues considered in negotiations; (ii) the 'extent' of bargaining, i.e. the proportion of a firm's employees to be covered by collective agreements, (iii) bargaining 'depth', i.e. the degree to which union representatives will be involved in the implementation of deals; (iv) bargaining 'level', i.e. whether agreements are to apply at the plant, company or industry level; and (v) the size of the bargaining unit (qv).

bargaining unit. The domain to which a collective agreement applies, e.g. a division of a firm, a subsidiary of a company, an entire business, an industry, etc. The size of a bargaining unit should depend on its ability to implement agreed decisions. For instance, there would be little point in, say, a shop steward (qv) negotiating with his or her head of department for a pay rise for union members in a certain section of a business if wage increases can only be sanctioned by the firm's top management.

Barnard, Chester (1886–1961). Businessman and influential writer on management subjects. According to Barnard, organisations are systems within which several sub-systems exist, interconnect and collectively determine the character of the organisation's interrelationships with the outside world. Barnard was a major precursor of the systems approach (qv) to management.

Barnum effect. The tendency of individuals undergoing psychometric tests (qv) to agree with the tester's conclusions regarding their personalities (even if the conclusions are objectively incorrect). It results from testers stating their interpretations in extremely general terms that could apply to *anyone* taking the tests.

BARS method. See BEHAVIOURALLY ANCHORED RATING SCALES.

Barth variable sharing scheme. A nineteenth century bonus system introduced by Carl Barth (1860–1939) to encourage less productive workers (trainees for example) to increase output. It allows high incentive bonuses at the lower ends of wage payment scales.

basic award. Compensation for unfair dismissal (qv) equivalent to the value of a normal redundancy payment (qv).

basic motion. In motion study (qv), a single complete movement of a body member. Hence, 'basic motion time' is the period needed for a basic motion taking account of distance moved, the visual attention necessary to perform the motion, degree of precision required and the extent of mental effort expended.

Basic Research in Industrial Technologies for Europe (BRITE). An EC-funded scheme for making low cost loans to small businesses that wish to undertake research and development intended to improve the competitiveness of European manufacturing industries.

basic time. The observed time taken by an operative to complete a job, multiplied by a subjective rating (qv).

basic work data. Published tables used in predetermined motion time systems (qv).

batch costing. The practice of treating each batch of production as a separate cost centre (qv).

batch production. Repetitive non-continuous production of small batches of output.

BCM programme. See BEHAVIOURAL CONTINGENCY MANAGEMENT PROGRAMME.

Bedaux, Charles E (1887–1944). An advocate of work measurement (qv) who suggested that all human effort is measurable in terms of a common unit comprising appropriate proportions for work and relaxation. The exact proportions of work and relaxation within the unit depended on the nature of the work, the intensity of effort and the recovery period necessary. *See* BEDAUX UNIT.

Bedaux points system. A wage incentive system devised by Charles Bedaux (qv) in 1911. Earnings were related to the number of minutes required to perform a specified job or operation according to a predetermined standard. Bonuses were awarded for output above this level.

Bedaux unit. A measure of work devised by Charles Bedaux (qv) defined as the amount of work a normal person is able to perform in one minute working at normal speed in normal working conditions.

behaviour expectation scales (behaviourally anchored rating scales). A technique of performance appraisal (qv) in which the assessor attempts to identify aspects of the appraisee's behaviour considered typical of that person when completing particular types of assignment.

behaviour-modelling training. An approach to training based on the theory of social learning (qv). Trainees are encouraged: (i) to notice the behaviour of role models (qv); (ii) to engage in vicarious learning (qv) and remember observed behaviours; and (iii) to copy the role model's behaviour. Motivation is built into the system via the reinforcement (qv) of appropriate actions.

behaviour therapy. Psychotherapy (qv) intended to cause an individual to *change* his or her behaviour, rather than merely analysing the person's mental and emotional condition.

behavioural contingency management (BCM) programme. Systematic and detailed specification of desired changes in the behaviour patterns of an organisation's members and of the conditions needed to achieve these changes.

behavioural engineering systems training (BEST). An approach to supervisory (first line) (qv) management training which instructs supervisors on how (i) to recognise excellent aspects of subordinates' performances, (ii) to inform employees about their performances and (iii) to reinforce good perfor-

mance through praise and congratulation. Supervisors are taught to build on subordinates' strengths by setting objectives and rewarding progress towards goal attainment.

behavioural sciences. Technically the subjects of psychology (qv), sociology (qv) and anthropology, although the social sciences of politics, history and economics (plus certain aspects of geography and law) are sometimes placed in the behavioural sciences group.

behavioural theory of the firm. According to R. Cyert and J. Marsh, the proposition that organisations do not normally take decisions according to rational and systematic procedures, but rather in consequence of the outcomes to internal battles for power among various interest groups.

behaviourally anchored rating scales (BARS). *See* BEHAVIOUR EXPECTATION SCALES.

behaviourism. The proposition that all human actions are primarily determined by environmental stimulus-response factors.

benchmark jobs. Jobs used as yardsticks against which the values of other jobs are assessed during job evaluation (qv) exercises. Benchmark jobs are usually drawn from the bottom, middle and top of the hierarchy of jobs within an organisation. Other jobs are then 'slotted in' to the hierarchy according to their content, value and importance compared to the benchmarks and to each other.

benchmarking, organisational. Measurement of an organisation's effectiveness compared to similar enterprises. 'Competitive' benchmarking involves the direct comparison of data on competitors and the firm in question. 'Internal' benchmarking means conducting an audit of activities within the firm and then inferring whether these activities are performed more or less efficiently than in competing organisations. 'Functional' benchmarking compares particular functions or processes. Generic benchmarking contrasts the overall administrative efficiencies of businesses.

Benson's relaxation response method. A stress management technique in which the stressed person repeats a word or fixes his or her gaze on an object, consciously maintaining a passive attitude and ignoring external intrusions.

BEST. *See* BEHAVIOURAL ENGINEERING SYSTEMS TRAINING.

BET. *See* BUSINESS AND ENTERPRISE TRAINING.

BETA. *See* BROADCASTING AND ENTERTAINMENT TRADES ALLIANCE.

B-forms. *See* F-FORMS.

bibliographic. A kind of database (qv) containing details of books and articles on a particular topic.

BIFU. *See* BANKING, INSURANCE AND FINANCE UNION.

biodata. Information about a job applicant's personal background collected in the belief that particular life experiences create attitudes and personalities that cause people to be suitable for certain types of work.

biofeedback. Information on selected physiological functions (blood pressure, heart rate, etc.) collected continuously and displayed (on a handheld VDU for instance) to a stress (qv) prone individual in order to enable that person quickly to withdraw from potentially dangerous stress situations.

biological clock. The hormonal and other physiological mechanisms that control the times of day a person feels tired and/or hungry. Shift work can severely disrupt these body rythms.

biorhythms. Recurring cycles in a person's biochemical mechanisms. Daily biorhythms such as tiredness, hunger or changes in body temperature are referred to as 'circadian' rhythms.

biosocial factor. An influence on individual behaviour caused by the interaction of biological and social influences.

black box approach. A term sometimes used to describe behaviourism (qv) because of its disinterest in explaining cognitive or motivational influences on human activity. Black box models of employee behaviour analyse behaviour by listing behavioural inputs and outputs rather than the precise mechanics of how causes are transformed into effects.

black economy. That part of the economy which depends on unrecorded work paid on a 'cash in hand' basis, without contracts of employment (qv), and undertaken by people who do not declare their incomes to the tax authorities.

blackcoated worker. Another term for a white collar worker (qv).

blacking. Refusing to deal with a firm or person or to take over someone else's work, e.g. employees blacking the duties normally performed by other workers currently on strike.

blackleg. A term of abuse applied to a strikebreaking worker.

blacklisting. Placing the names of certain individuals onto a confidential list circulated confidentially to potential employers, usually in order to warn them that the listed persons possess certain characteristics, e.g. being a known trade union activist or having a criminal conviction. Blacklisting is not illegal in the United Kingdom. *See* DATA PROTECTION ACT 1984.

blanket dismissal. Sacking several workers in circumstances where one of them is known to be guilty of an offence (theft for example) but cannot be identified because fellow employees (who are fully aware of the culprit's name) refuse to tell management about the guilty person. Such dismissals are not unfair (qv), *provided* the employer has carried out a reasonable investigation.

blanket pay agreement. A wage settlement negotiated between management(s) and trade unions and covering all grades of worker in a firm or industry.

block exemptions. Special European Commission (qv) rules exempting small firms from the competition laws of the European Community in relation to franchising (qv) and know how (qv) licensing, exclusive distribution and purchasing agreements, and collaborative research and development (qv) arrangements.

block release systems. Mixed work experience and training programmes in which trainees attend a college or other training establishment for several weeks or months at a stretch, without having to go to work within this period. Such schemes contrast with day release (qv) systems that only require one day a week at college.

block vote. *See* CARD VOTING.

blue chip company. A large, stable well-established public limited company with a sound reputation and shares that are generally considered a safe investment.

blue collar workers. Manual workers in industrial workplaces. Machine operators and assembly line operatives are examples.

blueprint. A drawing, plan or (latterly) mathematical model which specifies the dimensions to which an item is to be manufactured. The name derives from the cheap, low quality blue coloured paper on which such drawings were originally replicated.

body image. A person's self-perception of his or her own body as a physical object with spatially related parts. Individual body image has many implications for the ergonomic (qv) design of equipment.

body language. Non-verbal transmissions of information via gestures, facial expressions, posture, folding of arms or legs, limb movements, etc.

Bogardus scale. A means for measuring employee attitudes (qv) towards their working groups through questioning employees about their willingness to admit outsiders to these groups.

bona fide actions. Things done in good faith with no dishonest or misleading intentions.

bonus systems. Employee incentive schemes applicable either to individuals or entire working groups. There are two general types: 'effort' and 'value added'. Effort-based systems fix standard times (qv) for waiting time (qv), for clearing up, machine setting and similar duties. These periods are usually computed from past averages and are paid at a predetermined flat rate (qv). Added value schemes pay bonuses strictly proportional to the value of the worker's output. Alternatively, the bonus might relate to the monetary value of the time saved in completing a task.

boomerang effect. A term sometimes used to describe the phenomenon that occurs when workers subjected to measures designed to alter their attitudes in fact change their attitudes in the opposite direction to that intended.

boredom, causes of. Either the continuous repetition of a simple task, or the social environment in which tasks are undertaken. Thus, a job may be interesting but the worker could still feel bored because of its social isolation. Equally a repetitious and trivial job might not be boring, in consequence of the employee being able to communicate with others and find distractions.

borrowed employee. A worker lent or hired from one employer to another. Responsibility for the worker lies with the *first* employer, unless there is an agreement to the contrary to which the employee has consented.

bottom up planning. An approach to corporate planning (qv) whereby various departments and sections of departments generate their own plans for achieving broadly defined company goals. Proposals are then synthesised by senior management.

boundary spanning activities. Multifaceted work that involves diverse activities and significant uncertainty regarding which tasks will have to be completed and how they will be performed.

bounded rationality approach. A model of decision making which recognises the importance of limiting factors (qv). It asserts that it is frequently more logical to select a convenient and low risk outcome to a problem than attempt a theoretically superior solution.

Bowey's stability index. A labour turnover index that attempts to establish the extent to which a large proportion of a company's employees might all retire within a short period.

BR tax code. A tax code (qv) instructing an employer to deduct income tax from an employee's wages at the basic rate. Other non-numeric tax codes are NT (no tax to be deducted), OT (no tax free pay) and D, meaning that tax is to be deducted at the higher rate.

brainstorming. The process of generating a large number of new ideas, without considering their feasibility at the time they are put forward. All the ideas brought up by participants during a brainstorming session are listed, but not discussed. A separate meeting is then convened to evaluate the costs, benefits and implications of each idea. Only the most promising ideas are eventually followed up.

branch and bound technique. A problem-solving method that breaks down large and complex problems into a series of smaller manageable units ('branching'), and then imposes limits on the range of possible solutions to be considered (bounding).

branch committee. A committee comprising key members of the branch (qv) of a trade union (e.g. chairperson, secretary and treasurer). Branch committees are set up to deal with routine administrative union matters that do not require consideration by the entire branch.

branch of a trade union. The primary unit upon which trade union organisation is based. Branches normally cover a particular geographical area, with all union members who work for firms in that area being attached to the branch. Exceptionally, branches may be created for individual large firms that employ very many union members. The functions of a branch are to collect union dues, act as a forum for debate on union issues and elect representatives onto higher level union committees.

breach of a contract of employment. Breaking an employment relationship through (i) repudiation and refusal to perform an aspect of the bargain (e.g. not attending work or failing to pay wages) *or* (ii) incapability (e.g. falling ill and being unable to complete essential duties), *or* (iii) breaking a condition of the contract. An advance renunciation of a contractual obligation (e.g. a worker stating he or she is about to go on strike) is called an 'anticipatory breach'.

breakaway union. A trade union (qv) created by former members of another union who were dissatisfied with the latter's conduct and/or ability to represent their interests. An example is the Union of Democratic Mineworkers, which broke away from the National Union of Mineworkers.

breakeven point. The level of activity at which costs are covered by sales revenues.

Bridge programme. A European Community programme for funding research and development in biotechnology.

Bridlington agreement. An accord signed in 1939 by members of the Trades Union Congress (qv) whereby unions within the same industry or trade do not poach each others' members.

briefing session. A means for management/worker communication. Sessions involve face-to-face meetings of managers with groups of workers in order to present explain, receive and discuss information.

BRITE. See BASIC RESEARCH IN INDUSTRIAL TECHNOLOGIES FOR EUROPE.

British Association for Commercial and Industrial Education (BACIE). An organisation founded in 1919 which seeks to influence government and other bodies concerned with vocational training and education and to improve and extend the provision of vocational training. It publishes booklets and manuals on training methods and offers consultancy services to help firms devise training strategies.

British Executive Service Overseas Association. A charity run jointly by the Confederation of British Industry (qv), the Institute of Directors and the Overseas Development Association to send volunteer executives to work in developing countries.

British Health and Safety Society. An organisation formed to promote the exchange of information on UK occupational health and safety matters. It arranges conferences and publishes a journal.

British Occupational Hygiene Society. An organisation established to encourage the improvement of occupational hygiene in the UK. It arranges conferences and workshops and publishes a journal.

British Safety Council. A national organisation that provides accident prevention training programmes, a range of information sheets and booklets and a computerised information service.

broad based training. Courses undertaken by learners destined for a variety of occupations or by trainees who do not know the specific types of job they will eventually perform.

Broadcasting and Entertainment Trades Alliance (BETA). A trade union (qv) representing all grades of staff in the BBC and independent television companies, employees of radio contractors, and broadcasting freelancers.

broadly similar work. Jobs which under the Equal Pay (Amendment) Regulations 1983 (qv) have many common elements and insignificant differences (for example, a male 'chef' and a female 'cook' working in different canteens of the same organisation). Males and females undertaking broadly similar work are entitled to equal pay.

Brogden-Hunter method. A technique for utility analysis (qv) involving five stages. The firm computes the costs and benefits of selecting (i) a person at random and (ii) the perfect candidate. Then it estimates the increased employee performance likely to result from use of a particular selection method (psychometric testing (qv) for example); it now converts this into monetary terms, and finally evaluates the consequences of various outcomes for workgroup output.

Brussels Convention on the Jurisdiction and Enforcement of Judgments on Civil and Commercial Matters 1968. An agreement signed by all EC countries to prevent 'forum shopping'. In general, cases must go through national courts before they are heard by EC Courts, *unless* the case involves customs duties, social security matters, legal capacity, bankruptcy or matrimonial property rights.

BS 5378. A standard specification for safety signs, legally binding for all signs erected since 1981.

BS 5750. A quality assurance standard (qv), adherence to which enables firms to obtain British Standard Institute certification that their quality management systems satisfy certain minimum criteria. Customers of these businesses may then have confidence in their abilities to deliver goods of a certain level of quality and to maintain the quality of their output at a consistent level.

BTEC. *See* BUSINESS AND TECHNICAL EDUCATION COUNCIL.

budgets. Statements of intentions of and limits on the amounts of money that are to be spent by certain departments or on particular functions or activities. The term may also be applied to expectations of outcomes. Thus, for example, the phrase 'sales budget' is sometimes used to describe sales targets.

budget committee. A committee convened to allocate resources within an organisation. Its role is to establish criteria for determining budget allocations to formulate budget policy, and to plan and administer the budgetary system. The committee will usually be chaired by a senior executive and contain representatives of various departments and/or functional specialisations.

budgeting loans. Interest free government loans given at the discretion of state Social Fund officers to people receiving income support (qv) in order to enable them to meet essential intermittent expenditures. Similar arrangements apply to 'crisis loans', intended to help the poor cope with unexpected emergencies, and 'community care grants' which assist individuals move into the community from state institutions.

building trades tax exemption certificate. *See* 714 CERTIFICATE.

Bullock report. The 1977 report of a government enquiry into the possible introduction of compulsory employee representation in the management of large British firms. It recommended a $(2x+y)$ formula. The $2x$ comprised two equal groups of directors, elected by shareholders and workers respectively. A third group (y) would consist of outsiders chosen by both sides. The recommendations of the Report were never implemented.

bullying, responsibility for consequent damage. The vicarious liability (qv) of an employer for damages inflicted on one worker by another through bullying and/or intimidation. This arises in situations where (i) the employer knew or ought to have known that the bullying worker's actions were dangerous and did nothing to prevent them, and/or (ii) the bullying acts were committed in the course of the bully's employment.

Bureau for Action for Disabled People. A body established by the European Community to monitor EC programmes for helping mentally or physically disabled people. *See* HELIOS PROGRAMME; HORIZON.

bureaucracy. A form of organisation in which there are many rules, standard procedures, extensive planning, specialisation of functions and the complete separation of policy making from operational control. Precedents exist for most activities, and are always followed. Bureaucracy is rational, stable and self-perpetuating.

bureaupathology. Problems arising from dysfunctional behaviour patterns often encouraged by bureaucratic forms of organisation; notably, stress resulting in resistance to change, ritualistic attachment to routines and procedures, aloofness, insistence on petty rights, etc.

burnout. An extreme response to managerial stress (qv) whereby an individual becomes completely unable to cope with his or her job. It involves emotional and/or physical exhaustion, low job productivity and loss of self-esteem.

Burns, T., and Stalker, K.W. Industrial sociologists who investigated attempts made by Scottish companies to introduce new technologies during the 1950s and 1960s. They concluded that the nature, extent and rate of change of firms' outside environments affected their organisational structure and effectiveness. In stable environments, mechanistic organisations (qv) emerged which were not suitable for handling the problems created by technological change. Organistic (qv) forms of organisation were more appropriate for volatile environments.

burolandschaft. The 'landscaping' of open plan offices via the use of screens, furniture dividers, plants, indoor fountains, etc., in attempts to minimise the perceived lack of privacy and loss of individuality in large open plan offices.

Business and Enterprise Training (BET). A government training programme (previously known as 'Business Growth Training') intended to demonstrate to small to medium sized firms how effective training can lead to higher profits, and how they might train their employees. Responsibility for administering the scheme lies with the Training and Enterprise Councils (qv). Firms may choose from five schemes, covering business skills for owner/managers, the effective use of consultants, formation of business training plans, collaboration on training with other firms, and the practical implementation of company courses.

Business and Technical Education Council. A body formed from the merger of the Technician Education Council (set up in 1973) and the Business Education Council (established in 1974) which develops modular courses for use by colleges of further education. There are three levels of BTEC programme: general, national and higher national. 'General' courses are intended for people beginning their studies at age 16 without 'O' level passes. National awards are for those with 'O' levels or a credit pass at BTEC general. Higher national programmes have 'A' level or BTEC national entry requirements.

business game. A group training (qv) method in which a business situation is simulated and two or more competing teams required to take decisions, the predetermined consequences of which are monitored by an instructor. Participants are given certain objectives within present environmental circumstances determined by the rules of the game. Elements of chance are incorporated via random occurrences beyond the control of the players.

Business Growth Training (BGT). See BUSINESS AND ENTERPRISE TRAINING.

business management. The governance of all the administrative, technical and human processes involved in the generation of wealth. This differs from management (qv) generally, which applies to *any* form of organisation, including public sector bodies, non-profit organisations, government agencies, etc.

business plan. A document that examines impartially and systematically the feasibility of a business venture, usually in order to convince outside financiers of the merits of the proposal. Typical headings within a plan are: product offered; marketing methods; distribution system; nature of competition; key personnel; premises; organisation structure; cash flow forecasts and budget projections.

butty gang. A nineteenth century term describing a group of about a dozen labourers who would jointly negotiate a contract for doing a job in return for a single lump sum payment, which the gang members then shared out among themselves.

C

C - JAM. *See* COMPLETE JOB ANALYSIS METHOD.

C - Space. *See* CULTURE SPACE.

cabal. A collection of individuals who covertly unite in order to seize power within an organisation.

CAC. *See* CENTRAL ARBITRATION COMMITTEE.

CACC. The acronym for the Council for the Accreditation of Correspondence Colleges.

CADCAM. The acronym for computer aided design and computer assisted management.

cafeteria benefits. *See* FLEXIBLE BENEFITS.

CAL (computer assisted learning). *See* COMPUTER BASED TRAINING.

California Psychological Inventory. A standardised measure of personality (qv) compiled by giving questions to groups of people regarded by their peers as unusual or extreme in certain respects. Average responses to these questions are then taken to represent 'abnormal' answers to similar questions used in personality tests.

call back pay. A lump sum paid to a worker temporarily laid off but then asked to resume work in consequence of an upturn in demand for a firm's products.

CAM. *See* COMMUNICATIONS, ADVERTISING AND MARKETING FOUNDATION.

canteens, employers' obligations to provide. Government regulations requiring employers to provide canteens or other suitable messrooms for workers engaged in certain industries; notably building, cement and chemicals, laundries, glass bottle manufacturing, lead processing, pottery, sugar, and wool sorting.

capability of an employee. A worker's *learned* creative skills and competencies needed to complete vocational tasks. *See* COMPETENCY, OCCUPATIONAL.

capability profile. A listing of an individual's strengths and weaknesses as they relate to work.

capacity planning. A technique for relating the intensity of a firm's production operations to the forecast level of demand for its products.

capacity usage ratio. The ratio of the budgeted number of working hours to the maximum number of working hours potentially available in a certain period.

capital employed. The extent of the capital invested in a business, measured either as the value of its net assets (qv), or as shareholders' equity plus long term debts.

capital expenditure budget. A budget containing details of planned expenditures on plant and equipment (qv) likely to benefit the firm for several years into the future. Although capital assets might be paid for in a lump sum, it is conventional to set only a proportion of their total cost against the capital expenditure budget for a particular year.

capital intensive production. Manufacturing processes employing a high proportion of physical plant and equipment (qv), machinery, etc., to labour.

capital rationing. A constraint on new investment whereby only limited funds are available for fresh projects, regardless of the rate of interest. Expenditure on one investment automatically reduces the amount of money available for others.

captive pension scheme. *See* SELF-ADMINISTERED PENSION SCHEME.

card steward. A term sometimes used in the engineering industry to describe a shop steward (qv) responsible for ensuring that union members are up to date with their contributions.

card voting. The voting system used at the annual Trades Union Congress (qv). Representatives of various unions each cast a number of votes proportional to the size of their union. Thus a single delegate might be able to cast many thousands of votes.

cardinal traits. A term coined by the psychologist G. W. Allport to describe an individual's personality characteristics that come to the fore in all situations which he or she encounters. These differ from 'primary' traits, which emerge in some but not all situations; and 'secondary' traits that appear only occasionally.

career. A related series of jobs which (i) follow a fairly predictable pattern and (ii) follow a hierarchy of status.

career anchors. The basic principles, work philosophy, self-perceptions, values and attitudes towards others that a person applies to the determination of what sort of job he or she should do.

career clock. A self-imposed timetable for achieving certain career objectives (promotions or the completion of training courses for example) defined by an ambitious manager at the outset of his or her career.

career development. Training and planned experience deliberately acquired to assist individuals maximise their potential and contributions to employing organisations.

career expectations. Assumptions and forecasts that a person holds about his or her future career (qv), the rewards anticipated from a particular type of job and predictions concerning the timing and frequency of promotions.

career life cycle hypothesis. The proposition that managerial careers typically follow clearly defined and predictable patterns with distinct transitions between phases. First, individuals learn how to 'fit into' an occupation; then they begin to find themselves and to innovate, develop self-confidence, and become less reliant on existing occupational conventions.

career management. The forecasting of a firm's future demand for managers and the development of management succession programmes (qv) to ensure that appropriate employees acquire the training, guidance and experience needed to occupy higher level positions.

career pattern. A person's occupational history, how long the individual spent in various jobs, the frequency with which he or she was promoted, levels of work undertaken, etc.

career planning. Assessing the training and work experience requirements necessary for an individual to pursue a successful career. It examines the job opportunities available within an organisation and relates these to the capacities and aspirations of the employee.

Careers Service of local education authorities. Vocational guidance for school-leavers provided by local authorities under the 1973 Employment and Training Act. Local Careers Services liaise with schools careers guidance teachers and transmit to students and their parents information on further education, employment and training opportunities. Careers officers interview pupils at their schools, assist them to obtain employment and offer help and advice on problems encountered in school-leavers' first jobs.

Carr Committee. A government committee set up to investigate the causes of the acute shortages of skilled workers that occurred during the 1950s. Its report (published in 1958) concluded that the extent of UK skills training was inadequate and that its quality was generally poor. The committee suggested that the problem was attributable to industry itself. Hence, responsibility for increasing the supply of skilled labour should lie with industry, without government financial support.

cartel. A collection of firms that colludes to fix prices and levels of output in a certain industry or market. Cartels are generally illegal under the Treaty of Rome (qv) if they exceed a specified threshold value or cover a significant proportion of the total market.

case studies. A group training (qv) method involving the simulation and analysis of previously experienced real life problems. Each group member investigates and reports on a certain aspect of a case, and must criticise and assess the contributions of other participants. Case work encourages analytical approaches to problems and is intended to develop participants' diagnostic abilities.

cash flow forecast. A prediction of the timing and values of all a business's cash receipts and payments expected over a future period. Forecasts are typically broken down into monthly analyses.

casual labour. Temporary workers hired for short periods when demand is sufficient to justify their engagement. Casuals may or may not work part time. *See* PERIPHERAL WORKERS.

categorical data. Information on events, objects or people whose characteristics differ *qualitatively* rather than quantitatively, e.g. information about 'men' and 'women'. This contrasts with 'ordinal' data, whereby items are ranked in some sort of order.

catharsis. A form of abreaction (qv) in which a person relieves tension through expressing a previously repressed emotion or relives a painful memory.

CATS (Credit Accumulation and Transfer Scheme). *See* CREDIT TRANSFER SCHEME.

Cattell's 16 PF test. A personality test used for employee selection. It assumes the existence within people of 16 clusters of behaviour or 'factors'. The factors relate to (1) whether the person is easy going or reserved and formal, (2) intelligence, (3) emotional stability, (4) excitability, (5) assertiveness, (6) whether the subject is cheerful or depressed, (7) conscientiousness, (8) extroversion or introversion, (9) self-sufficiency, (10) vigour, (11) whether the person is cultured or uncultured, (12) trustfulness, (13) attitudes to conformity, (14) shrewdness, (15) self-confidence, (16) cognitive ability.

CBI. *See* CONFEDERATION OF BRITISH INDUSTRY.

CBSI. *See* CHARTERED BUILDING SOCIETIES INSTITUTE.

CBT. *See* COMPUTER BASED TRAINING.

CCTV training. *See* CLOSED-CIRCUIT TELEVISION TRAINING.

CD-ROM. *See* COMPACT DISK-READ ONLY MEMORY.

Cecchini Report. An economic analysis of the predicted costs and benefits of the creation of the European Single Market. It was funded by the European Commission and published in 1988.

CEDEFOP. The 'European Centre for the Development of Vocational Training', an EC body formed to promote recognition of vocational qualifications (including 'Certificates of Experience' obtained in various member states) across the Community.

CELEX. The official database (qv) of European Community law, including all primary legislation, proposals for new legislation and decisions of the European Court (qv). Secondary legislation (i.e. rules, orders, regulations, etc. made under primary laws) is contained in the database SCAD (Systeme Communautaire d'Acces à la Documentation).

cell organisation. *See* OPERATIVE CELL STRUCTURE.

centiminute. The decimal minute, used in work study (qv), whereby each (60 second) minute is divided into 100 units. This enables times to be expressed as minutes and decimal points of a minute. Decimal *hours* are also used in work study exercises.

Central Arbitration Committee (CAC). A government body established in 1975 to hear complaints from recognised trade unions (qv) about employers' alleged failures to meet disclosure of information requirements (qv). It also arbitrates in disputes referred to it by ACAS.

central disposition. A character trait that plays a key role in organising a person's perceptions (particularly first impressions) of others.

centralisation. The concentration of activities and/or decision making into the hands of just a few people.

centralised interpersonal communication network. An intra-group communication system in which one person has access to more channels of communication than others and hence is likely to process a greater amount of information than people who occupy peripheral positions. *See* GATEKEEPER.

centralised organisations. An organisation in which all major decisions are taken by a central administrative body which issues binding directives to lower levels. Subordinates are bound by fixed rules and procedures, and exercise little discretion in the course of their work.

centre of excellence. An organisation or section within an organisation singled out for additional funding and favourable treatment in consequence of its past achievements, e.g. successful research, implementation of cost cutting programmes, introduction of new products, etc.

CEO. *See* CHIEF EXECUTIVE OFFICER.

Certificate of Age Exception. A document issued by the DHSS attesting that a worker is above the age of retirement and hence not liable for Class 1 National Insurance (qv) contributions.

Certificate of Election. *See* CERTIFICATE OF REDUCED LIABILITY.

Certificate of Experience. A document attesting the experience acquired by a worker in a certain trade or industry covered by a European Community directive (qv) concerning that trade or industry. Under EC legislation a Certificate of Experience issued by the recognised authorities of one EC member country *must* be accepted by the authorities of other Community states.

Certificate of Means of Escape in Case of Fire. A document that has to be obtained by factories (qv) and certain other businesses from their local fire authority or, in some cases, the fire brigade. The certificate attests that the firm's premises have been inspected and that adequate means of escape in the event of fire exist.

Certificate of Pre-Vocational Education (CPVE). A qualification offered jointly by the City and Guilds of London Institute and the Business and Technician Education Council (BTEC). It is intended for students who wish to stay on at school beyond the age of 16 but have no specific vocational or academic objectives.

Certificate of Reduced Liability. A document issued by the DHSS attesting that a married woman is eligible to pay reduced rate Class 1 National Insurance Contributions (qv). Married women lost the right to pay lower National Insurance Contributions in April 1977, unless they were already paying lower rate contributions at that time and continued thereafter to be married (or separated but not divorced) and continuously employed. A widow has the right to reduced rate contributions only if she was paying the reduced rate immediately prior to her husband's death.

certification of training. The issue of a certificate, diploma or other written document formally attesting that a trainee has successfully completed a course.

Certification Officer. A government official responsible for (i) attesting the independence of trade unions (qv), (ii) maintaining lists of trade unions and employers' associations (qv), (iii) refunding the costs incurred by unions when balloting members and (iv) hearing complaints from union members regarding the conduct of union ballots.

CF 379. *See* EMPLOYEES WITH MORE THAN ONE JOB, NATIONAL INSURANCE AND.

CGLI. *See* CITY AND GUILDS OF LONDON INSTITUTE.

chain of command. The line of authority that runs from the apex of an organisation to its base and carries information and instructions.

chaining of responses. In operant conditioning (qv), a series of responses to a stimulus whereby each response leads directly to the next. Learning the words of a song is an example; the melody associated with the first line prompts the individual to remember the words of the next line, which triggers memory of the third, etc.

Chamber of Commerce. An association of local businesses and business people established to further members' interests and to promote business and industry in the local community. Chambers of Commerce offer a range of information and training facilities, especially in the import/export field. British Chambers of Commerce are private bodies with voluntary membership. In several Continental countries, however, Chambers of Commerce are state controlled, with compulsory membership for all local firms.

change agent. A person or institution responsible for initiating and implementing organisational change. Often the change agent is an external management consultant specifically recruited to undertake this task.

change in terms of employment. An alteration in the terms specified in a contract of employment (qv), which may or may not give rise to an action for constructive dismissal (qv). Under the Employment Act 1982 (qv), any change must be announced not more than one month after its occurrence and should be clearly communicated to each individual worker.

change, management of. Policies and procedures for implementing change. There are five major steps in the process: (i) precise definition of the changes required; (ii) specification of how these changes will affect particular individuals and groups; (iii) identification of the attitudes towards and perspectives on change currently held by employees and how these relate to proposed new methods; (iv) statement of the attitudes and perspectives necessary for employees to adapt successfully to new methods; and (v) implementation of measures designed to facilitate change.

change of practice agreement. An arrangement negotiated between a management and a firm's trade unions (qv) whereby no alterations in working methods are introduced unless a certain predetermined percentage of their financial benefits is distributed to employees as wage increases.

change of use certificate. A form of planning permission (qv) required for businesses which wish to enter the purpose for which their premises are used (e.g. from retailing to light engineering). Certificates are not normally withheld unless the intended new use of the premises would cause a public nuisance or a safety or health hazard.

charge hand. Another term for a supervisor (qv) sometimes applied in the manufacturing and construction (as opposed to service) industries.

charismatic leader. A group leader perceived by subordinates as possessing extraordinary powers, characteristics and abilities and who can inspire loyalty and enthusiasm among group members. See LEADERSHIP.

Chartered Association of Certified Accountants. See ACCA.

Chartered Building Societies Institute (CBSI). A professional body which offers examinations to people employed in building societies and associated institutions.

Chartered Engineer. An engineer who has satisfied the examination requirements of one of the major UK engineering institutions and has completed an appropriate period of practical experience.

Chartered Institute of Banking (CIB). A professional body offering examinations to people concerned with banking and financial services.

Chartered Institute of Management Accountants (CIMA). One of the leading UK professional bodies in the accountancy field. Prior to receiving a Royal Charter it was known as the Institute of Cost and Management Accountants (ICMA). CIMA students specialise in costing, investment appraisal and management accountancy (qv).

Chartered Institute of Marketing (CIM). A professional body offering examinations in marketing and sales management.

Chartered Institute of Public Finance and Accountancy (CIPFA). A chartered professional body (qv) which acts as the qualifying professional organisation for accountants in local authorities and other public sector services.

Chartered Insurance Institute (CII). A professional body concerned with education and training for the insurance industry.

Chartered professional body. A professional body (qv) granted a Royal Charter on the recommendation of the Privy Council, in recognition of its pre-eminence in a particular field. Examples are the Chartered Institute of Management Accountants, the Chartered Institute of Bankers, the Chartered Institute of Marketing and the Institute of Chartered Accountants of England and Wales.

Chartered Psychologist (C. Psychol.). A person recognised by the British Psychological Society as appropriately qualified in the field of psychology (qv). (It is also possible to become a Chartered occupational psychologist (qv).) Qualification is achieved through obtaining a relevant degree plus the completion of a period of work experience.

chattel. An item of property other than freehold land.

check-off agreement. An arrangement whereby an employing firm automatically deducts an employee's trade union subscriptions from his or her wages and passes the money directly to the union. The worker's permission is required before this may occur.

chief executive officer. The senior line manager (qv) within a business organisation, typically its managing director.

Children and Young Persons Act 1933. *See* EMPLOYMENT OF CHILDREN ACT 1973.

Chinese walls. Imaginary divisions within an organisation intended to prevent one division exchanging information with others.

chose in action. Rights over intangible resources not currently in a person's possession, e.g. debts or rights under insurance policies. This differs from a 'chose in possession', which relates to tangible items owned and possessed by a person or firm.

chronemics. The timing of verbal exchanges, e.g. the promptness of responses to questions.

chronobiology. The analysis of biorhythms.

Chronocyclegraph. *See* CYCLEGRAPH.

chunking. An aid to training and learning (qv) whereby instructional material is grouped together into meaningful segments in order to facilitate its memorisation.

CIB. *See* CHARTERED INSTITUTE OF BANKING.

CII. *See* CHARTERED INSURANCE INSTITUTE.

CIM. *See* CHARTERED INSTITUTE OF MARKETING.

CIMA. *See* CHARTERED INSTITUTE OF MANAGEMENT ACCOUNTANTS.

CIPFA. *See* CHARTERED INSTITUTE OF PUBLIC FINANCE AND ACCOUNTANCY.

Circadian rhythms. *See* BIORYTHMS.

CIRO method. An approach to the evaluation of training that analyses the usefulness of programmes under four main headings: context, input, reaction and outcome (hence the acronym CIRO).

CITB. The acronym for Construction Industry Training Board.

CITO. The acronym for Ceramics Industry Training Organisation.

City and Guilds of London Institute. An examining body particularly concerned with the training of craft workers (qv).

Civil and Public Servants Association (CPSA). A UK trade union (qv) that recruits civil servants. The Civil Service Union is also active in this field.

civil wrong. *See* CRIME.

class I body movement. A body movement involving just the use of the fingers. Class II movements require the use of fingers and wrist; class III movements need fingers, wrist and lower arm. A class IV movement is a class III movement with the addition of the upper arm. Class V requires the additional use of the shoulder. Work involving class III and IV movements is generally less tiring than that requiring classes I, II or V.

Class I National Insurance. NI contributions paid by employees of organisations, based on a predetermined percentage (varied periodically by the government) of the person's earnings up to a ceiling annual total amount. There are two types: contracted-out and not contracted-out. The former are for employees who belong to government approved company pension schemes, and are slightly lower than the latter. Non contracted-out employees automatically belong to SERPS (qv), unless they belong to an approved private pension scheme. Class 1 contributions may be grade A (standard rate), grade B (for widows and older married women), or grade C (for people over normal retirement age).

Class II National Insurance. NI contributions paid by the self-employed. They are flat rate and do not vary with earnings. Contributors do not qualify for unemployment pay or for SERPS (qv) benefits. Self-employed people also have to pay Class IV contributions according to the value of their profits between certain income levels.

Class III National Insurance. Voluntary NI contributions paid by people who for various reasons are not contributing under Classes I or II but who, nevertheless, wish to qualify for a limited range of benefits.

Class IV National Insurance. Earnings-related national insurance contributions paid by self-employed people in addition to Class II NI (qv) contributions. They are payable on profits above and below certain prespecified limits.

classical approach. A general approach to management which insists that there exist certain universally valid management principles that should be applied in all administrative and organisational circumstances.

classical conditioning. The connection of a neutral stimulus with a reflexive response. Neutral stimuli are unlearned and unconditioned; reflexive responses are responses controlled by the autonomic nervous system (qv) and involve such things as salivation, the secretion of adrenalin, changes in blood pressure, and so on. A famous example of classical conditioning was the experiments performed by the Russian Psychologist Ivan Pavlov, who rang a bell every time a group of dogs was shown food. Eventually, the dogs' mouths would water whenever they heard a bell, even though no food was offered: the dogs had become *conditioned* to respond to the sound of the bell. *See* CONDITIONING.

Classification, Packaging and Labelling of Dangerous Substances Regulations 1984. Legislation which controls the handling and conveyance of dangerous substances. It details required specifications for label sizes, warning signs, etc.

classified display. A form of newspaper recruitment advertising whereby all job advertisements are segregated into a certain section of a newspaper page.

clerical work measurement. Application of work study (qv) to determine the times necessary to perform clerical jobs. It seeks to reduce staffing levels, increase the efficiency of clerical procedures, record activities and generally improve administrative control.

clinical psychology. The application of psychology (qv) to the diagnosis of mental, emotional and behavioural disorders.

clinical selection of employees. Judgemental, impressionistic employee selection methods, usually based on job interviews. *See* ACTUARIAL SELECTION METHODS.

clique. A sub-group of individuals within a larger group, all of whom are more attracted to each other than to other members of the larger group. *See* SOCIOMETRY.

clocking in. The practice of workers inserting a 'time card' into a time recording machine on each occasion they enter and leave their places of work.

close company. A limited company with five or fewer stockholders or which is controlled by any number of directors who are also shareholders. Close companies are legally required to distribute most of their investment incomes to shareholders, who may be liable to

pay tax at a higher rate than the rate of corporation tax payable on funds left in the company.

closed-circuit television (CCTV) training. Filming of trainees as they complete tasks or make presentations in order to provide them with feedback on their performances and hence enable the identification of personal strengths and weaknesses.

closed loop system. A control mechanism whereby data on current performance automatically adjusts operations in order to rectify divergences between planned and actual output or activity.

closed question. An interview or written question with fixed alternative answers, e.g. a simple 'yes' or 'no'.

closed shop. An organisation or section of an organisation where all employees are members of a trade union and where there exists some means for preventing individuals who are not union members from being employed. Closed shops (which are generally unlawful in the UK) may be 'pre-entry', meaning that only existing members of a particular union are employed; or 'post-entry' whereby new recruits are obliged to join a certain union on entering the firm. *See* LABOUR SUPPLY SHOP.

closed system. *See* OPEN SYSTEM.

closure, mental. The process whereby the brain automatically attempts to complete and make sense of fragmented and incoherent information.

clothing, accommodation for. Facilities for storing and drying employees' clothing that is not worn during working hours, as required by the Factories Act 1961 (qv) and the Offices, Shops and Railway Premises Act 1963 (qv). Employers are obliged to consider the probability of theft when selecting a suitable location for this purpose.

cluster chain. A pattern of organisational communication whereby one person informs several others of a certain fact. Some of the message recipients do not pass on the information, but at least one person tells another 'cluster' of several individuals, the process being repeated several times. Cluster chains are common in organisational grapevines (qv).

CNAA. *See* COUNCIL FOR NATIONAL ACADEMIC AWARDS.

coaching. A method of instruction whereby a qualified and experienced person transmits knowledge to a trainee on a person-to-person basis. The instructor may vary the pace and content of the training to meet the recipient's particular requirements.

coaction. The process whereby persons with the same objective work towards the objective individually and without interacting or communicating with each other.

co-adaptation. Adjustments in an individual's behaviour implemented to enable the person to fit in with the norms of a group.

coalition bargaining. Negotiations (qv) that involve a number of trade unions (qv) collectively placing a joint demand to an employing organisation.

coalitions, bargaining theory of. A theory of bargaining which suggests that coalitions of parties to a negotiation will normally be unstable because those outside the coalition have an incentive to induce one or more coalition members to leave, and then form an alliance with someone else. This causes countermoves within the coalition and general instability.

Code of Practice. A document published by a government agency, professional body, trade association or other relevant authority outlining model procedures for good practice in a particular field. Codes give examples of excellent and bad behaviour, and recommendations regarding how things should be done. Government Codes of Practice (e.g. those issued by the Equal Opportunities Commission (qv), ACAS (qv), or the Health and Safety Executive (qv)) are not legally binding, but are looked at by Courts when adjudicating cases.

co-determination. The German system of worker participation in management. It provides for employee representatives on supervisory boards (qv), plus workers' councils and the provision of management information to employees.

coding of data. Categorisation of items of data by assigning to each item an indicator (e.g. a sign or number) which causes it to fall into a predetermined class.

CODOT. *See* COMMON OCCUPATION DIRECTORY OF JOB TITLES.

coercive power. Power (qv) derived from the ability of impose penalties on others or deprive them of rewards.

cognition. Mental processes concerned with thinking, reasoning, solving problems, language, reasoning and perception (qv). An individual's 'cognitive structure' is his or her complex of attitudes, beliefs and other aspects of his or her cognitive personality.

cognitive categorisation (conceptualisation). The psychological processes whereby a person places similar objects into a common mental category. Once a particular object is recognised as belonging to a certain category, its likely attributes may be predicted from previous experience with objects of the same class. This enables the conscious linking together of images, physical items, stimuli or events into 'concepts'. For example, apples, oranges and bananas are all separate and unique entities, but the brain will put them together into the single concept of 'fruit'.

cognitive consonance. Logical consistency among a person's attitudes (qv) and cognitions (qv).

cognitive dissonance. A state of mind in which an individual's perceptions (qv) of related objects, or circumstances are out of balance. Perceptions are inconsistent, causing the person to feel ill at ease.

cognitive psychology. That branch of psychology (qv) which focuses on the thought processes, e.g. attitude formation, information processing, rationalisation, decision making, perception etc.

cognitive resource theory. A leadership (qv) theory suggested by F.E. Fiedler (qv) according to which leaders in non-stressful interpersonal situations tend to use their *intelligence* more than their *experience* when managing a group, and vice-versa.

cognitivist approach to learning. A theory of learning (qv) which asserts that individuals learn not through operant conditioning (qv) but rather through being presented with information sufficient to enable them to plan ahead and act.

cohort effect. The influence on individual behaviour of a group of people, each member of which underwent a similar experience at the same time as the person concerned, e.g. training or exposure to certain norms (qv) or working conditions.

cohort of workers. A group of employees who all experience a certain event (recruitment or promotion for example) at the same time.

COHSE. *See* CONFEDERATION OF HEALTH SERVICE EMPLOYEES.

cold weather payments. State benefit paid for any consecutive seven-day period when the temperature falls below zero degrees Celsius to people on Income Support (qv) who have a child under five, or are disabled or in receipt of a state recruitment pension.

collective agreement. An outcome to collective bargaining (qv). Collective agreements can be incorporated into an individual employee's contract of employment if the affected person has previously agreed to this happening.

collective agreements, legality and enforceability. The rule that a collective agreement (qv) (e.g. one negotiated with an employer by a trade union (qv)) is not binding on a firm's employees unless (i) the worker's contract of employment (qv) contains a clause to this effect, (ii) there exists a statute compelling acceptance (as in the Health Service for example), or (iii) there has been long standing acceptance of collective agreements by everyone involved.

collective bargaining. The system whereby an employee's terms of employment are settled not by individual negotiation but rather by collective agreements (qv) reached between employee representatives (typically trade union (qv) representatives) and management. Agreements apply equally to many employees. *See* NATIONAL AGREEMENTS; LOCAL COLLECTIVE BARGAINING (WORKPLACE AGREEMENTS).

Collective Redundancies Directive 1975. An EC Directive that requires private sector employers to give prior notification to and consult with employee representatives when collective redundancies are proposed. The provisions of the Directive were incorporated into the Employment Protection (Consolidation) Act 1978 (qv), although they now only apply to recognised trade unions (qv). *See* NOTIFICATION OF PLANNED REDUNDANCIES.

collectively agreed terms. Express terms of a worker's contract of employment (qv) determined on the worker's behalf through collective bargaining (qv). Employees must indicate their willingness to accept these terms, e.g. through the incorporation of a written clause in their contracts of employment.

collectivism. The proposition that since society is an aggregation of groups with conflicting interests then institutions (e.g. trade unions (qv)) which represent group interests make important and useful contributions to social welfare overall. According to this view, governments should constrain and regulate individual activities and actively seek to protect disadvantaged groups.

Combination Acts 1800. Legislation intended to outlaw trade unions and all other combinations of workers. Organisation of employees into unions was regarded as a conspiracy, for which long terms of imprisonment or transportation could be imposed. Striking, attending union meetings and entering into contracts aimed at improving wages or working conditions became criminal offences.

combine committee. A committee of shop stewards (qv) representing the various subsidiaries and divisions of a large organisation.

COMETT. The acronym for an EC-funded programme, 'Community Action for Education and Training for Technology', intended to encourage joint ventures between EC universities and businesses. Universities conduct Community-financed technological research, while businesses draw upon and implement the findings.

comfort letter. A statement from the European Commission (qv) issued to a company stating that the Commission has no *prima facie* evidence to suggest that the company is acting unlawfully (e.g. in relation to EC equal opportunities or competition law) and hence that the Commission will not intervene in the company's affairs until the matter has been fully investigated. The firm cannot be sued or fined by the Commission until the investigation has been completed.

command. The process of issuing instructions to ensure that plans are implemented and targets met. *See* LEADERSHIP; DIRECTION.

commerce. The systems and procedures through which goods are traded and distributed. Hence it concerns wholesaling and retailing, foreign trade, finance, insurance and transport and communications.

Commission for Racial Equality. A quasi-autonomous publicly funded organisation which attempts to eliminate racial discrimination in the UK. It acts as a pressure group, conducts research, publishes pamphlets and issues Codes of Practice (qv) on the avoidance of unfair racial discrimination in recruitment and employment. Additionally the Commission will initiate test case legal actions against firms that unlawfully discriminate in circumstances where important matters of principle are involved.

commission, obligation to pay. The common law rule that employers who pay their staff via commissions are obliged to provide staff with the volume of work reasonably contemplated by the parties at the time their contract of employment (qv) was agreed.

Commissioner for the Rights of Trade Union Members. *See* EMPLOYMENT ACT 1988.

committee. A group of people to whom issues are referred for consideration, investigation or resolution. Committees can be temporary and *ad hoc*, or permanent. They may or may not be empowered to implement their decisions. *See* STANDING COMMITTEE.

Committee on Women's Rights. A committee of the European Parliament, established in 1981 to encourage the implementation of equality of employment opportunity for women.

common law. Law that derives from custom and tradition rather than from Act of Parliament.

Common Occupation Directory of Job Titles (CODOT). A categorisation of job titles into homogeneous groups determined by the UK Department of Employment.

communal occupation. A type of work where residential accommodation has to be provided as an essential part of the job.

communication. The exchange of information, opinion and sentiment. Information is encoded for transmission via a message that is decoded by the recipient. Decoding requires the interpretation of messages. 'Noise' is any form of interference with messages that produces extra and distracting information (technical jargon or overlong sentences for example). *See* COMMUNICATION SYSTEM; COMMUNICATION, VERTICAL AND HORIZONTAL.

communication barriers. Obstacles preventing the smooth flow of information through organisations. Examples are (i) overlong chains of command (qv) that lead to the distortion of messages as they pass through various levels of a hierarchy; (ii) individuals receiving so much information that most is disregarded; (iii) vague and meaningless sentences in written documents; and (iv) personal biases causing people to see only what they want to see and to hear only what they want to hear.

communication breakdowns. Communication (qv) difficulties created by problems such as delays in processing information, the distortion of messages as they pass through a chain of command (qv), information being sent to the wrong people, or managers assuming their colleagues have been informed of issues when in fact they have not.

communication overload. The situation that results from managers receiving so many messages that most are disregarded.

communication, paralinguistic. Communication (qv) via gestures and signals transmitted through the tone of voice adopted.

communication system. Arrangements and structures for linking together the constituent parts of an organisation through the creation, distribution and interpretation of information and the provision of feedback on events.

communication, vertical and horizontal. Flows of communication (qv) up and down an organisation (vertical communication), or laterally among colleagues of equal rank (horizontal communication). Channels for vertical communication are normally illustrated in a firm's organisation chart (qv) and (unlike horizontal communication) are an integral part of its formal authority system. Horizontal communications are not referred to higher levels. Rather they concern the exchange of news and opinion among people of equal rank.

Communications, Advertising and Marketing Foundation (CAM). A professional body set up by the major UK advertising institutions (the Advertising Association and the Institute of Practitioners in Advertising for example) to advance education and training in advertising and marketing. CAM offers examinations at the certificate and diploma levels.

community care grant. See BUDGETING LOANS.

Community Programme. A government job creation scheme that involved unemployed workers undertaking community projects. It offered participants work experience, but was criticised for not providing genuine vocational training. Hence it was revised in 1988 and incorporated into the Employment Training Scheme (qv).

commutation of an occupational pension. The exchange of pension rights for an immediate cash payment, e.g. when the beneficiary discovers he or she is fatally ill with only a short time to live. Whether commutation is possible, and if so the value of the payment, is subject to the rules of the scheme.

COMP scheme. See CONTRACTED OUT MONEY PURCHASE SCHEME.

compa ratio (comparative ratio index). A measure of the extent to which pay levels are clustered around the midpoint of a particular grade. It is calculated as the average of all salaries in a grade divided by the mid-point of the grade's salary range. A value exceeding one indicates unusually high salaries within the grade.

compact disk-read only memory (CD-ROM). A computer disk containing a DATABASE which the database producer sells to subscribers for a subscription or lump sum fee. The information on the disk cannot be altered, only read. However, the entire CD-ROM database will normally be updated every six or 12 months so that subscribers can buy periodically a new disk containing up-to-date information. CD-ROM contrasts with WORM (write once read many times) systems which enable subscribers to add material to the disk.

compact scheme. An agreement between a company and pupils in a local school (typically in an inner city area) whereby pupils are guaranteed a job with the company provided they attain prespecified goals in relation to attendance, standard of school work, punctuality, etc. Students spend short work experience periods with the company.

company agreements. See LOCAL COLLECTIVE BARGAINING (WORKPLACE AGREEMENTS).

company cars, contract purchase of. A means for acquiring company vehicles whereby a third party purchases and then leases them to a client business for a set period (normally four years), at the end of which they are sold to the client at a predetermined price. The system has significant tax advantages.

company law, fifth EC Draft Directive on. An EC proposal which, if adopted, will compel all EC companies employing more than 1,000 workers either to have a supervisory board (qv) responsible for general strategy and containing worker directors (qv); or a single board with a majority of non- executive directors (empowered to dismiss executive directors) and including worker directors. Between one third and one half of a single or supervisory board would consist of employee representatives. Alternatively, a company could implement worker participation in management decision making via a 'works council' that has representation on the board of directors.

company reports, employee information regulations. Requirements imposed by the Employment Act 1982 (qv), whereby public companies must include in their annual reports a statement describing the actions they have taken over the previous year to introduce or develop employee information arrangements, consultation procedures and/or employee share schemes.

company secretary. An official of a limited company (who may or may not be a director (qv)) responsible for certain legal duties, such as the maintenance of minute books and other statutory records. In law, the company secretary represents the company to the outside world. Every company is legally obliged to have a company secretary.

company town. A town or city heavily dependent for employment on a single large business.

company union. *See* STAFF ASSOCIATION.

comparability claim. A demand by workers for an improvement in their pay or other terms or conditions of service that will bring them into line with levels of pay and/or conditions of service granted to employees doing similar work within the same organisation or in other firms. Job evaluation (qv) is one means for dealing with comparability claims.

comparative estimating. A method of work measurement (qv) whereby the time needed to finish a job is determined from the times needed to complete the elements of comparable jobs which have already been studied.

comparative international management, study of. Analysis of the causes and consequences of differences in management style and practice between nations or groups of nations.

compensatory award. Compensation for unfair dismissal (qv) based on an assessment of the employee's loss of wages and benefits now and in the future.

competence based qualifications. According to the NCVQ (qv), certificates and diplomas which attest that the training a person has undertaken contributes directly to his or her ability to perform a job.

competence objective. An employee training objective expressed in terms of work activity. The phrase was used in the YTS programme to describe intended outcomes to YTS training.

competencies, managerial. Dimensions of managerial competence identified by the Occupational Standards Branch of the Training Agency (qv). The aim was to discover what managers do and hence establish the skills and experiences that need to be incorporated into management training courses. Three dimensions were identified: (i) 'managing resources and systems' (including managing people, financial control and other management functions);

(ii) 'personal effectiveness', incorporating communication and other interpersonal skills; and (iii) 'environmental sensitivity' to customers, the wider community, and to employees. *See* PERFORMANCE CRITERIA.

competency, occupational. An ability to perform the activities associated with an occupation including, according to the NCVQ (qv): (i) the ability to apply knowledge and skills at work and to transfer them to new situations; (ii) the organisation and planning of work; (iii) innovation; and (iv) coping with non-routine activities. The NCVQ relies upon experts from the appropriate sector of employment to determine the competencies required for each occupational area. Lead Bodies (qv) then decide the standards of competence necessary for a job and the level of performance required. Advice on the latter is given by individuals and organisations with expertise in education and training. The aim is that the process of setting standards be 'employment led'. *See* ELEMENT OF COMPETENCE; PERFORMANCE CRITERIA; UNIT OF COMPETENCE; COMPETENCIES, MANAGERIAL.

competitive benchmarking. *See* BENCHMARKING, ORGANISATIONAL.

competitive parity method. An approach to budgeting in which a firm estimates and copies the levels of budget allocated to various functions by major competitors.

competitive strategy. According to management theoretician Michael E. Porter, 'the art of relating a company to the economic environment within which it exists'. Porter identified four factors determining this environment: the ease with which competitors can enter the industry; bargaining powers of customers and suppliers; the ease with which substitute products can be introduced; and the extent of competition among existing firms.

complete job analysis method (C-JAM). A technique of job analysis (qv) which categorises tasks in terms of the times needed for their completion, their level of difficulty and the severity of the consequences of making a mistake.

complex man hypothesis. A proposition put forward by management theorist E.H. Schein suggesting that no single management style (qv) can improve the performances of all workers because individual motives are highly complex and liable to change both over time and with respect to the circumstances of work situations. This contradicts the 'self-actualising man' approach suggested by A. H. Maslow (qv); the 'economic man' view of human nature associated with scientific management (qv); and the 'social man' view of G. Elton Mayo (qv).

compliance. The process whereby an individual accepts the influence of another person or a group (e.g. by changing behaviour or attitudes) in order to to gain a favourable reaction from the other person or group. A simple example is an employee who laughs at the boss's jokes even when they are not funny. Note however that compliance does not necessarily imply the acceptance or internalisation (qv) of rules or orders, or identification with an employing organisation.

composite job advertisements. Single advertisements containing the details of several different jobs. Each entry is paid for by a different employing organisation. Sometimes the composite appears under the name of a recruitment agency, with the names of individual employers remaining anonymous.

compositing (grouping) of motions. The practice of combining together several motions on the same topic, all submitted for discussion and resolution to the annual national delegate conference of a trade union (qv) or to the Trades Union Congress (qv). Its purpose is the creation of a single motion that reflects the spirit of all the individual motions, so that just one motion may be debated, saving much time.

compressed working week. An arrangement whereby employees work fewer days per week by working an increased number of hours on the days they actually work, e.g. four ten-hour days following by a full day off.

compulsion. A irresistable urge to behave in a manner contrary to one's conscious wishes.

computer based training (CBT). Employee training via computer software packages. CBT is normally based on the principles of programmed learning (qv). Packages might include access to a public or custom built database. 'Adaptive testing' CBT allows trainees to predetermine the depth in which they wish to cover the subject. Thus, someone who only requires a brief overview of material will select an option that provides just the fundamentals of the subject, ignoring technical detail. Other options will examine the subject in greater depth.

computer integrated manufacture. Advanced CADCAM (qv) systems that have been extended to incorporate all aspects of production planning, operations, packaging and dispatch.

computerised testing. Use of computers to score and interpret standard psychometric (qv) tests administered by means of terminals and keyboards.

conceptualisation. *See* COGNITIVE CATEGORISATION.

concerted practice. A situation where the collective actions of a number of firms imply that they have colluded in order to violate the competition laws of the European Community, even through the firms have not entered a formal agreement.

concession bargaining. A form of collective bargaining (qv) in which management offers no wage increases or other improvements in terms and conditions of work, but instead threatens to create redundancies if productivity does not improve. *See* PRODUCTIVITY BARGAINING; MACHO MANAGEMENT.

conciliation. Use of an independent and fair minded third party to help settle an industrial dispute. The conciliator acts as a broker between disputants, advising each side of the other's feelings and suggesting possible compromise deals.

conciliation officer. A person employed by ACAS (qv) whose job is to encourage out-of-Court settlements in cases submitted to industrial tribunals (qv).

concurrent validity, establishing. Validation (qv) of a selection test by testing existing workers who undertake jobs similar to that for which candidates are to be tested. The aim is to discover the qualities needed for successful performance in the vacant post. Job applicants are then tested for evidence of these qualities and their marks compared with those obtained by currently employed workers.

conditional strokes. In transactional analysis (qv), pyschological rewards to a person for behaving in a certain manner. An example is a compliment to a subordinate for having remedied a deficiency (frequent latecoming for instance). Unconditional strokes, conversely, are general statements presented to a person which do not relate specifically to a particular act or mode of behaviour. Rather, they express overall appreciation of an individual's total worth.

conditioned response. In the theory of conditioning (qv), a response caused by a specific stimulus that comes to be associated with a certain event in the mind of the subject of the conditioning, e.g. feeling hungry on hearing the ringing of a dinner bell. Here, feeling hungry is the response that has been conditioned through the repeated association of the ringing of a dinner bell with taking food.

conditioned stimulus. An originally neutral stimulus (qv) that becomes associated with a conditioned response (qv) and is capable therefore of provoking a certain reaction. See CLASSICAL CONDITIONING.

conditioning. Learning (qv) through reinforcement (qv). See CLASSICAL CONDITIONING; OPERANT CONDITIONING.

Conditions of Employment and National Arbitration Order 1940. See MUNITIONS OF WAR ACT 1915.

Confederation of British Industry (CBI). A body formed in 1965 to represent the interests of UK businesses in their relations with government, the Trades Union Congress (qv), and other major organisations. It began from the merger of the Confederation of British Industries, the National Union of Manufacturers and the British Employers Confederation. The CBI lobbies government on issues affecting business, and generally expresses the employer's point of view.

Confederation of Entertainment Unions. A trade union (qv) confederation comprising various unions in the entertainment industry (Actors' Equity and the Musicians' Union for example) plus a number of writers' and journalists' unions, including the NUJ.

Confederation of Health Service Employees (COHSE). A leading UK trade union (qv) that represents health workers, especially people employed in the NHS.

Confederation of Industries of the European Community. See UNION DES INDUSTRIES DE LA COMMUNAUTE EUROPEENEE.

Confederation of Shipbuilding and Engineering Unions (CSEU). A trade union (qv) confederation founded in 1936 and comprising manual and white collar unions in the engineering and shipbuilding industries. Its aim is to provide a unified approach to national collective bargaining in these fields.

confederations of trade unions. Arrangements whereby several trade unions (qv) act jointly in order to further a mutual interest, e.g. by adopting a common position in pay negotiations with an employers' association (qv). Currently about 40 union confederations operate in the United Kingdom. They have their own administrative organisations and typically employ their own full time staff. Examples are the Confederation of Shipbuilding and Engineering Unions and the National Federation of Building Trades.

confidential information. Trade and other secrets belonging to employers which employees have a common law duty not to reveal to people outside the firm. The information must be genuinely secret, not already known to anyone else, and be such that its release would damage the firm or be advantageous to rivals. Examples are manufacturing secrets, designs, compounds and mixtures, lists of customers, and data concerning the financial state of a business.

confined spaces, entry regulations. Requirements under section 30 of the Factories Act 1961 (qv) controlling the circumstances in which employees or sub-contractors may lawfully be allowed access into confined spaces where dangerous fumes may be present. The definition of 'confined space' covers chambers, vats, pipes, tanks, pits, flues or similar places. Manholes must be provided, the employee should if possible wear ropes held by other workers outside the confined space and a sufficient number of workers must be trained in artificial respiration.

conflict between groups. Inter-group conflict arising from competition for limited resources, differing perceptions about the aims of an organisation, lack of co-ordination by higher management, attempts by one group to dominate others, etc.

conflict cycle. The stages through which an industrial dispute (qv) or interpersonal conflict typically passes. Stage one begins with a substantive issue that triggers the dispute. Tensions heighten and each side assesses the other's strengths and negotiating abilities. The parties then re-evaluate their initial feelings, and negotiations begin. Compromises emerge and the issue is finally settled.

conflict, functional and dysfunctional. Confrontations between members of an organisation that lead either to improved resource allocation, enhanced creativity and increased productivity (functional conflict); or to communication barriers and the organisation's inability to achieve its objectives (dysfunctional conflict).

conflict, institutionalisation of. Regulation of conflicts within organisations by the conscious application of norms (qv), rules and procedures.

conflict management. Implementation of policies for identifying sources of conflict within organisations and the creation of mechanisms for dealing with disputes. *See* PLURALISM.

conflict within groups. Intra-group disputes arising from personality clashes, breakdowns in communications, differences in perceptions of group objectives, changes in working methods and/or expectations of what might reasonably be demanded from membership of a group. Such conflicts create the need for readjustments in internal group relations, possibly including the introduction of new group norms (qv).

conformance quality. The degree to which a system or physical product satisfies predetermined technical standards. This differs from 'design quality', which relates to the attributes that customers perceive as contributing to the worth of a product.

conformity. An individual's inclination

to accept group norms (qv) and standards. This differs from 'persuadability', which is the extent to which a person is susceptible to influence by communications emanating from any source (not just group norms (qv)).

conglomerate. A collection of diverse businesses owned and controlled by a single holding company.

conjunctive negotiation. A negotiation in which the parties have no alternative but to reach a settlement. An example would be management and unions in a small subsidiary of a multinational corporation who are told by the parent organisation to reduce the size of the labour force, or face instant closure without further discussion. The question is not *whether* to discard staff, but *who* to dismiss.

conjunctive task. A group task comprising a number of highly interdependent subsidiary tasks, the successful completion of each of which is necessary for finishing the overall group project.

consciousness. An individual's subjective experience of reality. It includes perception (qv), memory, emotions and states of awareness.

consensual validation. Processes through which individuals attempt to validate their attitudes (qv) by seeking agreement with others.

consensus *ad idem.* The legal principle that a contract (e.g. a contract of employment) is only valid if the parties to it agree entirely about the exact details of its contents.

consequences analysis. A decision taking method based on analysing the effects of the likely outcomes from various alternative courses of action.

consequential loss insurance. Insurance against loss of business and the costs of disruptions occurring after an accident, fire or other disaster (quite apart from the loss of capital assets resulting from the catastrophe).

consideration. Evidence of the intention of the parties to a contract to enter a legally binding agreement. For example, the payment of wages in return for work undertaken is consideration in a contract of employment.

consideration style of leadership. A pattern of leadership (qv) that emphasises mutual trust and respect between manager and subordinate, concern for subordinates' feelings, and two-way communication (qv).

consolidation. The integration into a worker's basic wage of items of remuneration previously considered as bonuses and/or fringe benefits. Such items become *rights* rather than privileges.

conspiracy. A tort (qv) involving two or more persons agreeing to commit an unlawful act or a lawful act by unlawful means. The Conspiracy and Protection of Property Act 1875 (qv), converted certain conspiratorial actions into criminal offences, namely acts involving the use of violence, intimidation (qv), the persistent following of another person, 'watching or besetting', or hiding the tools or other property of other people. For conspiracy to be actionable, each conspirator must know and concur with the intentions of the other, and there has to exist an intention to execute the conspiracy.

Conspiracy and Protection of Property Act 1875. *See* CRIMINAL LAW AMENDMENT ACT 1871.

conspiracy theory. The perception held by some people that all industrial unrest is politically motivated and deliberately timed and co-ordinated by extremist left-wing agitators who possess sinister objectives.

constant attendance allowance. A form of Disablement Benefit (qv) payable to individuals who are totally disabled by industrial accidents or diseases and require constant attention from another person.

construct. A description of the relationships between objectives or events. Hypothetical constructs may be deliberately created in order to analyse issues and to ask 'what if' questions.

construct validity. The desirable property of a selection test that there exists, on average, significant relationships between candidates' test scores and other evidence (academic qualifications for example) concerning their levels of ability.

Construction (General Provisions) Regulations 1961. Rules which require excavations or openings to be securely fenced, fully illuminated and sur-

rounded by signs warning passers-by of the danger.

Construction (Working Places) Regulations 1966. Government regulations requiring that every side of a working platform from which a worker might fall more than six and a half feet must have a guard rail at least three feet high.

constructive dismissal. The resignation of an employee in consequence of the employer's breach of a fundamental term of his or her contract of employment (qv), thus entitling the employee to leave the firm (with or without notice) and possibly claim unfair dismissal (qv). A breach of contract is 'fundamental' if it goes to the root of the agreement, e.g. by halving the employee's contractually determined wages.

consultation. The process of informing subordinates of intended actions in order to canvass their views prior to taking decisions. This is not the same as negotiation (qv), because no willingness to compromise is implied.

consultation agreement. A document which specifies the topics upon which management is prepared to consult with employees and the administrative arrangements for consultation (qv) (e.g. the composition of consultative committees, frequency of meetings, procedures to be followed in the event of a deadlock, etc.).

Consumer Protection Act 1987. A statute which removed the need for an injured person to prove a supplier's negligence (qv) when claiming damages for injuries caused by defective products.

content theories. Motivation theories which focus on the precise definition and explanation of the needs that motivate workers to behave in certain ways.

content validity. The desirable property of a selection test that the questions it asks or the evidence of ability that it requires (typing or driving for example) are relevant to the quality or personal characteristic the test is seeking to measure.

contest mobility. A pattern of career (qv) development whereby individuals quickly assimilate job competencies, immediately utilise initial training and frequently move between jobs and employers. This is more common in competitive, rapidly expanding industries than in large and bureaucratic organisations. *See* SPONSORED MOBILITY.

contestable labour market. A situation in which there are no constraints on the entry of new workers to the market for labour of a particular type. Examples of non-contestable labour markets occur wherever there are legal entry barriers to an occupation (lawyers or accountants permitted to audit company accounts for instance), or where specialist skills and training are required.

continental shift system. A shift work arrangement in which employees regularly alter the shifts they complete.

contingency allowance. An addition to the estimated time required by an operative to complete a task to allow for unanticipated delays in the flow of production (machine breakdowns, non-availability of supplies, etc.).

contingency planning. Predetermination of the actions to be taken by individuals and departments in response to abnormal occurrences, opportunities or threats to an organisation.

contingency theory. The proposition that management styles and organisational structures should be tailor-made to suit the requirements of each particular managerial situation. It is the antithesis of the classical approach (qv).

continuation option. A clause in an occupational pension scheme whereby a member who leaves the scheme (e.g. in consequence of changing employers) is allowed to continue paying into the life assurance element of the scheme without loss of benefits from the life assurance policy.

continuing professional development (CPD). Acquisition by professionally qualified employees of new knowledge, skills and outlooks which enable them to maintain professional competence throughout their careers. CPD can occur via in-house training organised by firms and/or professional bodies, or through external courses in educational institutions.

continuous employment. A period of employment without gaps of more than a week's duration. Many employee rights depend on the worker having completed a minimum qualifying period of continuous employment, e.g. rights such as the length of notice to be given prior to dismissal; to redundancy (qv) pay; and to compensation for unfair dismissal (qv). Continuity is *not* broken by time off for holidays, sickness absence up to six months, or 'normal' layoffs pertaining to a particular occupation (college lecturers' long summer vacations for example).

continuous flow production. Mass production based on assembly lines, conveyor belts or other continuous supply systems used to create standardised and relatively homogeneous products. Typically, continuous flow production is capital intensive and involves robotics and automated production methods.

continuous reinforcement. In operant conditioning (qv), a situation where reinforcement (qv) *always* occurs immediately following a response to a stimulus. This differs from 'intermittent' reinforcement whereby reinforcement is delivered after some responses, but not after others.

contract costing. *See* JOB COSTING (TERMINAL COSTING).

contract for services. A contract with an independent contractor (qv). e.g. a company or self-employed individual, which is not a contract of employment (qv). Independent contractors provide *ad hoc* services and are paid on invoice. There is no 'wage', and the commissioning business does not deduct PAYE (qv) or Class I National Insurance (qv) from the payment. *See* EMPLOYEE.

contract hire of company vehicles. A means for leasing company cars whereby the lessor assumes total responsibility for repairing, maintaining and eventually replacing the vehicles.

contract in restraint of trade. *See* RESTRICTIVE COVENANT.

contract manufacturing. An arrangement whereby a firm engages a manufacturer to produce a large batch of output to precise specifications and solely for the use of the purchasing business. The latter then markets the output under its own (rather than the manufacturer's) name.

contract of employment. An agreement whereby one party provides work in return for wages and/or other emoluments (qv) paid by the other. Contracts contain *express* terms that precisely determine pay, hours of work, etc.; *implied* terms that arise from the nature of the relationship, custom and practice in a certain industry, and so on; and terms required by statute, e.g. the requirement that the employer provide safe and healthy working conditions. Implied terms cannot override statutory or express terms. A contract may be embodied in a letter of appointment, a written statement of terms, or in other documents (staff handbooks for instance). Contracts of employment can be struck orally but have to be confirmed in writing within 13 weeks of starting work. *See* CONTRACTS OF EMPLOYMENT ACT 1963.

contract of employment, unilateral variation of. A change in the terms of a contract of employment imposed by an employer without the employee's consent. Unilateral variations are fundamental breaches of contract. Hence affected employees are entitled to assume they have been constructively dismissed (qv).

contract of service. A contract of employment (qv) under which a worker becomes an employee (qv) rather than an independent contractor (qv).

contracted-out money purchase scheme. A form of money purchase occupational pension (qv) that enables an individual to contract out of the State Earnings Related Pension Scheme (SERPS) (qv), but results in a lower state retirement pension.

contracted-out occupational pension scheme. A private superannuation scheme recognised by the Occupational Pensions Board (qv) as providing benefits at least equal to those available under SERPS. Members of such schemes pay 'contracted-out' National Insurance contributions lower than the standard rate for other workers.

contracting out of political contributions. The situation where a trade union member must take the initiative in instructing the union not to use any part of his or her membership subscription for political purposes via the union's political fund (qv). This became legally necessary under the 1913 Trade Union Act. The Trade Disputes and Trade Union Act of 1927 imposed the condition that union members had to 'contract in' before any of their contributions could be put into a political fund, i.e. members had to inform the union that they wanted a percentage of their subscriptions to be used in this way, rather than the union paying these amounts into a political fund as a matter of course and only ceasing to do so when the member objected! This Act was repealed in 1945 and the 1913 position reinstated. Contracting out has continued to the present day.

Contracts of Employment Act 1963. The original statute specifying the minimum notice that has to be given to employees. It was subsequently updated and incorporated into other legislation, notably the Employment Protection Act 1975 (qv). Under the latter, an employee is entitled to receive within 13 weeks of commencing work a written contract of employment detailing:

(a) names and addresses of employer and employee;

(b) job title;

(c) date of commencement;

(d) the rate of pay and how and when payment will be made;

(e) terms and conditions regarding
   – sick pay
   – holiday pay
   – pension schemes;

(f) grievance and disciplinary procedures;

(g) special conditions relating to membership of a particular trade union;

(h) length of notice to be given by either side;

(i) arrangements for working overtime.

Employees working less than 16 hours a week are excluded, but those working between eight and 16 hours a week are entitled to a written statement within 13 weeks following completion of five years' service.

contracts of employment, EC Draft Directive concerning. A 1991 EC proposal whereby employers would have to issue to workers written contracts of employment (qv) within one month of the workers' recruitment, provided they work more than eight hours a week.

contraculture. The culture of a group which opposes the dominant culture of an organisation.

contribution. The difference between a product's sale price and its marginal cost (qv).

contribution holiday. An option available to the trustees of an occupational pension scheme the assets of which exceed its liabilities by more than 5 per cent. Employees' contributions to the scheme may be reduced or suspended for up to five years. *See* PENSION SCHEME SURPLUSES (ADMINISTRATION) REGULATIONS 1987.

contributions equivalent premium. An additional amount to be paid by an employee into SERPS (qv) following that person's resignation from a contracted out occupational pension scheme (qv), of which he or she was a member for only a very short period (so that no frozen benefits under the contracted out scheme are available).

contributory fault. The situation that sometimes arises in unfair dismissal (qv) situations where, although the dismissal was unfair, the employee contributed in some way to his or her sacking. The dismissed worker's basic (qv) or compensatory (qv) award may then be reduced.

contributory negligence. A worker's carelessness or indifference to obvious hazards which helps cause an accident injuring that person. Courts will reduce employees' compensation for damages suffered in accidents in such circumstances. The Court will apportion blame in an appropriate manner, e.g. by ruling that one third or one half the blame was attributable to the injured worker, so that his or her compensation is reduced by that proportion.

contributory pension scheme. *See* SUPERANNUATION SCHEME.

contrient interdependence. A competitive situation within a group whereby the actions necessary for one person to attain his or her goals necessarily have an adverse effect on other group members' abilities to achieve their objectives.

control. The process of (i) establishing standards and targets, (ii) monitoring activities in order to compare actual with target performance and (iii) implementing measures to remedy deficiencies.

control group. In an experiment concerning group behaviour, the practice of creating a separate group of individuals to perform the same operations as the subjects of the experiment, but who do not experience the same changes in environmental conditions as the experimental group. The purpose is to ascertain whether changes in conditions actually cause alterations in behaviour. This might be achieved through telling *both* the experimental and the control group that a change has occurred (whereas in fact the change only applies to the experimental group) and observing the results in both groups.

Control of Asbestos at Work Regulations 1987. Legislation intended to protect people working with or affected by operations involving asbestos. The Regulations cover exposure prevention and control, the amount of information to be given to workers, training and health monitoring and surveillance.

Control of Lead at Work Regulations 1980. Legislation compelling employers to protect employees and other persons against exposure to lead at places of work. Accordingly, firms are required to measure the extent of lead exposure and to implement adequate measures to prevent its diffusion. A detailed code of practice (qv) has been issued to explain the Regulations.

Control of Pollution Act 1974. A statute requiring firms (including sub-contractors) to dispose of waste materials in a prescribed manner.

Control of Substances Hazardous to Health Regulations 1989. Government rules requiring employers to prevent or properly control employees' exposure to substances which cause danger through contact, inhalation, ingestion or absorption. Medical records relating to these matters must be kept for at least five years.

Control of Substances, Hazardous to Health Regulations 1990. Government health and safety at work regulations which define the meaning of a 'dangerous substance' and impose on employers and self-employed persons a legal obligation (i) to identify and evaluate the risks associated with dangerous substances, (ii) to apply appropriate measures for storing and handling such substances and (iii) to prepare plans for coping with accidents or emergencies resulting from dangerous substances.

control test. A means for distinguishing between employees (qv) and independent contractors (qv) whereby a Court considers the extent to which an employer exerts control over a worker. The test is rarely used nowadays because in large and complex organisations detailed control over all a worker's activities is not normally possible. Rather, the control test is applied in conjunction with several other assessments. *See* INTEGRATION TEST; ECONOMIC REALITY TEST.

control theory of motivation. An approach to employee motivation (qv) which suggests that workers mentally compare their current job/task situations with desired (referent) standards and are then motivated to apply behavioural strategies intended to reduce discrepancies.

controlled imagery. *See* AUTONOMOUS IMAGERY.

convenor. The senior shop steward (qv) in a company or major division of a firm.

convergent thinking. *See* DIVERGENT THINKING.

conversion, psychological. An ego defence mechanism (qv) through which a person accommodates anxiety (qv) by converting it into a psychological disorder.

conversion training. Retraining of workers in new tasks and methods that differ from but relate to skills they possess already. An example is retraining a television repair person to become a video maintenance engineer.

convertibles. Company debentures (qv) that carry the option of conversion into company shares at some future date prior to the maturity of the debenture.

cooling-off period. A predetermined interval that the parties to an industrial dispute agree must elapse between when a dispute arises and when indus-

trial action takes place. This provides a 'breathing space' to enable both sides to calm down and reconsider their positions.

co-operative. A business that adheres to the principle of one vote per member rather than one vote per share – regardless of the extent of the member's investment in the enterprise. Members may be workers in the firm, or its customers. In the latter case the business is called at 'retail co-operative'.

Co-operative Research Action for Technology (CRAFT). An EC-funded programme for encouraging small businesses to co-operate in order to cut research and development costs.

co-option. The temporary attachment to a committee or an organisation of a person who has a particular skill or ability not possessed by other committee/organisation members.

co-ordination. Unification of the efforts of all the individuals, sections and departments within an organisation.

co-orientated peers. People who face the same life situation, share similar values, or possess identical interests and/or perspectives.

copyright. The legal ownership of original drawings, designs, written descriptions or computer programs, hence giving the owner the right to copy, publish or otherwise reproduce these items.

copyright clause. A clause in an employee's contract of employment (qv) which assigns to his or her employer the legal copyright over any model or document that results from any of the employee's inventions. Note however that the Copyright, Designs and Patents Act of 1988 effectively protects the employee from civil liability for infringement of this copyright, provided the invention legally belongs to the employee and not to the employing organisation.

Copyright, Designs and Patents Act 1988. *See* MUSIC IN FACTORIES, CANTEENS, ETC.

core skills. A basic competence embodied in NCVQ (qv) recognised qualifications. 'Group one' core skills are those essential for most work related activities: problem solving, communication, and 'personal autonomy' (e.g. ability to work in a group, recognition of individual strengths and weaknesses). 'Group two' skills are widely but not universally required, e.g. mastery of a foreign language, or mathematical ability. The third group comprises 'economic and industrial understanding', citizenship, and creative scientific/technical thinking. *See* COMPETENCY, OCCUPATIONAL.

core time. That period of the working day for which an employee engaged under a flexitime (qv) system *must* be present (the middle of the day for example).

core worker. A full-time permanent and (normally) superannuated employee.

corporate ability. The totality of a business's skills, taken in unison, which determines its general competence and capacity to outperform its competitors.

corporate bigamist. A term sometimes applied to a person who puts his or her work and career before family commitments.

corporate demographics. The age and skill distributions of a company's employees. Analysis of corporate demographics is necessary for the preparation of human resource plans (qv) and management succession (qv) programmes. It helps avoid situations where the skills essential for an organisation's survival are concentrated into the hands of a few ageing workers who might all leave or retire at the same time.

corporate objective. A key target that a business must achieve in order to fulfil its mission (qv).

corporate plan. A long-term plan describing how an organisation intends deploying its total resources in order to achieve its mission (qv).

corporate strategy. A statement of the general direction an enterprise should follow and the overall policies it will apply. It is a sort of route map for guiding the long-term progress of the firm. Five main steps are involved in determining and implementing a corporate strategy: definition of mission (qv); SWOT (qv) and PEST (qv) analysis; specification of alternatives; evaluation of options and choice of strategy; and the development of plans to meet strategic objectives.

corrective action request form. A document detailing a deficiency in a firm's operations and requiring a statement from the person responsible for the shortcoming to specify what he or she is doing to remedy the situation.

cost accounting. Computation of the costs of a business and the analysis of deviations of actual from expected costs.

cost-benefit analysis. The systematic analysis of all predicted costs and benefits arising from a a major project. It requires the allocation of monetary values to such intangibles as the effects of increased job satisfaction or the deterioration in the quality of life caused by external pollution.

cost centre. A department, person, item of equipment, activity or function to which costs may be allocated for the purposes of accounting, planning and control.

cost of living expense. A pay rise just sufficient to cover the rate of inflation that has occurred over the previous year.

cost of living index. *See* RETAIL PRICES INDEX.

cost premium bonus system. A group bonus scheme which compares actual with standard costs (qv) and distributes to workers an agreed proportion of observed savings.

cost-profit-volume analysis. Investigation of the relationships between a firm's costs, revenues and net incomes following changes in the level and its output. Examples of the technique include break even analysis, profit volume charts (qv), and standard costing (qv).

Council for National Academic Awards (CNAA). An educational body established by Royal Charter in 1964 to award degrees to students in polytechnics and other non-university higher education colleges. Today, many colleges award degrees under their own names, with the CNAA acting as a quality assurance agency for college programmes.

Council of Civil Service Unions. A trade union (qv) confederation representing non-industrial civil servants, e.g. members of the Civil Service Union, the Inland Revenue Staff Federation and the Prison Officers' Association.

Council of Ministers of the European Community. The major decision-making body of the European Community, consisting of a minister from each member country. However, the ministers change according to the matter being considered.

counselling. The process of helping employees recognise their feelings about issues, define personal problems accurately, find solutions or learn to live with a situation.

counter notice. *See* NOTICE OF INTENTION TO CLAIM.

countercyclical training. *See* TRAINING FOR STOCK.

County Courts. Courts established in 1846 to hear minor civil claims. They are presided over by a single judge who sits without a jury. County courts may deal with actions involving contract and tort (qv), but not defamation. There is an upper limit on the amount that can be claimed in a County Court action. Claims for higher amounts of compensation are heard in the High Court (qv).

coupled shift system. A shift work arrangement that incorporates an overlap between one shift and the next to ensure continuity of assignments.

course of employment, accident arising from. An accident occurring at work which is caused by the nature of the worker's employment. Accidents happening during tea or meal breaks, or even while a worker is acting carelessly are within 'the course of employment'. However, a heart attack experienced by an employee during working hours but due to a long standing coronory defect would not be covered.

cousin group. *See* STRANGER LABORATORY GROUP.

covenant, deed of. A signed and sealed document under which someone agrees to do something or to refrain from doing something.

Coverdale training. A group training method similar to T-group training (qv) intended to assist participants assess the relevance of their behaviour to the task in hand and the effects of their actions on other group members. It provides planned experience by taking the group through increasingly complex exercises, emphasising the emotional aspects of intra-group behaviour.

CPI (Consumer Price Index). *See* IMPLIED DEFLATOR FOR CONSUMERS' EXPENDITURE.

CPIS. The acronym for Computerised Personnel Information System.

CPD. *See* CONTINUING PROFESSIONAL DEVELOPMENT.

CPSA. *See* CIVIL AND PUBLIC SERVANTS ASSOCIATION.

C. Psychol. *See* CHARTERED PSYCHOLOGIST.

CPVE. *See* CERTIFICATE OF PRE-VOCATIONAL EDUCATION.

CQSW. The acronym for the Certificate of Qualification in Social Work.

CRAFT. *See* CO-OPERATIVE RESEARCH ACTION FOR TECHNOLOGY.

craft qualification shop. A pre-entry closed shop (qv) arrangement whereby employment is only given to individuals who have successfully completed an apprenticeship (qv) approved by a certain trade union, which might control the number of apprenticeships available to prospective trainees.

craft union. An early form of trade union (qv) for craft workers (qv), entry to which was restricted to persons who had served an apprenticeship (qv).

craft workers. Skilled employees who apply a wide range of competencies, exercise discretion and receive minimal supervision while completing highly complex non-repetitive (normally manual) duties.

craft workers in the European Community. *See* RECOGNITION OF CRAFT AND COMMERCIAL COMPETENCIES.

Crafts Council. A grant-awarding body that finances craft workshops used mainly for craft training.

'CRAMP' approach to training. A classification suggested by M. Belbin of the tasks that combine to create a job. It has five headings: Comprehension, Reflex development, Attitude formation, Memorising and Procedural learning.

crash cost critical path analysis. A term used in network analysis (qv) to describe the additional expenses (overtime working, higher input prices, etc.) required to complete a project in less time than initially anticipated.

creative conflict. According to Mary Parker Follett (qv), the deliberate and systematic examination of opposing viewpoints within an organisation in order to synthesise contrasting attitudes in a way that serves the common interest.

creative management. A management style (qv) that focuses on cognitive (qv) and affective (qv) aspects of decision making.

creche facilities, taxation of. The rule introduced in the 1990 Finance Act that if an employer provides a workplace nursery then the firm's employees are not liable for tax on the resulting benefit.

credentials of union officials. See ACCREDITATION OF UNION OFFICIALS.

credit accumulation and transfer schemes (CATs). Arrangements whereby learning obtained in any one of a wide range of institutions can earn credit towards a recognised qualification – provided the learning can be assessed. This enables trainees to build up the points needed to obtain an award by studying in several different colleges and/or by mixing college/employer based study with (for example) distance learning. See ECCTIS 2000.

credit transfer, NCVQ. The ability to transfer credit for completed units of competence (qv) from one NVQ to another without the need for further assessment or training. This reflects the fact that certain competencies (qv) are common to more than one type of occupation (driving a vehicle or handling commercial transactions for example).

credit transfer schemes. Agreements between educational institutions and organisations (professional bodies for example) whereby one body will accept a qualification awarded by others for the purpose of exempting the holder from a course contained in its own examination system.

crime. A wrong for which a person may be lawfully punished by fine or imprisonment. This differs from a 'civil wrong', i.e. a wrong committed against another person (rather than against the state), which is followed by civil litigation, normally including a claim for damages. Alleged civil wrongs concern disputes between individuals; there is no 'prosecution' and the police are not normally involved.

criminal damage. The deliberate or reckless destruction or infliction of damage on property belonging to another person, or damaging or destroying one's own property in such a way as to endanger others (e.g. racing a private car around a company car park and damaging other vehicles in the process).

Criminal Law Amendment Act 1871. Legislation which introduced the (then) new crimes of molestation and obstruction in relation to picketing (qv). The Act was superseded by the Conspiracy and Protection of Property Act 1875, which created specific categories of illegal behaviour such as the use of violence, persistently following an individual, and watching and besetting. Importantly, the 1875 Act stated that provided no crime is committed, actions taken by two or more people in contemplation or furtherance of a trade dispute (qv) is *not* of itself a criminal offence.

crisis loans. See BUDGETING LOANS.

crisis management. A reactive style of management that devotes most attention to dealing with immediate short-term difficulties as they arise rather than on planning and formulating long-term strategies.

criterion behaviour. A training term used to define the tasks, procedures, techniques and skills a trainee should have mastered by the end of a course of instruction.

criterion referenced interview. An employment interview in which each question asked relates to a specific aspect of the vacant position. Responses are recorded on a predetermined scale.

criterion referencing. Trainee assessment methods which evaluate trainees' performance against their ability to do certain specific things at a specified standard. Criteria for defining satisfactory performance are set independent of the body of learners, so that all or none of them might perform well or badly in the assessment, i.e. it is not the case that only a certain percentage will be allowed to pass or gain distinction.

criterion related validity. In employee selection (qv), the strength of the relationship between the selection method adopted (psychometric test, interview, biodata, etc.) and particular criteria attached to the selected person's job that indicate whether he or she is performing satisfactorily.

critical examination questioning technique. In method study (qv), the systematic analysis of activities through asking three series of questions: *primary questions* relating to present methods; *secondary questions* about available alternatives; and *tertiary questions* concerning preferred or new approaches.

critical function structure. A means for structuring an organisation (qv) that contains a single function considered so important for the organisation's success that it is split off and organised separately from the rest of the firm. Management deliberately creates an 'organisation within an organisation'.

critical incidents. Examples of exceptionally good or bad performance by subordinates considered by senior managers when appraising subordinates' performances. *See* PERFORMANCE APPRAISAL.

critical path. The sequence of activities which, if not completed on time, will hold up the completion of an entire project.

critical rate of unemployment. The level of unemployment at which money wage rates increase at the same level as productivity.

Crosby, Philip B. A pioneer of total quality control (qv) who developed a four-point plan for quality improvement: definition of conformance requirements; introduction of a quality maintenance system; establishment of zero defects goals; and the continuous measurement of the costs of low quality output.

cross chart. *See* RELATIONSHIP CHART.

cross-subsidisation of labour. The situation that occurs when employees in differing grades and occupational categories are paid a single uniform wage. Hence some workers receive wage levels above those justified by their marginal contributions, others receive less.

crown princes. Junior executives selected by their superiors to receive accelerated management training and development.

Crown servants. Workers employed by the state under a relationship analogous to, but not identical with, a contract of employment (qv). Employment protection and other statutes do not apply to Crown employees unless this is explicitly stated in the relevant legislation. Employees of nationalised industries and local government authorities are *not* Crown servants.

CSEU. *See* CONFEDERATION OF SHIPBUILDING AND ENGINEERING UNIONS.

CSU. *See* CIVIL AND PUBLIC SERVANTS ASSOCIATION.

cue control. Use of previously acquired information about how another person responds to certain stimuli in order to trigger desired responses in the other person. Cues are deliberately provided to elicit a habitual reaction from the individual involved.

cultural absolute. A value or norm (qv) considered by members of an organisation to be applicable in all circumstances at all times.

cultural imperative. Something that an individual must do in order to fit in with group norms (qv) and a firm's organisational culture (qv). This contrasts with a 'cultural exclusive', i.e. something that must *not* be done for the maintenance of cultural harmony, and a 'cultural adiaphora', which is an act without cultural implications.

cultural intervention. An organisational development (qv) term describing a change agent's (qv) attempt to alter an out-of-date or otherwise inappropriate organisational culture (qv).

culture. *See* ORGANISATIONAL CULTURE (ORGANISATIONAL CLIMATE).

culture fair test. An assessment procedure that purports to eliminate the effects of cultural variables. Such tests are typically dominated by 'performance' tasks such as assembling objects, drawing pictures, relating shapes, etc.

culture lag. The continuing existence of out-of-date attitudes and perspectives among employees following changes in organisational structure and working methods.

culture shock. Acclimatisation difficulties experienced by managers who move between firms that have different organisational climates. Examples are transfers from large to small companies, from centralised to decentralised administrative structures, or from a firm with an authoritarian management style (qv) to a firm in which participative management is common.

culture space (C - space). A term coined by Max Boisot to describe the cultural implications of the knowledge and information existing within an organisation and how they are used. Boisot distinguishes between personnel knowledge, organisational knowledge (e.g. patents and other intellectual property), public knowledge such as that found in textbooks and official reports, and 'common sense'. Organisations, he suggests, are typically based on just one of these types of knowledge. In consequence, particular patterns of interpersonal relationships arise.

cumulative timing. In work measurement (qv), the timing of entire job cycles rather than their individual components. *See* FLYBACK TIMING.

current assets. A business's stocks, debtors and cash in hand and at the bank.

current liability. An amount that a business owes to a creditor and which falls due within one year of the debt being incurred.

current ratio. The ratio of a business's current assets to its current liabilities.

curriculum vitae. A brief outline of a person's educational and other qualifications, work experience, achievements and biographical details. The term in Latin means 'course of life'.

custom and practice. Working practices and preassumptions which, although not actually written into contracts of employment (qv), are so well-established that they are legally binding on employees and employing companies. Examples are long-standing bonus payments, the right to work flexible hours,

deductions for bad work from employees' wages in certain industries, etc. For a 'custom' to be recognised by a Court of law it must be 'reasonable', unambiguous (and hence easily interpreted) and 'notorious', i.e. well known to everyone in the trade or industry concerned.

customary working day. According to the Shops Act 1950 (qv), the daily number of hours for which a shop assistant is normally employed in or about the business of his or her employing shop.

CV *See* CURRICULUM VITAE.

cybernetics. The study of control systems and, in particular, of the interrelations of machines and humans in the process of control.

cyclegraph. A work study (qv) technique used by F. B. Gilbreth (qv) to record short cycle work motions. Small lights were attached to a worker's wrists and/or other relevant body members and the work then photographed using an open shutter camera while the person was completing a task. This resulted in a photograph with traces of light indicating paths of the worker's body movements. A variation on this was the 'chronocyclegraph' wherein the light source was interrupted periodically in order to make the movement paths appear as a series of dots on the photograph.

cyclical unemployment. Unemployment associated with the trade cycle, i.e. alternate expansions and contractions in the level of industrial activity.

D

damage control procedures. Predetermined and standardised reporting and response mechanisms for dealing with incidents that cause damage to work-in-progress, property or production systems.

damages, legal. Compensation awarded by a Court to a litigant for any injury suffered by reason of some act or omission by another person or organisation. The Court will attempt to put the aggrieved party in as good a position financially as he or she occupied prior to the wrongful act or omission.

danger money. Additional payments to workers for accepting the risks of injury attached to certain kinds of inherently hazardous work. Payment of danger money does not absolve the employer from having to take suitable precautions against the possibility of accidents, but it does confirm that certain inevitable risks are involved in the job. This can affect the damages payable to an injured employee following an accident, since the legal principle of *volenti non fit injuria* (qv) ('those who consent cannot complain') may apply in such cases.

Dangerous Machines (Training of Young Persons) Order 1954. Government regulations specifying the types of machine that young people under 18 years of age are not permitted to operate unless they are fully trained or undergoing training on the correct use of the equipment.

Dangerous Substances (Conveyance by Road in Road Tankers and Tank Containers) Regulations 1981. Legislation requiring the carriers of dangerous substances to use only road tankers of adequate strength, proper design and suitable construction. Consignors must inform carriers of the details of the substances to be transported, and the details then must be passed on in writing to the drivers of the vehicles in-volved. Details should include instructions about measures to be taken if the substances escape. Tankers must carry hazard signs. The Health and Safety Executive (qv) publishes a list of dangerous substances which may be lawfully transported by road.

data processing. The transformation of raw data into useful information. Typically it involves sorting, storing, amending, performing calculations on, adding, deleting or retrieving items of data.

Data Protection Act 1984. A statute intended to protect individuals against the misuse of personal details held on a computer or word processor, and to provide a remedy if details are inaccurate. It is important to note that non-computerised records (card indexes for example) are not covered by the Act.

database. A collection of information held in a computer. 'Full text' databases contain every word of each document included (as opposed to summaries, titles or details of where to obtain further information). 'Numeric' databases contain mainly statistical information.

database hosts. Companies which own the computers on which database (qv) information is stored and which (for a fee) allow users to have on-line (qv) access to the information.

day release. A training facility made available by firms to certain employees, enabling the latter to attend college one day a week on full pay.

daywork. A wage payment system based on a fixed hourly rate multiplied by the number of hours worked. Additional payments (e.g. productivity and shift work bonuses) may be added to the basic day wage.

De Bono, Edward. Originator of the concept of 'lateral thinking', i.e. allowing one's mind to explore a problem in a random fashion and, in consequence, possibly discovering unconventional solutions.

death-in-service limit. The maximum tax-free benefit allowed under Inland Revenue rules for a superannuation scheme (qv) payout to the next of kin of a deceased worker. Currently this is four times the deceased person's annual salary.

death of an applicant to an Industrial Tribunal, continuation of case. The right under the Employment Protection (Consolidation) Act 1978 (qv) of the representative or next of kin to continue the Industrial Tribunal (qv) case of a person who died while instituting an action. The next of kin or representative may even *initiate* a case in appropriate circumstances, e.g. if the deceased was due a redundancy payment (qv).

death of an employee, National Insurance contributions and. The rule that Class 1 National Insurance (qv) contributions are not payable on the earnings of a worker who dies prior to the payment of his or her wages.

death of employer or employee, effects of. The legal rule that the death of either an employer or an employee does not affect rights accrued by the employee prior to the date of death of either party. Thus, employees are entitled to arrears of wages up to the date of death of an employer and, if the employer dies insolvent, they become preferred creditors for up to four months' wages (subject to a ceiling amount). However, employees have no right to wages after the employer's death. The estate of a deceased worker is entitled to his or her accrued wages.

debenture. A loan to a company, usually fixed term and fixed interest, secured against the company's assets.

debugging. Removal of errors from a system.

deceit. Leading a person to suffer financially by wilfully or recklessly causing that individual to believe and act upon a falsehood. *See* FRAUD.

decelerating bonus scheme. A wage incentive system that pays bonuses on the amount of time saved in a job, but where the percentage bonus falls as the amount of time saved increases.

decentralisation of organisations. The process whereby the senior management of an organisation devolves control over major operations to 'local' managers in departments, divisions, strategic business units (qv), or subsidiary companies. Managers of decentralised units acquire the experience needed for more senior management positions.

decentralised communication network. A communication (qv) system in which all members have access to the same number of communications channels and thus possess equal opportunities to acquire information from each other.

decision analysis. A means for determining an appropriate organisation structure for a firm, based on identification of the key decisions that have to be taken. The technique (first suggested by Peter Drucker) is intended to distinguish between a firm's *actual* decision taking and managers' *assumptions* about what decisions are required.

decision band method. An approach to work analysis and pay structuring that relates employee remuneration to 'responsibility', the latter being measured by the extent of decision making required in the job.

decision dynamics training. A group management training (qv) method that involves team decision making, interactive video (qv), role playing (qv) and business games (qv).

decision making. The process of (i) identifying the problems that need to be considered prior to taking a decision, (ii) examining the likely consequences of various courses of action and (iii) selecting one of the alternatives.

Decision of the European Court of Justice. A ruling in a test case put before the European Court of Justice in Luxembourg. The Court's jurisdiction covers the interpretation of Community legislation and disputes arising therefrom. Decisions of the Court have the force of law and are binding in all EC countries.

decision support system. All the software, models, algorithms and computerised information processing methods and systems used to solve problems and take decisions within an organisation.

decision tree. A diagram illustrating all the choices available in a multiple stage decision process. Each option leads to various consequences, which themselves have further consequences, etc.

declaration. A Court order which formally specifies the legal rights of employees under a particular statute. Its purpose is to clarify a complicated legal situation; the declaration has no binding force in itself.

deductions from wages, lawful. Deductions from an employee's wages allowed by the 1986 Wages Act and covering: (i) income tax and national insurance; (ii) attachment of earning orders (qv); (iii) payments requested in writing by the employee (trade union subscriptions for example); (iv) agreed deductions (embodied in a contract of employment (qv)) for lateness or poor work; (v) accidental overpayment of previous wages; and (vi) for retail employees (qv) only, deductions to make good cash shortages (e.g. money missing from a till) or stock deficiencies. Deductions must not exceed 10 per cent of wages due on any one pay day except for the last pay day before the employee leaves the firm, and must occur within 12 months of the detection of the deficiency.

deed of arrangement. A contract between a debtor and his or her creditors whereby the former's property is assigned to a trustee (qv) for administration on behalf of creditors.

defamation. Making public a statement which tends to lower the reputation of a person in the eyes of society or which causes society to avoid that person. Defamatory statements may be made in permanent form ('libel'), e.g. by writing and/or printing; or in temporary form ('slander'), e.g. by verbal utterances.

deferred compensation. Acquired entitlements (pension rights for instance) payable to workers at some future time (e.g. on retirement).

deferred payment of National Insurance contributions. See EMPLOYEES WITH MORE THAN ONE JOB, NATIONAL INSURANCE AND.

deferred wage theory. The proposition that through granting workers annual pay rises, employers cause employees to believe that each year's pay rise constitutes 'back pay' for effort expended over the previous 12 month period, i.e. to feel that existing pay levels should *automatically* be increased annually to compensate for last year's extra effort.

deflation. Economic recession, typically caused by government economic policies such as high interest rates, cutbacks in public spending and/or increased taxes.

Degimbe Report. A 1988 European Community report outlining the social dimension of the European Single Market and making a number of recommendations. The report formed the basis for the European Social Charter (qv).

deindividuation. Loss of individuality and feelings of personal autonomy that sometimes result from belonging to a large social group.

deindustrialisation. A term used to describe the dramatic decline of the manufacturing and secondary sectors (qv) of the UK economy that occurred in the 1970s and 1980s. Manifestations of deindustrialisation include reduced levels of employment and output in manufacturing industries and lower shares of international markets for UK manufactured goods.

delegate conference. Trade union (qv) meetings attended by representatives of large groups of workers in union branches, divisions, etc. See MANDATING.

delegation. The assignment to a subordinate of duties accompanied by the authority needed to complete them.

Delphi technique. An approach to forecasting based on consultation with experts on the subject in question, rather than on numerical extrapolation and statistical technique. The name derives from a famous oracle at Delphi in Ancient Greece.

DELTA. See DEVELOPING EUROPEAN LEARNING THROUGH TECHNOLOGICAL ADVANCE.

demand management. Government intervention in the economy via tax and interest rate changes, variations in money supply, public spending, etc. intended to smooth out fluctuations in the economy and promote full employment and price stability. See STOP-GO CYCLE.

demarcation disputes. 'Who does what' disputes regarding which tasks should be completed by which category of employee, e.g. whether changing a light bulb is an electrical worker's job or that of a maintenance technician.

de-merger. A term sometimes used to describe the process of breaking up a large organisation into smaller units and/or divesting the organisation of certain activities.

Deming, William E. An American management consultant substantially responsible for introducing to Japanese industry the concept of total quality management (qv) based on direct employee involvement with quality control and the complete integration of quality issues with *all* production processes. Deming asserted that the key to quality improvement is the reduction of variability in production processes.

democratic leadership. A leadership style (qv) in which the leader specifies overall objectives leaving the subordinate to achieve these as he or she thinks appropriate. There is much communication between the leader and the group, with group members actively contributing to the leader's decisions. An extreme form is *laissez-faire* leadership whereby subordinates are left completely alone to complete their work.

demographic time bomb. The adverse effects likely to result from trends in the age structure of the population. Examples include shortages of younger (and thus recently qualified) workers, a decline in the demand for products normally purchased by young people, and difficulties created by fewer employees contributing to company pension schemes.

demography. Analysis of statistics on birth and death rates, age structures of populations, ethnic groups within communities, etc.

denial. A Freudian ego defence mechanism (qv) which certain individuals use to distort reality and to push unwelcome facts from their minds. It involves the individual convincing him or herself that things are not as they really are.

department. A set of activities and subordinates under a manager's jurisdiction.

departmental purpose analysis. A means for improving the performance of a department through (i) determining its fundamental purpose, (ii) evaluating its capacities and (iii) establishing training programmes to equip departmental members with the skills needed to provide a better service.

departmentation. The process of creating departments within an organisation. Departments can be constructed around particular functions (accounts or marketing departments for example), products, markets (e.g. retail and wholesale), geographical regions or people. In the latter case, work is allocated according to the personal interests of the firm's heads of department, so that eventually each department controls a variety of unrelated duties.

dependence. A term used in social psychology (qv) to indicate one person's reliance on another for the satisfaction of his or her needs, e.g. effect dependence (qv).

depersonalisation. An individual's loss of self identity (qv) which occurs through his or her total conformity with organisational procedures and group norms (qv).

deposit administration scheme. A system for managing the insurance element of an occupational pension scheme. All the employee's insurance contributions (after deduction of a management charge) are paid into the equivalent of a deposit account with the insurance company and interest is added periodically. The interest rate applied is usually the equivalent of that available on building society deposits.

Deposit of Poisonous Waste Act 1972. A statute requiring firms (including subcontactors) to dispose of poisonous waste materials in a prescribed manner.

deposition. A signed written statement given under oath, e.g. to a Court official or notary public (qv).

depreciation. The decline in the value of a capital asset over time. An asset's value might be reduced by the same amount each year ('straight line' depreciation); or by a certain annual percentage ('diminishing balance' depreciation) so that lower amounts are written off as the asset becomes older. Tax allowances for depreciation are referred to as 'writing down' allowances.

depression. Permanent feelings of dejection and apathy. Work related depression may be *exogenous*, e.g. in consequence of failing to achieve an important objective or to gain promotion; or *endogenous* (i.e. within the person) resulting perhaps from innate feelings of hopelessness, personal inadequacy and inability to cope with events.

depressive neurosis. A form of neurotic behaviour (qv) in which a depressed individual experiences a protracted and exaggerated reaction to a disturbing event or a deep fear of added personal responsibility. It has been known to affect workers who are promoted to jobs beyond their levels of competence.

deprivation, feelings of. An individual's belief that he or she has been improperly denied ownership of or access to something considered essential to personal well-being.

depth interview. An interview in which the interviewer tries to probe the innermost feelings of the person being interviewed.

depth psychology. Analysis of the operation of the unconscious mind. *See* SUPEREGO.

deputy. Someone authorised to take over a superior's work in the latter's absence, as opposed to an 'assistant' who helps and completes assignments for a superior without being empowered to 'step into the shoes' of that person.

desensitisation. A means for overcoming a person's anxiety (qv) through training the individual to confront objects or events he or she finds disturbing, though in a controlled and relaxed environment.

design for safety technique. An approach to accident prevention which focuses on the incorporation of safety features into the basic design of a firm's products. It seeks to maximise the safety levels of all the materials and processes used in manufacture.

design quality. *See* CONFORMANCE QUALITY.

desk research. Research that relies on collating information from published materials and other sources (internal company records for instance), rather than gathering completely fresh information 'in the field'. *See* FIELD RESEARCH.

desk top publishing. Sophisticated word-processing packages that combine word-processing programs with computer graphics facilities. Text may be arranged in columns of variable width and in several different blocks within the same page; pictures, graphs and other illustrations may be inserted into documents at will. Hence, printed pages can be laid out in exactly the same format as in a magazine or newspaper.

deskilling. The reorganisation of working methods with the intention of substituting unskilled for skilled labour.

determinism. An explanation of behaviour which asserts that all observed occurrences are the inevitable consequence of previous events. For example, 'economic determinism' alleges that *all* economic and commercial conduct is the direct consequence of economic (rather than psycho-sociological) forces. Determinism suggests that genuine choices are rarely available, because everything depends on external influences.

deterministic system. A system for which it is possible to predict accurately all future states and circumstances.

de-unionisation. A management's unilateral decision to terminate recognition of trade unions, to suspend collective bargaining (qv), and to determine employees' pay through individual negotiations.

deutero learning. The process of learning how to learn.

Developing European Learning through Technological Advance (DELTA). An EC research programme intended to expedite the application of new technologies to learning systems, particularly in relation to open learning (qv) and distance learning (qv).

developmental press. The totality of an organisation's market research, product research, management development (qv), and deliberate introduction of technical and organisational change.

Devlin Commission. A 1972 enquiry into the role of employers' associations (qv). The Commission concluded that although employers' associations played a vital role in industrial relations (qv) they were inadequately staffed and grossly underfunded.

DGVT. The acronym for the Directorate General for Vocational Training of the European Community.

diacritical characteristics. Physical indications that distinguish the members of a certain group from other people. Examples are modes of dress, manner of speech, etc.

Diagnosis–Prognosis–Action (DPA) model. A framework for analysing business strategy and operations. It focuses on competitive strategy (qv) customer care and supplier relations.

diagnostic assessment. Evaluation of a trainee's progress in order to identify learning difficulties and/or individual problems and to discover means for overcoming them. It is an example of formative assessment (qv).

diagonal slice. See STRANGER LABORATORY GROUP.

DIANE. See DIRECT INFORMATION ACCESS NETWORK FOR EUROPE.

dichotomous question. A question that requires a choice of one out of two fixed alternative answers.

dictatorial leadership. An autocratic leadership (qv) style which entails the leader telling subordinates exactly what to do, without comment or discussion. Interpersonal relations are highly formal. There are rewards and penalties and threats of sanctions for underperformance. See PATERNALISTIC LEADERSHIP.

differential payments system. A wage incentive system whereby employees' remunerations increase by extremely large amounts for improvements in performance at high levels of efficiency, but by low amounts for improvements at very low levels of efficiency.

differential piecework. A piece rate (qv) wage system under which a bonus is paid according to the time saved by a worker while completing a job. The worker only receives a proportion (e.g. one half) of the monetary value of the time saved, so that the employing firm shares in the benefits of the worker's improved efficiency.

differentials. The amounts by which wage rates in different job grades or occupations differ.

differentiation of organisations. A term used by Lawerence and Lorsch (qv) to describe the process whereby many diverse sub-units of an organisation develop, each unit possessing differing perspectives, attitudes, hierarchies and communication systems. Differentiation results from uncertainty and change in the outside environment. See INTEGRATION OF ORGANISATIONS.

diffuse sanction. A penalty or threat of penalty imposed through the spontaneous behaviour of individual members of a group rather than through a formal procedure.

diffusion, cultural. The spread of cultural norms (qv) between organisations, and the acceptance of these norms over time by individuals and groups within the affected organisations.

diffusion strategies in negotiations. Methods of conflict resolution that seek to defuse potentially explosive bargaining situations by offering compromises, removing sources of disagreement, and if possible creating a common enemy to distract attention from problems.

dilutees. Unskilled workers engaged to complete skilled jobs following deskilling (qv) exercises.

dilution of labour. See DESKILLING.

dimensional motion time (DMT). A work measurement (qv) technique which analyses manual working methods into a number of basic motions and then assigns a standard time (qv) to each motion.

Dip.HE (Diploma of Higher Education). An educational qualification awarded on successful completion of a two-year course of advanced study in an institution of higher education. An extra year of study can be added to convert a Dip.HE into a degree.

direct consensus method. A variant on the time span of discretion (qv) approach to job evaluation whereby a committee uses the paired comparison method (qv) to rank jobs iteratively until consensus is reached on an appropriate hierarchy.

direct costs. The costs of input materials, labour and other expenses directly attributable to the production of a specific item. See OVERHEADS.

Direct Information Access Network for Europe (DIANE). An EC project intended to improve and increase the provision of Community-wide information services. It has developed an on-line (qv) data bank containing details of EC database producers and database hosts (qv). These details may be assessed through ECHO (qv).

direct labour. Labour (qv) used in manufacture, construction, mixing of materials, assembly or in otherwise altering the condition, shape or composition of a product. *See* INDIRECT LABOUR.

directed interview. An interview that requires the interviewee to answer a number of predetermined questions in a strict sequence, thus compelling the respondent to address particular issues.

directing. That part of management concerned with leadership (qv) and command (qv).

directive counselling. An approach to counselling (qv) in which the counsellor takes the initiative in suggesting to the counsellee various approaches to a problem and/or possible solutions. *See* NON-DIRECTIVE COUNSELLING.

Directive, European Community. An edict agreed by the member countries of the European Community. A Directive specifies a necessary outcome (e.g. to ensure that men and women completing work of equivalent value are paid equally) but then allows each Community state to introduce its own legislation to achieve the desired objective. There are important EC Directives affecting many aspects of personnel management, including equal opportunity in employment (qv), health and safety at work, mass redundancy and the protection of employees' interests following the transfer of ownership of a business or an employer's insolvency.

director. Technically a person elected by the shareholders of a company to protect their interests. In practice, however, the word is commonly used to describe any top administrator of a large organisation. Full-time directors are normally regarded in law as 'employees' rather than as self-employed persons.

Disabled Persons (Employment) Acts 1944 and 1958. Acts of Parliament intended to help disabled people secure employment through requiring firms with more than 20 employees to employ a quota of 3 per cent registered disabled (qv) workers.

disablement benefit. State support paid to ex-employees (but not to the self-employed) who become disabled in consequence of accidents occurring 'in the course of employment'. Benefit becomes payable once normal statutory sick pay (qv) is exhausted.

disaster control policies. Predetermined company responses to major catastrophes. Examples include fire, accident and evacuation procedures, contingency arrangements for alternative distribution systems following a strike by distributors' employees, etc.

disbursements. Cash payments, normally for incidental expenses such as hotel bills or travelling costs.

DISC test. A psychometric test (qv) developed from research on soldiers in the United States Army in the 1920s. It seeks to identify in job applicants the extent of the existence of four aspects of their personality: dominance, influence (or 'inducement'), submission (or 'steadiness') and compliance. Candidates are required to select between various words and phrases (e.g. persuasive, gentle, innovative) which they believe describe aspects of their personality most and least accurately. Results are plotted onto a star shaped graph which purports to indicate the test subject's self-image, actual personality and ability to cope with pressure.

discipline, progressive. Automatically graduated sanctions against employees imposed for offences such as persistent latecoming or unauthorised absence from work. Penalties become increasingly severe as the misconduct is repeated, beginning perhaps with a verbal warning, followed by a written warning, deductions from pay, higher deductions from pay, suspension, etc., and leading ultimately to dismissal from the organisation.

disclaimers. *See* UNFAIR CONTRACT TERMS ACT 1977.

disclosure of information requirement. The obligation under s. 17(1) of the Employment Protection Act 1975 (qv) of an employer to disclose to a recognised trade union (qv), on request, information without which the union would be 'materially impeded' in pursuing its collective bargaining objectives. Such information must be 'relevant and important'. If a request is refused the union can complain to the Central Arbitration Committee (qv). ACAS has issued a Code of Practice (qv) on the subject, outlining the sorts of management information that should and should not be disclosed.

disclosure of information to trade unions for collective bargaining purposes, ACAS Code of Practice concerning. A Code of Practice (qv) issued by ACAS in 1971 containing detailed guidelines about the nature and extent of information that employers should disclose to trade unions under the 1975 Employment Protection Act (qv). The information given should depend on the subject of the negotiations, the issues raised and the size of the bargaining unit (qv). It might include details of the organisation's pay structure (earnings analyses, results from job evaluation exercises, etc.); personnel policies in relation to recruitment, promotion and appraisal; cost structures and sources and uses of funds; and performance and productivity data.

discontinuous shifts. Shift work arrangements that involve gaps between shifts, as opposed to continuous 24 hours a day seven days a week operation.

discouraged worker hypothesis. The theory that many redundant workers remain unemployed for longer than is objectively necessary because the traumas attached to searching for a job when there are few local vacancies and the depressing impact of repeated rejections causes people to lose interest in making further applications for jobs, even jobs for which they are well qualified.

discovery learning. A training method in which the trainees find out for themselves the basic principles of their jobs and the best way to perform duties. The technique is trainee centred, immediately relevant to the worker's employment and teaches trainees to ask appropriate questions as well as find answers.

discrepancy theory of job satisfaction. The proposition that the extent to which an employee likes his or her job depends predominantly on the dif-

ference between the satisfactions the person expects from the job and the satisfactions he or she actually obtains.

discretionary pension scheme. A company pension scheme in which the employing firm decides which of its employees are to be superannuated. Typically, the benefits and contributions of each scheme member also vary according to the discretion of the firm's management.

discrimination. Treating certain people differently for unjustifiable reasons, particularly in relation to recruitment, training and promotion. *See* RACIAL DISCRIMINATION.

discrimination, psychological. A person's ability to perceive differences between objects, events or items of information.

diseconomies of scale. Increases in unit production cost resulting from large-scale operations. Examples of causes include excessive paperwork, bureaucracy, communication breakdowns and lack of co-ordination.

disengagement theory. The proposition that retirement from work is a natural (and for most people welcome) withdrawal from social relationships. Ageing is regarded as causing physical decline that inevitably results in decreased personal interaction with external environments. Retirement is seen as necessary to help the individual conserve his or her energies. *See* ACTIVITY THEORY.

disjointed incrementalism. A step-by-step procedure for taking decisions in organisations whereby a separate and independent decision is taken as each aspect of a problem unfolds. None of the 'incremental decisions' necessarily relate to preceding decisions. Rather, decisions move in new directions as increasing amounts of information are revealed.

dismissal. The termination of employment by (a) the employer, with or without notice, (b) the employee's resignation (with or without notice) in direct consequence of the employer's repudiation of the terms of a contract of employment, or (c) the failure of an employer to renew a fixed term contract. *See* CONSTRUCTIVE DISMISSAL; SUMMARY DISMISSAL; REDUNDANCY; UNFAIR DISMISSAL.

dismissal, ACAS Code on. An ACAS Code of Practice (qv) entitled 'Disciplinary and other Procedures in Employment', first issued pursuant to s.6 of the Employment Protection Act 1975 (qv) and periodically updated. It contains detailed guidance on the steps to be followed prior to dismissing a worker, on appeals procedures, conduct of disciplinary interviews, etc. Failure to observe the Code does not render the firm liable to legal proceedings, nor does it make a dismissal automatically unfair (qv); but the Code is admissible as evidence in cases before Industrial Tribunals (qv) and other Courts to illustrate what *should* have been done. *See* ANY DIFFERENCE RULE.

dismissal for trade union membership or activities or for refusing to join a trade union, special compensation for. Additional compensation of up to 104 weeks' pay (subject to an upper financial ceiling altered periodically) for a worker unfairly dismissed (qv) in connection with trade union matters. If a Tribunal orders the reinstatement (qv) or re-engagement (qv) of the dismissed worker and the employing firm refuses to obey then the number of weeks' compensation is raised to 156 and there is no upper limit to the value of 'a week's pay' used in the calculations.

disobedience, wilful. Deliberate refusal to obey an employer's reasonable, lawful and non-dangerous commands which are covered by the worker's contract of employment (qv). Wilful disobedience offers grounds for fair dismissal provided (i) it is critical to the employee's work, (ii) written warnings of previous disobedience have been issued and (iii) the sacking occurs within a reasonable period after the disobedience.

displacement. A consequence of frustration (qv) which involves the transfer of aggression away from the frustrating object, activity, objective or issue and towards something else.

dispute of interest. An industrial dispute involving a fresh claim for something not already available under an existing agreement. Examples are union demands for shorter working hours, and management demands that workers abandon restrictive labour practices (qv). Disputes of interest might be handled through negotiation (qv). *See* DISPUTE OF RIGHT.

dispute of right. An argument between management and employee representatives about the interpretation of an existing agreement, e.g. the calculation of bonus payments under a recently negotiated pay deal. Arbitration (qv) is normally a suitable means for resolving this type of dispute. *See* DISPUTE OF INTEREST.

disputes procedures. Procedural agreements (qv) between employers and trade unions (qv) that specify the steps to be followed when settling conflicts in industrial relations (qv).

dissociated emotion. Free floating emotional experiences not connected to objects or situations. Endogenous depression is an example.

dissociation, psychological. The splitting off of some aspects of an individual's personality (qv), which then develop independently. Certain creative abilities result from dissociation.

distance learning. Off-the-job (qv) training which enables people to study instructional materials without face-to-face contact with teachers. Distance learning can involve the use of videos, radio and television programmes, audio cassettes, and/or programmed learning (qv) manuals.

distributive justice. According to G. Homans, equity in the distribution of rewards to two members of a relationship; meaning that rewards are proportionate to each person's emotional and other investments. If distributive justice is not realised the under-rewarded person will feel angry while the over-rewarded person will experience a sense of guilt.

distributive learning. See LEARNING IN PARTS.

distributive negotiation. A negotiation concerning relative shares in a fixed quantity of resources that each party to the negotiation is to receive.

distributor. A person or firm holding the contractual right to sell goods on behalf of another business. Normally, distributors are *not* agents (qv).

district committee. The level of authority in a trade union immediately above the branch (qv). Members are elected by branches and exercise general control over all the branches in an area. Sometimes this function is undertaken by divisional committees (qv).

divergent thinking. Deliberately seeking several different and contrasting possible solutions to a problem. This contrasts with 'convergent thinking', which attempts to discover a single simple solution. *See* LATERAL THINKING.

dividends. Payments made to shareholders in companies. Since shareholders own the firm it is they who determine the amounts of dividends payable (rather than profits being retained within the firm for new investment). This is decided through a vote at the company's annual general meeting.

division of labour. The process of breaking work down into small, simple units that can be completed, repetitiously, by an unskilled worker. Employees then develop great speed at their work, and minimal job instruction is necessary. However, work may become boring and employee alienation (qv) may result.

divisional committee. A level of authority in a trade union immediately above the branch (qv) and in charge of branches in a specific industry. For example, a national engineering workers union might have separate divisions for its members employed in the steel industry, the motor car industry, the building industry, etc. *See* DISTRICT COMMITTEE.

divisionalisation. A form of decentralisation (qv) involving the establishment of self-contained units to undertake major responsibilities within an organisation, rather than setting up subsidiary companies. The work of divisions is co-ordinated by top management, with divisional managers being subject to central control.

dole. A slang expression for state unemployment benefit. Hence the terms 'on the dole' (i.e. being unemployed), 'dole queue' and 'dole money'.

domestic bargaining. Plant level ('local') collective bargaining (qv) between an employer and workers' representatives, as opposed to district, industry-wide or national negotiations.

dominance, psychological need for. The urge to control others and/or to possess a higher status carrying power (qv) over lower levels.

dominant factor approach. A method of job evaluation (qv) which identifies the single most important aspect of a job and then compares the values of all its other elements against this dominant factor.

dominant position. According to Article 86 of the Treaty of Rome (qv), a position of economic strength which enables an enterprise to prevent effective competition through its ability to operate independently of competitors and customers.

Donovan report. The final report of the Royal Commission on Trade Unions and Employers' Association, accepted by the government in 1968. Following the report, the government set up the 'Commission on Industrial Relations', the precursor to ACAS. Donovan drew attention to the fact that two parallel systems of industrial relations (qv) had arisen in Britain, a 'formal' national system and an informal local collective bargaining (qv) system based on word of mouth agreements between managers and shop stewards (qv).

doors, exits and lifts, fire precautions concerning. Legislation requiring that any door which opens onto any corridor or staircase from a room containing more than ten employees, and all other doors affording exit from a firm's premises, must open outwards. Windows on exit routes have to be conspicuously marked using large letters. Lifts must be completely enclosed with fire-resisting materials.

double day shift. A shift work arrangement that involves two consecutive shifts operating back to back between early morning and late evening, e.g. from 6.00 a.m. to 10.00 p.m.

double time. Hourly pay rates twice the level of normal wages.

double trust system. A method for appointing managers in certain Continental co-operative enterprises. Anyone appointed to a position of authority must be proposed at one level, and unanimously accepted at another level. Either the proposal comes from the higher level and is approved at the lower level, or vice-versa. The purpose of the system is the prevention of authoritarianism.

down loading. Reducing the scale of operations of a firm, department, section, project or function.

downtime. Periods when machines or equipment stand idle due to breakdowns or other unanticipated stoppages.

Draft Directives, European Community. Proposals of the European Commission accepted in principle by a majority of Community nations, but not implemented in consequence of opposition by one or more member states. At the time of writing there exist important Draft Directives on part-time workers, night and shift work, the protection of pregnant women, the provision of information to employees and on employee representation on the boards of large companies. *See* COMPANY LAW, FIFTH EC DRAFT DIRECTIVE ON; and VREDELING PROPOSAL.

drinking water requirements. Obligations imposed on employers by the Factories Act 1961 (qv) and the Offices, Shops and Railways Premises Act 1963 (qv) whereby firms must supply wholesome drinking water, cups (unless the water comes from an upward jet) and a means for rinsing them. Hot drinks must be provided to employees working in compressed air conditions.

drive. A source of human behaviour activated by need. Drives may be innate (the urge for sexual gratification for example) or acquired via learning (qv).

drivers of heavy goods vehicles, EC proposals concerning. Suggestions drafted by the European Commission for common criteria for the testing of drivers of heavy commercial vehicles. Currently, EC countries which require a special test for heavy good vehicles drivers waive such tests for foreign EC nationals and issue licences on proof of relevant experience.

driving hours of employees, EC Regulations on. Rules embodied in EC Regulations of 1977 and 1985 stipulating (i) minimum ages for drivers of various classes of commercial vehicle, (ii) that no-one may drive for more than ten hours in one day and (iii) that no more than four and a half hours can be spent at the wheel in any single stretch. A driver's working week may not exceed 56 hours, and has to be split up by predefined rest periods. Performance-related bonuses that could incite drivers to endanger road safety are forbidden. Also, tachographs (qv) are required on certain vehicles. *See* DRIVERS OF HEAVY GOODS VEHICLES, EC PROPOSALS CONCERNING.

DRO. The acronym for Disablement Resettlement Officer.

drop in and learn unit. *See* TRAINING RESOURCE CENTRE.

drunkenness, summary dismissal for. The sacking of a drunk employee on the spot, without notice. This is not unfair dismissal (qv) provided (i) the worker's intoxication causes a danger to safety, or (ii) the employee commits some other offence while under the influence of alcohol (swearing or violence for example), or (iii) the firm's disciplinary rules clearly state that instant dismissal will result from drunkenness, *and* – in all cases – (iv) it can be proven that the individual was actually drunk. *See* ALCOHOLIC EMPLOYEES, JOINT CODE OF PRACTICE CONCERNING.

DTI. The acronym for the UK Department of Trade and Industry.

dual career couple. A couple where both parties to the relationship have interesting and well-paid jobs. This might create conflicts between the partnership in that a promotion or job change that necessitates a geographical relocation for one of them could require the other to abandon his or her own career.

dual memory theory. The proposition that individuals can transfer large amounts of information from short-term memory to long-term memory by combining small units of information into larger blocs. This is only possible, however, if the learner *understands* each small unit and hence is able to place units into a meaningful context.

Dunlop, J. T. Influential writer on industrial relations who in 1958 presented a 'systems model' of the factors affecting industrial relations. The main factors were *actors* (employees, unions, employers' associations, managers and government); *context*, i.e. rules, procedures and the technical, market and legal environments within which an organisation operates; and *ideology*, i.e. the frames of reference (qv) of participants and the ideas that bind the actors together.

duopoly. A situation in which there are only two suppliers in an industry.

duopsony. A situation in which there are only two customers for a certain type of good.

dyad. A relationship between two people. Within a dyad each person develops expectations regarding the other's behaviour which, if not met, can create serious interpersonal conflict.

dynamic adaptive testing. Computerised testing (qv) of intelligence or ability whereby the level of difficulty of questions automatically increases as the candidate continues to give correct answers.

dynamic evaluation. Collection of data on (i) changes in output per person employed within a manufacturing business, (ii) the rate at which these changes occur and (iii) the change in the rate of change of per capita output. The results are plotted on semi-logarithmic graph paper.

dynamisation. A method for computing the final salary (qv) of a retiring employee in an occupational pension scheme. The employee's pension is based on his or her highest earnings in any one of the (say) five years preceding the date of retirement. However, the actual salary received in the employee's highest earning year is increased by the increase in the Retail Price Index between the end of the year in question and the retirement date, resulting in a 'final salary' equal to that which the employee would have received if peak earnings had continued and had increased in line with inflation.

dysfunctional change. An alteration in patterns of interaction among people within an organisation (qv) that worsens its efficiency.

dysfunctional system. A system with characteristics that impede the attainment of the objectives for which it was originally established.

E

early retirement. Retirement prior to the statutory age or age specified in a worker's contract of employment, normally accompanied by an enhanced pension and *ex gratia* (qv) lump sum payment.

earned income. According to the Inland Revenue, income obtained from wages, profits or pensions – as opposed to 'unearned income' that results from accumulated wealth (e.g. interest payments, dividends on shares, rent from property, etc.).

earnings-related benefits. National Insurance benefits (SERPS for example), the levels of which depend on recipients' previous earnings (and hence on how much they have contributed to the scheme).

easement. A right possessed by one person over the property of another.

EC nationals, rule on the employment of. The requirement specified by Articles 48 and 49 of the Treaty of Rome (qv) whereby citizens of one EC state do not require work permits (qv) to work in others, unless the person is from a country still within its EC seven-year transitional period. Admission to a country is for six months in the first instance, to allow the EC national to seek work. On finding a job the person must obtain a residence permit from the national authority of the country concerned. The permit will be for five years or the actual period of employment if the job lasts less than 12 months. EC workers in continuous employment for at least four years become entitled to live and work in the country permanently.

ECAS. *See* EURO CITIZEN ACTION SERVICE.

ECCTIS 2000 (Educational Counselling and Credit Transfer Service). A national computerised database set up to link educational and training courses with people seeking qualifications in various areas. It provides information on courses and their entry qualifications in UK further and higher education.

echelon. A level of rank, authority (qv) or command.

ECHO. *See* EUROPEAN COMMUNITY HOST ORGANISATION.

ECIS. The acronym for the Engineering Careers Information Service.

econometrics. Application of mathematical and statistical techniques to problems of economics and business forecasting.

Economic and Social Cohesion Initiatives. Proposals advanced in the European Community's 1988 working paper, 'The Social Dimensions of the Internal Market'. They concern (i) measures to alleviate the impact of unemployment via the retraining and redeployment of workers and (ii) the initiation of research into the consequences of the demographic time bomb (qv), into the special problems of disadvantaged population groups, and into the causes of and cures for long term and rural unemployment.

Economic and Social Committee of the European Community. A consultative body established under the Treaty of Rome (qv) comprising groups representing the interests of employers, trade unions and the general public (notably consumer, agricultural and commercial interests). All matters concerning the free movement of workers must be referred to the ESC for comment. The Committee has 189 members.

Economic and Social Council (ECOSOC - UN) of the United Nations. A division of the United Nations Organisation that co-ordinates the work of regional UN commissions concerned with economic and social affairs. It is not to be confused with the ECOSOC of the European Community.

Economic and Social Research Council (ESRC). A government body established to fund research into the social sciences.

economic man, model of. A hypothetical person who automatically responds to economic incentives, behaves in a perfectly rational way, is fully informed about the business environment and always acts in a manner intended to maximise personal satisfaction.

economic reality test. A means for distinguishing employees (qv) from independent contractors (qv) in which a Court evaluates a multitude of factors, including the engaging firm's rights (i) to appoint and control the worker, (ii) to suspend and dismiss, (iii) to determine the method of payment, working hours and methods and (iv) whether the worker provides his or her own tools or equipment. *See* CONTROL TEST; INTEGRATION TEST.

economies of scale. Reductions in unit production costs resulting from large-scale operations. Common examples are discounts obtained on bulk purchases, benefits from the application of the division of labour, integration of processes, the ability to attract high calibre labour and the capacity to establish research and development facilities.

economies of scope. Unit cost reductions resulting from a firm undertaking a wide range of activities, and hence being able to provide common services and inputs useful for each activity.

ECOSOC. *See* ECONOMIC AND SOCIAL COMMITTEE OF THE EUROPEAN COMMUNITY.

ECOSOC -UN. *See* ECONOMIC AND SOCIAL COUNCIL OF THE UNITED NATIONS.

EDI. *See* ELECTRONIC DATA INTERCHANGE.

EEF. *See* ENGINEERING EMPLOYERS' FEDERATION.

EEIG. *See* EUROPEAN ECONOMIC INTEREST GROUP.

EETPU. *See* ELECTRICAL, ELECTRONIC, TELECOMMUNICATIONS AND PLUMBING UNION.

effect dependence. The situation that arises when a member of a group is significantly influenced by the group through the group's ability to reward certain modes of behaviour and/or impose penalties.

effectance motivation. Motivation (qv) arising from an individual's belief that he or she can influence and ultimately master his or her environments.

effective date of termination of employment. For dismissal or resignation *with notice*, the date on which notice expires; and for dismissal or resignation *without notice*, the date the worker leaves the firm. These dates are important because many statutory rights (e.g. to a redundancy payment (qv) or not to be unfairly dismissed (qv)) depend on the employee having the appropriate qualifying period of service.

effector processes. Muscular contractions resulting from the use of body limbs while completing work.

efficacy, psychological. The extent to which an individual feels capable of influencing his or her environments and decisions that affect the person.

effort-based bonus schemes. Wage incentive systems that place a value on the effort that goes into the production of output, rather than on the value of the output itself. Certain predetermined time periods are allowed for waiting for work to arrive, for clearing up, machine setting, etc. Such periods are paid at a fixed standard rate. *See* OUTPUT-BASED BONUS SCHEMES.

ego. A term coined by Sigmund Freud (qv) to describe the means whereby an individual channels id (qv) impulses into socially acceptable behaviour. The id helps a person co-ordinate perceptions and hence cope with the realities of the outside world.

ego defence mechanism. A state of mind developed within an individual to enable him or her to cope with neurotic anxiety (qv).

ego extension. A person's belief that successes achieved by a group to which he or she belongs are also personal successes for that individual.

egocentricity. A person's (possibly incorrect) assumption that other people see things in the same way as that individual.

eighty-twenty rule. *See* ABC ANALYSIS (PARETO ANALYSIS).

elections for union officers. Secret ballots required by the Trade Union Act 1984 (qv) for the election of *all* members of the principal executive committees (qv) of an independent trade union (qv). Members of the union must vote by marking a ballot paper; not by a show of hands. No more than five years may elapse between elections.

Electrical, Electronic, Telecommunications and Plumbing Union (EETPU). A leading UK trade union (qv) representing electrical and plumbing workers. 'Electrical' is defined to include computer work, so the union also recruits in the computing field. In 1992 the EETPU merged with the AEU to form the Amalgamated Engineering and Electrical Union (AEEU) (qv).

electromyograph. A machine used in the biofeedback (qv) method of stress (qv) management. It emits a tone which changes frequency or has a dial which shifts position as a person moves from a relaxed to a highly agitated physiological condition.

Electronic Data Interchange (EDI). The fully integrated E-mail (qv) exchange of documents between companies using different types of computer system. *See* OSI.

electronic office. An office that uses microprocessors to integrate clerical procedures. Common features of electronic offices include E-mail (qv), computer conferencing, network linkages to outworkers, databases, integrated word processing and spreadsheet systems.

element of competence. A description of an action, behaviour, outcome or knowledge of what should be done in a workplace situation which a person needs to be able to demonstrate in order to obtain an NVQ. *See* NCVQ; COMPETENCY, OCCUPATIONAL.

elements of a job. The constituent parts into which a job can be broken down in order to conduct work measurement (qv). Each element will normally last between six and 30 seconds.

EMAS. *See* EMPLOYMENT MEDICAL ADVISORY SERVICE.

E-mail. Paperless electronic communications between workstations within and among organisations using desktop computers. Incoming messages are stored until accessed and read on a VDU by the recipient.

embezzlement. Dishonest use by an employee of money belonging to or intended for an employer.

embourgeoisement. The process whereby prosperous working class people might acquire middle class attitudes, perspectives and patterns of behaviour.

Emergency Powers Acts 1920 and 1964. Legislation that enables a government to take whatever measures it deems necessary to maintain the supply and distribution of food, water, fuel, etc., in order to 'ensure public safety and the life of the community'. The Acts have been invoked several times in the post Second World War period, typically in consequence of major industrial disputes (the 1973–74 miners' strike for example).

emoluments. Fringe benefits or other employee remuneration. The UK tax authorities define an emolument as 'any fee, salary, wage, perquisite or profit'. Examples are pension payments, holidays, special commissions, use of a car, company house, etc. *See* GIFTS TO EMPLOYEES.

empathy. In counselling (qv), the ability of a counsellor to understand the counsellee's feelings and to see issues from the latter's point of view.

empire building. Attempting to extend one's own power (qv), authority (qv) and influence, at the expense of seeking to achieve the aims of an employing organisation.

empirical sciences. Those sciences which seek to describe and explain real life occurrences by examining actual events and data, so that all propositions are checked out against available facts. This differs from the non-empirical sciences (e.g. theoretical physics or pure mathematics) which rely on logic and are not tested against reality in the first instance.

empiricism. The view that the best way to obtain fresh knowledge on a subject is to observe, measure and experiment.

employee. A person engaged under a contract of employment (qv) who is not an independent contractor (qv). To distinguish between 'employees' and 'independent contractors' a Court will examine the nature and extent of the control exerted over the work; the degree of integration of the worker with the firm's overall operations; whether the worker determines his or her working hours; whether the person is provided with a uniform, tools or equipment; and whether he or she is subject to internal grievance and/or disciplinary procedures.

employee information, EC Draft Directive concerning. A 1983 EC proposal that would compel large businesses to provide employee representatives with substantial general information on company plans and operations. Managements would also be required to consult workers' representatives on any decision likely to have serious implications for employees.

employee profile. See PERSON SPECIFICATION.

employee relations consultants. Public relations consultants who specialise in the design and production of employee handbooks, in-house brochures, company magazines, briefing documents, etc., using appealing typefaces, glossy multi-coloured covers and attractive illustrations intended to enhance employee motivation and to bond workers to their employing firms.

employee's obligations to an employer. The common law (qv) duty of an employee (regardless of his or her length of service) to work; co-operate; obey safe, reasonable and lawful commands; not work for any other business during working hours; respect the employer's trade secrets; and take 'reasonable care' to protect the employer's property and interests. See EMPLOYER'S OBLIGATIONS TO WORKERS.

employees with earnings from self-employment, National Insurance and. The rule that a person who works for a firm but is also self employed during periods not spent with the employer must pay *both* Class 1 *and* Class 11 National Insurance (qv) contributions. If this results in contributions exceeding the upper NI limit the worker is entitled to a refund at the end of the tax year. Alternatively the worker may apply to defer payment of Class II (but not Class I) contributions.

employees with more than one job, National Insurance and. The rule that a worker with several different jobs must pay Class I National Insurance (qv) contributions on earnings in every job up to a certain total earnings limit. Each employer is liable for contributions on the worker's earnings with

that firm, but need not know that the person is employed by other employers. Workers who expect to earn more than the upper ceiling may apply to the DHSS for a form CF379 which enables them to avoid NI contributions being deducted at source from their wages. Alternatively they may apply for a refund of excess contributions at the end of the tax year. Form CF28F is used for this purpose.

employees working abroad, National Insurance and. The rule that Class I National Insurance (qv) contributions are payable by both employee and employer on all earnings for the first 52 weeks of a UK employee's foreign posting.

employer. A person or organisation responsible for deducting PAYE and Class 1 National Insurance (qv) from workers' wages. Employers are vicariously liable (qv) for the wrong doings of employees (qv) provided the wrongs are committed in the course of the worker' employment. See INDEPENDENT CONTRACTOR.

employer-led standards. Criteria for evaluating the contents of training courses laid down by employers in a certain industry, profession or group of occupations. See LEAD BODY.

Employers and Workmen Act 1875. Legislation which formally stated that striking is not a criminal offence. See COMBINATION ACTS 1800.

employers' associations. According to the Trade Union and Labour Relations Act 1974 (qv), organisations of employers 'whose principal purposes include the regulation of relations between employers and workers or trade unions'. They consist of businesses in the same trade or industry which come together to (i) deal collectively with trade unions (qv), (ii) influence government, (iii) conduct research and provide advice, legal and other services to members and (iv) generally further the interests of employers.

Employers' Liability (Compulsory Insurance) Act 1969. An Act of Parliament requiring all employers to insure against possible liability for bodily injury or disease sustained by employees in the course of their work. A copy of the employer's insurance certificate must be displayed at the firm's premises.

Employers' Liability (Defective Equipment) Act 1969. An Act of Parliament which states that when an employee is injured through a defect in the equipment provided by his or her employer and the defect is the fault of a third party (e.g. the equipment's manufacturer) then the injury is deemed to be also attributable to the negligence of the employer, even if no actual negligence by the employer has occurred. The employer may then sue the third party for damages.

employer's obligations to workers. The common law (qv) duty of an employer to pay an employee's wages, to provide work, take reasonable care to protect the employee, indemnify the employee against losses sustained in consequence of performing his or her duties and treat the employee with reasonable courtesy. In the absence of a specific disclaimer in a worker's contract of employment (qv), he or she is entitled to expect these 'as of right'. *See* EMPLOYEE'S OBLIGATIONS TO AN EMPLOYER.

employer's premises, use for trade union ballots. The legal rule that a firm must allow its premises to be used for a ballot (qv) conducted by a recognised trade union (qv) in relation to a proposed industrial action or response to the employer's proposals on terms and conditions of work – unless the firm can demonstrate that it is not reasonably practicable for its premises to be utilised in this fashion.

Employment Act 1980. A statute that confirmed the legality of picketing, provided the workers concerned only picket their own places of work. Secondary picketing (qv) was declared generally unlawful, unless an associated company (qv) or other business connected with a dispute is involved (e.g. a company to which a firm has transferred its work during an industrial dispute (qv)). The Act also introduced the right of individuals not to be dismissed in consequence of their refusal not to join a trade union (qv).

Employment Act 1982. A statute which removed trade union immunities for unlawful acts committed outside a trade dispute, (qv) while simultaneously narrowing the definition of what a trade dispute involves. The Act also in-

creased substantially the level of compensation payable to workers unfairly dismissed for joining or refusing to join a trade union.

Employment Act 1988. A statute which declared unlawful all industrial actions (qv) taken to enforce or maintain a closed shop (qv). It also established the rights of a union member (i) not to be unjustifiably disciplined for failing to support a strike and (ii) not to be instructed to strike without a ballot of union members. Additionally the Act (i) forbade unions to compensate members for losses arising from unlawful actions (e.g. by paying a member's fine), (ii) required that all candidates in union elections be entitled to address voters (by post if necessary) and (iii) created a new government post, the Commissioner for the Rights of Trade Union Members, whose task is to assist individual union members claim their legal rights.

Employment Act 1989. A statute that removed most legal restrictions on the employment of women in 'traditional' male industries (coal mining for instance) and increased from six months to two years the period of employment that has to elapse before a worker is automatically entitled to a detailed written statement of the reasons for his or her dismissal. The Act also removed numerous restrictions on the hours of work of young people (e.g. restrictions on night shift working), and imposed the requirement that applicants to Industrial Tribunals (qv) pay a deposit of up to £150 if a pre-hearing assessment (qv) of the intended case considers the application to have no reasonable prospect of success or to be frivolous, vexatious or unreasonable.

Employment Act 1990. An Act which outlawed the pre-entry closed shop (qv) (i.e. refusing to employ someone because he or she is not a member of a particular union). Additionally it removed trade union (qv) immunity in respect of unlawful secondary action (qv), and made unions liable for the torts (qv) of all their officials (including shop stewards (qv)) unless they repudiate these actions in a prescribed manner. The Act also enabled employers to dismiss selected strikers involved in unofficial industrial action (qv) without the dismissal being unfair (qv). *See* STRIKERS, RULE ON THE DISMISSAL OF.

Employment Agencies Act 1973. A statute which required all UK employment agencies (qv) to possess a government licence.

employment agency. A business that, for a fee, introduces prospective employees to recruiting employers. Employment agencies require a licence from the Department of Trade and Industry.

Employment and Training Act 1972. The statute which established the Manpower Services Commission (qv).

Employment Appeal Tribunal (EAT). A Court that hears appeals against decisions of Industrial Tribunals (qv) (except in relation to matters concerning health and safety) or of the Certification Officer (qv). It is presided over by a High Court judge who, like the chairperson of an Industrial Tribunal, sits with two lay members drawn from each side of industry (employers' associations and trade unions). The EAT can only hear appeals on points of law, not on points of fact. Further appeals on points of law go to the Court of Appeal.

Employment Department Group. A division of government with particular responsibility for retraining the unemployed, especially those who have been out of work for a considerable period. It was the parent organisation of the Training Agency (qv).

employment exchange. *See* JOB CENTRES.

employment in licensed and unlicensed premises, regulations concerning. Rules contained in the Shops Act 1950 (qv), restricting to a maximum of 65 hours per week (excluding meal times) the working hours of shop assistants who serve refreshments or intoxicating liquor. Such employees, moreover, must receive 32 days holiday per year, including six consecutive days on full pay.

employment interviews. Interviews of job applicants intended to select the best candidate for the vacant position.

Employment Medical Advisory Service (EMAS). A branch of the Health and Safety Executive (qv) which advises on occupational health problems and supervises the medical examination of

employees engaged on hazardous processes.

Employment Medical Advisory Service Act 1972. A statute empowering medical advisers engaged under the Act to compel employers to have their workers medically examined if an adviser believes the health of employees is at risk.

Employment of Children Act 1973. A statute which in conjunction with the 1933 Children and Young Persons Act regulates the employment of young people below the statutory school-leaving age. The employment of children under the age of 13 is prohibited. Children between 13 and 16 can work part time, but not during school hours, or before 7 a.m. or after 7 p.m., or more than two hours in any day in which the child must also attend school. However, work experience placements for children in their last compulsory year of schooling are permitted.

Employment Policy 1944, Government White Paper concerning. A commitment undertaken by the 1944 wartime UK coalition government to seek as the primary objective of economic policy a high and stable level of employment in the post Second World War years. It led to the establishment of a permanent staff of economists and statisticians in the Civil Service responsible for interpreting economic trends and advising on policy matters. This commitment had to be abandoned in the 1970s, with the control of inflation becoming the main aim of government economic policy.

Employment Protection Act 1975. A statute that provided employees who have completed more than certain minimum periods of continuous employment (qv) with the rights not to be unfairly dismissed, and to receive redundancy (qv) payments. The Act also established rules concerning the implementation of redundancies. *See* EMPLOYMENT PROTECTION (CONSOLIDATION) ACT 1978.

Employment Protection (Consolidation) Act 1978 (EPCA). A statute which brought together certain elements of the Employment Protection Act 1975 (qv), and the Contracts of Employment Act 1963 (qv). The Act confirmed employees' rights to receive written contracts of employment (qv), maternity pay (qv), a written statement of reasons for dismissal, minimum periods of notice and paid time off work for public duties (qv).

employment relationship. A close and continuing relationship between a worker (who provides skill and labour) and an employer who pays wages. Employment can be for a fixed or an indefinite period or for the completion of a specific project or task.

Employment Training Scheme (ETS). A government-funded training programme that attempted to provide individually planned training experiences for the long-term unemployed. Trainees spent some time with an employer, but might also have attended a college and/or have worked on a community project. It was a voluntary scheme with participants receiving a small supplement to their normal benefits. See TRAINING AGENTS.

empowerment. The practice of giving employees the right to control their activities. Employees take executive decisions within certain prespecified limits and then experience and assume responsibility for the consequences of their actions.

enactive experience. An awareness of the meaning of an item through physical contact with it, e.g. by touching.

encounter group. A means of leadership, self-awareness and assertion training (qv) whereby individuals are encouraged to express their innermost feelings to other members of a group, and then receive feedback on other members' reactions to their comments.

enculturation. The acquisition by an individual of cultural norms (qv) via learning (qv).

end loaded wage agreement. A pay settlement which provides employees with two pay rises during a specified period; a rise immediately following the conclusion of the agreement and another shortly before the next scheduled round of pay negotiations.

endogenous change. See EXOGENOUS CHANGE.

Engel's law. The proposition that as a family's income increases, the proportion of income spent on necessities goes down.

Engineering Council. An organisation

established in 1974 to consolidate and integrate the training activities of the main UK engineering institutions and to represent the interests of professional engineers.

Engineering Employers' Federation. An organisation formed to represent at the national level the interest of local Engineering Employers' Associations.

engineering strategy. In organisational development (qv), the imposition of deliberate changes in working environments (plant layout, office design, control systems, etc.) in an attempt to alter employees' attitudes (qv). See POWER STRATEGY.

Enterprise Allowance Scheme. A government scheme established in 1983 to help unemployed people start their own businesses. Participants receive a (taxable) weekly allowance for 52 weeks. The allowance itself is below the level of income support paid to most unemployed people. To qualify for the scheme the applicant must be aged between 18 and 65 years, have been unemployed for at least eight weeks, be receiving unemployment benefit or income support and have at least £1,000 (possibly borrowed) to invest in the business.

enterprise culture. A social climate in which initiative, self-reliance and willingness to assume responsibility and take risks are highly respected.

enterprise zone. An area free from most governmental planning restrictions and with extremely low local authority business rates for new enterprises starting up in that region.

entrepreneur. The initiator and organiser of business activity. Entrepreneurs (i) decide how resources are deployed and utilised and (ii) carry the risks of businesses.

entrepreneurial structure. A form of organisation structure, common in small firms, whereby a single person or a small group dominates all activities, performs a wide range of duties and takes all significant decisions. Internal communications are highly informal and there is no coherent managerial hierarchy as such. Departments (qv) are constructed around the interests of the dominant individual or group.

entropy, social. The degree of randomness and uncertainty in a person's behaviour.

entry behaviour. A trainee's levels of skill, competence and ability prior to commencing a course of instruction.

Environmental Health Officer. A government official responsible for monitoring and implementing the environmental health requirements of the Health and Safety at Work Act 1974 (e.g. in relation to hygiene and cleanliness conditions in factory canteens and kitchens).

environmental scanning. The systematic analysis of an organisation's economic, market, legal, technological and other environments undertaken to predict and respond to external changes.

EPCA. *See* EMPLOYMENT PROTECTION (CONSOLIDATION) ACT 1978.

epistemic freezing. The situation where a person abandons all cognitive/mental activity and stops seeking information.

Equal Opportunities Commission. A body similar to the Commission for Racial Equality (qv) but responsible for encouraging gender equal opportunities.

equal opportunity in employment. The situation in which there is no unfair discrimination against either of the sexes or any ethnic or legally constituted social group in relation to access to jobs, terms and conditions of employment, promotion, training, remuneration or termination of employment.

Equal Pay Act 1970. A statute requiring employers to give equal treatment to men and women in relation to terms and conditions of employment for like work and work rated as equivalent. *See* EQUAL PAY (AMENDMENT) REGULATIONS 1983.

Equal Pay (Amendment) Regulations 1983. An update to the Equal Pay Act 1970 (qv) which entitled men and women to the same remuneration and conditions of service as members of the opposite sex in the same organisation doing similar work, or 'work which is of similar value (qv)', as judged by a job evaluation (qv) exercise.

Equal Pay Directive 1975. A European Community Directive which defined the meaning of the principle 'equal pay for equal work' as specified in Article 119 of the Treaty of Rome (qv). Under the Directive, equal pay for both sexes is required for 'the same work to which 'equal value' is attributed'. *See* SIMILAR VALUE WORK; UNEQUAL VALUE JOBS.

equality clause. A provision in a contract of employment (qv) stating that if a woman is employed to do work broadly similar (qv) to that of a man then her terms and conditions of employment will never be construed as less favourable than male workers. Courts will treat contracts of employment that do not include equality clauses *as if* such a clause had been explicitly included.

equitable wage structure. A remuneration system seen by employees as rewarding fairly each job within a enterprise in terms of (i) the skills and other qualifications needed for various positions and (ii) comparability with wage rates in other organisations.

equities. Technically the (risk-bearing) ordinary shares of a business. In practice however the word is commonly used to describe any kind of share capital.

Equity, British. *See* ACTORS' EQUITY ASSOCIATION, BRITISH.

equity theory. The proposition that employees' beliefs about whether they are fairly treated in relation to (i) their efforts and (ii) how other workers are treated are a primary determinant of motivation.

equivalent pension benefit. The right of an employee who belonged to an employer's contracted out superannuation scheme – but who quit his or her job – to receive pension benefits equal to those which the employee would be entitled to under the non-contracted-out state pension system. It is the former employer's responsibility to make up the worker's state pension contributions, unless the employee's pension rights are transferred to the superannuation scheme of another employer.

ERASMUS. A European Community programme implemented in 1987 to encourage student mobility and co-operation between universities in the Community.

ERC. The acronym for Employment Rehabilitation Centre.

ERDF. *See* EUROPEAN REGIONAL DEVELOPMENT FUND.

ERG theory. A restructuring of Maslow's need hierarchy (qv) into three categories of need: existence, relatedness and growth. (ERG is the acronym for these three words.) Existence needs correspondence to the physiological and security needs of the Maslow system. Relatedness needs include the needs for affection and for satisfactory personal relationships. Growth needs involve self actualisation (qv), the desire to take decisions, and the needs to exert effort and control.

ergonomics. The study of the relationships between employees and their working environments and how the latter can be adapted to meet human capabilities and needs. Practical applications include factory layout, lighting, acoustics, ventilation, design of office furniture and design of control panels and instruments.

erosion of differentials. The consequence of a remuneration policy (qv) that results in the wages of basic grade workers being near to or even higher than those of their supervisors.

escalation clause. A clause in a wage agreement whereby wage rates automatically rise by predetermined amounts once certain objectives have been attained or whenever prespecified rates of inflation are experienced.

escrow agreement. An agreement whereby a document is delivered to a third party (a trustee (qv) for instance) for safekeeping until some condition has been fulfilled or duty undertaken. For example, employers' signed agreements to award certain levels of pay increase may be held in escrow pending the outcome to arbitration (qv) proceedings.

ESF. *See* EUROPEAN SOCIAL FUND.

ESITC. The acronym for the Electrical Supply Industry Training Committee.

ESOP. The acronym for Employee Share Ownership Plan.

ESPRIT. The acronym for the 'European Strategic Programme of Research and Development in Information Technology', an EC-funded project designed to encourage businesses, universities, and research institutes to co-operate on specific information technology (IT) projects. *See* SPRINT.

ESRC. *See* ECONOMIC AND SOCIAL RESEARCH COUNCIL.

esteem. Social approval for a person's actions and/or level of performance.

ET. *See* EMPLOYMENT TRAINING SCHEME.

ethical investment funds. Unit trusts which either (i) decline to invest in certain industries or countries considered morally undesirable or (ii) will only invest in companies that adhere to certain principles.

ethical relativism. The proposition that moral rules can only be understood and explained by referring to the culture in which they operate.

ethics. Fundamental moral principles, judgements and values governing individuals and/or group behaviour.

ethnic minority. According to the definition applied by UK Courts a group distinguished from others by a combination of shared customs, beliefs, traditions and characteristics derived from a common or presumed common past, even if the distinctions are not biologically determined. For example, Jews and Sikhs have been accepted by the legal system as constituting distinct ethnic groups.

ethnocentrism. The tendency to regard one's own nation, group or culture as superior to others and to evaluate the standards of other nations, groups or cultures in the context of this belief. This contrasts with 'polycentrism', which regards other nations, etc., as different but equal; and with 'geocentrism', that sees some but not all nations, groups and cultures as being of equal value.

ETP in Japan. *See* EXECUTIVE TRAINING PROGRAMME IN JAPAN.

ETUC. *See* EUROPEAN TRADE UNION CONFEDERATION.

ETUI. *See* EUROPEAN TRADE UNION INSTITUTE.

Eureka programme. A scheme intended to encourage high-tech projects (especially in the fields of robotics (qv) and advanced manufacturing (qv)) by companies in 20 European countries. It has a permanent secretariat based in Brussels. The extent of public funding of projects is left to the discretion of national governments, although in practice most governments provide up to 50 per cent of the costs of approved schemes.

Euro Citizen Action Service (ECAS). A citizen's advice system established by the European Commission (qv) to advise EC citizens about their rights under Community law, particularly as these rights relate to equality of treatment for workers employed in foreign EC countries.

Euro executives. Geographically mobile and multi-lingual managers capable of adapting to the business culture and methods of any EC country. They are fully conversant with Community business laws, institutions and practices and regularly move between companies and locations.

Euro information centres. A network of business contact points established to inform industry about European Community activities and legislation, especially in relation to commerce and employment. They are mainly located in the libraries of Chambers of Commerce.

EUROCONFIN. An EC organisation established to co-ordinate information about the availability of financial backing (including venture capital (qv)) for small- and medium-sized enterprises.

Euroform. A European Community organisation established to co-ordinate member states' national training policies.

Europartnership. An EC-funded information system set up to provide firms that wish to co-operate with businesses in other EC or European Free Trade Association (EFTA) countries with information about prospective partners.

European Commission. Effectively the civil service of the European Community. The Commission initiates proposals to the Council of Ministers (qv) of the EC where, if accepted, they become 'Directives' that bind all member states. The Commission also issues 'Recommendations' (which are not law) on various matters.

European Community Host Organisation (ECHO). The European Commission's own database host (qv) which provides access to Commission sponsored databases, including important health and safety information.

European Court of Human Rights. A Court established in 1950 to hear complaints of violations of the European Convention of Human Rights. Applicants to the Court must first have ex-

hausted all national legal remedies for redressing their grievances. The Court is quite separate from the European Community and the European Court of Justice (qv).

European Court of Justice. A Court established under the Treaty of Rome (qv) and based in Luxembourg that supervises the judicial aspects of EC treaties and legislation. It has 13 judges, one from each member country.

European Documentation Centres. Definitive collections of European Community legislation and main administrative documents, housed usually in university or college libraries.

European Economic Interest Group (EEIG). A non-profit making unlimited liability joint subsidiary of at least two EC businesses in different countries formed to conduct market or other research, or to establish common distribution facilities or for some other collective purpose.

European Foundation for the Improvement of Living and Working Conditions. An EC-funded body that commissions and subsidises research into industrial relations (qv), the quality of working life (qv), health and safety at work, protection of the environment and the impact of new technologies on living and working conditions. It has 33 members drawn from EC governments, employers' associations, trade unions and the European Commission.

European Parliament Committee on Social Affairs, Employment and the Working Environment. A standing committee of the European Parliament which has the right to be consulted on draft legislation concerning employment matters before the EC's Council of Ministers (qv) takes final decisions. The committee prepares a report on each proposal and suggests amendments.

European Productivity Movement. An international organisation of western European countries that organised training in American management methods for European industrialists during the immediate post Second World War period.

European Regional Development Fund (ERDF). A financial reserve established by the EC in 1975 to finance public investment projects (notably for roads and telecommunications) in depressed EC regions.

European Remuneration Network. A consortium of EC management consultancies that collectively produces a survey of levels of executive remuneration in European countries.

European Social Charter. A list of basic social and employment rights intended for incorporation into the constitutional laws of EC member nations. The Charter demands the rights of EC citizens to: (i) freedom of movement; (ii) fair remuneration; (iii) freedom of occupation; (iv) improvement in living and working conditions; (v) social protection; (vi) freedom of association; (vii) freedom of collective bargaining; (viii) vocational training; (ix) equal treatment of men and women; (x) information about their employing firms and participation in management decision making; (xi) protection and safety at work; (xii) protection of young persons in employment; (xiii) a decent standard of living for the elderly; (xiv) social integration for disabled persons.

European Social Fund (ESF). A European Community fund established under Articles 123–125 of the Treaty of Rome (qv) to improve employment opportunities within the EC, particularly by increasing the occupational and geographical mobility of labour (qv). Currently most of its resources are devoted to measures aimed at reducing long term unemployment and integrating young people into the workforce, e.g. by training and the provision of information on job opportunities. Advice on the administration of the fund is given to the European Commission by a Social Fund Committee comprising representatives of national governments, trade unions and employers' confederations.

European Trade Union Confederation (ETUC). An association of 35 trade union organisations (e.g. the British Trade Union Congress) founded in 1973 from 20 European countries. It is particularly concerned with mitigating any adverse effects resulting from the harmonisation of employment rights and practices across the European Community.

European Trade Union Institute (ETUI). A research, information and education organisation founded in 1978 by the ETUC (qv), which publishes reports on European trade union matters and represents trade union interests to the European Commission and European Parliament.

Euroqualifications. Certificates and diplomas in languages and European management studies awarded under a joint examinations scheme administered by the London, Brussels and Bremen Chambers of Commerce and Industry.

Eurotech. A network of EC national research and development organisations (NRDOs) in which each national body acts as the local representative of other EC countries' NRDOs for the purposes of identifying contacts and licensing selected technologies.

EUROTECNET. An EC-funded programme that seeks to increase the availability of information technology training opportunities for people already in employment. It identifies and exchanges information about IT training initiatives in various EC countries.

EURYDICE. The EC's partially computerised education information exchange network.

eustress. A term coined by Hans Selye to describe aspects of stress (qv) that have positive connotations. Examples are falling in love, succeeding in a highly competitive situation, or receiving an award. It is the opposite of *distress*, i.e. negative and harmful stress.

evolutionary operation. Application of closed loop (qv) production control systems to assembly and continuous flow process industries.

ex gratia **payment.** An *ad hoc* payment made to a person without accepting any legal responsibility for the events that led up to the payment.

Exceptionally Severe Disablement Allowance. A special form of disability benefit (qv) payable in certain cases to victims of industrial accidents or diseases and whose injuries are so severe that they require the constant attention of a relative or some other person.

exchange theory. An explanation of social behaviour which asserts that interpersonal relations depend mainly on 'rewards' exchanged and 'costs' incurred in social interactions. Rewards include compliments, affection, gratification of emotional needs, etc. Examples of costs are feelings of anxiety, humiliation, rebukes or similar disagreeable outcomes.

exchange visits of young workers, EC Council Decision on. The European Council's 1984 decision to establish a programme to encourage the cross-border exchange of young workers within the Community. To qualify for funding, workers must be between 18 and 28 years of age, have started full-time work before the age of 20, and have received basic vocational training. There are two schemes: one for short exchanges lasting from three weeks to three months; the other for long visits of four to 16 months. The European Commission pays up to 75 per cent of an individual's travel costs plus a flat rate living allowance. The aim is to assist programme participants improve their occupational skills and knowledge of foreign languages.

executive. A middle manager responsible for tactics (qv), as opposed to a senior manager responsible for strategic management (qv). Executives are concerned with the acquisition and deployment of resources, allocation of duties, specification of secondary objectives, monitoring performance and reporting back to higher levels of authority.

executive director. A full time employee of a limited company who, as well as being in charge of a particular function (marketing, production or finance, for example) is also a director (qv) of the enterprise.

executive leasing. *See* LOCUM MANAGEMENT (INTERIM MANAGEMENT).

executive pension plan. An occupational pension scheme for the managerial employees of a company. Executives 'sacrifice' part of their current salaries in return for endowment assurance benefits that are largely free of income tax, capital gains, corporation and inheritance taxes.

executive search (headhunting). The use of external recruitment consultants to locate and approach suitable candidates (who are already employed by other companies) for management positions. Headhunters maintain files of possible applicants compiled from newspaper and magazine reports, informants, trade association yearbooks, etc. They will analyse a vacancy and advise the recruiting company on the salary and other benefits necessary to attract suitable people.

executive search, MCA Code of Practice on. A Code of Practice devised by the UK Management Consultancies Association which requires the Association's members engaged in headhunting to (i) ensure that the client firm really has a genuine vacancy (and is not using the exercise simply to obtain information on competitors), (ii) not charge fees to candidates, (iii) maintain total confidentially and (iv) not place a candidate with one client company and then approach the same person and introduce him or her to another firm.

executive share option scheme. *See* APPROVED DISCRETIONARY SHARE OPTION SCHEME.

executive training programme in Japan. An EC-funded management training and development programme which sponsors young European executives to undertake language and in-house company management training courses in Japan.

exhaustion of rights. A legal phrase meaning the exercise of a person's rights over his or her intellectual property (qv).

exit interviews. Interviews with resigning employees intended to discover the causes of their resignations and hence enable a firm to implement measures to prevent others leaving for similar reasons.

exogenous change. Change resulting from factors external to an organisation and beyond its control. This differs from 'endogenous' change, which emerges from *within* the organisation and is subject to managerial control.

expectancy theory. A theory of motivation (qv) which asserts that an individual's behaviour will reflect (i) his or her self-selected goals and (ii) what the person has learned or believes will help achieve them. Hence, people are motivated by their *expectations* that certain modes of behaviour will lead to desired ends.

expectations augmented Phillips curve. An economic model of how wage levels are determined. It assumes that the rate of change of wages depends on both the current rate of unemployment and the *expected* rate of inflation.

experiential learning. 'Learning by doing' in circumstances where the opportunities to develop competencies cannot be predetermined. What is learned depends on the situations that arise in a specific period.

experience curve effects. Cost reductions and efficiency increases attained in consequence of a business acquiring experience of certain types of project, function or activity. These effects differ from economies of scale (qv) in that they result from longer experience rather than a greater volume of output.

expert power. Power (qv) resulting from a person's special knowledge or ability to help attain a group objective.

expert system. A computer program that mimics the problem solving methods of a human expert.

expression of wish. In the context of an occupational pension scheme, a member's request that certain people or organisations receive the death benefits resulting from that person's membership of the scheme. Normally, pension scheme rules specify a strict order of next of kin entitled to receive benefit, and the trustees of a scheme will follow this exactly – they are not legally bound by an expression of wish that nominates other parties.

extension of working life. According to S. R. Parker, the situation that arises when a person extends his or her work attitudes into leisure periods, with no clear demarcation between work and leisure. Work becomes the central life interest of the individual.

extent of bargaining. *See* BARGAINING STRUCTURE.

external growth. *See* INTERNAL GROWTH OF A BUSINESS.

external locus. *See* LOCUS OF CONTROL.

externalities. Costs or benefits accruing to other people in consequence of the actions of a single individual. Externalities may be positive or negative. An example of negative externalities is a factory that pollutes the environment, thus imposing costs on the community as a whole.

extinction of behaviour. The weakening and eventual disappearance of a conditioned response (qv) through the absence of continuing reinforcement (qv).

extractive industries. Industries concerned with mining, quarrying, fishing, forestry and agriculture.

extrovert. Someone who is socially outgoing, freethinking and communicates easily with other people. Extroverts work well in group situations, but may not be able to function effectively if left alone. Also they are prone to impulsive behaviour and quickly lose patience with routine work. *See* INTROVERT.

extrinsic motivation. *See* INTRINSIC MOTIVATION.

eye-hand span. The extent to which a worker's eye movements precede the movements of his or her hands while performing a task. It is measured by plunging a workroom into total darkness and recording how much of an operation the person continues to perform.

Eysenck Personality Inventory. A personality test used for employee selection. It comprises a simple questionnaire requiring yes/no answers to questions intended to measure the degrees of a candidate's introversion/extroversion and stability/neuroticism. These dimensions are then broken down into numerous sub-categories. For example, 'stability' is divided into 'phlegmatic' and 'sanguine'; while 'phlegmatic' segments into: passive, careful, thoughtful, peaceful, controlled, reliable, even-tempered, calm.

F

face validity. The impression created by an employee selection test of measuring attributes that are directly relevant to the job for which applicants are being tested. This is regarded as a desirable quality in tests. An example is a test for the selection of trainee accountants that deliberately contains questions referring to practical financial situations, even when this is not strictly necessary.

face-to-face workgroup. A group of workers (usually comprising about half a dozen individuals) who are physically close enough to each other to interact directly on a personal level.

facework. A psychological term used to describe personal behaviour intended to enhance an individual's external image and/or to disguise his or her inner feelings.

facilitating question. A question intended to expedite an employment interview. Such questions ease the flow of conversation. They could take the form of an encouraging remark phrased as a question; a general question not specifically related to the job; or a summary (in question form) of something the candidate has already discussed.

facilitator. A committee leader who, instead of acting as a neutral chairperson, stimulates interest in the committee's work by suggesting new ideas and motivating participants. The facilitator might provide information, mediate between committee members and recommend certain courses of action.

facilities management. The practice of outside firms taking over an entire function (computerised records or export administration for example) within client companies. The facility management firm administers the function on the client's behalf, under the client's letterhead and possibly using the client's equipment and workers.

facility value. In an intelligence or aptitude test, the proportion of people taking the test who answer a particular question correctly.

factor comparison method. A technique of job evaluation (qv) that determines an employee's remuneration according to the existence of certain factors; notably mental skill and physical requirements, responsibility, and working conditions believed associated with a job.

Factories Act 1961. The basic statute governing health and safety requirements in factories, including regulations concerning the employment in factories of young people.

Factories (Cleanliness of Walls and Ceilings) Order 1960. Regulations exempting factories (qv) from the legal requirements to (i) wash or sweep floors at least once a week and (ii) whitewash walls and ceilings, provided the rooms involved are only used for storage, or the parts of the rooms not washed, swept or whitewashed are at least 20 feet above the floor.

factories, regulations for setting up. Obligations established by the Factories Act 1961 (qv), requiring employers who intend using premises as factories (qv) to inform a district factory inspector at least one month before opening up and to display an abstract of the Factories Act in a prominent position in the factory building. *See* FACTORY INSPECTORATE, HER MAJESTY'S.

factory. According to the Factories Act 1961 (qv), a place where persons are employed in manual labour in any process for or incidental to the making, repairing, altering, cleaning, adapting for sale or demolition of an article. *See* NOTIONAL FACTORY.

factory agreement. *See* LOCAL COLLECTIVE BARGAINING (WORKPLACE AGREEMENT).

Factory Inspectorate, Her Majesty's. Inspectors responsible to the Health and Safety Executive for monitoring the implementation of certain provisions of the Factories Act 1961 (qv) and the Health and Safety at Work Act 1974 (qv).

failure to agree. A written statement that formally records the fact that the parties to a negotiation (qv) have not been able to settle their differences. The statement will specify the precise reasons for the breakdown in negotiations and detail each party's current position.

failure to consult about intended redundancies. An employer's failure to follow the consultation procedures specified in the 1975 Employment Protection Act (qv) when implementing redundancies in a firm which recognises a trade union. The union is entitled to obtain from an Industrial Tribunal (qv) a protective order directing that threatened employees continue to be paid for a specified period.

fair dismissal. *See* UNFAIR DISMISSAL.

fair dismissal of a pregnant employee. The sacking of a pregnant woman on the (proven) grounds either that her pregnancy makes her physically incapable of performing the duties attached to her job, or that continuing to employ her would cause the employing firm to break the law, e.g. through having the woman continue to work in a 'dangerous occupation' where the employment of pregnant females is not legally allowed.

Fair Employment Act 1976. An equal opportunities statute applicable only in Northern Ireland. It seeks to confer on workers rights similar to those contained in the sex discrimination and race relations acts (qv), but for unfair religious and political discrimination.

fair procedures prior to dismissal. Rules which an Industrial Tribunal (qv) will expect a firm to have followed (taking account of the firm's size and resources) when dismissing workers. The main requirements are that employees should not normally be dismissed for a first offence, that proper warnings be given, that the accused person have an opportunity to state a case and that all the facts of the situation be taken into consideration.

Fair Trading Act 1973. A statute which consolidated existing Restrictive Trade Practices (qv) legislation, established the Office of Fair Trading (qv), and strengthened the investigatory powers of the Monopolies and Mergers Commission (qv).

fall back pay. A worker's guaranteed minimum weekly or monthly wage in a payments by results system.

false negatives. Trainees who fail an assessment (qv) not because they are incompetent, but rather through faults in the assessment process. 'False positives', conversely, are people who for the same reason pass an assessment which objectively they ought to fail given their level of ability.

Family Credit. Social Security benefit available to low income families with children and where at least one of the parents is in full time employment.

fares to work scheme. A government programme which pays 75 per cent of the taxi fares (up to a maximum weekly value) of registered disabled people unable to use public transport for journeys to and from work.

FAST. An EC-funded project established to forecast the pace and likely future directions of technological change.

fast tracking. A promotion system in which certain preselected employees are put onto accelerated training, planned experience and management development programmes and then presented with clearly defined targets, the attainment of which automatically leads to promotion.

Fatal Accidents Acts 1846–1959. Legislation which determined that where someone's death is caused by the wrongful act, neglect or default of another person then the latter is liable for damages *as if* the victim had not been killed. Prior to the legislation the relatives of people who died in accidents could recover nothing, whereas survivors could sue for compensation, i.e. it was 'cheaper to kill than to maim'. Actions under these Acts must commence within three years of the death of the victim.

fate control. The ability of one person to determine completely the outcomes available to another. Use of fate control to shape other people's behaviour is referred to as 'conversion of fate control'.

fatigue. A reduction in the energy available to perform a task. It results from physical changes occurring in the body in consequence of effort, and causes tiredness in the affected person.

faults analysis. The systematic diagnosis of the mistakes made by employees while performing certain types of job.

Fayol, H. (1841–1925). One of the key founders of the classical approach (qv) to management. According to Fayol, all business organisations are concerned with essentially similar activities, i.e. finance and accounting, technical operations, security, commercial activities and 'management'. The latter was said to have five aspects: co-ordination, control, planning, organisation and command. Fayol advocated unity of command (qv), specialisation of functions, use of organisation charts (qv), and the setting of objectives throughout the firm.

FDA. See ASSOCIATION OF FIRST DIVISION CIVIL SERVANTS.

featherbedding. See RESTRICTIVE LABOUR PRACTICES.

federal organisation structure. A form of organisation sometimes adopted by firms or other bodies employing large numbers of professionally qualified workers. The individual professional employee enjoys great autonomy over working processes, and is assisted by a separate administrative support unit responsible for routine management tasks.

Federation of Recruitment and Employment Services Ltd. A trade association for employment agencies. It publishes a yearbook detailing members' particular fields of interest.

feedback control system. A control mechanism in which information from the output of a system is instantly transmitted to the input stage so that (if appropriate) remedial action can be implemented. This differs from a 'feedforward' system, wherein forecasts of likely problems are attempted and current activities altered now to overcome predicted future difficulties.

feeling personality type. In the Jungian typology (qv), a person able to empathise with others. Such an individual is good at persuasion, conciliation and at identifying colleagues' personal needs.

On the other hand the 'feeling' person tends to be guided by emotion, disorganised and uncritical of issues and events.

felt-fair methods. Techniques of job evaluation (qv) that apply overall general assessments (rather than analytical methods) to the grading of employees' work.

fencing of machines regulations. Rules specified in the Factories Act 1961 (qv) governing the guarding of dangerous machines. The regulations state that all engines or motors, transmission equipment (belts, shafts, pulleys, etc.) and other moving parts of hazardous machinery must be securely fenced. However, a fixed guard need not be provided if the machine has a device which automatically prevents its operator coming into contact with moving parts.

F-forms. Standard forms, registers, placards and notices published by HMSO for use in factories (qv). Important examples are F-91 (record of inspection of lifting gear, scaffolding, etc.); F-2508 (notice of accident or dangerous occurrence); and F-996 (abstract of lead paint regulations). Some similar documents are prefixed by the letter B, and are thus known as B-forms, e.g. B1-2347 (placard warning of the presence of an abrasive wheel); and B1-9101 (cautionary notice of a fragile roof).

Fiche d'impact system. A scheme initiated by the European Commission (qv) to assess the consequences for business of new European Community legislation.

fidelity guarantee. An agreement whereby a third party (an insurance company for example) assumes liability for the consequences of the dishonest acts of named employees.

Fiedler, F. E. American writer on leadership who suggested that a small number of common factors typically determine the nature of leadership situations. Examples of these factors are the amount of formal authority vested in the leader, the nature of subordinates' tasks and the extent of subordinates' confidence in a leader's abilities.

field research. Social research that involves direct observation of behaviour and/or the interviewing of subjects at their places of work and other everyday locations.

field review. A method of performance appraisal (qv) in which a member of the firm's personnel department interviews heads of department about their subordinates' performances and then prepares appraisal reports, which have to be read and approved by the departmental heads. It is used when managers are unable or unwilling to assess their subordinates independently.

field theory. In psychology (qv), the proposition that human behaviour can only be understood through considering the totality of interacting elements that contribute to it, rather than studying a particular stimulus/response situation. It asserts that since the psychology of the individual person is integrated, holistic, and highly complex, then it is wrong to differentiate between the psychology of people at work ('industrial' psychology) and human psychology overall.

figure and ground theory. The proposition in gestalt (qv) psychology that individuals naturally separate things into figures or shapes set against a background.

final accounts. The trading and profit and loss account, manufacturing account (where appropriate) and balance sheet of a business.

final salary. The remuneration upon which a superannuated employee's retirement pension is based. Rules for calculating final salary are set down by the Superannuation Funds Office (qv) and allow final salary to be *either* the employee's average earnings during any three consecutive years in the ten years prior to retirement, *or* the employee's remuneration (i.e. basic wage plus 'normal' fluctuating emoluments (qv)) in any one of the five years preceding the date of retirement. Normal fluctuating emoluments are taken as the average over a three-year period. Golden handshakes (qv) cannot be included in the calculations.

finance lease. An equipment leasing arrangement whereby the leased item is used by a single firm until the end of its useful life.

financial accountancy. That branch of accountancy primarily concerned with the systematic recording, analysis and interpretation of a company's final accounts, i.e. its trading and profit and loss accounts and end of period balance sheet.

financial engineering. The techniques and procedures through which enterprises seek to finance their long-term operations at the lowest aggregate interest cost.

Financial Statement and Budget Report. A document published immediately after the Chancellor of the Exchequer's Budget statement to the House of of Commons. It provides a brief analysis of the Treasury's forecast of the effects on government revenues of tax and other Budget changes.

fine tuning. Economic demand management (qv) which seeks to vary the extent of government intervention according to forecast rather than current or past economic circumstances. It recognises that economic conditions may have substantially altered by the time that policies determined today actually begin to exert an influence.

fines on employees. Deductions from employees' wages for misconduct, shoddy work or stock deficiencies. These are illegal unless permitted by a statute relating to a particular industry or the worker has agreed to their imposition via a written term in his or her contract of employment or some other written agreement. *See* WAGES ACT 1986.

Fire Certificate. A document issued by a local fire authority under the Fire Precautions Act 1971 (qv), and legally required by any factory (qv), office or shop with more than 20 employees at any one time or ten or more employees anywhere other than on the ground floor. Premises that do not require a certificate but which employ more than ten people must have outwards opening exit doors and clear markings on all escape doors and windows.

Fire Precautions Act 1971. A statute that requires certain classes of premises to possess a Fire Certificate (qv). Under the Act, means of escape from the building and other fire precautions have to be 'adequate'; staff must be given training in evacuation procedures and use of fire-fighting equipment; and fire appliances must be inspected periodically and formally recorded as being in working order.

Fire Precautions (Non-Certificated Factory, Office, Shop and Railway Premises) Regulations 1976. Legislation concerning fire precautions in factories, offices and shops that do not require a Fire Certificate. Under the Regulations it is unlawful to lock or fasten any door through which employees must pass in order to leave the building. Suitable fire-fighting equipment must be provided, and quick exit from rooms must be possible in the event of fire.

first aid boxes, requirements for. Obligations laid down in the Factories Act 1961 (qv), and the Offices, Shops and Railway Premises Act 1961 (qv), for employers to retain first aid boxes under the charge of a responsible person who, if the organisation employs more than 150 people (50 for a factory) must be trained in first aid. *See* HEALTH AND SAFETY (FIRST AID) REGULATIONS 1981.

first aider. *See* HEALTH AND SAFETY (FIRST AID) REGULATIONS 1981.

first line manager. *See* SUPERVISOR.

five fold system. A standard format devised by J. M. Fraser for conducting employment interviews. Candidates are assessed under five headings: impact on other people; qualifications and experience; innate abilities; motivation; and emotional adjustment. *See also the* SEVEN POINT PLAN.

fixation. A consequence of frustration (qv) whereby an individual acquires a compulsion to continue doing something that has no objective value (e.g. obsessive continuation of outdated working methods).

fixed and floating charges. Security for a loan where the security relates to specifically named assets such as buildings or vehicles (fixed charges); or security against *all* the company's assets, so that lenders have no claim over particular assets if the borrower's business fails (a floating charge).

fixed assets. Assets such as land, buildings, motor vehicles, etc., that are purchased for use *within* a business rather than for resale at a profit.

fixed group bonus system. A collective wage incentive scheme which pays a fixed bonus per hour or per unit whenever the output of an enterprise or department exceeds a certain amount.

fixed shift system. A shift work arrangement under which groups of employees work together continuously, changing shift *en bloc* as required.

fixed term contract. A contract of employment (qv) which expires on a particular date. Contracts which state they will expire on the performance of a task or the occurrence of an event (finishing a project or following the withdrawal of external funding for example) but which fail to specify a termination date are *not* 'fixed term contracts'.

fixed term contracts, non-renewal of. Technically a form of dismissal. However, an employee with a fixed term contract for at least two years who signs an agreement not to claim compensation on expiry of the contract cannot then demand financial recompense if the contract is not renewed.

flat organisation. An organisation structure with wide spans of control (qv) so that many employees experience higher level work. Subordinates are not closely supervised while completing their duties. *See* TALL ORGANISATION.

flat rate wage. A fixed and predetermined hourly, daily or weekly wage rate that does not vary with respect to a worker's output.

FLAW. The acronym for 'foreign languages at work'. Numerous FLAW training programmes are currently in operation.

flexible benefits. Packages of company fringe benefits that allow employees to select whichever elements are best for them, given their personal situations. Thus, for example, holidays might be traded-off against higher levels of sick pay; longer maternity leave against pension rights, etc.

flexible budgeting. Budget systems that automatically respond to changes in a key performance index or to variations in external environments. Production budgets, for example, sometimes depend on the value of sales achieved – it is assumed that increasing sales will require additional resources to sustain the expansion. Rolling budgets (qv) are another example.

flexible manufacturing. Computer controlled machining and other production techniques that enable the manufacture of small batches of output, each modified to suit the requirements of a particular market segment. However, manufacturing economies of scale continue to be obtained.

flexible workforce. A workforce consisting mainly of casual, part time and other peripheral (qv) workers.

flexible working practices. Working methods and arrangements whereby employees are expected to move from task to task, section to section, machine to machine, and between different types of work as a normal part of their duties.

flexitime arrangements. Agreements with workers whereby employees themselves decide when to start and finish their daily work, subject to completing a predetermined minimum number of hours over a certain period – usually one week.

FLIC programmes. See FOREIGN LANGUAGES IN-COMPANY TRAINING.

flip-flop arbitration. See PENDULUM ARBITRATION.

floor inspection. Use of decentralised 'roving' inspectors to test the quality of materials and processes at different locations. Inspectors move around the premises identifying problems where and when they occur.

flow production. Continuous production with integrated processes, typically using conveyor belts, pipes, ducts, etc. There is minimal manual intervention between processes.

flowline. A factory assembly line on which employees have to keep up with each other. This contrasts with 'bench assembly' where employees can work at their own pace.

fluid intelligence. Intuitive ability, as opposed to 'crystallised' intelligence involving analytical thinking, reasoning, problem solving etc.

flyback timing. In work measurement (qv), the timing of individual elements of a job rather than the period taken to complete the job as a whole. See CUMULATIVE TIMING.

flying pickets. Workers who quickly move around from one subsidiary of a business to another in order to engage in picketing (qv). Their aim is to prevent a multi-site firm switching production between divisions or subsidiaries. Under the Employment Acts of 1980 and 1982 (qv), such picketing is lawful only if it is undertaken by workers directly involved in the dispute (e.g. as employees of the business).

FMCIT. The acronym for the Food Manufacturers Council for Industrial Training.

fog index. A measure of the degree of confusion created by a piece of writing. It is calculated from a sample of 100 of the writer's words through (i) dividing 100 by the number of sentences in the sample, (ii) counting the number of words in the sample that have more than two syllables and multiplying this number by the outcome to step (i) and (iii) multiplying the result by 0.4. The lower the index the clearer the communication. A value of 12 normally represents good writing.

folie a deux. A psychological term used to describe the transmission and sharing of delusions (especially delusions of grandeur) among two or more individuals.

Folkways. Norms (qv) that are not enforced by group sanctions.

Follett, Mary Parker (1863-1933). An influential management theorist who asserted that organisations worked more effectively when the 'personal' authority of managers (i.e. the formal authority vested in them) was replaced by 'functional' authority, (i.e. the authority necessary for particular activities to function efficiently in the context of the situation to hand). Follett adopted a holistic approach to management, emphasising the needs (i) to recognise the complexity of workplace behaviour and (ii) to interconnect human and mechanical aspects of industrial life.

fooling around. See PRACTICAL JOKES BY EMPLOYEES, LIABILITIES FOR DAMAGES.

FORCE. See FORMATION CONTINUEE EN EUROPE.

force field analysis. Systematic examination of those elements within an organisation that seek to promote change and those which resist new methods. It aims to measure the relative strengths of progressive 'driving forces' and inhibiting 'resisters' within organisations.

FORCE programme. A European Community funded scheme for developing continuous vocational educational training courses within the Community, especially courses intended for women who wish to return to work.

forced choice rating scale. A performance appraisal (qv) checklist comprising a list of statements arranged in pairs and requiring the assessor to tick which alternative statement in each pair is considered most descriptive of the employee's performance. Statements in each pair are intentionally not very different from each other.

forced distribution method. A technique of performance appraisal (qv) that requires assessors to grade less than a certain proportion (e.g. 40 per cent) of appraisees as 'average'. This prevents assessors describing all their subordinates as 'average' in every respect.

Fordism. A term sometimes used to describe the introduction of scientific management (qv) to assembly lines. The name derives from Henry Ford, one of the first entrepreneurs to apply the principles of scientific management to production processes.

foreign languages in-company (FLIC) training. Work-based language courses run by outside trainers within companies on a part-time basis, e.g. the first hour of every other working day.

foreign students, National Insurance and. The rule that students from abroad who take temporary employment during college vacations may defer payment of Class I National Insurance contributions (qv) for 52 weeks provided the work they do is related to their courses of study.

foreign workers in the European Community. Employees resident in the EC who are not nationals of any Community state and not entitled, therefore, to free movement within the Community or to protection against discrimination in relation to terms and conditions of work, social security, etc. However, Community legislation does provide for measures intended to ensure that the children of foreign workers receive intensive language training, and that foreign workers have the same rights to union membership as nationals of the host country.

foreign workers, National Insurance and. The rule that foreign workers employed in the UK are liable for Class I National Insurance (qv) contributions unless they are not ordinarily resident in the UK and have been sent here temporarily for less than five years by overseas employers. In the latter case, liability for NI may be deferred for up to 52 weeks. *See* FOREIGN STUDENTS, NATIONAL INSURANCE AND.

foreign workers, position of non-European Community persons. The absence of the rights of non-EC migrant workers (qv) to claim the freedoms of movement and residence, employment protection and social security benefits available to EC citizens. Such matters are left to national governments to decide.

foreperson. *See* SUPERVISOR.

forgetfulness, causes of. In training programmes, the inability to practise, lack of repetition of important points by the instructor, bad learning habits previously acquired and conflicts between new information and what trainees have already learned.

formal group. A group deliberately created by management to achieve a particular end. Management selects group members, leaders and methods for completing work. 'Informal' groups, conversely, can form without management support. They are established by people who feel they possess a common interest.

formal organisation. The organisation system imposed by management, comprising organisation charts (qv), official hierarchies, company rule books, operating manuals, official communication channels, etc. Formal organisation is intended to be permanent, to contribute directly to the attainment of a business's goals and to facilitate the efficient execution of work. *See* INFORMAL ORGANISATION.

Formation Continuee en Europe. An EC programme concerned with the development of continuous professional training. Its aims are to encourage innovation in professional education and to stimulate investment in the professional training field.

formative assessment. An assessment (qv) of a trainee's performance intended to provide feedback in order to enable the trainee (i) to review and reflect on his or her progress, (ii) to correct mistakes and remedy weaknesses and (iii) generally to improve the process of learning. Performance appraisals (qv) *ought* to be formative in nature. See SUMMATIVE ASSESSMENT.

Foundation for Business Education Partnerships. An organisation established to promote compact schemes (qv) between schools and employers and generally to improve school/industry relations.

foundation training. Broadly based occupational training intended to develop general vocational skills. Its purpose is to underpin subsequent specialist studies.

frame. In programmed learning (qv), a small unit of instructional material that the trainee must master before progressing to the next unit of work. Typically, each frame is followed by a list of questions that have to be answered correctly prior to the trainee moving on to another frame.

frames of reference. The attitudes and psychological influences that determine how a person perceives events and issues. See UNITARISM; PLURALISM.

Framework Directive 1989. An EC Directive on health and safety at work containing: (i) a statement of general principles to be adopted by member countries to encourage improvement of the health and safety of workers; (ii) the requirement that employers take measures to ensure the protection of employees' health and safety and eliminate health and safety risks; and (iii) a demand that businesses provide information on health and safety to their employees and consult with them on health and safety matters.

franchise. An exclusive right to use the name, products, business methods, logos, etc., of another organisation within a specified geographical area.

fraud. A false representation made (i) knowingly, or (ii) without belief in its validity, or (iii) recklessly or carelessly. See DECEIT.

fraudulent conversion. The crime (qv) of wilfully and knowingly converting the property of another person to one's own use.

fraudulent trading. Deliberately continuing to operate a company after it has become insolvent in order to obtain benefit, e.g. by running up its debts. A Court may identify particular individuals responsible for the fraudulent trading. Such persons are then liable for everything the company owes.

free cover. In an occupational pension scheme, the maximum death benefit available to a member's dependants without the member having to provide evidence of his or her good health. See EXPRESSION OF WISH.

free report method. A technique of performance appraisal (qv) in which the appraising manager writes what amounts to an essay about a subordinate's abilities. The criteria used in assessing the subordinate may be left to the appraising manager to decide, or certain matters that have to appear within the report might be specified, e.g. technical competence, enthusiasm, punctuality, job knowledge, etc.

free rider. A term of abuse used by union members against a fellow worker who accepts pay increases and other benefits negotiated by a trade union but refuses to join the union or contribute to its funds.

freedom of movement of EC workers. The requirements from 1993 onwards that workers be free (i) to seek employment in any EC member state; (ii) to reside in any Community country with their families for as long as they wish; (iii) to receive local unemployment benefit; and (iv) to have equal access to public housing and to education for their children.

freestanding AVC. An additional voluntary contribution (qv) made by a member of one occupational pension scheme into another, completely separate and independent, scheme. Individuals are not legally entitled to contribute more than a total of 15 per cent of their incomes to the various schemes.

Freud, Sigmund (1856–1939). Famous psychologist who suggested that a person's motivation and behaviour could be greatly influenced by his or her unconscious mind. See PERSONALITY, FREUDIAN THEORY OF.

frictional unemployment. Unemployment that occurs when there are unemployed workers of a certain occupation in one part of the country but a shortage of that type of worker elsewhere. It results from ignorance of available opportunities and from the immobility of labour (qv).

friend. In the industrial relations context, a person (typically a trade union representative) who accompanies a complaining worker in meetings connected with a grievance procedure, or who represents an accused employee during disciplinary interviews.

fringe benefits. Emoluments (qv) that are taxed, but not at source under PAYE. Examples are living accommodation provided to employees and/or their spouses, gift vouchers, and luncheon vouchers (though the first part of the cost of these is entirely tax free). Long service awards are taxed *unless* the award is in the form of a 'reasonably' priced tangible article, rather than cash. Twenty years' service is needed before a worker qualifies for a tax-free long service award, and no other award must have been received during the previous ten years. Employees' expenses paid by employers are tax free, including legal and survey fees, lodging and travel expenses, settling-in allowances and so on.

fringe turnover ratio. An index of labour turnover (qv) intended to measure the extent to which recently recruited employees are leaving a firm. It is calculated from the formula:

$$\frac{\text{Number of employees who joined and left within the last year}}{\text{Average number of workers employed during the year.}}$$

Fromm, E. An influential psychologist who asserted the existence of three basic dimensions of personality: receptivity, exploitation, and shaping. The 'receptive' person relies heavily on imposed authority, and looks to others for help and control. Exploitative individuals are highly competitive and will use other people's ideas for their own purposes. 'Shapers' will alter their orientations in order to fit in with the demands of specific situations.

front loaded training. Vocational training provided exclusively at the beginning of a worker's career. Although it is common, this is appropriate only for stable technical environments where skill requirements do not change over time. Otherwise regular updating and retraining are necessary.

frustration. The consequence of interference with an individual's attempt to achieve his or her desired objectives. It is commonly associated with lack of control over working methods.

frustration of a contract of employment. The situation that arises when, despite the good intentions of both parties, it is impossible to honour a contract of employment (qv) in the manner originally intended. Examples are an employee's long-term illness or imprisonment.

frustration-regression model. A hypothesis suggested by C. P. Alderfer in 1972 which asserts that if an employee's progress towards the fulfilment of a particular need is blocked, then the person will continue to seek to satisfy this need while simultaneously regressing towards the fulfilment of needs that are more easily gratified.

fugue. A psychological term sometimes used to describe a temporary shift in self identity (qv).

full time equivalents. Part time workers who by virtue of their lengths of service are covered by various employment protection laws. Typically the periods involved are two years' continuous services for those who work more than 16 hours a week, and five years for those working at least eight hours a week.

fumes, regulations on the control of. Rules specified in s.63 of the Factories Act 1961 (qv) which require employers to take all reasonably practicable measures to prevent employees inhaling dangerous fumes. Exhaust appliances must be installed wherever fumes present a potential danger. Internal combustion engines must be partitioned off and their fumes allowed to escape to the open air.

functional analysis. A technique for deriving standards of performance (qv) for units of competence (qv) in NVQs. A 'function' is regarded as a 'role expectation', i.e. an activity described in terms of what is expected of its outcome. Functions are identified first for an occupation as a whole and then for individual workers, who typically will undertake a number of functions. Examples of outcomes are 'providing information', or 'performing calculations'. *See* NATIONAL COUNCIL FOR VOCATIONAL QUALIFICATIONS.

functional authority. The authority of a staff manager (qv) to control the activities of people in other departments provided these activities (training for instance) relate to a particular function.

functional benchmarking. *See* BENCHMARKING, ORGANISATIONAL.

functional departments. Departments (qv) responsible only for a single type of activity, e.g. accounting, advertising, transport, personnel, etc.

functional job analysis. A technique of job analysis (qv) that defines jobs according to two criteria: 'work performed' and the 'traits' necessary in the person doing the job. Work performed is described in terms of its demands *vis-a-vis* contacts with other people, and involvement with materials and finished goods. Worker traits include training time needed, aptitudes, physical characteristics, interests and temperament.

functional organisation. Creation of an organisation structure (qv) based on specialisation of activities and functional departments (qv).

functional organisation of a personnel department. Segmentation of a personnel department according to particular specialist functions, with separate sections for recruitment, personnel records, welfare services, etc.

functionalism. The proposition that all social and cultural matters are necessarily interdependent.

funeral payments. State benefits paid to bereaved families currently receiving Income Support (qv), Family Credit (qv) or Community Charge Rebate to enable them to meet funeral expenses. Advances are then repayable from any money available from the deceased person's estate.

furniture lent to employees, taxation of. The rule contained in the 1976 Finance Act that if an employer equips an employee's living accommodation with furniture and fittings then the employee is annually liable for tax on 20 per cent of the market value of the asset as at the date it was first used.

fusion process. According to E. W. Bakke, the desirable process whereby an employee uses an organisation to satisfy his or her needs and to further personal ambitions; while the organisation simultaneously uses that individual to help achieve organisational objectives.

future autobiography method. A selection technique that requires candidates to state what they believe they will be doing in five and ten years' time. Responses are then examined for indications of applicants' ideals, of whether they perceive themselves as in control of their own destinies, and the contexts in which they place past and current experiences.

future shock. A term coined by A. Toffler to describe contemporary society's inability to cope with rapidly increasing rates of technical and environmental change.

G

G factor. *See* TWO FACTOR THEORY OF INTELLIGENCE.

galvanic skin response. A physiological measure of emotion obtained through the attachment to a person of an electronic device that assesses the drop in the electrical resistance of the skin that occurs following a person's emotional arousal.

game theory. A means for analysing the sources and consequences of conflict among individuals and between groups. Statistical probabilities are assigned to various possible outcomes in a competitive situation, which is then simulated and participants' behaviour observed. *See* ZERO SUM GAME.

Gantt, H. L. (1861–1919). An advocate of scientific management (qv) who pioneered the use of statistical production control. He devised performance charts for operatives, machines and processes allowing simultaneous comparison of several activities in terms of costs, idle time, stoppages, etc. Gantt collaborated with F. W. Taylor (qv) on a number of major assignments.

gap analysis. A technique of corporate planning (qv) in which management establishes targets based on its predictions of what seems reasonably attainable in the longer term and then compares these targets with forecasts derived from the projection of current activities into the future, assuming present circumstances remain constant. Divergences are then analysed and policies devised and implemented to bridge the gaps. *See* HUMAN RESOURCE PLANNING.

garbage in – garbage out (GIGO). A term used to state the fact that the quality of the outputs from a system (e.g. a data processing system) is critically dependent on the calibre of the inputs to it.

garnishee order. A Court order against a debtor compelling (named) people and institutions that owe money to the debtor to pay this to the Court (for distribution to creditors) and not to the debtor.

gatekeeper. A person who (i) communicates with the outside world on behalf of an organisation (formally or informally), (ii) gathers information from external sources and (iii) through being able to withhold this information from certain of the organisation's members is able to influence the decisions it makes.

gateways. Means whereby large companies can sometimes avoid UK and European Community anti-monopoly legislation by arguing that certain mergers, collusions, restrictive practices, etc., are in the public interest because they generate employment, exports, industrial research, improve public safety, and so on.

GDP. *See* GROSS DOMESTIC PRODUCT.

GDP deflator. A price index for total value added within the UK.

geared pay systems. Complex bonus systems intended to level out employees' piece work earnings.

gearing. The ratio of debt to equity capital in a company. A firm that borrows heavily relative to its share capital is said to be highly geared.

Gellerman grid. The categorisation of freshly recruited employees into two groups (those expected to do well and those not expected to do well) followed by a comparison of these predictions with employees' actual levels of job performance.

general adaptation syndrome. A response to stress (qv) that follows three stages: alarm reaction (qv) with attendant physiological change; 'resistance', as the body attempts to repair itself from the effects of the alarm reaction; and 'exhaustion' resulting from the body beginning to break down in consequence of continuing exposure to stressful situations.

General Federation of Trade Unions. A trade union (qv) confederation founded in 1899 to provide services (e.g. research and educational facilities) for small trade unions.

general manager. An executive whose span of control (qv) covers several different functional specialisations.

General Municipal and Boilermakers Union (GMB). One of the largest UK trade unions (qv), recruiting workers from almost every section of British industry. It works in unison with APEX under the name GMB–APEX.

General Register, requirement to maintain. A requirement of the Factories Act 1961 (qv) that a factory (qv) must list all accidents, dangerous occurrences and industrial diseases at a place of employment, the names of employees trained in first aid, and the dates of the painting of walls and the testing of fire alarms.

general secretary. The chief executive of a trade union (qv). General secretaries are normally full time officials and are responsible only to union national executive committees.

general strike. A simultaneous strike by workers in all industries in all parts of the country. Whether such a strike would be legal in Britain is a much debated issue, since immunity from civil liability does not extend to 'political' strikes.

general unions. Trade unions (qv) comprising unskilled and semi-skilled workers organised on a national basis. The Transport and General Workers Union and the General and Municipal Workers Union are examples.

generalised other. According to the psychologist G. H. Mead, an individual's overall perceptions of how other people wish that person to behave.

generativity. A desirable characteristic of certain organisations which devote effort and resources to the development of younger managers in order to ensure orderly management succession (qv) and continuity in administration.

generic benchmarking. See BENCHMARKING, ORGANISATIONAL.

generic skills. Occupational competencies that are easily transferred from one job or occupation to another, i.e. skills which apply to an entire class of activities.

genetic screening. Pre-employment genetical analysis of job applicants to identify persons with 'genetic defects' that might cause them to be damaged by exposure to certain toxic substances, radiation, etc.

gentleman's agreement. A contract that is binding in honour only.

genuine material factor. A legitimate reason for men and women not receiving equal wages for similar value work (qv). An example is higher pay for a man (say) with longer service than a woman in the same job, provided the higher rate is available to members of either sex with the appropriate amount of service.

genuine occupational qualification (GOQ). An aspect of a job that makes it suitable only for a member of one particular sex or ethnic group or for a single person. This has the effect of exempting the job from the provisions of the Sex Discrimination and Race Relations Acts (qv). Examples are actors who play male or female roles; Chinese waiters for Chinese restaurants; female workers in a women's prison, etc.

Geocentrism. See ETHNOCENTRISM.

gestalt. The overall form, shape and configuration of a consciously perceived environment or system.

gestalt psychology. An approach to psychology (qv) which adopts a holistic view of mental processes, rather than breaking them down into constituent elements. 'Gestalt laws' are the principles of perceptual organisation that determine how various perceptions are grouped together into larger wholes.

gifts to employees. Presents given to certain workers that are taxable only if they stem directly from employment. Thus, marriage gifts to employees, prizes for passing examinations, etc., are normally tax free because they are not part of the employment relationship. Such gifts must be unsolicited, non-recurring and of 'reasonable' value. See EMOLUMENTS; FRINGE BENEFITS.

GIGO. See GARBAGE IN – GARBAGE OUT.

Gilbreth, F. B. (1868–1924) and Gilbreth, Lillian (1878–1972). Management consultants and advocates of scientific management (qv) who analysed the human body movements used in work situations. They began with a detailed study of all the motions required for bricklaying, extending this to a comprehensive taxonomy of all body movements used in manual labour. *See* GILBRETH SYSTEM.

Gilbreth system. A categorisation into 17 basic motions of the human body movements needed for work. Its purpose was to enable jobs to be designed so as to avoid motions that use the entire arm and shoulder and motions involving only the fingers.

given up–giving up (GU–GU) complex. Psychological resignation to the fact that a certain goal cannot be attained, leading to a sense of relief from the strain of constantly trying (unsuccessfully) to achieve the objective. Regularly trying to achieve something but having to give up creates feelings of powerlessness, stress (qv) and uncertainty. Given up–giving up can restore stability and predictability to a person's life.

GMB. *See* GENERAL MUNICIPAL, AND BOILERMAKERS UNION.

go-slow. Deliberate non-co-operation of workers with their employer in order to pressurise the employer during an industrial dispute (qv). Workers engaged in go-slows are liable to be fairly (qv) dismissed (subject to their being given appropriate written warnings) provided their actions cause them to be in breach of their contracts of employment (qv). *See* OBEDIENCE, DUTY OF EMPLOYEES.

going concern. A commercial enterprise that is already in business and thus has existing customers, suppliers, staff, premises, administrative procedures, etc. *See* GOODWILL.

going rate. The market wage for a particular type of work.

goldbricking. The practice in certain piece rate wage (qv) systems of workers not declaring all their output on certain days, preferring to hold it back as a reserve for use on days when they wish to 'take it easy'. Consequently, daily pay averages out at a near constant level.

golden handcuffs. Remuneration arrangements whereby certain significant rewards do not become available until an employee has remained with a firm for an agreed minimum period.

golden handshake. An *ad hoc* termination payment made to an employee who leaves a firm, independent of pension arrangements. Such payments are taxable, but at relatively low rates.

golden parachute. An incentive offered to an existing director of a company takeover target to induce him or her not to oppose the attempted takeover, e.g. by offering the director large amounts of severance pay if his or her services are not required following the acquisition.

goodwill. The difference between the sale value of a business and the value of its physical assets, i.e. that part of the work of a business attributable to it being a going concern.

Gordon technique. *See* SYNECTICS.

government training and employment programmes, status of participants. The rule that a person on a long term government training scheme is *not* an employee even though he or she spends a considerable period working for an organisation. Conversely, individuals engaged on community programmes intended to create work for the long-term unemployed are regarded in law as employed workers.

graded hourly rate system. A wage payment method whereby each worker is paid an hourly rate that depends on his or her merit rating (qv).

grading system. A method of non-analytic job evaluation (qv) whereby management defines a number of grades into which all jobs in the organisation are fitted. Grades are differentiated with respect to the skill, responsibility, complexity, effort, supervision, etc., attached to the jobs within them.

Graicunas, V. A. A French management consultant who showed how wide spans of control (qv) create enormous numbers of cross-relationships with and among subordinates. For example, a span of control involving five subordinates generates the potential for 100 cross-relationships. Seven subordinates leads to 490 cross-relationships; ten subordinates to 5210!

grandfather system. The practice in performance appraisal (qv) of sending a manager's assessment of a subordinate to the appraising manager's own boss for review and comment.

grandiose self. *See* NOBEL PRIZE COMPLEX.

grapevines. Informal and unofficial communication channels that frequently arise in large organisations. They circumvent orthodox communication procedures and often carry malicious and unsavoury rumours, especially those of a personal nature.

graph theory. Detailed analysis of the flows of activity within a network. *See* PERT; NETWORK ANALYSIS.

graphology. The study of the shape, size and manner of a person's handwriting, including closure of letters, position of words on the paper and slope of the lines, in order to predict personality characteristics such as attention to detail, persistence, intelligence, etc.

gratuity. A gift (e.g. a tip) or reward for services rendered, such as long meritorious service. *See* GIFTS TO EMPLOYEES.

graveyard shift. A slang term for the night shift in a continuous three shift system.

great man theory. The proposition that an organisation's development and welfare depends almost entirely on the personal characteristics of a single individual who manages it.

green labour. Schooleavers or others new to industrial organisations and without work experience.

greenfield locations. Sites for industrial premises in non-industrialised areas. Businesses that develop greenfield sites usually qualify for numerous government subsidies.

greenlight session. In job evaluation (qv), a brainstorming session intended to analyse a particular job from the perspectives of the people who do it, focusing on what they dislike about the work.

greenmail. The purchase of a significant minority shareholding in a company followed by its resale at a higher price to major shareholders in the company in exchange for the predator abandoning the attempted hostile takeover.

grievance procedures. Mechanisms for hearing and dealing with workers' complaints. Normally the employee is required to approach his or her immediate superior in the first instance, possibly accompanied by a union representative. The matter is passed to higher levels of management and to the employee's union if it remains unresolved.

grievance procedures, Code of Practice concerning. A Department of Employment Code of Practice (qv), first issued in 1971, outlining model procedures for handling employee complaints. It embodies three basic principles: (i) that workers should have a contractual right to have genuine grievances redressed; (ii) that employee representatives be involved in drafting procedures; and (iii) that grievances be dealt with promptly and that natural justice (qv) apply.

grievance procedures, notification of details. The requirement of the Employment Protection (Consolidation) Act 1978 (qv), that all contracts of employment (qv) contain details of the employer's grievance procedure, specifying how grievances should be raised, time limits, stages of the procedure, whether representation is allowed, etc. This does not mean the employer *must* have a grievance procedure; only that if one exists then its particulars must be made known to workers.

gross domestic product (GDP). The output of the entire economy. In principle GDP can be measured from three sources: total production of goods and services; aggregate incomes; and total national expenditures. The figures from these measurements should in theory be equal, although in practice they differ.

gross profit. The value of sales less cost of sales and direct costs of production. Cost of sales consists of the worth of the firm's stock of goods at the start of the period plus purchases during the period less stock on hand at the period's end.

group absolutism. The tendency for members of certain groups to consider that their existing customs, mores (qv) and modes of behaviour are the only ones that are correct.

group appraisal. A method of performance appraisal (qv) that involves a number of interested and knowledgeable parties in the assessment of an individual's work performance. Normally the group includes the appraisee's direct superior, a subordinate and someone from another department. The group submits a report to the boss of the appraisee's immediate superior.

group capacity assessment. A method of clerical work measurement (qv) which uses synthetic times (qv) to determine the periods that ought to be taken by groups of clerks when completing collective duties.

group cohesion. The degree to which members of a group are prepared to co-operate, to continue their association with the group and share common goals and perspectives. Cohesion encourages conformity to group norms and causes stable group behaviour.

group dynamics. The consequences of the forces that operate within groups. Examples are the emergence of power and authority structures, of informal communication systems and conflicts within and between groups.

group norms. Group members' shared perceptions of (i) correct behaviour, (ii) how work should be completed and (iii) proper attitudes towards management and other groups, and related matters.

group selection testing. An employee selection method whereby a group of applicants is observed by an assessor as it performs various tasks, with or without an appointed group leader. Group tasks are designed to test candidates' interpersonal skills and abilities to work as members of a team (qv).

group technology. The geographical arrangement of factory processes, plant or equipment into relatively self-contained units that minimise the distances between each related process or item of plant or equipment.

group therapy. Collective psychotherapy (qv) involving the joint counselling (qv) of several people simultaneously. Group members share their experiences and provide each other with mutual assistance and emotional support.

group training. Training that involves participants learning from each other through pooling experiences and critically examining opposing viewpoints. *See* CASE STUDIES; T-GROUP TRAINING; BUSINESS GAME; ROLE PLAYING.

groupthink. The tendency for like minded people within a cohesive group to agree on issues without challenging each others' ideas or realising that the consensus which seemingly emerges may not represent the actual views of the group. The problem is commonest in groups with strong,

charismatic leaders and when group members devote little mental effort to analysing problems.

guarantee. A promise given by a third party whereby it assumes ultimate responsibility for the debts of another person or business. An 'indemnity' is a guarantee that makes the third party liable *no matter what the circumstances* of a debtor's default. Otherwise, guarantees only apply to matters covered by the terms of the agreement. For example, a firm that guarantees to meet a salesperson's travelling expenses would not be liable for hotel bills relating to the salesperson's spouse.

guarantee payment. The right conferred by the Employment Protection (Consolidation) Act 1978 (qv) whereby an employee is entitled to receive up to five days' pay during any three month period for time the worker is laid off because of shortage of work.

guaranteed annuity option. A provision in an occupational pension scheme whereby the proceeds of an endowment assurance policy included in the scheme may be used to purchase a retirement annuity (qv) at a guaranteed predetermined maximum price.

guaranteed minimum pension. A minimum value for the pension which an occupational pension scheme approved for contracting out (qv) purposes by the Superannuation Funds Office (qv) must pay to a retired employee.

Guard Dogs Act 1975. Legislation prohibiting the use of a guard dog in commercial premises without the presence of a handler capable of controlling the animal. A notice warning that a guard dog is present must be prominently displayed.

gu–gu complex. *See* GIVEN UP–GIVING UP COMPLEX.

Guildford–Zimmerman Temperament Survey. A personality test which uses a questionnaire that asks test respondents to express their feelings about certain subjects and situations.

Guilds. Associations of craft workers that developed during the fourteenth century for the purpose of improving members' remunerations and generally protecting their interests. They operated apprenticeship (qv) schemes and sickness and unemployment benefit systems. Guild members were self-employed, and individually negotiated the fees they charged to employing organisations. However, the craft guilds were an important precursor to modern trade unions. Guilds became illegal following the passing of the Combination Acts 1800 (qv).

guilty knowledge test. A method of polygraph (qv) testing which assumes that knowledge of certain information leads to enhanced physiological reactions to questions that relate to this information.

Guttman scale. A means for measuring attitudes (qv) which involves test subjects indicating their preferences in relation to sets of items ordered along a continuum of approval or disapproval.

H

habituation. Diminution of the strength of a person's response to a particular stimulus in consequence of repeated exposure to it.

haggling. In negotiations (qv) the processes whereby each party attempts to maximise his or her outcomes by making offers which fall short of other parties' demands, in the hope that compromises will emerge eventually.

half holidays for shop workers. The requirement of the Shops Act 1950 (qv), that a shop assistant must finish work before 1.30 p.m. on at least one week day in each week.

half life survival rate. The duration of the period by the end of which half of a particular group of recruits to a company has resigned, all of whom started at the same time. *See* SURVIVAL RATE ANALYSIS.

halo effect. The assumption sometimes made during employment interviews that because a certain candidate possesses one desirable characteristic then he or she must be equally worthy in other respects.

Halsey scheme. A bonus scheme developed in the 1890s in which half the time saved in consequence of an employee working faster accrued to the employee as a bonus expressed in terms of his or her flat rate wage. Total weekly earnings thus comprise hours worked times rate per hour plus half the time saved times rate per hour.

Hancock annuity. An annuity (qv) purchased by an employing firm for the benefit of a retiring employee at the time of the latter's retirement, or for the next of kin of a deceased worker. The name derives from a 1919 test case, Hancock *v* GRIC Ltd., which established the principle that the company purchasing the annuity may regard its cost as a business expense for tax purposes.

haptics. The use of touch while conversing with another person.

harmful agents, EC Draft Directive concerning. A 1980 EC proposal which recommend the imposition on employers and employees of certain basic responsibilities in relation to health and safety at work. It covers the prevention of accidents, first aid, hazard and fire safety, provision of information about dangerous substances to employees, and safety training.

Harrison, Roger. A leading advocate of the human relations approach (qv) to human resources management (qv). Harrison argues that organisations should be designed to satisfy the human needs of workers, rather than employees being 'slotted in' to existing organisational structures.

Hawthorne effect. Enhanced employee output and effort resulting from improved feedback to workers and the knowledge that management is investigating the behavioural effects of changes in working methods. Morale and employee interest in work increases, regardless of the particular types of changes in working conditions and methods imposed.

Hawthorne experiments. Research into workgroup behaviour conducted by G. Elton Mayo (qv) and associates at the Hawthorne plant of the US Western Electric Company in Chicago between 1927 and 1932. The investigators concluded that group norms (qv) and the social organisation and conditions of work were more influential in determining employees' behaviour than managerial directives and/or financial payments systems.

Hay/MSL method. A job evaluation (qv) method (developed in the United States by the E. N. Hay organisation) that breaks jobs down into three basic factors: know-how, problem solving, and accountability (qv).

hazardous substance. A substance potentially capable of harming a worker. Containers of hazardous substances must carry 'R phrases' (qv), 'S phrases' (qv) and/or hazard warning symbols according to industry specific health and safety legislation.

HCIMA. The acronym for the Hotel, Catering and Institutional Management Association.

headhunting. Another term for executive search (qv).

Health and Safety at Work, etc., Act 1974. The basic statute governing UK health and safety at work requirements. It imposes on employers a general duty to ensure, 'so far as is reasonably practicable', the health and safety at work of employees. Under the Act, any firm employing more than four workers must prepare a written statement of its policy on health and safety and bring this to employees' attention. Section 7 of the Act requires workers to co-operate with management on health and safety matters, although ultimate responsibility for ensuring that instructions on health and safety are obeyed lies with the employing firm. *See* SAFETY REPRESENTATIVES; HEALTH AND SAFETY EXECUTIVE.

health and safety at work, criminal liability of employers. Liability for criminal proceedings arising from sections 2 to 9 of the 1974 Health and Safety at Work Act or regulations made under these sections. Firms may be prosecuted (rather than facing civil actions) for obstructing inspectors, failing to implement inspectors' recommendations, or making false statements relating to information required under the Act.

health and safety at work, EC Framework Directive concerning. A statement of *general principles* concerning the protection of employees' health and safety at work, agreed by all EC member nations and requiring employers to take 'appropriate measures' to satisfy these principles, according to detailed rules imposed by national authorities. It obliges employers to prevent occupational risks, eliminate dangers, inform and consult with workers, and invite the 'balanced participation' of employee representatives when dealing with health and safety matters.

Health and Safety Commission. A government-appointed watchdog body that oversees the operation of the Health and Safety at Work Act 1974 (qv). The Commission has up to nine members at any given time. It advises the government on safety issues and supervises the Health and Safety executive (qv).

Health and Safety Executive. A government body set up to enforce the provisions of the Health and Safety at Work Act 1974 (qv). It has three directors plus a staff of factory and other inspectors. As well as conducting inspections the HSE issues numerous Codes of Practice (qv) on safety matters.

Health and Safety Executive Library and Information Service. An on-line database containing over 100,000 items of information relating to health and safety matters. It may be accessed through a number of database hosts (qv).

Health and Safety (First Aid) Regulations 1981. Legally binding government regulations defining the items that have to be included in factory and office first aid boxes. Additionally the Regulations require that there be sufficient people trained in first aid to deal with employees who are injured or taken ill. Such training may be evidenced by an employee's possession of a first aid certificate issued by the Red Cross, the St John Ambulance Brigade or, subject to Health and Safety Executive approval, an employing organisation.

Health and Safety Information for Employees Regulations 1989. Rules that require factories (qv) to distribute leaflets to workers or to display posters informing employees of their employing firm's obligations under relevant health and safety legislation.

Health Register. A document that the Factories Act 1961 (qv) requires be kept by factories to record details of medical examinations of employees engaged on hazardous processes.

heavy industry. A term used to describe traditional labour-intensive (qv) industries such as shipbuilding, coalmining and steelmaking. *See* LIGHT INDUSTRY.

hedonism. The proposition that all human behaviour is motivated by the desire to pursue pleasure and avoid pain.

helicopter factor. In transformational leadership (qv), the capacity of certain individuals to rise above immediate short run supervisory tasks and take a bird's-eye view of a complex situation.

HELIOS programme. A European Community action programme initiated in 1988 to help disabled people find and hold down a job. It covers vocational rehabilitation, education, training, mobility and housing for the disabled.

Hersey–Blanchard model. An approach to leadership (qv) which claims that the major factor affecting the suitability of a particular leadership style (qv) is the 'maturity' of the leader's subordinates. Maturity is defined as an employee's experience, ability level and willingness to accept responsibility.

Herzberg. F. (b.1923). An American psychologist who developed the two factor (qv) theory of motivation.

heuristics. A technique for applying *ad hoc* rules of thumb to the solution of complex problems. Results obtained are regarded as provisional and subject to alteration as circumstances change. The game of chess is an example.

H-form organisation. An organisation structure in which subsidiary businesses are owned by a holding company (qv), which leaves each subsidiary to manage itself as a quasi-autonomous unit. *See* M-FORM ORGANISATION (MULTI-DIVISIONAL ORGANISATION).

hidden agenda. Items implicitly arising during a negotiation (qv) but not appearing as formal agenda items. Discussions pertaining to these matters can dominate the negotiation and cause much conflict among participants. *See* SURFACE BARGAINING.

hierarchical task analysis. A technique of job analysis (qv) in which tasks are examined first in general terms and then in increasingly specific amounts of detail.

hierarchy. A pyramid of authority and decision making within an organisation, with a distinct chain of command (qv) from the apex of the organisation to its base.

hierarchy of needs. A rank order of needs which (according to A. H. Maslow) individuals attempt to satisfy sequentially. There are five levels: physiological, security, affection, esteem and self-actualisation (qv).

High Court. A system of civil Courts established in 1875 to deal with civil actions involving larger claims than can be handled by County Courts (qv). Most employment cases (e.g. wrongful dismissal (qv), compensation for industrial accidents) are heard in the 'Queen's Bench Division' of the High Court, while cases involving pension schemes, trusts (qv), partnerships (qv) and companies go to the 'Chancery Division'. Appeals from the High Court are directed to the Court of Appeal, then to the House of Lords and finally to the European Court of Justice (qv).

High Technology National Training. A government training programme incorporated into the Employment Training Scheme (ETS) (qv) and specially designed to increase the supply of qualified people in certain designated skill shortage occupations.

higher business control. A method devised by T. G. Rose for controlling large organisations. It involves the presentation to senior management of condensed reports on a firm's 'business position' (i.e. trends in sales and stockholding), 'technical position' (progress on research and development, productivity and output statistics), 'trading position' (current profitability, turnover per unit of capital employed (qv), etc.), and its 'financial position' (cash flow, returns on investments, and so on).

Higher Education Diploma. An educational qualification obtained after at least three years' study that is recognised in all EC countries. Anyone possessing the appropriate diploma is free to practise his or her profession in any member state.

Higher National Certificate/Diploma. Post 'A' level educational qualifications awarded following two years' advanced study. Those who study part time receive the HNC. Full time students are given the Diploma.

higher order conditioning. Classical conditioning (qv) in which a tertiary or higher order stimulus is introduced and to which test subjects are conditioned to respond. For example, Ivan Pavlov conditioned dogs to salivate not only in response to the ringing of a bell (a 'secondary stimulus') prior to their being fed, but also in response to things connected with the bell, e.g. showing them an object of a particular shape whenever the bell was rung.

Highly Flammable Liquids and Liquified Petroleum Gases Regulations 1972. Legislation requiring flammable liquids or containers of liquified petroleum gas to be stored and handled in a prescribed manner.

hilltop approach. In work study (qv), an audit of a system's procedures that takes a bird's-eye view of the interactions of processes, drawing together all their aspects. This contrasts with the 'reduction approach', which systematically breaks down the system into small parts.

historical costing. Computation of production costs *after* work has been completed, rather than predicting costs in advance of production, as occurs with standard costing (qv). It is appropriate where each batch has unique features, so that accurate estimation of likely costs is impossible.

HNC/HND. *See* HIGHER NATIONAL CERTIFICATE/DIPLOMA.

holding company. A company that possesses a majority shareholding in several other companies which it has either set up or acquired through purchase. The holding company and (normally) subsidiary units are regarded as 'associated employers' as far as industrial disputes (qv) involving employees of any one unit are concerned. Hence, striking employees may lawfully picket (qv) other units, and unfairly dismissed or redundant (qv) workers might be able to claim against the parent company organisation in an Industrial Tribunal (qv).

holism. An approach to social analysis that regards the whole of a system as more than the simple summation of its constituent elements. The totality of the system is seen as possessing its own unique characteristics.

homeostasis. A stable situation in an operational system, achieved through automatic intervention to counteract random disturbances.

homeworkers, reporting of activities regulations. Rules embodied in the Factories Act 1963 (qv), whereby a factory employer who uses employees who work from home (e.g. assembling components or making up materials)

is required to inform the local authority of the workers' names and addresses. The local authority is empowered to prohibit the work if it is considered injurious to health.

homogeneous organisation. A form of functional organisation (qv) whereby work of the same type is grouped together and performed in a department specialising in that sort of activity.

honesty tests. Selection tests intended to identify job applicants likely to steal from the employer, especially in retailing, data processing and the financial services sectors. Tests ask seemingly ambiguous questions about the candidate's opinions in relation to dishonest practices.

honeycomb organisation. A business organisation structure comprising a conglomeration of 'cells', each corresponding to a particular functional field. The firm recruits employees who are already trained and competent in relevant specialisations, adding or deleting cells as circumstances change. If for example a company acquires its own fleet of vehicles it might add a transport management cell to its organisation, hiring an experienced and qualified transport manager and ancillary staff from outside the firm. Honeycomb organisations can expand or contract their operations extremely quickly.

honorarium. A voluntary fee paid to someone who has provided professional services in the absence of a contract. *See* EX GRATIA PAYMENT.

HORIZON. An EC programme for the vocational rehabilitation of physically handicapped people. It covers education, training, employment, mobility and housing.

horizontal fast track. A planned experience job rotation scheme which gives the employee a larger number of postings – all at the same level of responsibility – within a certain period than is normal for employees on that person's grade.

horizontal integration. Mergers or takeovers of businesses operating at the same stage in the chain of production, distribution or supply (a merger between retail outlets for instance).

Horney, Karen. An influential psychologist who in the 1940s claimed there are three fundamental categories of personality: the compliant type, the aggressive type and the detached type. Compliant individuals are driven by the need for affection; aggressive types perceive other people as fundamentally hostile, causing aggressive people to seek to dominate those around them; detached types value privacy, autonomy and self sufficiency.

horns effect (cloven hoof effect). The reverse of the halo effect (qv). It involves the false assumption that since a job applicant demonstrates one or two bad points during an employment interview then he or she must be equally inadequate in all other respects.

hospital treatment allowance. A special disablement benefit (qv) payable in certain cases to victims of industrial accidents or diseases while the victims are in hospital receiving treatment.

host. *See* DATABASE HOST.

hot stove rule. According to Douglas Mc Gregor (qv), the best means for administering industrial discipline. Sanctions should be applied uniformly, immediately, predictably, consistently and impersonally – so that no precedents arise for non-enforcement of regulations.

house journal. A magazine or newsletter produced within a company by and for the information of its employees.

house loans to workers. *See* LOANS TO EMPLOYEES, TAXATION OF.

house party method. A group selection technique involving the observation of how candidates interact during a few days in an assessment centre (qv). The aim is to determine how each individual relates to working groups.

housing benefit. A government social security payment to families on low incomes and with low levels of savings. It covers their rent and up to 80 per cent of local taxation.

HSELINE. *See* HEALTH AND SAFETY EXECUTIVE LIBRARY AND INFORMATION SERVICE.

human factors engineering. The American term for ergonomics (qv).

human–machine interface. A system for bringing together and regulating relations between humans and machines and mechanical and/or electronic systems. Menu driven computer software packages are a simple example.

human relations approach. A general approach to management which suggests that human, psychological and (primarily) group influences are critical determinants of employee attitudes and behaviour.

human resource accounting. The systematic measurement and analysis of the costs and financial benefits of engaging and using human resources. Examples are recruitment and training costs, assessment of the consequences of staff development exercises, the monetary effects of various salary systems, etc.

human resource planning. The process of comparing an organisation's existing human resources with its forecast need for labour and in consequence specifying the measures necessary for acquiring, training, deploying, developing or discarding workers. It involves the estimation of the consequences of changes in working practices, and the preparation of skills inventories (qv).

human resources management. Those aspects of management which deal with the human side of enterprise and with employees' relations with firms. It covers, *inter alia*, elements of industrial psychology, personnel management (qv), training and industrial relations.

humanistic psychology. Aspects of psychology (qv) that focus on creative abilities and the emotional side of human development.

humidity monitoring requirements. Rules specified in the Factories Act 1961 (qv) requiring the installation of hygrometers in artificially humid factories (qv) and stating upper and lower permissible limits for humidity.

hygiene (maintenance) factor. An aspect of the working environment which, if satisfactory, an employee does not notice but which, if it is less than satisfactory, causes employee displeasure and low morale. Hygiene factors do not motivate employees.

hyperactive worker. Someone who undertakes tasks incessantly but without any concern for their meaning or relevance to his or her employing organisation.

hypochondriasis, retirement. Obsessive preoccupation with somatic problems that sometimes accompany retirement from employment. It is thought to result from loss of role (qv) and exclusion from previously familiar social and other environments. In becoming an 'ill' person, the individual creates a new role for him or her self.

hypothecation. The practice of pledging goods or property as security for a debt without transferring possession or title to them. Lenders have a lien on the pledged assets, i.e. they can keep the goods until the debt has been settled.

I

IAM. *See* INSTITUTE OF ADMINISTRATIVE MANAGEMENT.

ICFTU. *See* INTERNATIONAL CONFEDERATION OF FREE TRADE UNIONS.

ICO. The acronym for the Institute of Careers Officers.

ICOM. *See* INDUSTRIAL COMMON OWNERSHIP MOVEMENT.

ICSA. *See* INSTITUTE OF CHARTERED SECRETARIES AND ADMINISTRATORS.

id. According to the psychologist Sigmund Freud, a collection of inborn instinctual drives, present in each individual, which seeks gratification of a person's desires. The id has no inhibitions and cannot distinguish reality and fantasy or between right and wrong. *See* EGO.

identical elements, transfer of learning through. A theory regarding the transfer of learning (qv) which states that positive transfer occurs if parts of one task are the same as parts of another. For example, two office jobs may be different from each other except that both include telephoning and filing. A person transferred between the two jobs will benefit from a carry-over of previously acquired telephoning and filing skills.

identification. The process whereby one person assumes the attitudes, perspectives, behaviour patterns and/or attributes of another person or group because the characteristics adopted help that individual establish good relations with the other person or group.

identity crisis. Feelings of disorientation, anxiety (qv) (and possibly depression) resulting from self-perceived uncertainties regarding one's role (qv) and self-identity (qv).

ideographic data. Information on behaviour that is unique to a specific person.

ideologies, managerial. Socially determined sets of beliefs held by some senior managers that inwardly support and legitimise top management's elite status within organisations.

ideology. A body of beliefs and ideas that reflect the values of a certain group in society.

ideology, organisational. A body of ideas and/or way of thinking predominant within an organisation.

idle time. Periods spent by workers waiting for work to arrive. A flat rate (qv) hourly payment normally applies to such periods.

idle time variance. The financial cost of the difference between the anticipated number of hours that employees are idle due to abnormal circumstances and the actual number of idle hours.

IKBS. *See* INTELLIGENT KNOWLEDGE BASED SYSTEM.

illegal contract of employment. A contract of employment entered into in order to commit a crime or other unlawful act, or which violates a statute. Examples are contracts for the employment of prostitutes or for engaging as a driver someone who does not possess a driving licence. Such contracts are not legally binding; Courts will assume they do not exist.

illumination requirements. Minimum standards of illumination needed for various industrial tasks. These vary from 1500 lux for very fine assembly work, through 300 lux for medium assembly work, to 200 lux for sheet metal work. Background lighting should normally be at least 150 lux. (One lux is the light given by a standard candle at a distance of one metre from the work.)

ILO. *See* INTERNATIONAL LABOUR OFFICE.

ILO Yearbook. *See* YEARBOOK OF LABOUR STATISTICS.

I.Mech E. The abbrieviated version of the name 'Institution of Mechanical Engineers'.

imagery, mental. Subjective experiences involving recollections, thoughts or imaginations that reproduce previous sensory experiences.

imitative learning. *See* VICARIOUS LEARNING.

immobility of labour. Unemployed workers' inability or unwillingness to move to other areas where jobs are available. It results from housing difficulties, moving expenses, problems with finding new schools for children, reluctance to leave friends and family, etc.

immunity of trade unions. The legal exemption of certified independent trade unions (qv) from civil liability for breach of contract, inducement or threatening to break a contract, or other claims for damages by employers or third parties affected by an industrial action – provided the action is in contemplation or furtherance of a trade dispute (qv). Immunity is restricted by several Employment Acts (qv).

imperfect competition. A market situation in which there is a large number of suppliers but where entry barriers and other market imperfections cause price to be higher and output lower than in genuinely competitive conditions.

impingement pay. Extra wages paid to employees who work during their contractual holiday entitlement.

implicit personality theory. The proposition that individuals perceive issues, events and objects according to a relatively fixed set of biases, i.e. that without realising it people have definite views about what things should be like, and that these views affect judgements.

implied deflator for consumers' expenditure. A measure of inflation sometimes cited in union claims for wage increases. It is computed by dividing the current value of consumers' expenditure by an estimate of the volume of total consumption measured at constant prices. *See* RETAIL PRICES INDEX.

impression management. Techniques used by individuals to present certain (possibly misleading) impressions of themselves to the outside world. Examples are flamboyance, ingratiation, concealment of particular facts about a person's background, etc.

imprest system. A means for ensuring that an account (petty cash for instance) always has sufficient resources

to meet the demands placed upon it. Amounts spent from the account during (say) each month are automatically made good at the month's end so that the next month begins with the same balance as at the start of the last one.

Improvement Notice. An order issued by a Health and Safety Executive (qv) or other government inspector compelling a firm to take positive action to deal with a health or safety hazard within 21 days. *See* PROHIBITION NOTICE.

imputation. An estimate of the value of property or (more commonly) a service. For example, the estimated value of a personnel department's contribution to the work involved in filling a vacancy might be charged to the section in which the vacancy arose, to indicate how much the section would have had to pay to an outside recruitment agency for similar services.

IMS. *See* INSTITUTE OF MANAGEMENT SERVICES.

IMSSOC (Institute of Manpower Studies System of Occupational Classification). *See* INSTITUTE OF MANPOWER STUDIES.

In Place of Strife. A 1969 government White Paper which proposed substantial reforms of trade union law and organisation. It provoked bitter hostility from the trade union movement and was quickly withdrawn. However, the TUC promised to undertake voluntary internal reforms of certain aspects of union structure and behaviour.

incapability. A reason for fair dismissal which encompasses incompetence and inability to perform work through injury or ill health. The law requires that prior to a dismissal on these grounds the employer explain to the worker why his or her work is sub-standard, allow reasonable time for improvement and issue written formal warnings detailing the inadequacies and stating the consequences of non-improvement.

incentive. A prospective reward or punishment capable of motivating an individual to greater effort. Examples include financial bonuses, status symbols and possibilities of promotion or demotion.

incidental act. An activity indirectly related to the fulfilment of a contract of employment and included therefore in a worker's course of employment. Examples are arriving early for work, going to the toilet, collecting wages, etc. Employers are liable for damages resulting from accidents to workers occurring during the completion of incidental activities.

incidental learning. Learning (qv) that occurs casually and effortlessly, normally through experience.

income and expenditure account. The equivalent of a profit and loss account, but drafted by non-profit organisations (clubs and charities for example).

income benefit insurance. An element of certain superannuation schemes (qv) whereby the next of kin of a deceased superannuated employee who died before retirement is paid a guaranteed income for life or for a specified number of years.

Income Support. State benefit available to unemployed people who are ineligible for unemployment pay (qv) or for whom the level of unemployment pay is insufficient to meet their needs. Claimants must be over 18 years of age (16 in cases of exceptional hardship) and have savings of less than a certain amount. Strikers, students and people working more than 24 hours a week are not eligible.

Incomes Data Services Ltd. A research organisation that conducts salary surveys and issues reports on a variety of personnel, employment and industrial relations issues. It publishes a monthly review of salaries and benefits, a directory of salary surveys, international reports and a monthly analysis of trends in top people's salaries.

incomes policies. Laws or government exhortations which seek to restrict workers' pay rises, typically through establishing a 'norm' for the level of wage increase to be paid in a given period.

incorporated associations. Organisations which for legal purposes have their own legal identities which are completely independent of the legal identities of their members. Companies are the commonest example. Hence, company creation is frequently referred to as the 'process of incorporation'. An incorporated association may enter contracts and sue and be sued in its own name. It is responsible for its own debts thus limiting members' liability for these debts to the values of their investments. *See* UNINCORPORATED ASSOCIATIONS.

increment. A periodic salary increase, usually of a predetermined amount. Each grade within a salary structure will contain a certain number of increments, through which employees in that grade progress over time.

incremental learning. Learning (qv) that occurs through a series of logically planned exposures to instructional materials and/or experiences.

indemnity. *See* GUARANTEE.

indemnity of employees, liability of employer. The implied common law duty of an employing organisation to settle expenses necessarily incurred by workers during the course of their employment.

indenture. A contract of employment (qv) for an apprentice (qv). This must be in writing and be for the apprentice's benefit. Apprentices may not leave their employers unless the latters' conduct indicates an unwillingness to provide proper instruction.

independence. In a group communication network, a person's relative autonomy as determined by his or her position in the system.

independent contractor. A self-employed person or firm engaged under a contract for services (qv). Independent contractors are not employees (qv) and thus cannot claim unfair dismissal (qv), redundancy payments (qv), statutory sick pay (qv) or other benefits available to employed workers.

independent trade union. According to the Trade Union and Labour Relations Act 1974 (qv), a trade union (qv) not dominated by an employer and not liable to interference by an employer through the provision or withdrawal of financial or other support.

index linked wages. Employee remuneration packages which provide for automatic wage rises following increases in the rate of inflation.

indexed final remuneration. *See* DYNAMISATION.

indicative planning. National economic planning via the setting by the government of targets which the government then seeks to persuade industries and large organisations to seek to achieve.

indicators of industrial activity. Statistics relating to economic development in 25 OECD countries, categorised by industry. They are compiled by the OECD and published in Britain by HMSO.

indirect costs. *See* OVERHEADS.

indirect discrimination. Unfair sex or race discrimination resulting from the imposition of a condition likely to result in a disproportionately small number of one of the sexes or a certain ethnic group being able to meet the condition. An example is a job advertisment which states that applicants must be over six feet tall, hence indirectly discriminating against women. 'Direct' discrimination, conversely, means treating people less favourably on account of their race, sex or because they are married. An example is a job advertisment specifying 'males only need apply'. *See* VICTIMISATION.

indirect labour. That part of a firm's workforce which does not contribute directly to the production of goods. Examples are secretaries, general administrative staff, cleaners, etc.

individualism. The proposition that people work best when left alone to pursue their own self interest. An implication of the principle is that individuals should not be subjected to state regulation or control by institutions such as trade unions (qv).

individuation. Acquisition of a unique and distinctive role (qv) by a member of a group.

indivisibilities, existence of. The situation that occurs when productive capacity must either be fully used or not used at all, i.e. operations may be 'switched on' or 'switched off ', but cannot be partially completed.

induction. The process of introducing recruits to an organisation and of informing them about company procedures and where to go for assistance if they experience problems.

indulgency pattern. According to A. Gouldner, a management style (qv) based on informality and a relaxed approach to regulations, hopefully leading to harmonious and friendly interpersonal relations.

industrial accident. An accident covered by the Health and Safety at Work Act 1974 (qv), i.e. one which occurs at work and results in at least three days' absence from employment.

industrial action. A sanction imposed by employees (normally acting through a trade union (qv)) against an employing firm in furtherance of an industrial dispute (qv). Action might begin with employees withdrawing their co-operation and refusing to do anything not strictly covered by their contracts of employment (qv). Then the workers may ban overtime, refuse to cover for sick colleagues and so on. Ultimately a strike may be called. *See* DISOBEDIENCE, WILFUL.

Industrial and Provident Society. A limited liability organisation registered as a co-operative (qv) with the Registrar of Friendly Societies. At least seven members are required and certain rules must be written into the organisation's constitution. These rules relate to such matters as the scope of membership of the co-operative; returns to members and others who lend it money; and how its surplus assets are to be distributed on the dissolution of the enterprise.

Industrial Common Ownership Movement (ICOM). A privately funded organisation formed to promote worker co-operatives. It provides preprinted packages of documents for firms that wish to register as co-operative Industrial and Provident Societies (qv).

industrial democracy. A term used to describe a variety of measures for involving employees in the management decision making of their firms. Possibilities range from complete workers' control (as in a producers' co-operative) to participation schemes, works councils (qv), worker directors (qv), consultation agreements, and straightforward collective bargaining. *See* COMPANY LAW, FIFTH EC DRAFT DIRECTIVE ON; BULLOCK REPORT.

industrial dispute. A dispute between a firm and its workers. Independent trade unions (qv) registered with the government Certification Officer (qv) are exempt from civil liability in respect of damages suffered by employers and third parties during industrial disputes, provided the action is not directed against an employer whose employees are not involved in the dispute. Definitive listings of the matters that may be regarded as *bona fide* industrial disputes are contained in the Trade Union and Labour Relations Act 1974 (qv), and the Employment Act 1982 (qv). Disputes among different groups of workers are not industrial disputes. *See* SECONDARY ACTION; TRADE DISPUTE.

industrial dynamics. Application of cybernetics (qv) to business systems and decision making.

industrial engineering. The application of analytical techniques commonly associated with science and engineering to the management of production. It is particularly concerned with work study (qv), quality management and production planning and control.

industrial espionage. Obtaining confidential information about a rival organisation without the latter's knowledge or permission. Industrial espionage is not of itself illegal in the UK (unless actual theft (qv) is involved). Examples are following competitors' delivery vehicles and noting the addresses of the customers to whom they make deliveries.

industrial estate. An area within or around a town or city specially designated for industrial or commercial use. Buildings on an industrial estate are designed for easy conversion into factories (qv) or office premises; there is ample access for vehicles; warehousing facilities, etc.

Industrial Fatigue Research Board. An organisation set up in 1917 to investigate the relations between employees' health and productivity. It was particularly concerned with improving the efficiency of wartime munitions workers, and to this end established multidisciplinary teams of medical doctors, engineers and social scientists to analyse the ergonomic (qv) aspects of work.

Industrial Injuries Advisory Committee. A committee set up by the Department of Health and Social Security to advise on (i) the payment of benefits to victims of industrial accidents and diseases and (ii) the deployment of the resources of the UK Industrial Injuries Fund (a central fund administered by the DHSS for the purpose of compensating those involved in industrial accidents).

Industrial Injuries and Diseases (Old Cases) Act 1975. Legislation which continued the right of workers injured by industrial accidents or diseases occurring before 5 July 1948, to receive the compensation to which they were previously entitled under the Workmen's Compensation Acts 1925–1945 (qv).

Industrial Injury Benefit. *See* SOCIAL SECURITY ACT 1975.

industrial momentum. The phenomenon of industries continuing to exist in particular geographical areas long after the conditions that led to their development are no longer present. Reasons for this include the availability within a community of a pool of skilled labour, and the emergence of service industries to support the main industry in the region.

Industrial Participation Association. An organisation established to undertake research into industrial participation and to promote employee involvement in the management of enterprises.

industrial psychology. A previous name for work psychology (qv). Today the term is reserved specifically for aspects of psychology which relate only to industry (e.g. the psychological consequences of repetitive assembly line operations) rather than to work as a whole.

industrial relations. Rules, practices and conventions governing interrelations between managements and their workforces, normally involving collective employee representation and bargaining. The rules of industrial relations define procedures for settling wages and conditions of work, for resolving disputes, dealing with conflicts and a wide range of grievance and disciplinary processes. Rules may be written or verbally agreed, internally formulated or externally imposed, e.g. through government legislation.

Industrial Relations Act 1971. A statute which sought to create a stable and legally enforceable framework for the conduct of industrial relations (qv). It was a contentious Act, fiercely opposed by the Trades Union Congress (qv). The Act was repealed in 1974 although many of its provisions were reinstated via the Employment Acts (qv) of 1980 and 1982.

industrial relations audit. A systematic appraisal of the effectiveness of a company's entire range of industrial relations policies and procedures, including its collective bargaining (qv) arrangements, grievance procedures (qv), works councils (qv), consultation methods, the work of its negotiating committees, and so on.

Industrial relations, Code of Practice on. A Code of Practice (qv) issued under the Industrial Relations Act 1971 (qv) but retained when the latter was abolished. It recommends: (i) the establishment in firms of orderly procedures for collective bargaining and for settling disputes; (ii) the freedom of workers to join trade unions; (iii) that managers be given training in industrial relations; and (iv) that clear and comprehensive employment policies (on recruitment, promotion, control of grievances, redundancy, etc.) be applied.

Industrial Relations Review and Report. A journal which summarises current developments and recent legal judgments pertaining to personnel management and industrial relations. Additionally it conducts surveys of trends in earnings in various industries and publishes the results.

Industrial Reorganisation Corporation. A government agency formed in 1966 to promote structural change in the British economy through encouraging the merger of selected companies. Grants were offered to finance takeover bids in approved cases. The Corporation was disbanded in 1970. *See* NATIONAL ENTERPRISE BOARD.

industrial revolution. The rapid transformation of an agrarian economy into one based on industry and manufacturing. Britain was the first country to experience an industrial revolution. This happened in the eighteenth and early nineteenth centuries.

Industrial Safety Advisory Council. A government committee established by the UK Department of Employment to report on matters relating to industrial safety.

Industrial Society, The. A private foundation comprising representatives of employers' associations, trade unions, large UK companies and government agencies. Its purposes are to provide training for industry (particularly in the fields of supervisory management and interpersonal skills (qv)) and to offer to the business community general advice on personnel management (qv) and industrial relations (qv).

industrial sociology. A branch of sociology particularly concerned with working groups, work behaviour, interpersonal relations in employment and attitudes towards jobs and employing organisations.

Industrial Training Boards (ITBs). Organisations established following the Industrial Training Act of 1964 and empowered to maintain lists of all employers in certain industries and to impose a levy on them. Monies received are used for employee training in those industries. Appeals by firms against being defined as falling within a levied 'industry' are heard by Industrial Tribunals (qv). By 1981 there were 23 ITBs in existence. Successive governments reduced their number until, by 1981, only seven remained. In 1989 the government decided to abolish all ITBs and levies except for the construction industry. Several ITBs were replaced by non-statutory training organisations (qv).

Industrial Tribunal. A three-person Court, with a qualified solicitor or barrister in the chair plus two lay members, that hears cases relating to alleged unfair dismissal, health and safety at work, equal opportunities and related employment matters. Each of the lay members represents one of the two sides of industry (unions and employers' associations). *See* PROCEDURE IN INDUSTRIAL TRIBUNALS.

Industrial Tribunal (Rules of Procedure) Regulations 1985. Rules that regulate procedures in Industrial Tribunals (qv). They provide for pre-hearing assessments (qv) at the request of either party, and for new systems intended to speed up Tribunal hearings.

industrial union. A trade union (qv) that seeks to unite all the employees of a particular industry into a single union, regardless of their occupation or level of skill. The National Union of Mineworkers is an example.

industry. A collection of businesses all involved in the same type of activity, e.g. producing similar products or serving the same market.

Industry Training Organisations. *See* NON-STATUTORY TRAINING ORGANISATIONS.

inferiority complex. Feelings of personal inadequacy leading to resentment, depression and, ultimately, to abnormal behaviour.

inflation accounting. Adjustment of a company's financial accounts to allow for the effects of inflation. This enables management to assess how much of a reported increase in profits is attributable to a higher volume of sales and/or improved efficiency rather than to rising prices.

inflation tax, proposal for. A suggestion (never implemented) that employers who give their employees wage rises above a predetermined rate (determined annually by the government) should pay a tax equal to the difference between the value of the pay rise awarded and the government norm. The arguments against the idea are that policing would be difficult and that it would itself be highly inflationary, as firms might simply raise their prices to cover the tax.

informal organisation. An unofficial organisation system that arises naturally and spontaneously within a business as individuals begin to interact. Informal groups emerge to represent people with common interests, each group possessing its own norms (qv), perceptions and internal communications. *See* FORMAL ORGANISATION: FORMAL GROUPS.

informal warning. An unrecorded warning issued to a worker following a breach of discipline. Such warnings cannot in law be used to justify disciplinary action following a repetition of the offence (a formal written warning is required for this purpose).

information overload. The situation that occurs when an individual is bombarded with so much information that he or she is unable to cope. In consequence the person simply ignores most of the information.

information processing, psychological. The mental processes whereby external stimuli are perceived, interpreted and acted upon. *See* COGNITIVE CATEGORISATION (CONCEPTUALISATION).

information sub-system. Those aspects of an organisation (qv) concerned

with (i) collecting and analysing information, (ii) internal and external communication (qv) and (iii) taking decisions.

information technology. The acquisition, processing, storage, analysis and dissemination of information using computers.

information theory. A field of study concerned with the structure and characteristics of information systems; including how much unnecessary data they contain, their efficiency and the rules they apply to the categorisation of items of information.

infrastructure, economic. All the services that support an industrial society, e.g. road and rail networks, the education and training system, public utilities (qv), the telecommunications system, etc.

ingroup. A group comprising individuals who feel a sense of affinity with each other and of belonging to the group. An 'outgroup', conversely, consists of a group of persons possessing a characteristic that sets them apart from the ingroup.

inherent risk. Dangers associated with certain types of work (steeplejacking for instance) which an employer cannot obviate. Firms are not generally liable for injuries attributable to inherent risk, provided they were not negligent and had warned employees of the existence of such risk (unless the risk is patently obvious).

inhibition. Interference by one psychological process in the operation of another, e.g. fear paralysing a worker thus preventing him or her avoiding an accident.

inhibition in work. *See* WORK INHIBITION, FREUDIAN THEORY OF.

initiating structure. An approach to leadership (qv) involving close supervision of subordinates, highly detailed job descriptions and the division of subordinates' work into simple tasks.

initiation ceremony. A ceremony or practical joke inflicted on an employee soon after he or she has started work in order to induct that person into a group. The employer is liable for injuries suffered by an employee during an initiation ceremony if the employer knew about it and did not implement steps to prevent it taking place.

injunction. A Court order requiring that something be done (a 'mandatory' injunction) or not be done (a 'prohibitory' injunction). *See* INTERLOCUTORY INJUNCTION.

Inner City Task Forces. Government organisations established in 1988 to stimulate economic development in inner cities. Their role is to co-ordinate the efforts of government departments, local authorities and private firms concerned with inner city industrial rejuvenation.

inner directed person. Someone who is creative, individualistic, and inclined to do things in his or her own way. An 'other directed person', conversely, is conformist and easily influenced by external events.

inner self awareness. An individual's cognitions of his or her own thoughts, feelings and reactions. This differs from 'outer' self awareness, which concerns a person's awareness of the effects of his or her behaviour on others.

input driven learning. Training that follows a preset syllabus using predetermined training techniques. It seeks to guarantee that learners will acquire certain knowledge and/or abilities. This contrasts with 'outcome led' learning whereby a training programme is adapted according to how well trainees are coping with the course, e.g. by devoting more time to certain topics or by lowering target standards of achievement in response to trainees' slow progress.

INSEAD. A prestigious European business school located at Fontainebleau near Paris.

in-service training (INSET). Training undertaken in the course of employment and directly related to the development of occupational skills. INSET is typically an important feature of management development schemes.

INSET. *See* IN-SERVICE TRAINING.

insight learning. Cognitive learning (qv) involving understanding through self-discovery, as opposed to learning by rote (qv).

Insolvency Act 1986. The major statute governing bankruptcy and company liquidation (qv) in the United Kingdom. For bankruptcy, the Act adheres to the well-established principle that although bankrupts must use their personal assets to meet their debts, they should then be free to start again following a reasonable period (currently three years for someone declared bankrupt for the first time; ten years for people with previous bankruptcies).

Insolvency Directive 1980. An EC Directive granting employees of insolvent businesses the right to claim against the state for unpaid wages, accumulated holiday entitlements, etc., at the time of their employer's insolvency. All the demands of this Directive were incorporated into the 1978 Employment Protection (Consolidation) Act (qv) which provides for the government to pay workers in insolvent firms up to eight weeks' arrears of wages, maternity pay, wages for statutory periods of notice, holiday pay for up to six weeks in the prior 12 months, and basic compensation (qv) for redundancy (qv) or unfair dismissal (qv).

insolvency practitioner. An individual who advises insolvent persons or businesses about the courses of action necessary to honour their debts. Under the Insolvency Act 1986 (qv), anyone holding the office of receiver, administrator, trustee or other formal bankruptcy or company liquidation appointment must be a licensed insolvency practitioner.

Inspection Report. A form completed by a safety representative (qv) following an inspection. A copy is sent to management which is obliged under the Health and Safety at Work Act 1974 (qv) to fill in a blank section headed 'Remedial Action or Explanation' in relation to potential hazards identified by the representative.

inspectors, DHSS. Government inspectors empowered to make spot checks to ensure that employers are only reclaiming the statutory sick pay (qv) to which they are entitled. Inspectors may enter firms' premises at any time, examine any document and question any person. An employer's refusal to co-operate with an inspector can lead to an initial fine plus further penalties imposed on a daily basis.

inspectors, legal powers of. Statutory rights of Health and Safety Executive (qv) and local authority inspectors (Environmental Health Officers for example) to enter firms' premises at will, take photographs, examine and photocopy documents, question anyone on the premises, require individuals to sign written statements and conduct any investigation relevant to the efficient conduct of an investigation.

instinct. An innate unlearned pattern of feelings or behaviour. People are born with instincts, rather than their being acquired.

Institute of Administrative Management. A professional body (qv) offering examinations to students concerned with general administrative management.

Institute of Chartered Accountants. A professional body (qv) for accountants who qualify via the Institute's examinations and who serve a period of 'articles' (i.e. planned experience) under the supervision of an existing Chartered Accountant. Separate Institutes exist for Chartered Accountants in England and Wales, Scotland and Ireland. Members are statutorily authorised to audit company accounts.

Institute of Chartered Secretaries and Administrators. The professional organisation for company secretaries. It is a chartered professional body (qv), entry to which is entirely by examination. The Institute publishes a magazine (*The Administrator*) and maintains an extensive library of materials on company law and administration.

Institute of Management Services (IMS). A professional body (qv) for individuals concerned with work study (qv), organisation and methods (qv), and related management services (qv). It offers a series of examinations for people wishing to qualify as management services officers.

Institute of Manpower Studies. A research organisation founded in 1969 and based in the London School of Economics and the University of Sussex. The IMS publishes reports on matters of interest in human resource planning (qv), plus a 'System of Occupational Classification' similar to CODOT (qv) but containing more detail.

Institute of Personnel Management (IPM). A professional body (qv) for those concerned with personnel management. It emerged from the UK Welfare Workers' Association, founded in 1913. Today the IPM operates an education scheme to prepare students for a career in personnel management, provides information and advisory services to members, arranges conferences and workshops and publishes books and monographs in the personnel field.

Institute of Training and Development (ITD). A professional body (qv), concerned with training and the development of human resources. It offers a programme of examinations for people wishing to qualify in the training field, organises conferences and exhibitions connected with training issues and publishes a journal.

institution. An organisation with members who tend to behave in a regular, predictable and standardised manner according to preset rules, norms (qv) and folkways (qv).

institutional discrimination. Unfair race or sex discrimination resulting not from individual initiative, but rather from individuals conforming with racist or sexist norms (qv) embedded in an organisation's structure, rules and procedures. An example is a firm that only recruits from certain schools or universities the overwhelming majority of the graduates of which are male and/or white.

institutionalisation. Conformance by an individual to a standardised pattern of behaviour and behavioural expectations in consequence of his or her protracted involvement with an institution (qv).

instructional technology. The rigorous analysis of training methods and processes. See SYSTEMATIC TRAINING.

instrumental orientation. An attitude (qv) towards work that focuses on pay and job security. Employees with instrumental attitudes regard work as a *means* to achieving improvements in living standards; they are not concerned with whether their jobs are innately interesting.

instrumentality. In the expectancy theory (qv) of motivation, how a worker perceives the correlation between performance levels and possible rewards. The relation can be positive or negative.

instrumented T-group technique. A method of T-group training (qv) that requires participants to respond to written questionnaires, answers to which form a basis for group discussion.

insufficient notice, damages against employees. Compensation awarded by Courts to employers who sue employees for leaving their employing firms without giving sufficient notice. Examples of the damages claimable include the administrative costs of finding a replacement (advertising expenses for instance) and the value of the production lost from failure to give proper notice.

insured occupational pension scheme. See SELF ADMINISTERED PENSION SCHEME.

intangible assets. Valuable assets that do not possess a physical identity. Examples include goodwill (qv), ownership of patents and other intellectual property, brands and trademarks, etc.

Integrated Services Digital Network (ISDN). A networked computer system that permits fast, high quality transmission of data, voice, text and graphics.

integration of organisations. A term used by Lawrence and Lorsch (qv) to describe the creation within organisations of unifying devices intended to integrate activities into a united whole capable of achieving organisational objectives. Devices include rule books, codes of conduct, the establishment of norms (qv), use of standard procedures, appointment of co-ordinators, etc. See DIFFERENTIATION OF ORGANISATIONS.

integration test. A means for distinguishing employees (qv) from independent contractors (qv) whereby a Court evaluates whether a person's services are an integral part of an organisation or merely an accessory to its operations. The test is useful for situations involving professionally qualified people (chartered accountants or solicitors for example) where the engaging firm does not control the method of performance of duties. See CONTROL TEST; ECONOMIC REALITY TEST.

integrative negotiation. A negotiation in which the parties seek a common position on an issue.

intellectual property. Rights over inventions, patents, trade marks, designs and any other copyright material. Such rights normally belong to the employers of individuals who make inventions, devise new processes, write computer programs, etc., rather than to the individuals themselves. See INVENTIONS; KNOW-HOW.

intelligence quotient (IQ). An index comparing a person's performance in an intelligence test with the performances of others. For children, IQ is measured by dividing the individual's 'mental age', i.e. his or her ability to solve puzzles that the average child of a certain age can handle, by his or her chronological age. In adults, IQ is assessed by dividing a person's score in an IQ test by the average score for the entire test sample. Thus an individual with an IQ of 100 has a score just equal to that of the average.

intelligence tests. Selection tests intended to assess the calibre of an applicant's intellect, particularly vis-a-vis his or her reasoning and thinking abilities, perceptiveness, self-awareness, learning capacity and critical and organisational faculties. Tests might seek to measure numerical ability, physical dexterity, verbal fluency and/or spacial perception.

Intelligent Knowledge Based System (IKBS). Integrated computer systems based on the latest developments in information technology (qv). Research into IKBSs attracts much financial support from the UK government and the European Community.

interact news. A multi-lingual European Community publication intended to provide useful information to disabled people, especially news of employment opportunities.

interaction process analysis. A technique for recording and analysing the processes of social interaction that occur within a discussion group. An observer places each statement or idea mentioned into one of 12 categories, noting who made the remark and to whom it was addressed. The results are then analysed to discover the role structure of the group and the patterns of interaction among participants.

interactive skills. Interpersonal communications skills that involve initiating messages and responding to the face-to-face communications of other people.

interactive video. A video of a simulated interpersonal communication situation that maps out the background to the depicted events. Actors in the video assume various managerial/employee roles. The film builds up to a climax, at which point the video stops abruptly leaving the viewer to say how he or she would handle the next stage in the situation. A class discussion follows.

interest group. A collection of individuals who share common perspectives, views, objectives or economic interests. Examples are various grades of employees, shareholders, members of a department, professional groups, etc.

interest on awards of Industrial Tribunals. Interest levied on an employer on the value of an Industrial Tribunal (qv) award that remains unpaid 42 days after the Tribunal's decision. The rate of interest charged is related to market levels and is altered periodically.

interface. A common boundary between two systems, e.g. the human–machine interface (qv) or a common link between various makes of computer.

interference pay. Compensation to workers operating under a piece rate (qv) payments by results system for low output levels caused by workers being shifted to other duties or departments to help with urgent projects, thus preventing their achieving normal piecework performance.

interfirm comparison. Use of financial ratios and other essential information to compare the operating performance of one organisation with others.

intergroup relations. See INTRA-GROUP RELATIONS.

interim management. See LOCUM MANAGEMENT (LOCUM LEASING).

interim relief. A temporary order by an Industrial Tribunal (qv) compelling the re-employment of an employee sacked allegedly for no other reason than joining or refusing to join a trade union (qv), until the Tribunal has time to hear the worker's complaint. Application for interim relief must be submitted within seven days of the sacking.

interlocutory injunction. A Court order restraining named individuals or organisations (a trade union for example) from carrying out certain acts which the person obtaining the injunction alleges are unlawful. The injunction remains in force until a full trial hearing can be arranged. Refusal to obey an interlocutory injunction constitutes contempt of court, for which large fines may be imposed.

internal benchmarking. See BENCHMARKING, ORGANISATIONAL.

internal growth of a business. Development of a firm's productive potential through new product development, retention of a large part of the business's earnings for new investment, the acquisition of fresh plant and equipment (qv), entry to new markets, etc. This differs from 'external growth', which involves the acquisition of other businesses.

internal justification. Changing one's internal beliefs, frames of reference (qv) and attitudes (qv) in order to overcome cognitive dissonance (qv).

internal labour market. The supply and demand position in relation to workers already employed within a firm.

internal locus. See LOCUS OF CONTROL.

internal markets, creation of. A method for allocating resources within large organisations (including the public services) whereby managers are expected to behave *as if* they are entrepreneurs and thus subject to market forces. Units of the organisation submit competing bids for resources. Successful bids are rewarded with internal 'contracts' for the supply of in-house services.

internalisation. The process whereby an individual accepts the social influence of others because the latters' behaviour or attitudes fit in with the value system of the person concerned. The induced attitude or behaviour is itself intrinsically rewarding.

International Confederation of Free Trade Unions (ICFTU). An international organisation founded in 1949 to act as a forum for discussions between representatives of trade unions in Western bloc countries. Currently it has 142 member organisations from 97 nations. It meets biennially, and has a 30-strong secretariat responsible for implementing agreed decisions.

International Labour Office (ILO). A United Nations agency founded by the

League of Nations in 1919 and based in Geneva, Switzerland. Its aim is to improve labour conditions, living standards and economic and social stability via international action involving the participation of employee representatives, employers and national governments. The ILO commissions research and publishes the results of investigations into various aspects of employment and management.

International Packet Switching Service (IPSS). A computerised communications network that enables customers of a database host (qv) in one country to gain access to database hosts in other nations.

International Standard Classification of Occupations (ISCO). A taxonomy of occupations (qv) developed by the International Labour Office (qv).

International Trade Secretariats (ITSs). International trade union (qv) organisations covering trade unions in a certain industry in various countries. They are associated with the International Confederation of Free Trade Unions (qv).

interpersonal attraction, Newcombe's theory of. The proposition advanced by the psychologist T. M. Newcombe in the 1960s that people with similar attitudes are attracted to each other. According to the theory, individuals feel a need for the support of others in relation to their beliefs and attitudes, and thus feel uneasy when confronted by people with attitudes contrary to their own.

interpersonal process recall. A method of self-awareness and interpersonal skills (qv) training in which a conversation or interview is recorded and then played back in order to stimulate participants' recall of their thoughts, feelings and intentions at the time of the conversation or interview.

interpersonal skills. Skills used when relating to and communicating and dealing with other people. Examples are negotiating (qv), counselling (qv), letter and report writing, and making presentations.

interventions. Initiations of change within organisations, typically by change agents (qv) such as management consultants. Examples include training interventions, structural reor-

ganisations and attempts to alter the organisational cultures (qv) of enterprises.

interview, active. An interview in which the interviewee does more than simply answer questions with fixed alternative answers.

interview funnel. An employment interview (qv) technique whereby the person conducting the interview begins with broad, open ended questions but then systematically narrows the scope of the questions asked; eventually focusing on a small number of topics specifically related to the vacant position. See INTERVIEWING, REVERSE FUNNEL METHOD.

interview, passive. An interview in which the interviewee does little more than answer closed questions (qv). This contrasts with the 'open ended' interview which does not require fixed response answers.

interview, qualitative. An interview that uses questions the answers to which cannot be quantified in a straightforward manner.

interview, unstructured. An interview that does not follow a predetermined pattern.

interviewing, reverse funnel method. An interviewing technique which begins with questions involving fixed alternative answers, followed by open ended questions to which any answer may be given.

intimidation. A threat to commit an illegal act that will cause damage to another person, hence giving rise to tortious liability. Note however that the Trade Union and Labour Relations Act of 1974 (qv) stated that threats to break contracts of employment (qv) are not actionable in tort. This was amended by the Employment Acts of 1980 (qv) and 1982 (qv) which extended tortious liability to threats to break contracts where secondary actions (qv) are involved. See TORT.

intra-group relations. Interpersonal contacts and relationships *within* a group, as opposed to contracts and relationships *between* different groups.

intrapreneurship. The existence of innovative, risk taking entrepreneurial attitudes within employees of large organisations. It can be encouraged by allocating budgets (qv) to individuals rather than departments, through establishing strategic business units (qv), creating self-contained task forces, and so on.

in-tray exercise. An employee selection test in which the candidate is asked to deal with a batch of miscellaneous documents which the person is supposedly likely to find in his or her in-tray when actually undertaking a job. The assessor does not need to be present during the exercise, but will examine the completed documents and the candidate's written responses to each item. The latter are then matched against the competencies being assessed.

intrinsic motivation. Motivation that results from the wish to fulfil deeply felt personal needs. This differs from 'extrinsic' motivation, which offers the person various external rewards (money, promotion, fringe benefits, etc.) provided he or she attains certain objectives.

intrinsic reinforcement. In classical (qv) and operant conditioning (qv), a reinforcement (qv) resulting from positive inner feelings following the performance of a particular activity.

intrapunitive aggression. Aggression directed by a person against him or her self. 'Extapunitive' aggression, conversely, is directed against other people and things.

introvert. A personality (qv) type characterised by diligence, introspection, independence and the ability to work alone. However, introverts sometimes misunderstand other people's intentions, have difficulty coping with interruptions and need peace and quiet to complete their work.

intuitor personality type. In the Jungian typology (qv), a person who is an imaginative problem solver and who feels at home with complex theories and new ideas. However, the intuitor is easily bored by practical detail and tedious work.

invalid care allowance. State benefit payable to individuals who cannot go out to work because they are looking after severely disabled persons in their homes.

Invalidity Benefit. A state pension which replaces state sickness benefit and becomes payable after 168 days of incapacity.

inventions by employees, compensation for. See PATENTS RULES 1978.

inventions, ownership of intellectual property resulting from. The common law rule that the benefits of an employee's invention belong to his or her employing firm, provided (i) the ideas leading to the invention arose during the course of the worker's employment and (ii) the invention might reasonably have been expected to result from the employee's duties.

inventory, personal. A measure of a person's characteristics in a certain area, e.g. personality (qv) or vocational interests (qv), Such assessments differ from 'tests' in that they have no cut-off point defining 'pass' or 'fail'. Rather they enable individuals to determine their strengths and weaknesses in various dimensions of their personalities and related fields.

inverted appraisal. Performance appraisal (qv) in which a subordinate evaluates the behaviour, strengths and weaknesses of senior managers in the organisation, including the appraiser's own immediate superior.

investment appraisal. Assessment by a firm of the profitabilities of various possible capital projects in order to determine which of them should be undertaken.

investment trust. A public limited company that purchases shares in other companies and makes further investments in any area (property for example) which it believes will yield satisfactory revenues. A member of the public who buys shares in an investment trust thus effectively obtains a stake in a broad spectrum of investments. The trust pays dividends to its own shareholders from the revenues it receives from its investments.

Investors in People Kitemark. Awards given by Training and Enterprise Councils (TECs) (qv) to public and private sector organisations that achieve certain prescribed standards of training and staff development. Winners may display the Investors in People Kitemark on their commercial literature.

involuntary unemployment. The excess of the supply of labour over the demand for labour by firms at the going wage rate.

IPM. *See* INSTITUTE OF PERSONNEL MANAGEMENT.

IQ. *See* INTELLIGENCE QUOTIENT.

ipsative tests. Selection or other tests in which the subject is required to choose between several alternatives when answering each question.

IPSS. *See* INTERNATIONAL PACKET SWITCHING SERVICE.

IRIS. A European Community initiative intended to promote the training of women. The scheme is not itself a source of funding for training. Rather it seeks to provide an information exchange facility and to influence policy on vocational training for females. Thus it identifies appropriate training schemes, organises exchanges and visits for instructors, arranges seminars, etc.

Iron and Steel Trades Confederation (ISTC). The leading trade union (qv) in the UK iron and steel industry.

ISCO. *See* INTERNATIONAL STANDARD CLASSIFICATION OF OCCUPATIONS.

ISDN. *See* INTEGRATED SERVICES DIGITAL NETWORK.

ISTC. *See* IRON AND STEEL TRADES CONFEDERATION.

IT1. *See* NOTICE OF APPEARANCE.

ITBs. *See* INDUSTRIAL TRAINING BOARDS.

ITD. *See* INSTITUTE OF TRAINING AND DEVELOPMENT.

item information in employee records. Data in an employee's personal file that relates to his or her biographical details, qualifications, training courses attended, etc.

item response testing. A method for psychometric testing (qv) which asks different candidates different questions of different levels of difficulty, depending on the known background and ability level of the candidate concerned. It thus seeks to avoid giving candidates questions which for that person are absurdly easy or far too hard.

itemised pay statement, right to receive. The right under the Employment Protection (Consolidation) Act 1978 (qv) of an employee (qv) to receive a pay statement at the time of or before receiving pay. This must detail the gross amount, all fixed and variable deductions, the net amount payable and how the money is to be paid (e.g. by direct credit into a bank account).

ITSs. *See* INTERNATIONAL TRADE SECRETARIATS.

J

job. A collection of work activities performed as a condition of employment.

job analysis. The systematic examination of all the characteristics, attributes, responsibilities and special requirements of jobs in order to prepare job descriptions (qv) for use when recruiting staff and/or in job evaluation (qv) exercises.

job centres. Government-funded offices which provide information on job vacancies in a local area and where unemployed workers can register their availability to prospective employers. The latter may use a job centre's facilities free of charge.

job characteristics model. A means for evaluating the effects of job enrichment (qv) programmes on employee attitudes (qv) and behaviour. The psychological consequences of alterations in the dimensions of a job are predicted. Changes in workers' attitudes and performance are then measured (using questionnaires) and compared with the predictions.

job components inventory (JCI). A job analysis (qv) technique that identifies, analyses and seeks to quantify the occupation-specific skills necessary to do a job, and their importance relative to alternative types of work.

job costing (terminal costing). Ascertainment of the costs of jobs or contracts that are kept quite separate from others during the course of their completion.

job cycle. The entire set of operations that a worker must perform in order to complete a certain task satisfactorily.

job depth. The degree of decision making and personal control exercised by an employee when completing a job.

job description. According to the UK Department of Employment's *Glossary of Training Terms,* a broad statement of the purpose, scope, duties and responsibilities of a job. *See* JOB SPECIFICATION.

job design. Determination of the content of a job through choosing the methods by which it will be completed, the extent of its responsibilities and the tasks to be undertaken.

job enlargement. Allocation to workers of wide varieties of tasks of approximately the same level of difficulty. It seeks to make work more interesting, thus improving employee motivation.

job enrichment (vertical job enlargement). The allocation to a worker of (i) additional responsibility, (ii) more complex and difficult tasks and (iii) greater scope to make decisions. It aims to make a job more interesting and/or to train and prepare the employee for higher level duties.

job evaluation. The process of placing jobs in order of their relative worth so that employees may be fairly paid. It focuses on the characteristics of each job rather than on the personal attributes of the occupants of particular positions. *See* ANALYTICAL and NON-ANALYTICAL JOB EVALUATION.

job extension. A term used to describe both job enrichment (qv) and job enlargement (qv).

job fragmentation. The process of splitting a job into a number of small sub-units and then incorporating these sub-units into other existing or newly created jobs.

job hopper. Someone who is incapable of holding down any one job for any significant period.

job introduction scheme. A government programme implemented to encourage employers to offer trial periods of employment to disabled workers. Employers receive (currently) £45 per week for six weeks (13 weeks if the disabled person needs a longer period to demonstrate his or her ability).

job production. A production situation in which articles are manufactured to clients' precise specifications. Examples are bookbinding, shipbuilding and housing construction.

job release schemes. Government programmes to encourage the employment of young people through paying cash subsidies to older workers who accept early retirement. One variation also paid a contribution to the employer's wage cost of employing the young person.

job restructuring. Changing the duties, responsibilities and working methods associated with a job. *See* JOB ENLARGEMENT; JOB ENRICHMENT.

job rotation. The practice of having employees regularly change jobs within a department or organisation, either to relieve the boredom of repetitive work or as a component of a training or staff development programme.

job satisfaction. The extent to which an employee perceives his or her work favourably. High job satisfaction indicates a strong correlation between a person's expectations of the rewards accruing from a job and the rewards the job actually provides. However, high job satisfaction does not necessarily lead to improved performance: a worker may be happy with his or her job, yet still create sub-standard output.

job sharing. The practice of having two (or more) people complete a single job, each working on a part time basis. *See* TWO MONDAY MORNINGS SYNDROME.

job simulation exercise. An employee selection task that seeks to replicate key tasks and situations experienced in the job for which the candidate has applied. Tasks may involve decision making, groupwork, fact finding, negotiating, etc.

job specification. A detailed statement of the physical and mental details involved in a job and (where appropriate) a description of the environment in which work is undertaken. Job specifications are usually expressed in terms of what the worker has to do and the knowledge and judgements required for successful completion of duties.

job ticket. A document recording the times spent on a particular job by various workers, who circulate the ticket from one operative to another as the work changes hands.

Job Training Programme. An MSC sponsored scheme intended to increase the supply of workers possessing skills known to be in high current demand. It was eventually incorporated into other government training initiatives.

jobshare scheme. A government scheme for encouraging firms to create part time jobs for the unemployed. Employers receive £1,000 for each job that is divided, e.g. by converting existing full-time jobs into part-time jobs, by splitting a fresh full-time job into two new part-time jobs, or by combining overtime into regular part-time employment.

Johari window training. A technique for improving individual perception (qv). It trains people (i) to appreciate how others react to their behaviour and (ii) to increase the openness of their relationships.

joinder of parties. The statement of the names of the intended parties to a legal action appearing at the head of the writ of the summons used to commence a Court case.

joining of respondents in cases of alleged unfair dismissal. A procedure made available by the Employment Act 1980 (qv) whereby a union or union official may be held partially liable for the compensation awarded to a worker unfairly dismissed for refusing to belong to a trade union. For such an action to succeed, the union or union officer must have exerted pressure on the employer to sack the worker, e.g. by threatening a strike.

joint and several liability. The (unlimited) liability of members of a partnership for all debts entered into by any one partner on behalf of the firm. If some partners have no assets on termination of a partnership its creditors can claim from the remaining partners all they are owed.

joint consultation. Meetings between management and employee representatives to discuss matters of mutual concern. It does *not* involve negotiations (qv), but rather the exchange of information and views in order that management may take mutually acceptable decisions. Note that employee representatives do not control managerial decision making.

Joint Industrial Councils. Bodies set up following the 1917 report of the Whitley Committee (qv) to facilitate collective bargaining (qv) between employers and unions in certain UK industries.

joint negotiating committees (joint union committees, works councils). Committees comprising representatives of management and all unions operating within a company. JNCs normally meet at predetermined intervals to deal with problems arising since the last meeting. Each side promises not to initiate hostile actions prior to a matter being discussed in the JNC.

joint notice. A form used in an occupational pension scheme, signed by both the individual member and the pension provider declaring that the scheme is a contracted-out occupational pension scheme (qv) and that the individual will not be contributing to SERPS (qv).

joint shop stewards committee. A committee containing lay workplace representatives of all the unions in a company.

joint venture. A business project financed and controlled by two or more enterprises each of which retains its separate identity.

Jonah complex. According to Abraham Maslow, fear of the possible negative consequences of a promotion, e.g. of not being able to do the job, or of social isolation from subordinates.

journeyman. A skilled craft worker. Historically the journeyman was an independent self employed person who 'journeyed around' seeking work rather than being employed by a single organisation.

judgment debtor. Someone who has been successfully sued by a creditor and ordered to pay to that person a certain sum of money. *See* ATTACHMENT OF EARNINGS ORDER; GARNISHEE ORDER.

judgemental personality type. In the Jungian typology (qv), someone who is decisive, orderly and can be relied upon to complete a task. Such individuals make quick decisions, but tend to be dominated by their own plans.

Judgments Conventions, EC. *See* BRUSSELS CONVENTION ON THE JURISDICTION AND ENFORCEMENT OF JUDGMENTS ON CIVIL AND COMMERCIAL MATTERS 1968.

judicial precedent. The doctrine that a court of law is not entitled to make new laws, but exists merely to decide cases in accordance with existing legal rules.

Jung, Carl Gustav (1875–1961). Swiss psychiatrist and psychologist and pioneer of analytical psychology. An early colleague of Freud (qv), Jung developed the system of archetypes and the collective unconscious from studying patients' dreams. He extended his work outside conventional psychology in his writings on religion, philosophy and mythology.

Jungian typology. *See* MYERS–BRIGGS TYPE INDICATOR.

junior board. A technique of management development (qv) whereby junior managers remain in their existing jobs but acquire experience of senior management work by simulating the work of their board of directors. The junior board is given the same information on an issue as the senior board; members discuss this and suggest a course of action, which is then compared with the decision of the main board.

Juran, J. M. A pioneer of total quality control (qv) who developed a quality management system based on the inculcation of awareness of the need for quality improvement among all members of an enterprise. The system itself involved training, goal setting, establishment of quality councils, the appointment of quality facilitators and giving recognition and rewards to employees who exceeded quality targets.

just-in-time methods. Production and inventory control systems in which workflows are scheduled so precisely that only the barest minimum stocks of work-in-progress need be held. This is made possible by inputs from the previous stage in the production process arriving 'just-in-time'.

K

Kaizen system. An approach to employee participation in management decision making, based on quality circles (qv), that encourages groups of workers continually to improve the work of their sections via a cycle of 'planning, doing, checking and actioning'.

Kanban system. A method of just-in-time (qv) control of work-in-progress whereby each stage in the production process calls for supplies at just the moment they are needed, rather than holding inventories. Hence, materials are 'pulled' through the system and not 'pushed' into stocks.

Kanter, Rosabeth M. American academic who in 1983 published a highly influential study of barriers inhibiting the introduction of change in a sample of 115 US companies. She concluded that certain common factors prevent change, e.g. management through committees, absence of employee participation in management decision making, excessive criticism of employees by supervisors, suspicion of new ideas, and the exercise of tight control over subordinates.

KBA. See KNOWLEDGE BASED ASSESSMENT.

Kelly's repertory grid. A personality test that requires candidates to compare choices (A with B; B with C; C with A; etc.) in order to establish a hierarchy of preferences. The result is supposed to reveal a candidate's frame of reference (qv) regarding the outside world.

Kepner–Tregoe problem analysis technique. An approach to problem solving that seeks to identify changes in variables connected with, but not an integral part of, an issue. For example, an increase in labour turnover might be connected with some environmental factor not immediately apparent from an appraisal of a firm's pay and working conditions.

key economic indicators. Economic statistics which give an idea of how well or badly some aspect of the economy is performing. Examples are indices of wages and prices, unemployment rates, trends in national income, etc.

key person insurance. An insurance policy providing for the payment of compensation for loss of business and/or organisational disruption following the death or illness of a critically important employee.

key task analysis. A method of job analysis (qv) that focuses on the central tasks within a job. It is especially suitable for work which involves a large number of disparate duties, many of which require little or no training.

Keynesian economic policies. Interventionist demand management (qv) government economic policies involving regular tax and interest rate changes plus deliberate variations in public spending intended to regulate aggregate economic activity.

kickback. An underhand payment (possibly a bribe) given for services rendered, e.g. to influence a buyer to place a contract with a certain supplier, or to persuade an interview panel to appoint a certain candidate.

kinaesthesis. In the context of motion study (qv), the processes whereby a person knows the position and movement of limbs through messages received from muscles and tendons.

kinaesthetic reaction. A term used in ergonomics (qv) to describe the phenomenon that occurs when a person feels sensations of movement in human muscles or joints in response to a stimulus, even though no body movement has actually occurred.

kinaesthetics. The analysis of human body movements, as used in motion study (qv). See GILBRETH SYSTEM.

kinemics. The study of gestures. See BODY LANGUAGE.

kinesic communication. Communication (qv) through body language (qv).

kinetogram. A photograph or set of photographs showing the path travelled by a limb or other body member while completing a task.

Kleig light effect. A term used to describe the Hawthorne effect (qv) in certain industries.

know-how. Confidential non-patented technical knowledge concerning the methods and manner in which work is completed. It is possible for one firm to licence another to use its know-how. The licence agreement may lawfully restrain the licensee from exploiting the licensor's know-how in territories not covered by the contract. *See* CONFIDENTIAL INFORMATION.

knowledge based assessment (KBA). Assessment (qv) of a trainee's possession of knowledge rather than his or her ability to apply that knowledge in a work situation. The problems with KBA are that (i) knowledge acquired can quickly become out of date and (ii) knowledge is but one component of the ability to work effectively. *See* PERFORMANCE BASED ASSESSMENT.

knowledge based industry. An industry based on the possession and communication of information, rather than on manufacturing. Information technology (IT) is an example. Employees in such industries are sometimes described as 'knowledge workers'.

knowledge of results. Feedback given to trainees concerning their level of performance which enables them to assess how well they are progressing.

Koch block design test. An intelligence test comprising a set of 17 three by four inch cards showing a series of coloured patterns, plus 16 cubes with various colours and combinations of colours painted on their faces. Candidates are required to create the designs printed on the cards using the coloured blocks. The test is intended to measure attention, adaptation, self-criticism and intelligence.

Kondratieff cycles. Long-term trade cycles (qv) of expansion and recession extending over an average period of about 55 years, supposedly caused by periodic bouts of new technological innovation, followed (inevitably) by depressions.

Kuder Preference Record. A vocational interest inventory (qv) that lists triads of activities from which the subject must choose his or her most and least preferred activity. Interests are assessed under ten occupational headings: mechanical, computational, scientific, outdoor, persuasive, artistic, musical, literary, social and clerical. The subject's responses are then compared with people already working in various occupations.

L

laboratory training. *See* T-GROUP TRAINING.

labour. Mental or physical work that contributes to the output of goods or services.

labour force. All persons employed, self-employed or available for employment during a specified period.

labour-intensive methods. Production techniques that involve a high ratio of labour (qv) to plant and equipment (qv).

labour law. Aspects of law concerned with industrial relations (qv), trade unions (qv), working conditions, contracts of employment, health and safety, individual employment protection and collective bargaining (qv).

labour market, contestable. *See* CONTESTABLE LABOUR MARKET.

labour-only sub-contracting. The practice of firms using sub-contractors to provide labour rather than directly employing their own labour.

labour pool shop. *See* LABOUR SUPPLY SHOP.

labour rate variance. The cost of the difference between anticipated and actual wage rates paid to workers employed on a particular job or project over a certain period.

labour stability index. A measure of labour turnover (qv) showing the percentage of the firm's employees with at least one year's service. It is computed from the formula:

$$\frac{\text{Number of employees with more than one year's service}}{\text{Total number of people employed one year ago}}$$

Note that this does not reveal the average length of service of employees, which needs to be computed separately. *See* SURVIVAL RATE ANALYSIS.

labour supply shop. A pre-entry closed shop (qv) in which a particular trade union (qv) supplies the firm with labour. This differs from the 'labour pool' pre-entry closed shop whereby employers only recruit workers who are members of and have registered with a certain union, but where the workers thereafter move freely from firm to firm without needing to inform the union. Such arrangements were declared unlawful by the Employmnet Act 1990 (qv). *See* PROMOTION VETO SHOP; CRAFT QUALIFICATION SHOP.

labour theory of value. The proposition that the value of an item depends predominantly on the amount of labour needed for its production.

labour turnover. The extent to which freshly recruited workers enter and existing workers leave an organisation.

labour turnover index. The ratio of the number of workers who left an organisation during a certain period (normally six months or a year), to the average number of workers employed by the organisation during the same period. Note that the resulting figure will be artificially high if just one or two posts are filled and vacated many times during a particular period.

labour utilisation budget. That part of a company's production budget which deals with the costs of employing, deploying, and servicing labour (e.g. training and recruitment costs).

labourers. Unskilled manual workers engaged on heavy physical duties, e.g. lifting, shovelling, hod-carrying, etc.

ladders, regulations concerning. Rules contained in the Construction (Working Places) Regulations 1966, whereby ladders used at work must be inspected by a competent person prior to their use in order to ensure that they are in a safe condition. Ladders must extend beyond three feet six inches above the floor, and rise at an angle of one foot out from the wall for every four feet increase in height. Any ladder used for a long period in a single location must be tied, taken down at the end of the working day and stored overnight in a secure location.

laissez-faire government policies. Deliberate non-intervention in economic affairs by government in the belief that business and industry should be left to manage itself without state control or interference.

larceny. Theft from anyone other than an employer.

lateral communication. Exchange of information among employees of equal occupational status. Such communication is normally conducted less formally than vertical communication (qv).

lateral thinking. An approach to problem solving in which possible solutions are obtained by investigating the problem from odd or unusual angles.

laundering of money. Conversion of money obtained illegally or through tax avoidance into bona fide bank account or other balances.

LAUTRO. The acronym for the Life Assurance and Unit Trust Regulatory Association.

law of effect. A theory proposed in 1911 by the psychologist E. L. Thorndike according to which behaviour accompanied by pleasureable (rewarding) outcomes will tend to be repeated, whereas behaviour with disagreeable consequences will tend to be avoided.

law of the situation. A proposition advanced by Mary Parker Follett (qv) suggesting that managerial efficiency increases when the 'personal authority' of senior executives (i.e. the authority vested in them as individuals) is replaced by 'functional authority', namely the authority perceived by subordinates as necessary for a manager to ensure that specific activities function effectively, depending on the situation to hand.

Law Reform (Contributory Negligence) Act 1945. A statute enabling the victims of industrial accidents to claim partial compensation from their employers even if the accidents causing injury were partly their own fault.

Law Reform (Personal Injuries) Act 1948. A statute that enabled Courts to deduct from the damages awarded to workers injured in industrial accidents caused by their employers appropriate proportions of amounts already paid to these workers in the form of statutory sick pay or disability benefit. The purpose is to prevent workers being over-compensated for their injuries.

Lawrence, P. R., and Lorsch, J. W. Management theorists who in the 1960s suggested an 'environmental' approach to work, technology and the theory of organisation. They claimed that organisations are formed to solve environmental problems. Thus, organisations develop separate units (divisions, departments, specialist functions, etc.) to deal with various aspects of the outside world. *See* DIFFERENTIATION OF ORGANISATIONS; INTEGRATION OF ORGANISATIONS.

lawyers practising in the European Community, EC Directive on. A 1977 EC Directive (qv) enabling qualified lawyers to offer their services in any EC member state, although a migrant lawyer must practise under the same rules and conditions as local lawyers and may be required to be accompanied in Court by a colleague who practices full time in the country in question.

lay off. According to the Employment Protection (Consolidation) Act 1978 (qv), a period of four consecutive weeks, or a broken series of at least six weeks in a 13-week period, during which an employee (qv) receives no pay of any kind. Following a lay off a worker is entitled to claim a redundancy payment (qv).

lay person. Someone who undertakes duties voluntarily, usually without significant payment. Examples are shop stewards (qv) or the lay members of Industrial Tribunals (qv).

layout planning. Determination of the physical layout of plant and equipment (qv) and offices (qv). Equipment can be grouped together according to the specific process for which it is used or to the product it helps manufacture. *See* GROUP TECHNOLOGY.

LCCI. *See* LONDON CHAMBER OF COMMERCE AND INDUSTRY EXAMINATIONS BOARD.

lead body. A committee comprising representatives of professional bodies, government departments and occupations concerned with a particular industry or business function. Its role is to devise criteria for measuring the competence of employees in the relevant industry or function. These criteria form the basis for training courses that lead to awards of the National Council for Vocational Qualifications. There are currently about 140 lead bodies in the UK.

lead bonus. A wage supplement paid to workers who are required to assume additional responsibilities or practise extra skills.

leaderless group discussion. An employee selection (qv) method in which applicants are invited to discuss a subject among themselves while being observed by assessors. The assessors record each candidate's willingness to introduce topics, reactions to other participant's comments, articulateness, ability to cope with criticism, etc.

leaders. Persons who direct and control others and initiate activities within a group.

leadership. The ability to influence the thoughts and behaviour of others. A leader's position may be formal and result from designated organisational authority (qv), or informal and depend on the individual's personal ability to exercise power (qv). Unofficial group leaders frequently emerge in large organisations. Thus, 'leadership' is not *necessarily* the same as 'management' of a working group.

leadership, paranoid. Leadership (qv) behaviour characterised by delusions of persecution, suspicion of subordinates' motives, inability to accept criticism and the constant search for praise from superiors. Megalomania and illusions of grandeur might also be present.

leadership style. A leader's ambience towards subordinates and the methods he or she adopts for getting work completed. There is a continuum of possible leadership styles extending from complete autocracy at one extreme to total democracy at the other. Different phrases are used to describe various approaches. F. E. Fiedler, for example, distinguished between 'permissive' and 'directive' modes of behaviour. R. Blake and J. Mouton referred to 'concern for people' as opposed to 'concern for production'. R. Likert de-

scribed 'job-centred' versus 'employee-centred' management. Other phrases have included 'task-orientated' (i.e. autocratic) and 'people-centred' (democratic) styles, 'tight' and 'flexible', 'co-operative' versus 'dictatorial', and so on. *See* AUTOCRATIC LEADERSHIP; DEMOCRATIC LEADERSHIP.

leading indicator. A measure of economic or business performance which changes in advance of other variables, hence providing an early warning of likely future events.

leapfrogging. The situation whereby unions in different firms or industries demand from employing organisations pay rises at levels above those achieved elsewhere in the immediately preceding period. This leads to constantly escalating wage settlements. *See* SYNCHROPAY.

learned helplessness. The situation that arises when long term unemployed people 'learn' that it is futile continuing to apply for jobs. This learning (qv) causes depression and persists even when job markets improve and genuine chances of employment exist. Individuals become convinced they will not be able to get jobs and thus are not motivated to seek retraining.

learner centred learning. Training programmes that seek to transmit only the knowledge and skills that trainees need to learn rather than sticking rigidly to institutional syllabuses or traditional subject disciplines.

learning. The absorption of knowledge, acquisition of skills and/or assumption or fresh attitudes. Learning results in a permanent change in ability or behaviour.

learning by rote. Memorisation of a set of facts by regular repetition without any concern for their significance or interrelationships.

learning curve. A graph showing on one axis the amount a trainee has learned, and on the other the time spent learning the material. *See* LEARNING PLATEAU.

learning families, creation of. A method for facilitating skill ownership (qv) whereby training and job experiences are grouped together into broad occupational categories. Hence the trainee learns a variety of skills within a particular family and (hopefully) will easily be able to transfer these skills between specific jobs. Examples of families are 'manufacturing and assembly', 'clerical and administrative', and 'scientific and technical'.

learning in parts. Breaking down material to be learned into small self-contained units, each of which is learned separately and in such a way that the learner can (i) learn the first section, (ii) practise the first section, (iii) learn the second section, (iv) practise the second section *and* the first, and so on. Thus the learner systematically builds up an inventory of skills. *See* WHOLE LEARNING.

learning networks. Arrangements within or between organisations whereby individuals offer to share with others their recently acquired skills and knowledge of advanced techniques. *See* SKILLS EXCHANGE SCHEME.

learning plateau. A time interval during a course of instruction when the trainee's level of ability remains constant. Often, learners develop quickly at first, then learn nothing more for a certain period, until eventually they once again begin to make progress. Plateaux result from loss of motivation, from trainees being overloaded with information which they need time to digest, lack of opportunity to practise, or trainees' failure to recognise the importance of certain aspects of the training.

learning theory of personality. Approaches to personality (qv) which emphasise the importance of parental influences, child rearing practices and early experiences on the development of individual personality.

least preferred coworker (LPC) scale. A means for analysing a manager's approach to leadership devised by F. E. Fielder (qv). It requires the test subject to identify a person with whom he or she has worked and who was least preferred as a coworker. Then the manager must describe this person under 16 headings. Managers who characterise their least preferred coworkers relatively favourably receive a high LPC score, suggesting a relationship-orientated (rather than task-orientated) leadership style, and vice-versa.

leave of absence agreement. A document which sets out the circumstances in which a firm will allow employees to take paid time off additional to holiday and sick pay entitlements. It will define, for example, the meaning of 'close relative' for bereavement leave purposes, the maximum periods available, reporting procedures, etc.

leaver's statement (Form SSP1[L]). A document that a firm is obliged to issue to a worker whose contract of employment has expired and who recently received statutory sick pay (qv). It must show the period of incapacity for work and details of the SSP paid to the worker, who passes the leaver's statement to his or her new employer.

Leavitt, Harold. An influential organisational behaviour (qv) theorist who asserts the existence of three distinct types of manager: the 'implementer' who is action orientated, extrovert and operates mainly through other people; the 'problem solver' who adopts a logical and systematic approach; and the 'pathfinder' who is analytical, inquisitive and thinks deeply about issues.

LECs. *See* LOCAL ENTERPRISE COUNCILS.

lecturers, teachers and instructors, National Insurance and. The rule imposed by the DHSS that part-time lecturers, teachers and instructors engaged to teach four or more days over a period of up to three months are liable for Class I National Insurance (qv) contributions.

legitimate power. Power (qv) which derives from a person's position of authority in an organisational hierarchy being perceived by subordinates as right and proper. It can result from the person's formal appointment to a top job, from election, or some other conspicuous act of recognition.

letter of attorney. A document, signed and witnessed by the person issuing it, formally authorising someone to act on his or her behalf within the terms of the letter.

levels of competence, NCVQ. Five levels of occupational competence determined by the National Council for Vocational Qualifications, Level I involves basic routine duties; Level II coves a broader range of activities with greater personal responsibility; Level III is for skilled and supervisory work; Level IV concerns complex, technical and specialised tasks; while Level V embraces senior occupations or professions requiring extensive job knowledge and application of a significant range of fundamental techniques and principles.

levels of management. The three basic types of management in the managerial hierarchy: strategic, tactical and supervisory.

leverage buyout. A company takeover financed by borrowed funds that are secured against the target firm's assets.

Lewin, K., Lippett, R., and White, R.K. Leadership (qv) theorists who in 1939 published a highly influential study on the effectiveness of autocratic (qv) and democratic leadership (qv) styles. Democratic approaches were observed to be more productive.

lex mercatorum **(law of merchants).** Customary practices that regulate the conduct of commercial transactions.

lien. The legal right of someone owed money to retain (but not sell) the debtor's goods until an outstanding balance has been settled.

lieu payments. Emoluments (qv) to workers to compensate them for a loss or a service rendered in excess of normal obligations. Examples are payments in lieu of workers not being allowed to work out their notice of dismissal, extra holidays in lieu of overtime worked, etc.

life position. A term used in transactional analysis (TA) (qv) to describe a person's dominant way of relating to other people. There are four possible TA life positions. The 'I'm OK, you're OK' position is held by individuals with healthy and positive attitudes towards themselves and others. The 'I'm OK, your not OK' position applies to someone with high self-esteem but low regard for other people. The 'I'm not OK, you're OK' state is a childlike position where the individual looks to others for direction. Worst of all is the 'I'm not OK, your not OK' position in which a person has a low opinion of him or her self and of other people.

life skills. Individual competencies needed to deal with other people and to cope with social and work environments.

life space. According to K. Lewin, the totality of elements in a person's physical and social environments.

life-table. In occupational pension schemes, a statistical summary of the mortality rates and life expectancies of various cohorts of members over time.

LIFs. See LOCAL INITIATIVE FUNDS.

lifting equipment. According to the Factories Act 1961 (qv) hoists and lifts, chains, ropes, cranes, overhead travelling crane devices and other lifting tackle. Note however that fork lift trucks are not included. Under the Act, all lifting equipment must be properly constructed, of adequate strength and soundly maintained.

lifting injuries. Typically back injuries, slipped discs, hernias and sprains and strains resulting from attempting to lift a load too heavy for the injured worker. There is no definition of a 'safe' weight that an employee may lawfully be required to lift, although an important test case (Fricker *v.* Perry 1974 16 K.I.R. 235) suggested that workers should not be asked to lift more than 140 lb in normal circumstances (subject to the size and shape of the load, individual strength and experience, and other safety factors).

light industry. A term used to describe assembly and manufacturing industries that are less labour intensive than heavy industry (qv).

lighting in factories, requirements for. Rules embodied in the Factories Act 1961 (qv) which oblige employers to provide sufficient and suitable lighting in places of work and passages in Factories (qv). The duty is absolute. Hence even a single light bulb that fails just before an accident can render the employer liable for damages.

like work. Jobs done by men and women that are broadly similar (qv) in terms of the type of work involved and the skill and knowledge required for their completion. It is *not* necessary for jobs to have the same job title or contracted obligations in order for them to represent like work.

Likert, Rensis (1903–1981). A management theorist who presented a four-fold categorisation of leadership style (qv). System 1 leaders were totally authoritarian; System 2 leaders offered subordinates some flexibility over how they completed their work (but only to a limited extent and still remained autocratic and remote); System 3 leaders discussed goals with subordinates, leaving them to decide for themselves how to complete tasks; while System 4 leadership involved group rather than individual decision making.

Likert scale (summated attitude scale). A means for scoring self-report questionnaires intended to reveal test subjects' attitudes (qv). The questionnaire contains a large number of statements that are either pro or anti the matter being considered, and the respondent indicates his or her agreement or disagreement with each statement. Only those items to which the test subject responds in the same consistent way on at least two occasions are included in the final scoring.

Limitation Act 1939. A statute which determined that legal actions for tort (qv) or breach of contract cannot be brought after the expiry of six years from the date of the alleged civil wrong. Actions for negligence, nuisance or breach of duty involving personal injury became 'statute barred' after three years; actions relating to contracts under seal evidenced by a deed are statute barred after 12 years.

limited liability company. A business in which the liability of the owners (shareholders) for the firm's debts is restricted to the value of their investment in the company.

limited partnership. A partnership (qv) in which the liability for the firm's debts of at least one of the partners is limited to the extent of his or her investment in the business. Partners with limited liability are called sleeping partners (qv).

limited revaluation premium. An *ad hoc* payment into SERPS (qv) by an individual who leaves an employing firm that operates a contracted-out (qv) occupational pension scheme. In return for the premium the person receives an enhanced guaranteed minimum pension (qv).

limiting factor in decision making. A constraint or barrier that stands in the way of achieving the best solution to a problem, thus restricting the range of decisions that can be taken. *See* BOUNDED RATIONALITY APPROACH.

linage (run on) advertisements. Job advertisments that follow each other in a column of a newspaper.

line manager A manager who possesses executive authority to take and implement decisions.

line of balance A production scheduling and control technique intended to show the number of items that need to be completed at various 'milestones of progress' during a production plan, and how many items should have been partially completed at previous stages of production by these dates in order to guarantee completion of the required output by the end of the production period.

LINGUA An EC-funded programme intended to promote training in the official languages of the European Community. LINGUA is setting up a network of university language departments and introducing measures to encourage the development of foreign language teaching within the business community.

LINK scheme. A government-sponsored project designed to encourage the commercial exploitation of scientific and technological research by linking up academic institutions with commercial firms.

linking pin organisation. A form of organisation (qv) recommended by R. Likert (qv) whereby each manager is required to act as a 'linking pin' between the three distinct groups: (i) the manager's peers on the same level of authority, (ii) superiors and (iii) subordinates. Accordingly the manager has to sit on various committees each containing representatives of the three levels.

liquidation of a company. The winding up of a limited liability company. Liquidation may be voluntary or at the insistence of unpaid creditors. On liquidation, shareholders are only liable for the company's debts up to the value of their shareholding in the firm.

listed company. A public limited liability company, the daily share price of which is quoted on the London Stock Exchange.

living accommodation for employees, taxation of. Rules contained in the 1976 Finance Act whereby an employee who is provided with living accommodation by an employer is liable to pay tax on the annual rental value of the property, plus Community Charge and the expenses of occupation (such as lighting and heating), but excluding repairs and insurance. However, no tax liability arises if the person must occupy the accommodation in order to do a job properly *and* it is customary for accommodation to be provided for that type of work. See FURNITURE LENT TO EMPLOYEES, TAXATION OF.

loans to employees, taxation of. The rule contained in the 1976 Finance Act that if an employer provides an employee with an interest free or cheap loan then the difference between the actual interest rate paid and an annually 'prescribed' rate (related to current market levels) is chargeable to the employee's tax. This applies equally to a loan to an employee's relative. If the loan is written off it is regarded as employee remuneration. Loans for the purchase of a house are exempt from the interest tax provided the house is the employee's sole or main residence and the mortgage does not exceed a certain maximum value.

local collective bargaining (workplace agreements). Determination of pay and working conditions through collective bargaining (qv) at the workplace level, typically between local management and shop stewards (qv).

Local Employer Networks (LENs). Organisations sponsored by the Association of British Chambers of Commerce, the Confederation of British Industry and the Training Agency (qv) to provide a mechanism through which employers in a particular area can influence local colleges and education authorities. They provide information and advice on vocational training and arrange for employer representation on the governing boards of education establishments and college/industry link bodies.

Local Enterprise Councils (LECs). The Scottish Equivalent to Training and Enterprise Councils.

Local Initiative Funds (LIFs). Money made available to Training and Enterprise Councils (TECs) (qv) by the Training, Enterprise and Education Directorate (TEED) (qv) to develop and finance training programmes other than Emplyoment Training

(ET) (qv) and Youth Training (YT) (qv).

lock-in effect. The situation that can arise during negotiations (qv) whereby one of the parties deliberately adopts a certain ambience (e.g. of extreme friendliness) in the opening stages of the negotiation in order to create a particular mood for the meeting and, in consequence, 'lock' the opponent into certain patterns of behaviour.

lock out. Refusal of an employer to allow workers to undertake their work (or to pay their wages) in retaliation for workers taking industrial action (qv).

locum management (interim management, executive leasing). The practice of senior company managers or management consultants hiring themselves out to other organisations for short periods, e.g. because the lessor company has reached a high level of efficiency at which it possesses spare capacity in its top management. Consultants specialising in locum management will often handle the work of several clients at the same time. A number of bodies operate locum placement employment agencies, including the CBI.

locus of control. A psychological term meaning the extent to which people feel they are in command of their own destiny. Someone with an 'internal locus' believes he or she possesses direct and personal control over what happens. Individuals with an 'external locus' assume their life experiences are determined by external forces and/or other people.

logging in. Gaining access to a computer system, normally through the user identifying him or her self via a number and a list of initial commands.

logical positivism. See POSITIVISM.

logical systems analysis. A method of systems analysis (qv) which begins from a specification of the target output of a system and then identifies the inputs and procedures needed to generate that output.

logistics. Analysis of the costs, efficiencies and feasibilities of the various modes of transport and temporary storage needed to shift goods to their destinations – safely and with minimal pilferage and materials loss – at the right time.

London Chamber of Commerce and Industry Examinations Board. One of the oldest and largest business studies examining bodies in the world, responsible or about half a million examination scripts annually. LCCI is particularly active in the secretarial, book-keeping and accounting fields.

long service awards. *See* FRINGE BENEFITS.

long-term disability cover (permanent health insurance [PHI]). Payments by employers, usually through company superannuation schemes (qv), to sick or injured employees after the provisions of a company sick pay arrangement have expired. Currently the norm is for 50 to 75 per cent of salary, payable for three to six months following six months of sickness absence.

longitudinal surveys. In social science, empirical studies in which data on sample groups are gathered in different time periods.

looking glass self. According to the social psychologist G. H. Mead, those aspects of a person's self-image which are based on the reactions or judgements of others.

lower earnings limit. The minimum weekly earnings that an employee needs to receive prior to having to pay state National Insurance contributions. Once the limit is exceeded the person becomes liable for contributions on *all* earnings, both above and below the limit.

LPC scale. *See* LEAST PREFERRED CO-WORKER SCALE.

Luddites. Workers who destructively seek to prevent the introduction of new technology. They derive their name from that of Ned Ludd, the leader of a group of 19th century textile workers who smashed new machinery they regarded as threatening their livelihoods.

lump labour. Workers who offer their labour to organisations as self-employed sub-contractors rather than as 'employees' in order to enable employing enterprises to avoid having to pay employers' National Insurance and/or assume other employers' obligations. The term originally derived from the practice of groups of workers regarding themselves as independent partnerships providing employment services to clients in return for a lump sum payment.

luncheon vouchers. A fringe benefit issued to employees enabling the latter to purchase meals or light refreshments from restaurants and traders prepared to accept the vouchers as a means of payment. Vouchers are redeemed with the central organisation which sold them to issuing companies in the first instance. Part of the cost of a luncheon voucher is tax free for both the firm and the worker.

lying time. The period that elapses between the end of a working period and the day that wages for that period are actually paid.

M

McCallum, Douglas Craig (1815–1878).
A railway engineer who pioneered the
study of supervisory management and
the use of organisation charts (qv).
McCallum adopted an autocratic approach to leadership, advocating specialisation and the division of labour
(qv), frequent inspection of subordinates' work, rules and sanctions and
daily reports on subordinates' efforts.

McCarthys Ltd *v.* Wendy Smith 1980.
An important legal case on gender
equal opportunities (qv), heard in the
European Court of Justice (qv) and
which forced the British government
to introduce legislation bringing UK
equal pay law and practices in line with
the requirements of the EC's 1975
Equal Pay Directive (qv).

McClelland, D.C. A management theorist who in 1961 published an influential study on the characteristics of
achievement-orientated people, concluding that such individuals tended
to (i) prefer tasks for which they had
sole responsibility, (ii) avoid risk and
(iii) monitor continuously the effects
of their actions. 'Need achievers', as
McCelland called them, worked extremely hard and constantly sought to
improve their performances.

**McClelland power-affiliation-achievement
model of motivation.** A theory of motivation suggested by D. C. McClelland
(qv) which groups people according to
the strengths of their self-perceived
needs for power, achievement or involvement with others. Power seekers are
motivated by the prospect of controlling subordinates. Achievers are looking for occupational success, are task
oriented and self-reliant. Affiliators
want pleasant relationships with colleagues and to help other individuals.
McClelland used the term nAff to
characterise an individual's need for
friendly relations with others. People
with a high nAff have strong desires

for approval by peers and in consequence tend to adopt conformist attitudes when working in groups. The
term nPow was applied to describe an
individual's need to control others, to
influence people and be responsible
for them.

McGregor, Douglas (1906–1964). An industrial psychologist and leading pro-
ponent of the human relations
approach (qv) to management.
McGregor developed the Theory X
and Theory Y (qv) concepts of managerial behaviour.

Machiavellian management. A mangement style (qv) that involves opportunistic, manipulative, selfish, cunning
and generally amoral behaviour. The
name derives from the fifteenth century Italian diplomat Niccolo Machia-
velli, who wrote about such matters.

machine ancillary time. Deliberate stoppage of a machine for maintenance,
clearing, inspection, etc. *See* DOWN-
TIME; IDLE TIME.

machine bureaucracy. A bureaucracy
(qv) which relies totally on its members
strictly adhering to rules governing all
aspects of the organisation's work.

machine hour rate. A means for allocating overheads (qv) to machines. The
running time of each machine is
divided into the value of the overheads
to be apportioned.

machine idle time. Periods when a machine is not producing due to delays
in the arrival of raw materials or sub-
assemblies from a previous stage of
production.

machine loading. The amount and timing of work scheduled to be undertaken on a particular machine.

macho management. A tough, aggressive and uncompromising approach to management, particularly in
respect of industrial relations (qv).

macro-analysis. The study of social affairs on the aggregate level. For

example, macro-economics is the analysis of the workings of the entire economy, taken as a whole, rather than of individual economic units. *See* MICRO-ANALYSIS.

Madrid Protocol. An agreement proposed by all EC (and many other) countries for the implementation of a common system for registering trade marks, using a single set of (French language) documents and hence securing protection in all participating states. The system is to be administered by the World Intellectual Property Organisation (WIPO) based in Geneva.

main duties weighting. An approach to job analysis (qv) that focuses on three criteria: the importance of each element of a job in relation to its successful completion; the level of difficulty of each element; and the frequency with which elements are undertaken.

mainframe computer. A large and powerful computer serving several departments or organisations simultaneously, as opposed to a personal desktop computer.

MAITA. The acronym for Marine and Allied Industries Training Association.

make work programmes. Government job creation schemes implemented to keep workers in employment rather than their being on the dole.

management. An ongoing process that seeks to achieve the objectives of organisations (qv) in the most efficient ways possible. It is particularly concerned with the deployment of material, human and financial resources, with the design of organisations, their structure and development, the specification of objectives and the choice of criteria for evaluating organisational efficiency. *See* BUSINESS MANAGEMENT.

management accountancy. That branch of accounting primarily concerned with the preparation of the financial information needed for operational decision making. It is particularly concerned with cost accounting (qv), the design of management information systems, investment appraisal and budgetary planning and control.

management audit. A systematic analysis of the effectiveness of an organisation's policies and administrative procedures. Comprehensive audits should be undertaken periodically (every three or four years for instance) or whenever the firm's trading environments significantly change. Minor audits, taking one department or function at a time, might be completed between major analyses.

management buy-out. The purchase of an existing firm using funds raised by members of its current management. This differs from a management 'buy-in' in which the finance for the purchase is arranged by an outside team that subsequently contributes to the operational management of the business.

management by exception. A control technique that requires the application of corrective actions only when operations vary from predetermined norms by more than prespecified values.

management by objectives (MBO). A management control technique whereby company objectives are segmented into departmental, sectional and, ultimately, individual targets for managers. It involves performance appraisal (qv), planning, co-ordination and operational control. Superiors and subordinates meet and jointly agree the latters' goals.

management by walking around (MBWA). An approach to management control recommended by Tom J. Peters (qv) which requires managers to look and listen, talk to people at all levels within an organisation and become *personally* involved in happenings at subordinates' places of work. Specific MBWA activities include (i) regular reviews of sources of information, (ii) learning how employees think and *feel* about the organisation and (iii) finding out how staff perceive customers and whether they regard themselves as individually responsible for customer care.

management committee. A committee (qv) empowered to take and (importantly) implement decisions that relate to a particular function or field of operations.

management development. A series of planned training activities and work experiences designed to improve a manager's performance and equip him or her for higher level work. It could involve attendance at short courses, coaching (qv), counselling (qv), job rotation, understudying (i.e. spending a short period as a personal assistant to a more senior manager), attachments to project committees and special working parties, action learning (qv) and the completion of longer term academic qualifications in the management field.

management earn out. A company takeover or management buy-out (qv) in which the provision of external funds is made conditional on the acquired business achieving preset profit targets for an agreed period following the takeover.

management information system. The methods and procedures whereby an organisation procures, integrates and interprets the internal and external information needed for effective decision taking, planning and control.

management metaphors. Comparisons of organisations and management functions/issues with things totally unrelated to management in order to gain useful insights into the nature of managerial problems. Thus, for example, organisations have been likened to machines, the human brain, political systems and psychic prisons (qv).

management science. The application of statistical and operations research methods to managerial problem solving and decision making. This is *not* the same as scientific management (qv).

management services. A collection of activities concerned with improving productivity and employee performance. Examples include organisation and methods (qv); work study (qv); industrial engineering (qv) and organisational development (qv).

management style. The ambience towards employees displayed by an individual manager or by an entire management team.

management style, compulsive. A hyperactive, frantic management style (qv) characterised by the inability to attain objectives, thus creating stress (qv) and compulsive, ritualistic work activity intended to overcome personal deficiencies

management style, defensive. Managerial behaviour characterised by denial of reality, underachievement (qv), and outward aggression towards subordinates and other colleagues. It results in resistance to change, stress (qv) and lack of job satisfaction.

management style, reactive. A management style (qv) sometimes adopted by recently promoted managers who, unsure of their role (qv) and capabilities, focus all their efforts on responding to subordinates' actions rather than themselves initiating events.

management succession programme. A systematic plan to ensure that individuals are available to take over the work of senior managers following the latters' retirement, promotion, death in service, resignation or transfer. Devising such a programme requires career planning (qv), human resource planning (qv), training and staff development. *See* MOTHERHOOD ORGANISATION.

management training. Training that seeks either to improve a manager's current performance or to contribute to a management development (qv) programme. Typically it covers training in interpersonal skills, background information on the employing company and its trading environments, management techniques, problem solving, analytical skills, organisation, delegation and control.

managerial economics. A branch of economics that deals with the theory of the firm, market structures, decision making, costs, resource allocation and investment.

managerial grid. A technique of management training devised by R. Blake and J. Mouton intended to help managers improve their leadership ability. Managers are classified according to their concern for production on the one hand, and their interest in the human needs of subordinates on the other.

managerial prerogative. The right of management to manage without interference from employees or their representatives. Advocates of this view justify its propriety against the fact that managers represent the owners of the business.

Managerial, Professional and Staff Liaison Group. A voluntary grouping of trade unions (qv), associations and independent organisations without party political affiliations formed to represent middle managers and professional employees in various industries and occupations.

managerial responsibility. The deliberate restraint of corporate power in order to help others. It is manifest in concern for the physical environment, seeking to be a good neighbour and employer, involvement in community projects and so on. Examples are monopolies that do not exploit consumers, firms in high unemployment areas that do not pay low wages and companies owed money that do not take legal action against destitute debtors.

managerial sub-system. Those elements of an organisation (qv) concerned with setting objectives, designing its structure and relating its activities to the outside world.

managing director. The chief executive of a company. Rules concerning the appointment and powers of a managing director are usually included in the company's Articles of Association (qv). Examples of such rules include whether the managing director is to be elected by a majority vote of other directors or by shareholders at the company's annual general meeting.

mandating. The practice whereby someone involved in a negotiation (qv) has permission from his or her principal to agree a settlement only within prespecified limits. For example, a personnel officer representing a company in wage negotiations with a union might be mandated by the firm's senior management only to accept a wage demand of (say) not more than 10 per cent.

mandatory signs. *See* SAFETY SIGNS REGULATIONS 1980.

manifest need theory. The proposition advanced by H. A. Murray that most human needs are learned rather than inherited and come to be felt in direct consequence of signals received from the outside world. Individuals typically possess an extremely large number of potential needs, most of which are never activated. Particular needs become manifest only when triggered by environmental circumstances, otherwise needs are said to be 'latent' and unactivated.

Manpower Services Commission (MSC). The forerunner to the Training Commission (qv).

manual handling of loads, EC Directive concerning. A European Community Directive intended to control manual handling activities which involve a risk of injury. Under the Directive, employers are required to take appropriate steps to prevent the manual handling of dangerous loads without mechanical assistance. If manual handling is essential, employers must assess and minimise the risk of injury, taking into consideration the nature of the load and the characteristics of the working environment.

manual labour. Work done primarily or substantially with the hands rather than with the brain.

manual skills analysis. A technique of job analysis (qv) derived from work study (qv) and intended to identify the competencies employed by experienced workers when undertaking short cycle repetitive operations which require a high level of manual dexterity.

manufacturing account. The account in which a manufacturing business calculates the costs of acquiring input materials, manufacturing wages and factory overheads.

manufacturing automation protocol. Integration via computers of assembly lines and offices in different locations into a single self-contained manufacturing system.

manufacturing resource planning. An extension of materials requirements planning (qv) to include computerised purchasing, capacity planning (qv), automated stores procedures and other aspects of operational control.

Manufacturing, Science and Finance Union (MSF). A large trade union (qv) representing white collar workers (qv).

margin of error. A range of error regarded by management as acceptable. *See* MANAGEMENT BY EXCEPTION.

marginal cost. The additional cost of producing one extra unit of output. For example, if it costs £5,500 to produce 947 units and £5,525 to produce 948, the marginal cost of the extra unit is £25.

marginalisation. The banishment of a person or issue to the outer regions of an enterprise, thus excluding the person or issue from the organisation's mainstream activities and discussions.

MARIS-NET. A computerised information service providing on-line data on opportunities for distance learning and other vocational training and education. It is operated by Materials and Resources Information Services Limited and includes databases on open learning materials, management training, computer-based training (qv) and interactive video (qv).

market economies. National economic systems based on (i) private ownership of the means of production, distribution and exchange and (ii) free competition between businesses.

market level indicator. An index of share and fixed interest security prices used to adjust the amounts of national insurance premiums payable by certain classes of contributors. See LIMITED REVALUATION PREMIUM; PENSIONER'S RIGHTS PREMIUM; ACCRUED RIGHTS PREMIUM.

market wage. The 'going rate' for a job established in the labour market through the interaction of supply and demand.

marketing concept. The proposition that the supply of goods and services should be a function of the demand for them.

marketing services industry. The industry that supports and provides ancillary services to the marketing function. It includes advertising and public relations agencies, consultants, telemarketing firms, list brokers, direct mail fulfilment houses, etc.

married people, rules prohibiting unfair discrimination against. Regulations contained in the Sex Discrimination Act 1975 (qv) that prohibit direct or indirect discrimination against married people on account of their marital status. These rules were introduced to prevent employers issuing contracts of employment that required the automatic resignation of female employees on their marriage. It is not unlawful to discriminate against people because they are single.

masking, psychological. Mental processes that lead to one sensory stimulus being blocked by another, so that no reaction occurs.

Maslow's need hierarchy. The five levels of need which psychologist A. H. Maslow (1908–1970) suggested that individuals attempt to satisfy in ascending order. Initially, Maslow asserted, a person is concerned with *physiological* needs such as food, heat and shelter. Then, he or she seeks *security* via insurance, pension arrangements, etc. Third, the individual looks for *social* satisfaction (by joining social and recreational organisations for example). Next the person wants *esteem*, evidenced perhaps by status symbols, authority over others, recognition by peers, and so on. Finally, once all other needs are satisfied, the individual seeks self actualisation (qv).

mass production. Large-scale automated production of standardised output using the division of labour (qv) and fast moving assembly lines. See SCIENTIFIC MANAGEMENT.

master budget. A firm's central budgetary control document which draws together all anticipated operating and capital expenditures, grouped together under appropriate headings.

materials requirements planning. A computerised production scheduling technique which analyses end products and required customer delivery dates in order to determine the raw materials, components and sub-assemblies needed to manufacture and deliver customer requirements on time.

maternity absence, notice of. Statutory notice that a pregnant worker must give her employer 21 days prior to the date she intends starting her maternity absence. Notice must be in writing if the employer so requires. If less than 21 days' notice is given the employer has discretion whether to accept the shorter period and, if the shorter period is not accepted, no statutory maternity pay need be offered. In the latter case the woman may demand a written statement of the employer's reasons for not accepting the shorter period and may then appeal to the DHSS that it was not reasonably practicable for 21 days' notice to be provided.

maternity pay. Wages that by law must be paid to a pregnant employee while she is absent from work in order to have a child. There are two levels of payment: 'higher' and 'lower'. If the woman has worked with the same employer doing more than 16 hours a week for at least two years (five years if she has worked between eight and 16 hours a week) she can claim from her employer 90 per cent of her normal weekly pay (less the value of state benefit) for six weeks, plus the 'lower' rate (set by statute) for up to 12 further weeks. Women with between six months and two years' service are entitled to the lower rate for up to 18 weeks. The money is paid by the employing firm, which then reclaims it from the Department of Health and Social Security.

maternity pay fund. Government money used to compensate employers for maternity pay (qv) given to pregnant employees. The employer pays the worker and then deducts an equivalent amount of the monthly cheque it sends to the Inland Revenue to cover the tax and National Insurance contributions deducted from employees' wages.

maternity pay, qualifying week. The 15th week prior to a pregnant employee's expected week of confinement. To qualify for statutory maternity pay the woman must have accumulated 26 weeks' continuous employment (qv) by the qualifying week. Also, the woman must still be in employment with her previous employer during the qualifying week, although employment for a single day within that week will suffice to meet the condition.

maternity rights. Rights conferred by the Employment Protection (Consolidation) Act 1978 (qv) on a pregnant woman who has completed at least two years' continuous service (i) to receive maternity pay (qv); (ii) not to be dismissed because of her pregnancy; (iii) to attend ante-natal appointments on full pay; and (iv) to reinstatement following the birth of the child (qv). Special provisions embodied in the Employment Act 1980 (qv) allow firms with less than six employees not to reinstate a woman who has taken maternity leave back in her old job, provided it is 'not reasonably practicable' to reemploy that person.

matrix organisation. A system for organising managers from different departments into teams constructed to complete specific projects or oversee particular functions or tasks.

mathetics. A method of programmed learning (qv) which works backwards from the information or action to be learned to the determination of the instruction to be given. It begins with a task analysis (qv), followed by a detailed examination of the order of stimuli and responses involved in completing each task. Then a lesson plan is devised and programmed learning frames (qv) are written.

maturation. The process by which an individual's capacity for intellectual reasoning develops over time.

maturity curve. A graph which plots the median salaries of groups of workers against their age, thus enabling the firm to predict possible increases in its wages bill if the average age of its workforce increases.

maximum working area. The maximum amount of workbench space covered by a worker's hand and arm movements during the completion of a task. *See* GILBRETH SYSTEM.

Mayo, G. Elton (1880–1949). Industrial psychologist and leading advocate of the human relations approach (qv) to management. *See* HAWTHORNE EXPERIMENTS.

meal times for shop workers. The requirement of the Shops Act 1950 (qv) that shop assistants not be employed for more than six hours without a meal break of at least 20 minutes. If the hours of employment include 11.30 am – 2.30 pm then at least three quarters of an hour must be allowed. This period increases to one hour if lunch cannot be taken on the shop's premises. Moreover, a break of at least half an hour must be available between the hours of 4.00 pm and 7.00 pm. Shops which only employ members of a single family are exempt from these requirements.

measured day work. A payments system, based on work study, in which management insists that workers produce a prespecified daily output in return for a fixed daily wage. Employees are not expected to exceed or to produce less than target output.

mechanisation. The introduction of machines to undertake work previously done by humans.

mechanistic learning. Learning (qv) that results from stimulus/response factors, supplemented by practice. This differs from 'organic learning', which involves a change in a person's entire perspectives rather than simply what he or she can do.

mechanistic organisations. Bureaucratic organisations with fixed hierarchies and procedures and highly formal internal communication systems. Individual tasks are clearly defined and there is much specialisation, division of managerial labour and rigid administrative routines. Mechanistic organisations are highly resistant to change.

mechatronics. The integration of mechanical engineering with micro-electronics and computer control.

mediation. Intervention by a third party in an attempt to settle an industrial dispute. The mediator informs each party of the other's views and requirements, without the disputants necessarily having to meet face-to-face. Where appropriate the mediator will suggest compromises and ways to reconcile positions.

medical certificates. Evidence of sickness supplied by workers to their employers in order to claim statutory sick pay (qv). Workers must inform employers of their illnesses within seven days of incapacity (unless they are too sick to do this). For absences longer than seven days a doctor's statement on a prescribed form is necessary. Otherwise workers may attest their own illnesses. If statutory sick pay is refused the employer can be made to justify the decision in writing. The matter is then referred to a DHSS adjudication officer.

medical examinations, rule on. The common law (qv) rule that employees cannot be made to undergo medical examinations unless the requirement to submit to examinations is specified in their contracts of employment (qv), or unless the employer can demonstrate a genuine doubt concerning a worker's fitness for employment.

medical suspension, right to. The right of a worker injured in consequence of any of the health and safety hazards specified in schedule 1 of the Employment Protection (Consolidation) Act 1978 (qv) to receive pay for up to 26 weeks of medical absence, provided he or she (i) has been with the firm for at least one month, and (ii) has not refused an offer by the employer of alternative work that he or she is capable of performing. Workers refused medical suspension pay can complain to Industrial Tribunals (qv).

membership group. A group to which a person belongs which is *not* a reference group (qv).

memorandum of association. One of the key documents used to form and register a limited company. It contains a statement of the objects (contractual powers) of the business and details of its share capital.

mental age. The age for which a certain level of intelligence is normal, e.g. a child of 12 who is capable of completing puzzles that the average 15-year-old can do is said to have a mental age of 15 years.

mental association. Establishment of psychological associations between certain events or objects, normally in consequence of experience rather than conscious intent.

mental closure. *See* CLOSURE, MENTAL.

mental set. A person's expectations concerning a particular event believed likely to occur in the immediate future.

mentor. A senior manager who promotes the career development of a favoured subordinate through providing the latter with advice, resources, privileged information, introductions to influential people, and help and assistance when things go wrong.

mento-work factor method. An extension of the work factor (qv) motion study method to encompass mental processes. The latter are allocated to categories for: observation, discrimination, identification, conversion, memory and recall, computation, and decision.

merit rating. A term sometimes used to describe techniques for appraising the performances of manual and clerical workers. *See* PERFORMANCE APPRAISAL.

meritocracy. A promotion system based on ability and relevant experience rather than on personal contacts, nepotism or the social backgrounds of candidates.

meta analysis. A technique of mathematical statistics which combines the results from several different empirical studies into a larger analysis in order to improve the reliability of predictions. Meta analysis has been applied extensively to research concerning the reliability of psychometric tests (qv) and other selection methods.

metaphorical generalisation. Use of analogies to describe personality types, e.g. describing someone as warm, cold, rigid, flexible, shallow, etc.

metaphors, use in management. See MANAGEMENT METAPHORS.

metatask capacity. An organisation's ability to reorganise itself quickly following an environmental disturbance.

method study. The analysis of how work is performed in order to simplify work and avoid duplication of effort. A six-step procedure is commonly applied: (i) selection of tasks for study; (ii) recording of methods currently in use; (iii) examination of methods; (iv) development of better methods; (v) installation of revised systems; and (vi) maintenance of the new system.

methodology. All the procedures of enquiry, techniques of analysis and rules and methods used to study a subject.

methods audit. In method study (qv), a systematic appraisal of current working methods and procedures.

methods time measurement (MTM). A form of predetermined motion time system (qv) which uses published tables of standard times (qv) to assess the periods needed to complete basic operations undertaken in various work situations. MTM times contain no relaxation allowances (qv), but have instead a work study rating (qv) of 83 on the ILO scale (qv).

metropolitan shift system. A shift work arrangement that requires employees to change shifts two or more times each week.

M-form organisation (multi-divisional organisation). An organisation structure in which a firm's activities are grouped together into divisions corresponding to the various products or services it supplies. A functional organisation (qv) system is then applied within each division, leading to some duplication of effort within the enterprise. Divisions are co-ordinated from head office. See H-FORM ORGANISATION.

micro-analysis. The study of human behaviour at the level of the individual decision-taking unit, especially the factors that motivate decision takers to pursue particular courses of action.

micromotion analysis. Detailed method study (qv) of short cycle motions used when completing manual work.

mid-career crisis. A period mid-way through a person's career when he or she reassesses past successes and failures and has to come to terms with future options. The individual must re-evaluate original career aspirations and reconcile them with currently available possibilities.

middle manager. See EXECUTIVE.

migrant workers. Employees who work in counties different to those of their normal residence and/or places of birth. European Community legislation under Articles 48–51 of the Treaty of Rome (qv) requires that migrant workers who are EC nationals have the right to equal treatment with local people. However, each EC state is free to determine its own definition of a 'national' of its own country, so that a person can be classed as 'foreign' (as opposed to European Community) by the authorities of some countries but not by others. Foreign workers (qv) do not have the rights to freedom of movement and equal treatment enjoyed by EC migrants.

militancy. The tendency of certain individuals to initiate frequent industrial actions (qv) against their employing companies and to pursue these aggressively in order to achieve their goals.

milk round. The annual tour of universities, polytechnics and other higher education institutions by prospective employers in search of recruits.

minimum efficient scale of plant. The size of a business that is just able to achieve the lowest average unit cost of production for the industry in which it operates.

minimum resource theory. A theory of bargaining and coalition formation which suggests that the weaker parties to a negotiation will tend to form alliances with each other rather than with a stronger participant. It assumes that weaker parties do not believe that strong and powerful parties will appreciate and reward weaker parties' contributions to a coalition. *See* COALI-TIONS, BARGAINING THEORY OF.

Minnesota Multiphasic Personality Inventory (MMPI). A standardised measure of personality compiled through questionning people who have been clinically diagnosed as suffering from personality defects or mental disorders.

minors, contracts of employment with. Contracts of employment (qv) between employers and young people under the age of 18 years. Such a contract is binding on the employee if it is substantially for the employee's benefit. *See* EMPLOYMENT OF CHILDREN ACT 1973.

Mintzberg, Henry. An influential management theorist who in the 1970s categorised managerial work into three broad classes: (i) *interpersonal* duties involving leadership (qv), acting as a figurehead, co-ordinating and communicating with others; (ii) *informational* responsibilities that include collecting, analysing and distributing information; and (iii) *decisional* tasks which require the manager to plan, organise and initiate change. Mintzberg argued that all managerial activity was characterised by pace, frequent interruption, fragmentation of effort and the needs for quick thinking and regular verbal communication.

misconduct. A reason for fair dismissal that encompasses idleness; misbehaviour (such as theft, wilful disobedience or physical violence); or other disciplinary offences including persistent absenteeism, lateness or carelessness while completing work. Misconduct must be 'gross' in order to justify a sacking, and reasonable behaviour (qv) is expected of the employer at all times. *See* MISCONDUCT OUTSIDE WORK, DISMISSAL FOR.

misconduct outside work, dismissal for. Sacking a worker for misbehaviour outside working hours and not on the firm's premises. Examples are dismissals following workers' convictions for criminal offences (a school teacher sacked immediately after a conviction for child-molesting for instance), or where a person's actions or statements cause damage to the business. A Court will examine whether the alleged outside misbehaviour made the individual unsuitable for his or her work or unacceptable to fellow employees.

misrepresentation. Making false statements that are genuinely believed to be true ('innocent' misrepresentation) or giving false statements recklessly or knowingly ('fraudulent' misrepresentation).

mission statement. A brief explanation of the fundamental purpose and objectives of the firm, including how it wishes to relate to its environment and to other groups and organisations.

mistake proofing. Designing production or administrative systems to prevent activities from occurring which might cause errors were they to take place.

mitigation of loss, obligation to seek. The legal requirement that an unfairly dismissed worker seek alternative employment as quickly as possible. Hence the dismissing firm is not obliged to compensate the ex-employee for lost wages during an 'unreasonable' period of unemployment.

MITO. The acronym for the Meat Industry Training Organisation.

MMPI. *See* MINNESOTA MULTIPHASIC PERSONALITY INVENTORY.

MNTB. The acronym for the Merchant Navy Training Board.

mobility allowance. Weekly social security payments to disabled people in order to help them become more mobile. Claimants must be unable to walk or be deaf or blind. *See* FARES TO WORK SCHEME.

mobility of labour. The extent to which workers are willing and able to move between regions and occupations. Barriers to labour mobility include housing shortages in certain areas, lack of training, inability to transfer skills from one job to another, having children at school, etc.

models. Representations of reality intended to reduce complex problems to a small number of manageable variables, which the analyst may then study in depth.

module training. Training programmes comprising interconnected units, each of which can be taken separately and aggregated with others to form an end qualification.

Molestation of Workmen Act 1859. A statute which protected from criminal prosecution individuals engaged in peaceful picketing (qv).

monetarist economic policies. Government economic policies based on (i) tight control of the money supply, (ii) the creation of a stable private enterprise economic environment and (iii) the absence of government intervention in the economy.

money illusion. In pay bargaining, the belief by workers that money has the same purchasing power as it had in the past, when in fact the value of money has been eroded by inflation.

money purchase scheme. An occupational pension arrangement whereby contributions are a predetermined percentage of earnings, but the eventual benefits from the scheme (notably the value of a person's retirement pension) are unknown because benefits are contingent on the returns to the scheme's financial investments. Hence, benefits depend entirely on the value of the member's contributions, rather than on his or her final salary (qv).

Monopolies and Mergers Commission. A government body to which the Secretary of State for Industry may refer intended large scale takeovers for analysis and comment. See FAIR TRADING ACT 1973.

monopoly. Technically, a situation in which there is only one supplier in an industry. In practice however, 'monopoly' situations are said to exist when a single business holds in excess of about 25 per cent of a market.

monopsony. A situation in which there is only a single buyer of a certain type of goods.

moonlighting. The practice of employees simultaneously holding more than one job, usually without any individual employer knowing the employee is also working elsewhere.

mores. Social norms (qv) that are enforceable via sanctions.

morphogenesis. A change in the basic form, structure or state of a system.

morphological analysis. A brainstorming (qv) technique for the geometric generation of new ideas through cross-referencing concepts.

Morrisby differential test battery. A series of selection tests intended to assess candidates' verbal, numerical, spatial, quick thinking and mechanical skills. The aim is not only to determine test scores, but also to itemise the specific strengths and weaknesses of candidates.

mortgage. A loan secured against tangible assets (usually property) whereby the borrower possesses and uses the assets but does not own them until the final mortgage repayment.

mortgage debenture. A debenture (qv) secured against a mortgage (qv) on property owned by the borrowing firm.

motherhood organisation. An organisation system structured around generalist managers who are recruited young and without experience, but then trained and developed within the company. Staff are immersed in the culture of the employing business, undertake a wide range of duties, experience many types of work and are expected to remain with the firm for long periods.

motion study. The analysis of the human body movements needed for work. Its purpose is to identify and then eliminate unnecessary or especially tiring movements. See GILBRETH SYSTEM.

motivating factor. Something responsible for creating satisfaction at work, in contrast to hygiene (qv) factors. Examples are recognition from other members of an organisation, responsibility assumed, varied and interesting work and prospects for promotion. See TWO FACTOR THEORY OF MOTIVATION.

motivation. All the drives, forces and conscious or unconscious influences that cause an employee to want to behave in a certain manner.

motivation potential score. A measure of employee motivation suggested by J. R. Hackman and G. R. Oldham. It contains elements for: (i) each of the skills needed to complete the worker's job; (ii) the degree to which the job leads to a clearly identifiable outcome; (iii) the effect of the job on other people; (iv) the extent of the worker's ability to exercise discretion while completing duties; and (v) how easily the employee can assess the calibre of his or her performance. Information on these matters is obtained from a questionnaire completed by the job holder.

motor response. A body movement that results from the receipt of messages from the brain. *See* SKILL.

motor skill. A skill needed for a repetitive mechanical activity (typing for example). *See* PSYCHOMOTOR SKILL.

motorisation. A term sometimes used to describe the groundwork that needs to be done prior to the implementation of new methods, systems or equipment.

MPG. *See* MANAGERIAL, PROFESSIONAL AND STAFF LIAISON GROUP.

MSF. *See* MANUFACTURING, SCIENCE AND FINANCE UNION.

MSL Index. An index of trends and movements in the executive job market, published by the MSL organisation.

MTM. *See* METHODS TIME MEASUREMENT.

multi-option facility. A financing arrangement whereby a consortium of lenders makes available to a borrower a certain amount of funds over a long period. Each member contributes varying sums for short durations during the term of the agreement.

multiple activity chart. A bar chart used in work study (qv) to indicate the time requirements and sequencing of tasks.

multiple questions. Vaguely worded interview questions which enable candidates to interpret their meanings in several different ways and then choose which interpretation to answer.

multiple step day work system. *See* SINGLE-STEP DAY WORK SYSTEM.

multiple trial career. A career (qv) in which the individual regularly switches occupation as he or she becomes bored with contrasting types of work.

multiskilling. Working systems in which employees regularly exchange and share tasks. No job is undertaken exclusively by a single individual.

multi-unionism. The presence within an organisation of several trade unions (qv), each demanding separate negotiations with management. *See* DEMARKATION DISPUTES.

Munitions of War Act 1915. Wartime legislation that outlawed strikes and lockouts and imposed compulsory arbitration of industrial disputes. The Act was repealed in 1918. Similar prohibitions were embodied in the Conditions of Employment and National Arbitration Order of 1940, repealed in 1951.

Murrell, K. F. H. The major pioneer of ergonomics (qv) who in the 1940s investigated the design of machines, equipment and workstations in order to match them to human capacities and limitations.

mushroom theory of management. A humorous management metaphor (qv) likening certain organisations to mushroom farms where the 'mushrooms' (employees) are kept in the dark, and periodically have bucketfuls of manure thrown over them.

music in factories, canteens, etc, regulations concerning. Legislation (notably the 1988 Copyright, Designs and Patents Act) that defines music played during working hours in factories, canteens, offices, etc., as constituting 'public performances', which are unlawful without a licence from the Performing Rights Society Ltd. The Post Office Television and Radio Licence does *not* authorise the playing of copyright materials via a radio or television in a factory, office or canteen. *See* TARIFF 1.

mutual society. A legal structure for organisations the owners of which are also its customers, who take shares of the profits of the enterprise. Certain life assurance organisations are mutual societies.

mutuality agreement. An agreement negotiated between management and a firm's trade unions whereby management promises not to alter any aspect of working methods or conditions without the consent of shop stewards (qv) or other union representatives.

Myers–Briggs Type Indicator. A personality test based on psychologist Carl Gustav Jung's fourfold categorisation of individual tendencies. The categories are: introvert/extrovert; objective/intuitive; logical/emotional; decisive/hesitant. Subjects are required to complete a checklist questionnaire asking them to express their preferences in relation to various issues and situations.

N

NACDET. The acronym for the National Association of Colleges in Distributive Education and Training.

NACEDP. The acronym for the National Advisory Committee on the Employment of Disabled People.

nAch. *See* McCLELLAND, D.C.

NACRO. The acronym for the National Association for the Care and Resettlement of Offenders.

NADO Regulations. *See* NOTIFICATION OF ACCIDENTS AND DANGEROUS OCCURRENCES REGULATIONS.

NAFE. The acronym for Non-Advanced Further Education.

nAff. *See* McCLELLAND, D.C.

NAIRU. *See* NON-ACCELERATING INFLATION RATE OF UNEMPLOYMENT.

naive relativism. *See* RELATIVISM.

NALGO. *See* NATIONAL AND LOCAL GOVERNMENT OFFICERS' ASSOCIATION.

national agreements. Settlements between employers' associations and trade unions that determine employees' terms of employment across an entire industry or occupation. Agreements specify *minimum* rates of pay for various categories of worker (skilled, semi-skilled, etc.); minimum holiday entitlements; working hours and overtime rates; and so on. *See* COLLECTIVE BARGAINING.

National and Local Government Officers' Association (NALGO). A large UK Trade Union (qv) representing administrative, technical, clerical and professional workers in local government, the NHS, higher education, and the gas, electricity and water supply industries.

National Association of Pension Funds Ltd. An organisation formed to represent large self administered pension schemes (qv). It publishes an annual yearbook listing member companies plus details of their pension arrangements.

National Communications Union (NCU).

A trade union (qv) that recruits employees in British Telecom, the Post Office and Girobank. It has separate divisions for clerical and engineering workers.

National Council for Vocational Qualifications (NCVQ). A government body set up in 1986 to implement a national framework for vocational qualifications (qv) and to determine national standards of occupational competence. The latter are intended to act as the basis for national vocational qualifications (NVQs). Examining bodies that desire NCVQ accreditation must develop courses which correspond to NCVQ criteria laid down by 'industry lead bodies (qv)'. The NCVQ does not itself award certificates or diplomas, but rather will 'hallmark' approved qualifications, thus indicating that the holder has achieved a nationally recognised level of knowledge, skill and understanding of the subject at a certain prespecified level. NVQs are supposed to be free from specific course patterns and from unnecessary barriers to access.

National Database of Vocational Qualifications. A database (qv) established by the NCVQ (qv) to provide details of over 1,600 qualifications, 5,000 NVQ units of competence (qv), 200 awarding bodies, and the relationships between the levels of various qualifications. Searches can be undertaken across courses/units corresponding to qualification titles, occupation or industry. Subject searches are possible via the system's superclass (qv) subject classification scheme. The latter is useful when looking for particular individual units.

National Economic Development Council (NEDC). A forum for the discussion of national economic and labour issues by government, trade union and employers' association representatives.

National Enterprise Board. A government body formed in 1975 to co-ordinate government intervention in the economy and to act as a holding company for government investments in companies (especially companies in danger of going bankrupt). It was disbanded in 1981.

National Examination Board for Supervisory Management (NEBSM). An independent government sponsored body (now operating under the umbrella of the City and Guilds of London Institute) that offers Introductory, Certificate and Diploma level examinations in supervisory management. The examinations are run on a national basis and externally moderated to ensure consistency of standards.

national executive committee. The highest level of authority in a trade union (qv). The Trade Union Act 1984 (qv), requires that all NEC members be directly elected by the union's entire membership.

National Graphical Association. A trade union (qv) that recruits employees in the printing industry, including craft and professional workers.

National Insurance, exemptions from. Rules allowing workers who are either (i) below 16 years of age, or (ii) over the state retirement age, to avoid paying Class 1 National Insurance (qv) contributions. Employers do not have to pay NI for employees under 16, but do have to pay contributions for workers over the age of retirement.

National Insurance (Industrial Injuries) Acts 1946 and 1965. Legislation introduced to provide a comprehensive scheme of state insurance for injuries or deaths caused by industrial accidents or diseases. The Acts were subsequently consolidated into the Social Security Acts of 1965, 1986 and 1988.

National League of the Blind and Disabled (NLBD). A trade union (qv) formed in 1899 to represent blind (and subsequently disabled) workers mainly in the clothing and light engineering industries.

National Management Salary Survey. An annual survey of middle to senior management pay levels conducted and published by the British Institute of Management.

National On-line Manpower Information System (NOMIS). An on-line database (qv) produced for the Department of Employment and containing information on UK employment and vacancies. It is updated on a monthly basis.

National Record of Vocational Achievement. A document for recording an individual's employment plans and achievements. It comprises four sections: a personal record giving information on achievements in education, training and leisure; an action plan listing achievement targets and how they are to be attained; an assessment record charting progress made towards targets; and a catalogue of the individual's certificates, diplomas and other qualifications.

National Service Act 1948. Legislation giving members of the Reserve and Auxiliary forces who are called up for temporary military service the legal right to reinstatement in their previous employment on their return to civilian life.

National Training Awards scheme. A government-sponsored annual contest intended to draw public attention to the efforts of firms with excellent training records. There are three main categories for entries: innovation in training methods; training given by employers; and training organised and delivered by outside providers.

National Training Index. A directory of business training courses available in the UK. It covers college courses, distance learning programmes, company training schemes, training films, computer-based training (qv) packages and course organisers. NTI is financed by about 1,000 UK commercial organisations and government departments, and is only available on subscription.

National Training Task Force (NTTF). The government body responsible for co-ordinating the work of training and enterprise councils (qv).

National Union of Civil and Public Servants (NUCPS). A trade union (qv) formed in 1988 from the amalgamation of the Society of Civil and Public Servants and the Civil Service Union. It represents a wide spectrum of types and grades of civil servant.

National Union of Journalists (NUJ). A trade union (qv) that recruits members in the newspaper, periodicals and book publishing industries, in radio and television broadcasting, public relations and information services, plus photo-journalists and freelance writers.

National Union of Public Employees (NUPE). A leading UK trade union (qv) representing employees in local authorities and the NHS. Eighty per cent of members are manual workers. A number of nurses also belong. Three quarters of the total membership is female.

National Union of Railway Workers (NUR). One of the major UK rail unions. The other is the Associated Society of Locomotive Engineers and Firefighters (ASLEF).

natural justice. Rules that a Court of law will expect an employer to have applied during disciplinary procedures. They include requirements that accusations be supported by evidence, that the accused person be informed of the details of the complaint, that the accused be allowed representation when stating a case, be allowed to hear the other side's evidence, and be able to cross-examine witnesses. Committees considering disciplinary matters should act in good faith, not prejudge the issue and not include the other party to the dispute.

natural rate of unemployment. The unemployment rate that exists when the economy is in equilibrium, i.e. where the supply and demand for labour are equal in all sectors.

natural wastage. Reductions in the size of a company's labour force caused by workers resigning, retiring, etc., and not being replaced.

natural work unit. A collection of tasks that presents the employee with a self-contained, meaningful and interesting job.

naturalisation. The process whereby a person obtains citizenship of another country, e.g. by marriage to an existing citizen or following a certain period of residence in the country concerned.

NAYPCAS. The acronym for the National Association of Young People's Counselling and Advisory Services.

NCDB. *See* NATIONAL LEAGUE OF THE BLIND AND DISABLED.

NCU. *See* NATIONAL COMMUNICATIONS UNION.

NCVQ. *See* NATIONAL COUNCIL FOR VOCATIONAL QUALIFICATIONS.

NEBSM. *See* NATIONAL EXAMINATIONS BOARD FOR SUPERVISORY MANAGEMENT.

NEDC. *See* NATIONAL ECONOMIC DEVELOPMENT COUNCIL.

need achievement (N-ach). *See* McCLELLAND, D.C.

negative clearance. A decision by the European Commission (qv) to exempt a large firm from the rules on business competition contained in the Treaty of Rome (qv).

negative income tax. A taxation system (not used in the UK) whereby anyone earning less than a certain wage automatically receives state benefit to bring his or her income up to a minimum specified level.

negligence. A person's failure to exercise the amount of care that an average reasonable person would exercise in a particular situation. For negligence to be legally actionable there has to exist (i) a duty of care and (ii) a breach of that duty by the negligent individual or organisation. Also the damages suffered by the injured part must be a direct consequence of the negligence. *See* CONTRIBUTORY NEGLIGENCE; TORT.

negligence, professional. Breach of a duty of care in relation to one party's reliance on the advice of another. However, advice given casually without any intention of it being relied upon, or advice suggested by someone who does not claim expert knowledge of the matter in question cannot give rise to a claim for damages.

negotiated environment. A situation wherein a management colludes with other stakeholders (qv) of an enterprise (trade unions or staff associations for example) to create a stable environment and the ability to take managerial decisions which have predictable consequences.

negotiation. Discussions between parties with conflicting interests on an issue in order to agree a solution. It implies willingness to compromise, to forgo certain objectives and to implement decisions. *See* JOINT CONSULTATION.

nemawashi. A Japanese word used to describe group effort combined with collective responsibility.

nepotism. The practice of an organisation's owners or managers showing favouritism to their relatives, regardless of the latter's competence. This may create resentment among other employees, stifle initiative, and discourage and demotivate persons of ability who work alongside favoured individuals.

net assets. Fixed plus current assets less current liabilities. Current assets comprise stocks, debtors and cash on hand and at the bank; current liabilities are liabilities that fall due within a year.

net profit. Gross profit (qv) less administrative and other expenses, with or without adjustment for tax and interest payments.

net worth. Another term for capital employed (qv).

network analysis. A planning technique that breaks a project down into logically ordered components and estimates the minimum time needed for the project's completion.

network group structure. A collection of workers who operate independently but, nevertheless, consciously seek to co-ordinate their activities. Each person takes decisions autonomously and there is no coherent chain of command. Members are (usually) of equal rank and accountable only to a single central control.

networking. A means for organising the work of a business so that employees and/or sub-contractors operate from home, communicating with head office via a computer, telephone calls and face-to-face meetings at prearranged times.

neuro-linguistic programming. Training in the identification and control of interpersonal communication (qv) styles.

neurotic behaviour. Irrational conduct characterised by extreme anxiety (qv), obsessions, and emotional instability.

neutral stimulus. In classical conditioning (qv), a signal (e.g. ringing a bell or turning on a light) which has no special meaning in itself but which, if it is associated with another signal that does have a special significance, will lead to certain expectations. For example, ringing a dinner bell every time food is eaten will create expectations of food whenever the bell is rung and hence will produce salivation.

New Earnings Survey. An annual survey of earnings and working hours by industry, region, occupation, age and sex conducted by the UK Department of Employment. It is published by HMSO.

New Method Study. An approach to method study that embraces a wider range of techniques and devices than are applied by orthodox practitioners. Examples of the techniques adopted include brainstorming (qv), simulation analysis (qv), lateral thinking (qv) and creative management (qv).

New Opportunities for Women (NOW) scheme. An EC project financed by the European Social Fund (qv) to provide training opportunities in skills shortage areas (especially those involving information technology (qv)) to women who intend returning to work.

new technology agreement. An accord whereby management and unions jointly consider, negotiate and agree procedures for the introduction of major technical innovations.

New Training Initiative. A set of government policies introduced following the publication in 1981 of a White Paper, *A new training initiative – a programme for action*. Policies were intended to ensure that all young people under 18 years of age not in full time education received some vocational training, and that opportunities for adult training would increase. Major outcomes were the Youth Training Scheme (qv) and TVEI (qv).

new unionism. The emergence in the 1850s of craft unions with broadly based support among employees, a centralised organisation with national headquarters, a national executive committee (qv), full time officers, and regional structures. Members of these unions paid high financial contributions, thus providing substantial resources for sickness, unemployment and other benefits.

NGA. *See* NATIONAL GRAPHICAL ASSOCIATION.

NHSTA. The acronym for the National Health Service Training Authority.

NIACE. The acronym for the National Institute of Adult Continuing Education.

NICEC. The acronym for the National Institute for Careers Education and Counselling.

night and nightshift working, EC Draft Directive concerning. An EC proposal to impose on night shift workers statutory daily and weekly rest periods, plus limits on the amounts of overtime that nightshift workers are allowed to complete. Night workers would not normally be permitted to work more than eight hours in any 24 hour period, and overtime would not be allowed without special permission which, if granted, could only last for up to six months. Workers on nightshifts would have to be given additional paid time off to compensate for their working unsocial hours, rest periods of at least 11 consecutive hours, and a minimum of one day off each week. Individuals would be entitled to a free medical examination prior to starting night work and to further medical examinations periodically thereafter.

NLBD. *See* NATIONAL LEAGUE OF THE BLIND AND DISABLED.

Nobel Prize complex. According to the psychologist Helen Tartakoff, a narcissistic mentality involving the wish to be regarded as exceptional when compared to one's peers. Individuals possessing the complex have 'all or nothing' attitudes towards their work.

noise, EC Directives concerning. European Community Directives (qv) intended to restrict noise levels deemed to affect working performance and/or damage employees' hearing. There are Directives covering pneumatic drills, jackhammers, welding equipment, excavators, concrete breakers and mechanical picks.

noisy conditions. Working environments where the noise level is above 80 decibels. The scale of decibel measurement is logarithmic, so that an increase in noise from (say) 70 to 80 decibels means the sound is ten times louder.

NOMIS. *See* NATIONAL ON-LINE MANPOWER INFORMATION SYSTEM.

nomogram. In work study (qv), a diagram containing information on more than three dimensions of a job.

Non-accelerating Inflation Rate of Unemployment. That rate of unemployment which causes neither upwards nor downwards pressure on the current rate of inflation (through workers increasing or decreasing their wage demands).

non-analytical job evaluation. Felt-fair (qv) methods of job evaluation (qv)

that involve subjective, impressionistic assessments. There is no attempt to quantify the relative significance of particular aspects of a job. *See* RANKING SYSTEM, GRADING SYSTEM.

non-compliance award. Additional compensation payable to an unfairly dismissed (qv) worker whose ex-employer refuses to comply with an Industrial Tribunal (qv) order to re-engage (qv) or reinstate (qv) that person. The award can vary between 13 and 26 weeks' pay or, in cases of sex or race discrimination, between 26 and 52 weeks' pay.

non-contributory pension scheme. An employee superannuation scheme (qv) financed entirely by the employing organisation and hence involving no deductions from employees' wages.

non-directive counselling. An approach to counselling (qv) which assumes that only the counsellee is actually capable of defining his or her problems accurately. Hence, the role of the counsellor is merely to encourage the counsellee to talk about his or her situation and thus determine a solution. *See* DIRECTIVE COUNSELLING.

non-discrimination notice. A document issued by the Commission for Racial Equality (qv) to an employer considered by the Commission to be in contravention of the Race Relations Act 1976 (qv). The Commission must give the firm advance notice of its intention to issue the notice and allow at least 28 days for the firm to reply. If no reply is received or the response is deemed unsatisfactory the Commission serves the notice, which requires the employer to cease committing discriminatory acts immediately. Thereafter the Commission may take legal action against the employer.

non-empirical sciences. *See* EMPIRICAL SCIENCES.

non-executive directors. Part time members of a company's board of directors (qv) who (normally) are not employees of the firm and who bring particular specialist skills to the board's operations. Examples are accountants, legal advisers, technical experts and other specialist consultants. Non-executive directors bring a breadth of experience and objective outlooks to the work of a board. See EXECUTIVE DIRECTORS.

non-market activities. Work and wealth creation that is not counted in the gross domestic product (qv). Examples are farmers who consume part of their own output and employees who receive part of their wages in the form of room and board.

Non-Statutory Training Organisations (NSTOs). Industry training organisations responsible for predicting future skill requirements and for co-ordinating training activities in specific industrial sectors. There are more than 100 NSTOs in the UK. They have no statutory authority and are funded on a voluntary basis by the industries they serve. Some NSTOs provide direct training, others do little more than monitor and comment on the quality of training offered by external bodies.

norm based referencing. Trainee assessment (qv) methods which provide information on a learner's achievements in relation to other people in the trainee's group. The purpose is to differentiate between the individuals being assessed. A majority of trainees will be expected to obtain marks which cluster around the average mark, with just a few people doing extremely well or badly. The definition of satisfactory performance is determined by the proportions of trainees that the person or organisation conducting the assessment deems appropriate should pass or fail the assessment. See CRITERION REFERENCING.

normative approach to industrial relations. The view that the best way to achieve order and stability in industrial relations (qv) is to have clear and binding laws that apply to all parties. Participants then know precisely what is expected of them, although possibilities for flexibility in negotiating agreements are lost. See VOLUNTARISM.

normative control. Determination of patterns of interaction within a group via norms (qv) that establish rules regarding the division of rewards and costs among members. This avoids the need for recurrent interpersonal bargaining or for certain members to impose their power (qv) on others.

normative decision-making model. A contingency (qv) theory of leadership (qv) proposed by V. H. Vroom and P. H. Yetton (qv) which identifies five decision-making styles (ranging from complete autocracy through to consensus decision making) and specifies a series of diagnostic questions (arranged in the form of a decision tree) that managers should ask in order to determine which style is most appropriate in a particular situation.

normative function of a reference group. The ability of a reference group (qv) to control members' behaviour by evaluating how closely each member conforms to group norms (qv), and rewarding or punishing members on the basis of this criterion. This can only happen if the individuals concerned value or aspire to membership of the reference group.

normative statement. An expression of opinion about what ought to be, rather than a straightforward statement of facts.

norms. Expected modes of behaviour, attitudes or belief established formally or informally within a group. See GROUP NORMS; SOCIAL NORM; INCOMES POLICIES.

norm-set criterion referencing. A process for deriving criterion referencing (qv) from norm-based referencing (qv). Norm referenced assessments are conducted and the results noted. A decision is then taken regarding what constitutes satisfactory performance – given the results from the sample data. This decision forms the basis for the future criterion referenced assessments.

no-strike agreement. A clause in an employee's contract of employment (qv) which forbids the worker from going on strike. The Trade Union and Labour Relations Act 1974 (qv) states that such a clause is legal only if it is in writing, is made known to the employee and is agreed by an independent trade union (qv).

notary public. A person legally qualified to attest and certify deeds and other official legal documents. In Britain, solicitors typically undertake this role.

Notice of Appearance (IT1). The form on which the defendant in a case before an Industrial Tribunal (qv) writes out his or her grounds for defending the action.

notice of intention to claim. A written statement that workers on short time (qv) must submit to their employer within one month of the last qualifying week of short time working, informing the employer of the worker's intention to quit. The firm might then issue a 'counter notice', claiming that normal work will resume within the next month and is expected to last for at least three months. If this is the case the employees will not be entitled to redundancy payments if they proceed with their resignations.

notice periods, statutory. Minimum periods of notice of dismissal laid down in the Employment Protection (Consolidation) Act 1978 (qv). Workers with at least one month's service are entitled to a week's notice; those with at least two years' service to two weeks' notice plus an extra week for each further year of service up to a maximum of 12 weeks. These are minimum periods. If an employee's contract of employment (qv) provides for a longer period then the latter will apply (unless the employee is summarily dismissed (qv)).

Notification of Accidents and Dangerous Occurrences Regulations. Detailed government rules concerning employers' obligations to report the occurrence of various categories of industrial accident to appropriate health and safety enforcement authorities.

notification of planned redundancies. The requirement under the Employment Protection (Consolidation) Act 1978 (qv) that firms notify the Department of Employment if they are contemplating making ten or more employees redundant. Thirty days' notice is required for redundancies involving between ten and 99 workers over a period not exceeding 30 days. Ninety days notice is necessary for planned redundancies of 100 or more employees over a period of 90 days or less.

notional factory. Premises not concerned with manufacture as such, but still regarded as factories (qv) for the purposes of the Factories Act 1961 (qv). Examples include electrical stations; charitable institutions and prison workshops where articles are adapted for sale; docks, wharfs and harbours, and works of engineering construction (qv).

novation. The substitution of a new legal obligation for an old one with the consent of all the parties concerned, e.g. an incoming member of a partnership agreeing to take over all the business debts of a retiring partner, with the full approval of the creditors of the firm.

novus actus interveniens. See REMOTE DAMAGE.

NOW. See NEW OPPORTUNITIES FOR WOMEN SCHEME.

nPow. See McCLELLAND, D.C.

NSTOs. See NON-STATUTORY TRAINING ORGANISATIONS.

NTI, See NEW TRAINING INITIATIVE.

NTTF. See NATIONAL TRAINING TASK FORCE.

NUCPS. See NATIONAL UNION OF CIVIL AND PUBLIC SERVANTS.

nuisance. A failure to carry out a legal duty or the committing of an unlawful act which has the consequence of endangering the lives, safety, health or comfort of others. Examples are the discharge of fumes from factories, accumulating rubbish in public places, creating excessive noise levels, etc.

NUJ. See NATIONAL UNION OF JOURNALISTS.

NUM. The acronym for the National Union of Mineworkers.

NUPE. See NATIONAL UNION OF PUBLIC EMPLOYEES.

NUR. See NATIONAL UNION OF RAILWAY WORKERS.

nurses practising in the European Community, EC rules concerning. Regulations introduced in 1977 to enable qualified nurses to practise anywhere in the European Community, subject to their satisfying certain minimum training requirements. Comparability of training standards is achieved via an Advisory Committee on Training in Nursing, comprising three expert representatives from each member state.

NUS. The acronym for the National Union of Seamen.

O

O and M. *See* ORGANISATION AND METHODS.

OATC. *See* OPEN ACCESS TRAINING CENTRE.

obedience, duty of employees. The common law obligation of a worker to obey all the reasonable, lawful and non-dangerous commands of his or her employer, provided these are covered by the employee's contract of employment (qv). Employees who disobey their employers' instructions may be fairly dismissed, but only if the disobedience is wilful and crucially important to the employee's work. Written warnings must have been issued unless the disobedience warrants summary dismissal (qv). *See* FAIR DISMISSAL.

obiter dictum. A statement of law made by a judge 'in passing' when ruling on a particular case even though the statement itself does not form the basis for the judge's decision.

objective knowledge. Knowledge gained by an employee in consequence of his or her involvement with a particular employee and which is, therefore, the intellectual property of the employer. Objective knowledge can be protected through a restrictive covenant (qv) incorporated into a worker's contract of employment (qv).

objective test. A selection test (qv) designed in such a way that each question only has one correct answer, hence avoiding the need to interpret candidates' responses.

objects clause. An important component of a company's memorandum of association (qv), specifying the firm's contractual powers. Contracts entered into by the company which are not covered by its objects clause are *ultra vires* (qv) and not legally enforceable.

obligation to provide work. The duty implied in every contract of employment (qv) whereby the employer must provide employees (qv) with the opportunity to do their work whenever it is available. Thus, unless the employee's contract states otherwise, laying workers off without pay constitutes a fundamental breach of contract, entitling the worker to claim constructive unfair dismissal (qv).

Oblomov syndrome. Impaired work performance resulting from an employee's apathy, passivity, laziness and indolence. Real life action is replaced by fantasies and daydreams. The name derives from a fictitious character created by the Russian novelist Ivan Goncharov.

observed time. In work measurement (qv), the period taken by an employee to complete a task while being observed by a work study officer. *See* RATING STANDARD.

obsolescence, managerial. A consequence of rapid changes in technology, management practices and the type of knowledge needed for managerial occupations. It occurs when executives are unwilling or unable to upgrade their skills or retrain in new competencies.

occupation. A category of work that is independent of the firm or industry in which it is performed.

occupational analysis inventory technique. A method of job analysis (qv) based on 622 descriptions of work activities and conditions, grouped into five categories: information received; mental activities; observed behaviour; work outcomes; and work context.

occupational pension funds, EC Proposal concerning. A 1990 Proposal of the European Commission to open up the market for voluntary pension funds to Community-wide competition, hence enabling cross-border membership of occupational (and other) pension schemes.

Occupational Pension Schemes, Notes on Approval. Documents issued pursuant to the Finance Acts of 1970 and

1971 which grant the Superannuation Funds Office (qv) discretionary powers to approve company occupational pension schemes for the purpose of contracting out from the state scheme. *See* CONTRACTED-OUT OCCUPATIONAL PENSION SCHEME.

Occupational Pensions Board (OPB). A government body established in 1975 to issue certificates to occupational and personal pension schemes (qv) which qualify to contract out of the State Earnings Related System (SERPS) (qv). Additionally, the OPB examines and reports on matters connected with pensions referred to it by the Secretary of State for Social Security.

Occupational Personality Questionnaire. A personality test (qv) similar to Cattel's 16PF (qv) test but specifically related to occupational requirements (the 16PF is such that it seeks to measure general rather than vocational personality characteristics).

occupational psychology. Those elements of work psychology (qv) that deal mainly with individuals, rather than with the psychology of organisations or groups.

occupational sick pay (OSP). Payments to sick or injured employees independent of statutory sick pay (qv). The level of OSP is determined entirely by the employee's contract of employment.

Occupational Social Security Directive 1986. An EC directive (qv) prohibiting discrimination on the basis of sex, marital or family status in state social security or private occupational pension schemes for employees or the self employed.

occupational standards. Norms of performance or quality recognised by an industry, profession or training organisation as being necessary for the satisfactory completion of work.

occupational therapy. Psychotherapy (qv) in which the subject performs occupational tasks (preferably in a workplace setting) in an attempt to improve his or her self-esteem and feelings of personal value.

occupational union. A trade union (qv) concerned with organising employees within a certain (usually non-manual) occupation. The National Union of Bank Employees is an example.

Occupiers' Liability Acts 1957 and 1984. Acts of Parliament requiring occupiers of premises to take reasonable care to ensure that visitors will be safe when using the premises for the purposes for which the visitors were invited to be there.

oceanic power, feelings of. According to M. Kets de Vries, inner sensations of unity, competence and boundless energy that give rise to charismatic leadership (qv).

oculesics. Use (or avoidance) of eye contact in interpersonal communication.

OECD. *See* ORGANISATION FOR ECONOMIC CO-OPERATION AND DEVELOPMENT.

office. According to the Offices, Shops and Railway Premises Act 1963 (qv) any building or part of a building where administration, writing, bookkeeping, filing, typing, duplicating, calculating, drawing, handling money or telephone operating is carried out by at least one employed person.

Office of Equal Opportunities, European Community. A specialist EC body attached to the Directorate General for employment and social affairs and required to promote the equality of opportunity for women workers within member states.

Office of Fair Trading. A government body established under the Fair Trading Act 1973 (qv) to examine complaints from the public in relation to alleged unfair trading practices and to advise the Secretary of State for Industry on consumer affairs.

Offices, Shops and Railway Premises Act 1963. The basic statute concerning health and safety in shops and offices in the UK. It applies to all offices, even those used for other purposes (e.g. for manufacture or warehousing) although temporary offices or those operated for less than 21 hours a week are exempt. The Act covers such matters as the minimum amount of floorspace per person, minimum temperatures, washing facilities, etc.

official dispute. An industrial action (qv) formally sanctioned by a trade union (qv). Sometimes, actions begin unofficially but are then declared 'official' following a (possibly lengthy) administrative procedure.

off-line quality control. Consciously designing a product in such a way that it can be produced with the minimum item to item variation in its performance and dimensions.

off-the-job training. Training undertaken away from the workplace, either externally in a college or training centre, or internally within the firm in a section of its premises specially reserved for this purpose.

Ohmae, Kenichi. Influential Japanese management consultant who argued that international companies should locate in the world's prosperous areas (Europe, Japan and the developed Pacific Rim, and the US). According to Ohmae, cheap labour in underdeveloped countries should not be a major determinant of the capital investment decision because the proportion of labour costs in the total cost of production in these countries is rapidly declining in consequence of technological advance. Also, the expertise acquired through operating in one industrialised region is readily transferred to others.

Ohno, Taiichi. Executive director of the Japanese Toyota Motor corporation during the 1970s and inventor of the kanban (qv) just-in-time production control system.

oligopoly. A situation in which there is only a small number of firms in an industry relative to the volume of industry sales.

oligopsony. A market situation in which there is only a small number of buyers. In consequence buyers are able to influence suppliers' pricing and other decisions.

omnibus test. A test involving questions which are not grouped together into categories dealing with particular topics or types of ability.

ONC/D. *See* ORDINARY NATIONAL CERTIFICATE/DIPLOMA.

one-parent benefit. Additional state child benefit payable for the first or only child in a one-parent family. A 'parent' is any lone person entitled to claim child benefit (a grandparent for instance).

one stop shopping, consultancies and. The ability of a large human resources or general management consultancy to satisfy *all* a client's needs, rather than the client having to obtain advice and services on different aspects of personnel work from separate consultancies (e.g. a headhunter, a training consultant, a job evaluation expert, etc.).

one way communication. *See* TWO WAY COMMUNICATION.

one worker–multiple machine (OWMM) production. An assembly or production line which requires each worker simultaneously to operate several different machines.

on-line information. Information contained in a database (qv) that a user may access via a modem from his or her own computer terminal.

on-the-job training. Training undertaken at the place of work while the employee is simultaneously contributing to the employer's business. Typically it involves verbal instruction regarding equipment, procedures and working methods. *See* OFF-THE-JOB TRAINING.

OPB. *See* OCCUPATIONAL PENSIONS BOARD.

open access training centre (OATC). A training resource unit with training facilities available throughout the week (including evenings and Saturdays) so that students may attend at times particularly convenient for them. An OATC might contain computer-based training (CBT) (qv) hardware and software, interactive video (qv), training manuals, reference books and other conventional training materials.

Open College. An operation similar to the Open University but concerned with training and reskilling people at work and individuals seeking fresh employment. There is complete open access; no entry qualifications are necessary prior to enrolling for a course. The College inherited materials from the Open Tech (qv) when the latter was disbanded. No degrees or diplomas are awarded, although successful completion of certain units can count towards nationally recognised qualifications.

open ended questions. Interview questions that require candidates to discuss topics, express opinions and explain their feelings about issues and events. An example is the question, 'What made you decide to concentrate on personnel management while you were at college?'

open ended settlement. An agreement negotiated between a management and a trade union that is subject to cancellation and renegotiation at the behest of either party.

open learning. Off-the-job training (qv) in which a central organisation (usually a college) supplies trainees with a package of learning materials (manuals, videos, computer-based training (qv) packages, etc.) and provides trainee support services such as tutor back-up, telephone counselling, face-to-face instruction at 'surgeries' held on certain evenings each month, etc.

open loop system. A feedback control system (qv) requiring human intervention to remedy difficulties.

open question. An interview or written question to which any response may be given.

open system. An organisation (such as a business) that cannot survive without interacting with the environments within which it operates. A 'closed' system can continue indefinitely without such interaction. *See* SYSTEMS FACTORS.

Open Systems Interchange. Computing systems that enable the interconnection of computers from different manufacturers, enabling them to communicate and operate together.

Open Tech programme. A collection of open learning (qv) initiatives sponsored by the Manpower Services Commission (MSC) (qv) in the early 1980s. Instructional materials created for the programme were taken over by the Open College (qv) in 1987.

operant behaviour. Individual behaviour that results from a person's interactions with the outside world. It does not result from automatic physical responses to stimuli. Rather, it is *learned* via the process of operant conditioning (qv).

operant conditioning. Learning through trial and error. According to behaviourists (qv), correct behaviour that leads to a reward will be repeated. Thus, actual behaviour is determined by its perceived *consequences*. This theory has important implications for the theory of training.

operating lease. An equipment leasing system whereby the leasing company expects to lease the same item to many customers and where the leasing company is responsible for the item's repair and maintenance.

operational approach to budgeting. A budget allocation method whereby individual managers are asked how much they need in order to achieve certain prespecified objectives. Resources are then distributed and the people involved assume personal responsibility for administering their budget allocations.

operational game. A form of business game (qv) which simulates a real life situation experienced by the participants' employing company and which requires each player to assume a role and take appropriate decisions. Senior management then gives feedback on the likely effects of the decisions taken.

operational leverage. The ratio of fixed costs to total costs in a firm or department.

operations management. Management of all the processes necessary to transform tangible resource inputs into outputs of goods and services. It is particularly concerned with industrial engineering (qv) and the organisation of manufacturing.

operations research. According to the UK Operational Research Society, the application of 'the methods of science to complex problems arising in the direction and management of large systems of people, machines, materials and money in industry, business, government and defence'.

operative cell structure. A way of organising the workforce of a manufacturing company. Workers in each cell are made responsible for quality, production control and the movements of work from one cell to the next. They are expected to function as a team (qv) and to cover for each other's absences, late-coming, etc.

operative performance index. A measure of employee efficiency expressed as the ratio of what a worker should have produced in a certain period to what he or she has actually produced.

opportunistic theft. Theft (qv) resulting from the thief being tempted to steal in consequence of poor security in a firm's premises (unlocked offices, valuables left lying around, etc.).

optimised production technology. An approach to manufacturing that focuses on the identification and removal of bottlenecks in materials flows.

Ordinary National Certificate/Diploma (ONC/D). A post 'O'level two-year educational qualification that used to be offered by colleges of further education. Part time students were awarded an ONC; full time students received the Diploma. These qualifications were largely replaced by BTEC certificates and diplomas.

ordinary shares. Shares that have no special rights or privileges in relation to dividends or the division of assets on dissolution of a company. Ordinary shares with votes are called 'B' shares; those without votes, 'A' shares.

organic learning. See MECHANISTIC LEARNING.

organisation and methods (O & M). The application of work study (qv) to clerical and administrative procedures; notably to form design, office layout, analysis and measurement of clerical work, and the use of information technology. The aim is to simplify and improve existing procedures, particularly in relation to the elimination of unnecessary paperwork and the speeding up of the flow of documents between departments.

organisation chart. A diagram showing patterns of authority, responsibility and communication within an organisation.

organisation, classical approach to. The proposition that there exist certain universally valid principles of organisation that should be applied in all situations. It advocates narrow spans of control (qv), unity of command (qv), specialisation of functions and management by exception (qv). Employees should be selected and trained to meet the needs of the organisation rather than the organisation being restructured to suit the social and human requirements of its employees.

organisation, contingency approach to. The view that each organisation should be individually structured to suit the requirements of its particular circumstances and operating environments.

Organisation for Economic Co-operation and Development (OECD). An international organisation founded in 1961 by the leading western industrial countries. It collects statistics and publishes reports on the economic prospects of member states.

organisation man. Someone who naturally and effortlessly fits into bureaucratic organisations.

organisation manual. A booklet that specifies in detail the duties attached to each position in an organisation chart (qv).

organisation of work. Breaking down the totality of work that has to be completed within an enterprise into units for allocation to people and departments plus the specification of authority, responsibility and accountability systems. See ORGANISATION STRUCTURE.

organisation planning. Determination of the objectives of an enterprise's organisation structure and of the best means, via organisational design (qv), for achieving them. See ORGANISATIONAL DEVELOPMENT.

organisation structure. The system for distributing tasks within an enterprise and defining the general framework within which activities occur.

organisation theory. Critical analysis of the structure, functions, performance and control of organisations and of the behaviour of individuals and groups within them.

organisational analysis. The study of the configurations of organisations, of organisational communication networks, organisational command and control systems, authority structures and related organisational concerns.

organisational anarchy. The situation that exists when the managers of an organisation do not know how it works and behave in unpredictable ways. Consequently there is little forward planning, and decisions are taken in response to events rather than to initiate activities.

organisational behaviour, as an academic subject. The study of how organisations function and how people relate to them through their conduct, perceptions and intentions, individually or in groups.

organisational behaviour modification programmes. Application of the principles of operant conditioning (qv) to organisational problems. OBM programmes identify desired behaviour patterns and create reinforcement contingencies (qv) to encourage them. *See* BEHAVIOURAL CONTINGENCY MANAGEMENT PROGRAMME.

organisational culture (organisational climate). The totality of the attitudes, norms, beliefs and perspectives shared by the majority of the members of an organisation.

organisational design. Decisions concerning the makeup of the constituent elements of an organisation (departments, divisions, strategic business units (qv), etc.), how the elements are united, and on such matters as spans of control (qv), authority (qv) and responsibility structures, delegation (qv) and so on.

organisational development. The process of periodically reviewing the adequacy of a firm's organisation structures, communication systems, authority and responsibility systems, etc., in the context of its current and predicted organisational needs.

organisational drama. A situation that arises when a manager's subordinates begin to share the delusions of their superior and deliberately act out the latter's fantasies, e.g. by pretending to recognise enemies in other departments. *See* TRANSACTIONAL ANALYSIS; FOLIE A DEUX.

organisational learning. The processes whereby freshly discovered solutions to administrative problems pass into the firm's 'managerial memory', hence becoming integral parts of the organisation's mechanism for reacting to future events. A consequence is that decision-making procedures are continuously modified and adapted in the light of experience.

organisational life cycle hypothesis. A theory concerning the stages through which business organisations supposedly progress. Four stages are said to exist: the entrepreneural stage at the start of an organisation's existence (characterised by one person control); the 'collectivity stage', in which a coherent organisation structure emerges; the 'formalisation stage' that involves the establishment of a bureaucracy; and the 'elaboration stage' during which the bureaucracy is streamlined and working methods rationalised.

organisational morphology. The physical configuration of an organisation.

organisational nihilism. Complete denial of the legitimacy of an organisation's authority system, resulting perhaps from alienation (qv), boredom, depression or feelings that the organisation's work is trivial.

organisational pathology. According to C. Argyris, the analysis of the 'health' of an organisation. The members of a healthy organisation are in touch with reality, able to cope with change and share common perspectives regarding the organisation's goals.

organisational slack. Inefficiencies within an organisation (overmanning (qv) for instance) that management consciously tolerates in order to enable it to withstand environmental shocks, e.g. sudden upsurges in the demand for its output.

organisations. Social entities deliberately created to achieve certain objectives. Organisations are characterised by the division of labour (qv), power (qv) and authority (qv) systems, and a force (management for example) which guides them towards attaining their goals.

organistic organisations. Flexible and relatively informal organisational structures with effective communication systems, overlapping responsibilities and willingness to adapt to change.

organogram. *See* ORGANISATION CHART.

orientation programme. *See* INDUCTION.

original motion. A proposition put to a committee (qv) for debate and resolution.

Originating Application (ITI). The form completed by an aggrieved person in order to initiate a case in an Industrial Tribunal (qv). The form briefly outlines the nature of the allegation and the personal details of the applicant (length of service for example).

OSI. *See* OPEN SYSTEMS INTERCHANGE.

OSPRA. *See* OFFICES, SHOPS AND RAILWAY PREMISES ACT 1963.

other directedness. Exceptional sensitivity to the actions and wishes of other people. *See* INNER DIRECTED PERSON.

outcome led learning. *See* INPUT DRIVEN LEARNING.

outdoor management training. Management training based on outdoor pursuits such as rockclimbing, orienteering, canoeing, etc. Its advocates argue that there exist direct parallels between the personal qualities necessary for successful business management (planning, team-building, leadership, motivation, dealing with uncertainty and so on) and those needed to complete outdoor management development exercises.

outer self awareness. *See* INNER SELF AWARENESS.

outgroup. *See* INGROUP.

outline process chart. A diagram showing an overall view of a process and indicating the points where materials are used and the sequence of its activities and operations.

outplacement. Activities designed to help redundant employees find other jobs. Examples are career counselling (qv) and psychometric testing (qv) intended to discover the individual's suitability for alternative types of work.

output-based bonus schemes. Wage incentive schemes based on the value of output rather than the value of the effort necessary for the output's production. Workers receive no payment for waiting time, machine setting, clearing up, etc. *See* EFFORT-BASED BONUS SCHEMES.

outsourcing. Obtaining resources (including human resources) from external sources rather than from within the firm.

outworker. An employee who performs work at home, usually on a part time or casual basis.

overachiever. A person who is desperately anxious to succeed, even to the extent of attempting tasks beyond his or her level of ability. This contrasts with the 'underachiever' who possesses a low opinion of his or her capacities and hence does not try hard enough, consequently failing to meet expected levels of performance.

overcompensation, psychological. A response to a personal deficiency in one area that involves putting enormous effort into succeeding at something else.

overcrowding regulations. Rules embodied in the Factories Act 1961 (qv) requiring that each worker employed in a factory (qv) has at least 11 cubic metres (400 cubic feet) in which to work. Airspace more than 4.2 metres above ground is disregarded. Similar provisions apply to offices covered by the Offices, Shops and Railway Premises Act 1963 (qv).

overhead absorption costing. The selection of appropriate cost centres (qv) and the allocation to them of relevant shares of the total overheads (qv) of the firm according to a predetermined formula.

overheads. Costs that are not attributable to specific products, relating instead to the upkeep of the environment in which production occurs. Examples are rent, maintenance of buildings, secretarial and administrative services, heating, etc. Normally, overhead costs do not vary with respect of the volume of production.

overlearning. Practising a skill or reading instructional materials many more times than is objectively necessary for learning (qv) to occur.

Overseas Labour Section of the Department of Employment. A government body that provides advice to foreign nationals about UK work permits, the circumstances in which they are required, the procedures involved, the probability of approval, etc.

overseas students, employment of. Hiring overseas students during their free time or vacations. The employer must obtain permission for this from the Department of Employment. Permission will be granted only if the firm provides to the DOE evidence that the work will not interfere with the person's studies, that no suitable local labour is available, and that the terms and conditions of employment are not less favourable than those available in the local area.

overtime. Work done beyond normal working hours. It is normally paid at premium rates, e.g. at time and a half or double time.

overtrading. The situation that arises when a firm expands its operations too rapidly, leading to cash shortages (and hence the need to borrow at high rates of interest), to excessive levels of credit sales, delivery problems and general operational inefficiencies.

OW forms. Forms that a prospective employer must submit to the Department of Employment to obtain work permits (qv) for foreign workers or to employ overseas students (qv).

Owen, Robert (1771–1858). Owner of cotton mills and early pioneer of personnel management. Owen developed welfare services within his factories and experimented with incentive systems. He also devised appraisal systems, target setting schemes and systems for training and controlling workers.

OWMM. *See* ONE WORKER-MULTIPLE MACHINE PRODUCTION.

Own-Initiative Opinion. A view expressed by the Economic and Social Committee (ECOSOC) (qv) of the European Community, even though the matter on which the view is expressed was not referred to it by the European Commission (qv). ECOSOC is empowered to issue Own-Initiative Opinions on any subject it chooses, making it a powerful lobbying organisation in relation to labour and social affairs.

P

P11. The record of the tax deducted by a firm from employees' pay. Each month the employer must send to the Inland Revenue a cheque for all tax stoppages, together with a form P30 ('Remittance Card'). Annual totals are declared on form P35 ('Annual Declaration Certificate').

P35. A form that employers must complete annually to state how much tax and National Insurance they have deducted from their employees' wages.

P38(S). An Inland Revenue form signed by a student to enable his or her employer to avoid deducting tax from wages earned during college vacations.

P45. A form issued to an employee on leaving an employing firm stating the pay and tax deducted by the employer during the tax year up to the date of leaving. On beginning another job, the individual hands over his or her P45 to the new employer, who then applies the tax code stated on it to that person's earnings. If a recruit has no P45 the employer informs the Inland Revenue on form P46. Once a tax code is established the employee is notified of this on form P2.

P60. A form stating the value of pay and tax deducted from an employee's wages by an employer during a tax year.

paid up benefits. Rights under an occupational pension scheme that are automatically preserved following a member's resignation from the scheme (e.g. in consequence of changing jobs).

paired comparison method. A technique of job evaluation (qv) whereby the characteristics of each job are compared in turn with those of all the other jobs to be evaluated until a consistent hierarchy of jobs emerges.

Palmer, George (1809–1906). Biscuit manufacturer and early advocate of job security, staff training and development and sick pay for workers.

panel interviews. Employment interviews where candidates simultaneously face several interviewers. Problems include the theatrical atmosphere created by the situation, the possibility that some panel members will not be genuinely interested in the proceedings, and different interviewers applying different criteria to the evaluation of candidates.

panoramic office planning. The arrangement of open plan offices in such a way as to create self-contained work units within a wider open space. Filing cabinets, desks, plants, acoustic screens, etc., are strategically positioned to break up the floor area and promote the atmosphere of a conventional office.

paralinguistics. Non-verbal aspects of speech, e.g. tone of voice, accent, speed of delivery, chronemics (qv), loudness, etc.

paranoid behaviour. Irrational suspicion of the motives of other people and excessive sensitivity to perceived threats.

parental leave, EC Draft Directive concerning. A 1983 draft directive (qv) intended to provide for at least three months' leave for *either* parent at the end of the mother's statutory maternity leave. Employers would not have to pay wages during this period (the parent would obtain state benefit) but would be required to offer reinstatement. The proposals also apply to adopted children.

Parkinson's law. The proposition that employees will fill out their work unnecessarily in order to make it last as long as the maximum time available for its completion.

part time workers, Draft EC Directive concerning. An EC Draft Directive (qv) intended to improve the employment rights and terms and conditions of part time EC workers. It provides for wage payments and holiday entitlements strictly proportional to those of full timers doing equivalent work, for the same access to vocational training and pension schemes as full time employees, equal rights in relation to health and safety and the right of a part timer to claim unfair dismissal on the same basis as full time workers. Unfair discrimination against part timers when selecting workers for promotion would become illegal. The proposal applies to all part timers working at least eight hours a week. Employers would have to pay national insurance for *all* workers employed more than eight hours a week, including those earning less than the current NI threshold. *See* TEMPORARY WORKERS, DRAFT EC DIRECTIVE CONCERNING.

partial (intermittent) reinforcement. A learning (qv) situation in which reinforcement (qv) follows some but not all occurrences of the responses being encouraged.

participant observation. A method of field research (qv) in which the researcher becomes an integral part of a social group in order to study its behaviour in a natural society.

participation. Employee involvement in management decision making. It can occur individually via quality circles (qv), management by objectives (qv) and performance appraisal (qv) exercises, or collectively through employee representation on works committees, supervisory boards (qv), joint negotiating committees (qv), advisory groups, etc. *See* HUMAN RELATIONS APPROACH; CONSULTATION.

participative learning programmes. Training courses which actively involve learners in the *design* of training activities. Hence, trainees are made partly responsible for their own learning, rather than merely following a prearranged programme.

partnership. A collection of between two and 20 people (10 for banking firms) who form and run a business without limited liability. Partners are jointly responsible for the firm's debts.

Partnerships Directive 1990. A European Community Directive (qv) that requires limited partnerships (qv) or partnerships containing a limited liability company as a member to publish audited accounts. (Small businesses are exempt from this Directive.)

partnerships, rules on equal opportunities. Provisions of the Sex Discrimination Act 1975 (qv) which prohibit partnerships from discriminating against either of the sexes when taking new partners or in the partnership terms offered; including benefits, facilities or services.

passing off. A tort (qv) that involves trading in such a manner as to mislead the public into believing that a firm's goods or services are in fact the goods or services of another.

patents. *See* INTELLECTUAL PROPERTY.

Patents Rules 1978. A statutory scheme for rewarding employees responsible for new inventions deemed to belong to the employing firm. The scheme is run by a government Comptroller who awards compensation regarded as just and equitable having regard to the benefits received by the employer, the nature of the employee's duties, the employer's contribution and the employee's effort and skill devoted to making the invention. Applications for compensation must be registered within 21 years of the file of the patent.

paternalistic leadership. An autocratic leadership (qv) style similar to dictatorial leadership (qv) but where the leader genuinely attempts to gain the respect and allegiance of subordinates. Team members who always do as they are told receive special favours and limited dissent is tolerated.

Paterson's decision band method. A method of job evaluation (qv) that focuses exclusively on the amount of decision making required by a job. Six bands of decision making responsibility are identified: (i) policy making; (ii) implementation of policies; (iii) interpreting policies; (iv) routine decision making; (v) taking decisions automatically according to prespecified criteria; and (vi) deciding how to follow existing procedures.

path-goal theory. An approach to leadership (qv) based on the expectancy theory (qv) of motivation (qv). According to the theory, subordinates see their leaders as the source of rewards. Thus, leaders should clarify to subordinates the paths they must follow to obtain various rewards (higher wages, promotion, encouragement and support, job security, etc.). According to the theory, an effective leader is one who can identify which rewards are perceived as critically important by each subordinate.

Paula principle. The proposition that many competent women fail to achieve promotion to their levels of ability because their incompetent male bosses regard them as a threat to their own positions.

pay anomalies. Significant differences in the pay levels of various occupational groups whose work requires similar levels of skill, effort, responsibility, decision taking, educational qualifications, etc. Anomalies typically result from labour shortages that cause members of some groups to be recruited at high starting salaries, whereas existing employees in other occupational groups whose skills are not in such heavy demand receive minimal pay increases.

Pay As You Earn (PAYE). The income tax system for Schedule E (qv) taxpayers introduced in 1944 to enable employees to pay their tax gradually over the year, and to place the administrative responsibility for tax collection on employers.

pay freeze. A temporary but statutorily enforced national prohibition on the payment of wage increases to employees.

pay parity. Equality in the wage rates paid to workers (possibly in different firms or industries) who perform the same type of work.

pay review body. A government-appointed committee established to recommend levels of pay increase for certain groups of state employees (judges or hospital doctors for example).

pay round. The order in which managements and unions in various industries negotiate and settle annual pay rises and improvements in workers' terms and conditions of service within a particular year. A settlement emerging from one set of negotiations might be used by union representatives in another firm or industry as the starting point for their own next claim. *See* LEAPFROGGING.

pay under notice, right of employees to. The right conferred by the Employment Protection (Consolidation) Act 1978 (qv), of an employee to be paid in full while under statutory notice (qv), even if there is no work available for the employee to do.

payback period. The period needed for a capital investment project to recoup its initial capital cost.

PAYE. *See* PAY AS YOU EARN.

Payment of Wages in Public Houses Prohibition Act 1883. A statute that made illegal the practice of certain employers paying employees' wages in public houses at the end of the working week. The Act excluded publicans' employees.

payments in kind. Remunerations to workers paid as fringe benefits (qv) rather than as wages *per se* in order to minimise the recipient's tax liability.

payoff matrix. A rectangular array of numbers showing the returns to various courses of action under alternative assumptions.

payroll system. A set of procedures whereby data are collected on employees' wage rates, overtime details, etc., and then converted into payslips and monetary transfers into employees' bank accounts.

payroll tax. A tax levied on firms according to the number of workers they employ. The aim (apart from raising revenue for the government) is to encourage employers to increase their efficiency by economising on labour.

Pearson Commission. A Royal Commission which in 1978 reported on the extent of injury through accidents in the United Kingdom and the implications of these for the law of Civil Liability. It pointed out that nearly one quarter of all personal injuries result from accidents at work.

peer group. A collection of persons that an individual perceives as being of equal status or as possessing a common interest with the person in question, who will compare his or her performance or rewards against those of peer group members.

peer group appraisal. Performance appraisal (qv) conducted by colleagues of equal rank to the appraised person who do not have the power to impose sanctions. The advantage claimed is that peer group appraisals may analyse issues more honestly and critically than when the appraisee fears the career consequences of admitting mistakes to an immediate superior.

peer review. A method of validating and approving training and educational courses whereby experts from industry, commerce, the professions and educational institutions express an opinion on whether a course is of a proper standard.

penalty clause. A provision in a contract whereby payments for work or services rendered are reduced if the work is not completed on schedule.

pencil and paper test. A test that requires written answers to questions.

pendulum arbitration. A method for fixing the level of pay increase to be awarded to a group of workers. Management and (usually) a trade union each submit to an independent arbitrator figures they believe to be reasonable. The arbitrator selects one figure or the other: the parties are not allowed to haggle.

Pension Scheme Surpluses (Administration) Regulations 1987. Legislation compelling the trustees of any occupational pension scheme that has assets which exceed liabilities by more than 5 per cent to dispose of the surplus via improved pension benefits, increases in payments to surviving dependants, enhanced early retirement provisions, or contribution holidays (qv).

pension schemes, EC Directive on equal treatment for men and women. A 1986 EC Directive compelling member nations to prohibit sex discrimination in occupational pension schemes. Discrimination could occur either directly, or indirectly by reference to a particular marital or family status. The Directive does not apply to executive pension plans (qv), to schemes where an employer is providing for only one employee, or to options available under a pension scheme (thus for example the extent to which men and women may exchange pension rights for immediate cash payments on retirement may differ).

pension schemes for controlling directors, taxation of. The rule contained in the 1970 Finance Act that income tax relief of up to 15 per cent of earnings is available to directors contributing to a self-adminsitered pension scheme (qv).

pensionable earnings. The level of remuneration which determines a retired worker's occupational pension (e.g. his or her final salary (qv)). Pensionable earnings may differ from take home pay in consequence of excluding such items as overtime, commissions, bonuses, etc.

pensioner trustee. A person or organisation approved by the Superannuation Funds Office to ensure, in his or her capacity as trustee of a self-administered occupational pension sheme (qv), that if the scheme is wound up then its assets are distributed to members in the form of deferred pensions payable from the normal date of retirement. The pensioneer trustee is jointly and severally liable (qv) for the debts of the trust along with other trustees.

pensioner's rights premium. An additional payment into SERPS (qv) made by an employee or his or her employing organisation when the occupational pension scheme to which he or she belongs ceases to be contracted out of the state system. In return SERPS will take over the obligation to pay that person the guaranteed minimum pension (qv) specified in the previous scheme.

Pensions Ombudsman. A person appointed by the government under the Social Security Act 1990 to arbitrate in disputes concerning allegations of injustice or malpractice in occupational pension schemes (qv). The Ombudsman is empowered to impose his or her decision.

perceiver personality type. In the Jungian Typology (qv), someone who can see all sides of a problem and is flexible in his or her approach. However, such individuals may be reluctant to commit themselves and prone not to finish tasks.

perception. The process through which an individual interprets sensory inputs such as sight, sound, smell, taste, feelings of being hot or cold, etc.

perceptual defence. The process of blocking out disturbing information from conscious perception (qv).

per diem. A daily allowance.

performance appraisal. The analysis of an employee's recent successes and failures at work and/or the assessment of that person's suitability for promotion or training. *See* PERFORMANCE REVIEW; BEHAVIOUR EXPECTATION SCALES, (BEHAVIOURALLY ANCHORED RATING SCALES); POTENTIAL REVIEW.

performance-based assessment. Assessment (qv) of a trainee's knowledge, skills and competence while undertaking actual work activities. *See* KNOWLEDGE-BASED ASSESSMENT.

performance criteria. A definition of the expected level of performance for an element of competence (qv). Criteria are described in terms of 'outcomes' (i.e. what must be *achieved*) rather than the process of learning.

performance-related training. The development of competencies that directly assist job holders achieve their immediate objectives. Training is specifically related to performance requirements.

performance review. An analysis of an employee's activities over the previous six months or year undertaken in order to find ways of improving his or her performance. The review will investigate the appraisee's personal strengths and weaknesses, critical incidents (qv), reasons behind successes and failures and the barriers that might have prevented better performance.

performance standards. *See* STANDARDS OF PERFORMANCE.

Performers' Protection Acts 1958–1972. A statute giving legal protection to performers against other persons making unauthorised recordings of their work. Under the Act, original performances are protected for 50 years from the date of their occurrence.

period of disqualification. A period during which a pregnant employee is not entitled to receive statutory sick pay (qv). It runs from the eleventh week before the date of the woman's expected confinement to the actual date of confinement. *See* MATERNITY PAY.

period of entitlement. A period within which an employee can claim (but is not necessarily entitled to receive) statutory sick pay (qv). Periods begin with the onset of the sickness and end when the employee becomes fit for work (provided this happens within 28 weeks), or when the employee leaves or resigns, or when a pregnant employee reaches her period of disqualification (qv).

period of incapacity for work (PIW). Four or more days' incapacity for work, whether or not the employee would have been required to work had he or she been well. Workers who are ill for a PIW are entitled to receive statutory sick pay (qv).

peripheral workers. Part time or casual employees hired and fired according to the organisation's immediate short term needs. *See* CORE WORKERS.

permanent health insurance (PHI). *See* LONG TERM DISABILITY COVER.

permanent position. A term used to describe a full time (usually pensionable job). It does *not* mean the occupant has lifelong job security.

Perrow, Charles. An industrial sociologist who in 1970 published an influential study of technical systems, categorising technologies into two classes: (i) those involving routine, predictable and familiar tasks; and (ii) those in which problems are diverse, unpredictable and will not have been previously experienced. According to Perrow the distinction is important because it affects employee motivation, the extent of the division within an organisation, degree of centralisation, management methods and leadership style.

person specification. A pen portrait of the ideal occupant of a particular job, specifying that (theoretical) person's background, training, experience, personality and other characteristics. The specification might detail the mental disposition needed for the work, appearance requirements, special abilities (leadership or the capacity to cope with stress for example), and so on. Person specifications are used for employee selection (qv) in order to evaluate candidates against this hypothetical ideal applicant.

personal effectiveness. Dimensions of occupational competence determined by personal attributes rather than job knowledge. Examples are maturity, self-confidence, initiative and interpersonal skills (qv).

personal pension scheme. A pension scheme administered (usually) by a large insurance company rather than an employing organisation and not linked to any particular employer. Personal Pension Schemes are portable between employers and can be maintained even when the employee is not working. Holders of schemes approved by the Occupational Pensions Board (qv) may contract out of SERPS (qv).

personal preference schedule. A personality test which presents the candidate with a number of statements itemising alternative modes of response to various situations. Respondents express their most and least desired ways of behaving. The same technique is sometimes used to measure personal values.

personal space. The psychological distance that a person wishes to maintain between him or her self and other people.

personality. The totality of an individual's attitudes, perspectives, beliefs, values, dispositions and motives, mental and other personal characteristics. These factors may be biologically or environmentally based, or arise from the interaction of environmental and biological variables.

personality, Freudian theory of. The suggestion by the psychologist Sigmund Freud (qv) that personality is the consequence of a mixture of early childhood experiences and instinctual drives. According to Freud, an individual's personality emerges from a three-cornered struggle between the 'id' (a mass of impulses lacking any direction or control), the influence of the outside environment, and the 'superego' (or 'conscience' as it could be loosely termed).

personality sub-systems. The various mental states said to co-exist within an individual (ego states (qv) for example).

personality tests. Selection tests which seek to identify in applicants personality traits such as introversion, extroversion, assertiveness, ability to cope with stress, etc. See MYERS–BRIGGS TYPE INDICATOR.

personnel audit. A comprehensive review of a firm's personnel policies and procedures; including the costs of recruitment, the effectiveness of training and management development and succession programmes, health and safety policies, grievance procedures, etc.

personnel management. That part of human resources management (qv) concerned with staffing the enterprise, meeting the needs of people at work and the practical rules and procedures governing relationships between employees and the organisation.

persuadability. See CONFORMITY.

PERT. See PROGRAM EVALUATION REVIEW TECHNIQUE.

PEST analysis. Systematic examination of the political, economic, social, technical and similar factors in the environments in which a business operates.

Peter principle. The idea that since individuals are often promoted in consequence of successes achieved in their current jobs they will rise through the ranks of an organisation until they eventually occupy a position in which they are useless. They then cease being promoted and stay in those positions indefinitely as incompetent employees.

Peters , Tom J., and Waterman. R. H. Influential management consultants whose writings in the 1980s challenged the usefulness of traditional line (qv) and staff (qv) organisation systems and western industry's lack of concern for customer care. They asserted that effective corporate leadership requires (i) the creation of an appropriate organisational culture (qv), (ii) the motivation of employees through managers' direct and personal involvement in subordinates' work and (iii) the incorporation of customer care considerations into all aspects of company planning and control. See MANAGEMENT BY WALKING AROUND.

Petra programme. A European Community action programme intended to improve the vocational training of young people and prepare them for working life.

phenomenology. An approach to human behaviour which asserts that observed conduct cannot be straightforwardly explained through scientific analysis. It assumes that people are basically unpredictable and subjective and that each individual is motivated by a unique set of complex factors. This contradicts behaviourist (qv) and rationalist (qv) views on the subject.

PH1. *See* LONG TERM DISABILITY COVER.

Phillips curve. A hypothesised inverse relationship between the level of unemployment and the rate of change of money wage rates. This implies the existence of a trade off between the rate of wage increase and unemployment. It is named after the economist A. W. Phillips, who published a highly influential article on the subject in 1958. The Phillips curve has not predicted the level of UK unemployment at all well since the 1960s.

Philosophy, Organisation, Information, Strategy and Efficiency (POISE) model. A framework for analysing business strategy and operations which begins with the drafting of a mission statement (qv), followed by environmental scanning (qv) and SWOT analysis (qv). It focuses on the critical examination of business systems, especially the firm's management information, procurement, research, organisational development (qv) and marketing systems.

phobic reaction. A form of neurotic behaviour (qv) involving an irrational fear of a normally harmless object or event.

physiological psychology. That branch of psychology (qv) which deals with the relationship between mind and body, e.g. the physiological consequences of stress (qv) at work.

picketing. Attempts by strikers (qv) to persuade fellow workers not to enter their places of employment. Picketing is only lawful when undertaken by persons in contemplation or furtherance of a trade dispute (qv), although an outside trade union official may join in the picket providing he or she is representing union members lawfully involved in the dispute. It must be peaceful and intended merely to communicate information to non-striking workers. Under the Employment Act 1988 (qv) trade unions lose their immunity from actions for civil damages if they picket a firm that refuses to enforce a closed shop (qv).

picketing, Code of Practice on. A Code of Practice (qv) produced in 1980 by the Secretary of State for Employment which recommended that the number of pickets be restricted to six at each entrance and that the union responsible for the picket consult and co-operate with the police. It also required that pickets not interfere with emergency or other local essential services. The Code is not law, but is used by Courts and Industrial Tribunals (qv) as a guide to what *should* have happened in particular cases.

PICKUP. *See* PROFESSIONAL, INDUSTRIAL AND COMMERCIAL UPDATING.

piece-price system. A sub-contracting system whereby a contractor, who does not supervise work undertaken, supplies raw materials to other people or businesses and pays these sub-contractors for each piece of finished output produced to an acceptable level of quality.

piece rate wages. Employee remuneration based on the number of units of output the worker produces rather than the time spent on the job.

pilferage. Theft of goods during transit.

plaint note. A legal document in which the plaintiff in a Court case sets out his or her cause of action against the defendant.

planned maintenance. The practice of servicing or replacing equipment at regular predetermined intervals rather than waiting for equipment to fail. This should pre-empt production difficulties resulting from unexpected breakdowns.

planning permission. Authorisation to operate a business that every firm must obtain from its local authority. An application for planning permission must include details of the existing and proposed use of the business's premises, how many people the firm will employ and their working hours, the movement of vehicles to and from the premises and the parking space available, plus information on waste disposal methods and requirements for storing any hazardous materials.

plans. Predetermined responses to anticipated future events; as opposed to forecasts, i.e. predictions of future situations, and objectives, which are statements of things that need to be achieved for the organisation to fulfil its mission (qv). Plans convert into tactics (qv) and hence into operational activities.

plant and equipment. Fixed assets (qv) employed within a business. 'Plant' is physically immovable; 'equipment' may be shifted from place to place.

plant bargaining. *See* LOCAL COLLECTIVE BARGAINING (WORKPLACE AGREEMENTS).

plant register. A detailed catalogue of the origin, cost, date of purchase, location and operating difficulties experienced with each item of a company's plant (qv).

plant utilisation budget. The budget (qv) that controls details of the planned costs of operating various categories of plant and equipment (qv).

plateauee. A manager whose career development has ceased and is content to operate competently for a long period at his or her present level. Plateauees typically adopt low profiles within organisations. They experience a limited amount of job satisfaction and are not subject to excessive stress (qv).

playboy Directive. A European Commission Directive (qv) granting the right of residency in any Community state to persons of independent means.

pluralism. An approach to decision making (especially in industrial relations) which asserts that the best way to achieve consensus and the long term acceptance of agreements is to recognise that parties to a negotiation necessarily possess conflicting interests and differing attitudes and views.

PMT system. *See* PREDETERMINED MOTION TIME SYSTEM.

Pneumoconiosis, Byssinosis ad Miscellaneous Diseases Benefit Scheme 1983. A DHSS scheme introduced to provide disablement benefit (qv) to workers affected by slowly developing diseases (qv) caused by employment prior to 5 July 1948, and who did not qualify for compensation under any other legislation.

Pneumoconiosis, etc. (Workers' Compensation) Acts 1979–1991. Legislation providing for lump sum payments from the state Social Security Fund to victims of slowly developing industrial diseases who received no compensation from their employers and whose employers subsequently went out of business.

PODSCORB. The acronym for the basic management functions of planning, organising, directing, staffing, co-ordinating, reporting and budgeting.

POEU. Acronym of the Post Office Engineering Union.

points system. A technique of analytical job evaluation (qv) whereby management (i) lists a set of factors deemed relevant to all the jobs that are to be evaluated and (ii) allocates a points value to each factor identified in each evaluated job. The more demanding the job relative to a particular factor the more points are awarded for that factor in that job. Examples of factors are numerical ability, dexterity, supervision of others, responsibility for equipment, extent of decision taking or the amount of training required.

POISE. *See* PHILOSOPHY, ORGANISATION, INFORMATION, STRATEGY AND EFFICIENCY MODEL.

poisonous substances regulations. Regulations specified in the Factories Act 1961 (qv) which prohibit employees from taking meals in rooms containing poisonous substances or where dust or fumes have been generated by lead or arsenic. The firm must provide alternative rooms for workers to take their meals and/or have rest periods. *See* CONTROL OF SUBSTANCES HAZARDOUS TO HEALTH REGULATIONS 1989.

poka-yoke. A Japanese mistake proofing (qv) technique which designs operative's jobs in such a way that it is near impossible for them to take incorrect actions.

Police Act 1919. Legislation forbidding police officers from joining any union other than the Police Federation and prohibiting the latter from organising strikes.

political funds. According to the Trade Union Act 1913, funds used for contributions to a political party or payment of its expenses, for the provision of services or property for the party's use, payments to holders of political office, or the production of any publicity materials intended to promote the interests of a party or candidate. The Trade Union Act 1984 (qv) widened the definition of the political activities on which a union can spend money, and required that its members be balloted every ten years to approve the continuing existence of a political fund. The latter must consist solely of sums given by members for this purpose (other union finances cannot be transferred into the political fund). Members who do not wish to contribute to a political fund cannot be compelled to do so. Complaints regarding these matters are dealt with by the Certification Officer (qv).

political power of a business. The ability of a large corporation to influence public opinion, politicians and senior civil servants, and to gain access to other powerful representatives of community groups. Such power typically results from the company's role as a major employer of labour and its contributions to national exports.

politics, organisational. Negotiations (qv) and settlements within organisations made necessary by the existence of contrasting interests and the differing perceptions (qv) of various organisation members. Political activities lead to compromises, toleration and a stability of relationships which enable the organisation to survive.

polycentrism. *See* ETHNOCENTRISM.

polygraphy. Use of lie detector machines for employee selection. Its purpose is to detect deception through measuring the test subject's psychophysiological responses to a set of questions. This is done by comparing physiological responses to 'relevant' items (i.e. those under discussion) and 'control' questions that have the same arousal potential but bear no relationship to the matters being investigated.

polyvalence. The desirable property of certain types of training that the competencies acquired are useful in several occupations, thus avoiding the need for occupational specialisation too early in a person's career.

portable pension. A pension with rights that can be transferred between different employing organisations.

Porter, L. W. and Lawler, E. E. Motivation (qv) theorists who sought to explain the nature of the relationship between effort and performance. Effort is said to depend on (i) the extent to which the rewards from an activity are likely to satisfy the individual's needs for security, esteem, independence and personal development and (ii) the individual's expectation that effort will lead to such rewards. Hence, the higher the probability that the reward depends on the exertion of effort the greater the effort a person will devote to an activity.

Porter, M. E. Influential American academic who developed a theory of competitive strategy, which he defines as 'the art of relating a company to its economic environment'. Porter uses economic and statistical analysis to derive general conclusions regarding competitive behaviour. In 1990 Porter extended his work to cover the competitive advantages obtained by entire nations, arguing that product and process innovation is today the primary determinant of competitive gain, rather than cheap labour or other cost considerations.

Position Analysis Questionnaire. A standard questionnaire used to gather information in job analysis (qv) studies. It asks questions on 187 job elements organised into six categories: information input, mental processes, work output, relationships with colleagues, job context and 'other relevant characteristics' (speed of work for example). The questionnaire cannot normally be used for managerial or professional jobs.

positive discrimination. Actions intended to favour a racial group or one of the sexes in order to redress a racial or sexual imbalance within an organisation, e.g. giving special access to training, or encouraging members of a certain race or sex to apply for work or promotion. This is permitted under equal opportunity legislation provided the favoured group was seriously under-represented in the group over the previous 12 months.

positivism. An approach to social analysis which asserts that the only knowledge which is truly genuine is that which is discovered via scientific observation, rather than through imagination or conjecture. Logical positivism is a derivative of this view, insisting that the only valid statements are those derived from systematic analysis and which can be verified through empirical observation and testing.

post-contractual statement. A declaration by an employer or a worker intended to alter the terms and conditions of the employee's contract of employment (qv) *after* the contract has been agreed. Such a statement has no legal validity unless both parties have previously undertaken to honour it. A written contract sent to a worker after a verbal offer of employment and which alters the terms of the verbal offer does *not* supersede the verbal offer, which remains binding.

post-industrial society. A term used to describe the social situation arising from the replacement of most manual labour by machines and robotics (qv) and the development of the service sector as the major provider of income and jobs.

potential review. An analysis of an employee's capacity to undertake higher level and more demanding work and an assessment of the speed at which he or she is capable of advancing. Individuals are advised of their prospects and what they must do to enhance their career prospects. *See* PETER PRINCIPLE.

poverty trap. The situation that arises when an unemployed person becomes financially worse off through taking a low paid job, losing in consequence a variety of state benefits only available to the unwaged.

power. An individual's or group's ability to initiate activity or to change the attitudes or behaviour of other people. This differs from authority (qv) in that a person need not be appointed by management to a position of command in order to exercise power. Appointed leaders *might* be powerful as well as occupying positions of authority. Equally, however, an official leader might not possess real power. Determinants of power include a person's ability to reward or punish others, personal charisma, capacity to satisfy group needs, control over information and resources, possession of expert knowledge and the extent to which group members identify with the values of the powerful person.

power of attorney. Legal authority to act on behalf of another person. This must be documented and signed by the individual granting the power.

power strategy. In organisational development (qv), the deliberate involvement of all the influential people within an organisation in the implementation of change. This contrasts with an engineering strategy (qv), and with an 'economic strategy' whereby management attempts to 'buy' the acceptance of change by rewarding various interest groups.

practical jokes by employees, liability for damage. The vicarious liability (qv) of an employer for damages caused by a worker fooling around or playing a joke on another employee in circumstances where (i) the joker's conduct is related to his or her job or (ii) previous potentially dangerous incidents have been reported but ignored.

pre-contractual statement. An express oral or written statement made by an employer or an employee concerning the precise terms of a proposed contract of employment (qv) but made prior to the formation of the contract. Examples are statements made during job interviews or in letters of appointment or other correspondence between the parties. Such statements form an integral part of the eventual contract and may not be altered without the consent of both sides. *See* POST-CONTRACTUAL STATEMENT.

Predetermined Motion Time (PMT) system. A motion study (qv) scheme based on the supposition that since the body movements of different people are essentially similar then the task completion times of various people should be approximately equal. It assumes that every job can be broken down into a series of standard movements for which known completion times have already been computed. Then the times that ought to be spent on each element are aggregated to give a standard time (qv) for the entire job. This was supposed to avoid the need for subjective work study rating (qv) of employees' efforts. *See* METHODS TIME MEASUREMENT.

predictive validity. The desirable property of a selection test that there exists a significant correlation between candidates' performance in the test and subsequent levels of ability in the job for which they were tested.

pregnant employees, Draft EC Directive on the protection of. A 1990 EC proposal that would oblige employers to adapt – without loss of pay – a pregnant woman's hours, duties and working conditions to ensure her health and safety. Pregnant employees normally engaged on night work would have to be given alternative day jobs for a 16-week period, of which eight weeks would have to be prior to the expected date of birth of the child. Fourteen weeks' maternity leave on full pay would be available, with no loss of employment rights (including the right to reinstatement). Two of the weeks would have to be taken immediately before the expected date of birth. Pregnant employees would be protected against dismissal on the grounds of pregnancy, regardless of their lengths of service. The proposal also requires the protection of pregnant women from specific harmful processes or substances.

pre-hearing assessment. A sitting of an Industrial Tribunal (qv) that occurs if, following a superficial examination of the facts of an application, the Tribunal suspects that one party's case is bound to fail. If appropriate, the Tribunal will warn that party that its case seemingly has no foundation in law. If the party receiving the warning wishes to proceed with the case it can do so (before a different Tribunal), but if it loses may be required to pay the costs of the other party to the case.

prejudice in employee selection. Selection procedures based on unreasonable biases that create feeling of dislike and intolerance towards candidates of a particular race, sex, religion, minority group, etc.

preliminary hearing. A sitting of an Industrial Tribunal (qv) to establish whether the Tribunal has authority to hear a case, e.g. if an employer claims that a sacked employee has not completed the period of continuous employment (qv) necessary to claim unfair dismissal (qv).

premium bonus scheme. Another term for differential piecework (qv).

prepotency need theory. The proposition that a person's human needs can be listed in a hierarchy of importance, with the most basic at the bottom and the most sophisticated (self-actualisation (qv) for instance) at the top. According to the theory, an individual's lower level needs take precedence over higher level needs, and that person will not attempt to satisfy the latter until the former have been largely met. *See* MASLOW'S NEED HIERARCHY.

preproduction programming. Work planning, process engineering (qv) and choosing the rate and quantity of production.

pre-selection. Procedures for reducing to manageable dimensions an extremely large number of applications received in response to a job advertisement. Examples are the rejection of all candidates who fail to satisfy preset criteria (possession of a certain educational qualification for instance), or the examination of candidates' vocational interests and/or biodata (qv).

prescribed disease. Any one of about 50 industrial diseases specified by the Department of Health and Social Security as injurious to health. Workers contracting a prescribed disease are automatically entitled to receive industrial injury benefit (qv).

prescribed element. That part of an award made by an Industrial Tribunal (qv) which covers the aggrieved worker's lost earnings. *See* RECOUPMENT OF STATE BENEFITS.

prestige. Status acquired through an individual's personal qualities rather than from his or her appointment to an official position.

pre-vocational education. Measures to inform young people about the world of work before they enter the labour market. It could include formal lectures, visits to firms and short work experience placements. *See* CERTIFICATE OF PRE-VOCATIONAL EDUCATION.

price–earnings ratio. The current market price of a share divided by its earnings during the reported accounting period.

Priestman plan. A group bonus scheme through which each member of a group that exceeds its target is given a wage increase proportional to the magnitude of additional output.

primacy effect. The consequences of allowing first impressions and early information about a subject to influence one's evaluations.

primary group. A group consisting of members who come into direct face-to-face contact with each other. This contrasts with the 'secondary' group in which there is little if any direct contact between members. Examples of primary groups are small departments within a firm, or project teams or committees that meet frequently. Secondary groups might be factories, long assembly lines with little interpersonal contact among operatives or geographical divisions of a firm.

primary labour market. The supply and demand situation relating to workers who possess a specific type of skill that is directly connected with a particular occupation.

primary mental abilities. A set of discrete independent abilities sometimes used to categorise the subjects of intelligence tests (qv). They comprise: spatial ability, numerical ability, memory, inductive reasoning, speed of perception, verbal meaning and verbal fluency.

primary negotiating demands. Demands put to an opponent in a negotiation (qv) and for which no concessions are possible. 'Secondary demands', conversely, are subject to compromise. The choice of which demands are primary and which secondary is subjective, and might alter as negotiations develop.

primary reinforcement. An event that *reinforces* behaviour without any need for prior training.

primary rewards. In classical and operant conditioning (qv), rewards connected with the satisfaction of physiological needs such as food, water, sleep, removal of pain, etc. Such rewards are gratifying in themselves and hence do not require any learning. *See* SECONDARY REWARDS.

primary sector. Sections of the economy concerned with agriculture, forestry and fishing, and the extraction of minerals, oil and other raw materials.

principal. In the context of trade, the person ultimately responsible for fulfilling an obligation, e.g. for goods purchased in the principal's own name, or for the actions of an agent. In the context of investment, the initial sum of money invested.

principal executive committees. The key decision-making bodies of trade unions (qv). Examples are national executive committees, regional/divisional policymaking committees, industry committees, etc. Under the Trade Union Act 1984 (qv), every voting member of a principal executive committee must be elected by the union's membership.

Elections have to occur once every five years at most.

principal limiting factors (principal budget factors). The major constraints that restrict an organisation's activities and hence its ability to spend. Possible principal limiting factors are sales revenue (which normally determines how much money is available to purchase inputs), shortages of labour, scarcities of raw materials or restricted machine capacities. Budget systems are usually constructed by first preparing the budgets most affected by relevant principal limiting factors.

principle of closure. In cognition (qv), the tendency of an individual to fill in gaps in information, perhaps unconsciously. Related concepts are the 'principle of proximity', i.e. mentally grouping things together if they are physically close, and the 'principle of similarity', which is the tendency mentally to group together similar items.

principle of correspondence. The proposition of the classical approach (qv) to management that delegation (qv) of responsibility to subordinates should always be accompanied by the delegation of sufficient authority (qv) to instruct others to perform essential tasks.

principle of supportive relations. A proposition suggested by R. Likert (qv) that a manager should behave in such a manner that subordinates perceive his or her actions as building and maintaining subordinates' feelings of personal importance and worth.

priority based budgeting. An approach to budgeting that deliberately allocates generous amounts of resources to top priority projects, if necessary by cutting expenditures elsewhere.

privileged correspondence. Letters between a solicitor and his or her client, or without prejudice communications (qv). Such documents cannot normally be used as evidence in Court actions.

privity of contract. The principle that the legal effects of a contract are confined to the contracting parties. Thus, for example, a contract of employment between a firm and a worker cannot impose any obligations on the worker's spouse.

proactive inhibition. *See* RETROACTIVE INHIBITION.

probationary employee, dismissal of. Sacking an employee during or on termination of a prespecified trial period. If the dismissed worker has completed the appropriate period of continuous employment (qv) then a claim of unfair dismissal (qv) may be registered. Industrial Tribunals (qv) will expect the employer to have regularly appraised the probationer's work, to have informed the probationer about standards expected and given appropriate help and guidance.

problemistic search theory. The proposition that, typically, managements only begin to look for solutions to new problems when the use of existing precedents and decision-making procedures fail to provide remedies. The search will then seek to discover as quickly as possible the first usable solution that may be conveniently located, rather than the best. For example, a firm confronted by heavy short-term financial losses may simply decide to declare a part of its labour force redundant, without considering wider-ranging possibilities for introducing new products, entering unfamiliar markets, administrative cost cutting, etc.

procedural agreement. An agreement negotiated between management and trade union representatives covering the methods, rules and procedures to be used when settling disputes.

procedural default (dismissal and). Failure to comply with a contractually agreed grievance, disciplinary or appeals procedure when dismissing an employee (qv), or a breach of natural justice (qv). A procedural default may result in a dismissal being unfair (qv). *See* ANY DIFFERENCE RULE.

procedure in Industrial Tribunals. The order in which arguments are put to Industrial Tribunals (qv). First the respondent (qv) (or the applicant (qv) if the case involves alleged sex or race discrimination) presents a brief opening statement. Witnesses are called and examined, are cross-examined by the other party and then questioned by the Tribunal. The process is repeated by the other side. Then both sides sum up. The Tribunal is entitled to alter this order of presentation if it believes this is appropriate.

procedure map. A method study (qv) diagram showing the flow of documents within an organisation and indicating what happens to them at each stage in the flow.

process chart. A diagram showing the sequence of operations involved in a group task.

process consultancy. Consultancy services which seek to create in the client the capacity to solve problems independently by transferring to the client appropriate diagnostic and analytical skills.

process curriculum. A training curriculum designed to equip trainees with the abilities to think for themselves and to cope with constantly changing states of knowledge. Trainees are taught how to develop and structure their own training.

process engineering. Choice of production methods, tools and equipment.

process, factory. According to the Factories Act 1961 (qv), a continuous activity that occurs as a normal ongoing part of a factory (qv) operation, rather than an isolated or *ad hoc* event.

process innovation. Improvements in the way existing methods and procedures are undertaken, as opposed to the invention of completely new methods or products.

process loss. Loss of weight in materials arising from the process of manufacture, rather than from pilferage (qv).

process skills. *See* PRODUCT SKILLS.

process theories. Approaches to the theory of motivation which examine the thought processes that underlie individual motivation to behave in a certain manner.

product portfolio analysis. A technique for deciding which of its products and/or activities a company should retain, develop or discard.

product skills. Competencies that can be measured quantitatively, e.g. the ability to type at 40 words per minute. This differs from 'process skills', which do not possess clearly definable outcomes. Examples of process skills are organisational ability, problem solving, capacity to learn, etc.

production. The conversion of raw materials and/or components into finished items.

production budget. A budget (qv) that details the expected costs of creating the outputs specified in a company's sales forecast.

production line balancing. Allocation of equal amounts of work to each work-station in a production line, so that all stages in the system must process the same number of items at any one time.

production points scheme. A group bonus system based on points relating to the amount of work each member of a group should do in one minute, making allowance for contingencies and relaxation. A proportion of the group's excess of points over standard is paid as bonus.

productive potential of an economy. A country's ability to produce. This de-pends on the quality of the nation's natural resources, plant and equip-ment, financial capital and markets, the skills and aptitudes of its work-force, and how well these factors are combined.

productivity agreement. The outcome to successful productivity bargaining (qv). A productivity agreement will provide for improvements in terms and conditions of employment in exchange for workers altering their working practices in order to increase produc-tivity. Specific changes in work meth-ods and procedures will be detailed, together with the measures to be taken to mitigate their adverse consequences on employees. The circumstances in which the agreement can be revised or terminated will also be outlined.

productivity audit. A comprehensive re-view of a firm's productivity situation in relation to its workers, physical re-sources and operating environments. Resource factors include plant and equipment (qv), capacity utilisation and production planning and control systems. Examples of employee-related factors are incentive schemes, training and supervision arrangements, perfor-mance standards, job design, workers' attitudes (qv), and the overall culture of the enterprise.

productivity bargaining. Negotiations between managements and trade unions through which workers accept significant changes in working meth-ods (particularly the removal of ex-cessive overtime, demarcation (qv) and other restrictive practices) in ex-change for a package of output-related pay rises. *See* PRODUCTIVITY AGREEMENT.

productivity measure. A yardstick against which the efficiency of workers is evaluated. The commonest criteria is output per employee, although other approaches are possible, e.g. value added per direct worker, time saved per job, effort expended while com-pleting duties (e.g. the number of calls made by a salesperson) and so on.

productivity planning. Specification of programmes for work simplification, automation (qv), introduction of robo-tics (qv), improvement of scheduling (qv) procedures, materials require-ments planning (qv) and the introduc-tion of advanced manufacturing methods.

profession. A line of work, the mastery of which requires several years of seri-ous study. Practitioners of the profes-sion take a genuine pride in their activities and feel loyalty towards the profession as well as to employing or-ganisations. The knowledge obtained during training for the profession should distinguish practitioners from others working in the same field.

professional body. An organisation that seeks (i) to maintain or improve its members' occupational status and (ii) to enhance members' standards of performance through the provision of training and a system of certification, usually (but not always) involving examinations.

professional bureaucracy. An organisa-tion that depends heavily on the con-tributions of professionally qualified workers and which is structured to meet the special requirements of the professional employee, e.g. by having decentralised administration and pro-fessional support units with their own clerical/administrative staff.

professional indemnity. Insurance taken out by businesses that provide profes-sional services (accountants or man-agement consultants for example) to protect them against claims arising from inaccurate or negligent advice being given to customers and causing the latter to incur financial loss.

Professional, Industrial and Commercial Updating (PICKUP). A government training scheme launched in 1982 that involves the design of tailor made in-plant and open or distance learning packages, short courses and other training programmes intended to update the skills of UK workers. PICKUP itself does not pay directly for courses. Rather, it encourages and organises the provision of suitable programmes in colleges, polytechnics and universities.

profile information. Data extracted from employee records to enable a company to define the main characteristics of typical incumbents of various types of job. Examples are age and sex distributions of workers in certain occupations, levels of educational attainment, etc.

profile of a trainee. A report containing information on a variety of attributes and characteristics possessed by a trainee, rather than a grade for an assessment (qv). Profiles are a means for recording information about people; not methods of assessment or grading.

profit and loss account. The account in which a business computes its net profit (qv).

profit-related pay, taxation of. The rule introduced in the 1987 Finance Act that half the proportion of an employee's pay that moves up or down in line with the employing company's profits is free of tax, up to a ceiling value. To qualify for relief the employer's profit-related pay scheme must be registered with the Inland Revenue.

profit volume chart. A diagram that relates changes in the volume of a firm's output to changes in its profits.

profitability analysis. Use of key indices to measure a business's profitability. Indices commonly used include the rate of return on capital employed (qv), earnings per share, profit per unit of sales, and the ratios of profits to fixed assets and to working capital (qv).

Program Evaluation and Review Technique (PERT). A technique of network analysis (qv) used where the durations of the major activities necessary to complete a project are uncertain.

programme budgeting. An approach to the budgeting of large, expensive and complex projects. The contributions of various activities to a project's overall aims are evaluated and the maximum and minimum cost of each activity assessed. Individuals and sections are then held accountable for achieving carefully defined targets within preset budget constraints.

programmed decisions. Decisions taken automatically according to a predetermined criterion, e.g. the decision to place an order to replenish the firm's stock of a certain item whenever some specified minimum inventory level is reached.

programmed learning. A training technique whereby the trainee is presented with instructional material in small units (called 'frames') immediately followed by a list of questions that have to be answered prior to moving on to more difficult assignments. The questions are an integral part of the scheme and designed in such a way that it is not possible to complete the programme without answering them.

progress chaser. An employee whose sole task is to check on work in progress, identify bottlenecks and co-ordinate activities at the shop floor level to ensure that jobs are finished on time.

progressive bonus scheme. See RE-GRESSIVE BONUS SYSTEM.

prohibition notice. An order issued by a Health and Safety Executive (qv) or other government inspector compelling a firm to cease a dangerous activity. Appeals against such notices are heard by Industrial Tribunals (qv), and normally assert that it is 'not reasonably practicable' to comply with the notice, i.e. that the risk of injury is minimal whereas the costs necessitated by the notice are extremely high.

prohibition signs. See SAFETY SIGNS REGULATIONS 1980.

project management, requirements of. The special skills needed for successful completion of self-contained projects. Such competencies include: co-ordination, motivation, planning and scheduling tasks, determining priorities, crisis management, setting targets, resource allocation, plus a knowledge of tendering procedures and the legal aspects of contracts.

projection. An ego defence mechanism (qv) which causes an individual unconsciously to attribute to another person a characteristic which in fact is possessed by the individual concerned. For example, someone who feels extremely aggressive in consequence of neurotic anxiety (qv) may (wrongly) perceive the presence of aggression in someone else.

projective sensitivity. A person's ability to identify accurately other people with feelings, emotional reactions, attitudes and perceptions similar to his or her own.

projective tests. Personality (qv) tests which supposedly require candidates to reveal their personalities by describing what particular shapes or objects mean to them. *See* RORSCHACH INK-BLOT TEST.

promotion depression. Depression (qv) sometimes experienced by recently promoted managers in consequence of being treated with excessive deference by subordinates or feeling excluded from social interactions among subordinates and of becoming the target of subordinates' resentments (and perhaps jokes).

promotion veto shop. A closed shop (qv) arrangement in which an employee's promotion to a higher grade depends on the length of the period that he or she has been a member of a certain union.

promotive interdependence. A stimulus to co-operation within a group whereby group members' destinies are so intertwined that they can only achieve their objectives through acting in unison.

proper job evaluation. An analytical job evaluation (qv) acceptable to an Industrial Tribunal (qv) as having been thorough in analysis, impartial, not sexually or racially discriminatory, and having taken into account all important factors. To be 'proper', the evaluation must be 'consistent', i.e. not undertaken casually by different people at different times.

protean career. According to D. T. Hall, a career pattern determined entirely by an individual and not by his or her employing organisations. The person involved deliberately alters career direction as his or her circumstances alter (having a child for example).

protected pension rights. Certain benefits in a private occupational pension scheme which by law must be at least equal to those available under SERPS (qv).

Protection of eyes regulations 1974. Government regulations which obliged employers to supply suitable goggles or eye screens in a wide range of occupations where there is special risk of injury to employees' eyes. The screens or goggles provided must protect the worker's eyes 'effectively' in all 'reasonable circumstances' arising from his or her employment. However, they are not expected to *guarantee* complete safety in all circumstances.

protective award. A payment to an employee threatened with redundancy (qv) whose union has successfully complained to an Industrial Tribunal (qv) that the employer failed to adhere to the consultation requirements of the Employment Protection Act 1975 (qv). The employer is obliged to pay the worker's full wages for a period of between 28 and 90 days, depending on the total number of employees being made redundant.

protective clothing. Helmets, goggles, gloves, overalls, aprons and safety boots necessary to prevent injury to workers. The Health and Safety at Work Act 1974 (qv) requires employers not only to provide necessary protective clothing but also to ensure it is worn.

proxemics. Use of space in communications, e.g. by standing or sitting close to another person.

proximate cause. The direct and immediate cause of an event (an accident for example).

proximity, principle of. *See* PRINCIPLE OF CLOSURE.

psychic income. Feelings of well-being derived from job satisfaction (qv) and/or the status attached to a certain occupation (qv).

psychic prisons, organisations as. A metaphor suggested by G. Morgan as a means for conceptualising a certain type of organisation, namely those managed by people who perceive themselves narrow mindedly and who relate current events to past achievements, operations and values even when the past is not relevant to the demands of the modern world.

psychodiagnostics. The systematic analysis and interpretation of individual personality (qv).

psychodrama. *See* SOCIODRAMA.

psychogenic illness. An illness simultaneously affecting many members of an organisation, seemingly without any identifiable physiological cause. Examples are fainting, rashes, headaches, stomach upsets, etc. Outbreaks tend to occur in businesses with rigid rules and highly structured organisational procedures and where the work done is tiring, boring and repetitious.

psychogroup. A social group characterised by mutual agreement among members, each of whom satisfies other members' social and emotional needs.

psychological contracts. Employees' opinions about how much work they should do and how they should be treated by their employing organisations. *See* WAGE EFFORT BARGAIN.

psychology. The study of human thoughts, behaviour and emotions either in isolation from social contexts or in direct relation to a specific social environment. It seeks to determine the nature of individuals: their needs, motives, personalities, how they learn, how they modify their behaviour, etc. 'Psychiatry' is a specialised branch of psychology which deals with mental disorders. *See* COGNITIVE PSYCHOLOGY; SOCIAL PSYCHOLOGY; PHYSIOLOGICAL PSYCHOLOGY.

psychometric tests. Selection tests that seek to quantify psychological dimensions of job applicants. Examples are tests of intelligence, personality and motivation.

psychomotor skill. A skill (qv) that involves the co-ordination of thought and physical action. Information is organised in the brain and used to initiate appropriate bodily movements.

psychosis of association. Another term for folie a deux (qv).

psycho-social sub-system. Those aspects of an organisation (qv) which determine the modes of interaction between its members. The sub-system is affected by individual perceptions (qv), group dynamics (qv) and roles (qv).

psychosomatic disorders. Illnesses substantially caused by psychological factors. For example, stomach ulcers are frequently ascribed to tension and anxiety (qv) rather than to organic failure.

psychotechnics. Psychological techniques employed to control human behaviour.

psychotherapy. Treatment of disturbed behaviour and anxiety (qv) using nonphysical methods, usually involving counselling (qv).

psychotic behaviour. The actions of a person who has lost contact with reality and who experiences extreme levels of anxiety (qv).

public corporations. State enterprises, the directors of which are appointed by a government Minister.

public duties, time off for. The right under the Employment Protection (Consolidation) Act 1978 (qv) of an employee (qv) to take reasonable amounts of paid time off work to perform duties attached to the occupancy of certain public positions, i.e. magistrates, local authority councillors, members of statutory tribunals and members of education, health and water authorities.

public good. An economic term used to denote anything that benefits the entire community rather than specific individuals within it (clear air for example). Consumption of a public good by one person will not deprive others of its benefits.

public liability insurance. Insurance taken out by employers to protect them against claims by members of the public who allege they have suffered damage in consequence of the firm's actions.

Public Order Act 1986. A statute which (among other things) created the offence of 'causing harassment, alarm or distress' in situations of public disorder, e.g. unlawful picketing (qv). Disorderly behaviour can involve threatening, abusive or insulting words spoken or displayed on banners.

public utilities. Industries supplying basic services to the community, e.g. postal and telecommunications, transport, etc.

purpose organisation. *See* FUNCTIONAL ORGANISATION.

putting out fires. A term sometimes used to describe crisis management (qv).

putting out system. A sub-contracting arrangement whereby a contractor supplies raw materials to an individual or family to process within the home, and then purchases the finished output.

pygmalion effect. The phenomenon that sometimes occurs when a manager is led to believe that a subordinate is of high calibre and expected to do well, and the subordinate does then succeed – mainly in consequence of the manager being a mentor (qv). The subordinate involved might only be of average ability.

pyramid structure. A line (qv) and staff (qv) organisation structure with narrow spans of control (qv), unity of command (qv), unbroken chains of command (qv), and many levels of management between the top and bottom of the enterprise.

Q

Q-data. Information about an individual's personality (qv), obtained via a self-evaluation report.

QPMI. *See* QUALITY PERFORMANCE MEASUREMENT INDICES.

qualified acceptance. Acceptance of a contract subject to the fulfilment of a stated condition before the contract takes effect.

qualifying day. A day for which an incapacitated employee is entitled to receive statutory sick pay (qv). Normally a qualifying day is a day the employee would have worked if he or she had not been ill (including a weekend day if this is standard trade practice). *See* PERIOD OF INCAPACITY FOR WORK.

quality assurance standards. Procedures applied within a company in order to assure customers that certain prespecified minimum quality requirements are being met, e.g. that only materials of a particular type and quality are used in manufacture or that only properly trained and certificated workers are employed on a job.

quality circle. An employee discussion group, usually comprising production operatives under the guidance of a specially trained group leader. Circles meet periodically to consider, analyse and resolve quality and production control difficulties.

quality management. A holistic approach to quality issues which regards inspection and quality control (sampling, adherence to machining tolerances, probability calculations, etc.) not as independent functions but as integral and inseparable components of the *total* production system, intimately connected with all other aspects of work.

quality of working life (QWL). The totality of human satisfaction at work. Determinants of QWL include working conditions, the extent of employee participation in decision making, interpersonal and intergroup relations, and the culture of the organisation in which the individual is employed.

quality performance measurement indices (QPMIs). Quality performance standards established following a quality improvement programme. Indices can be constructed to identify operator inadequacy, management inadequacy and environmental problems that cause low quality output.

quality versus acceptability of decisions. The conflict that sometimes arises between the *quality* of a decision in terms of its use of objective facts, expert knowledge and/or sophisticated decision-making systems: and its *acceptability* to the people who must carry it out. Acceptable decisions tend to be those which satisfy subordinates' needs and generate positive rewards for interested parties.

QUANGO. *See* QUASI-AUTONOMOUS GOVERNMENTAL ORGANISATION.

quantum meruit damages. In breach of contract cases, damages payable when someone is prevented from completing his or her side of a bargain by the behaviour or repudiation of the contract by the other side. Suppose for example that an employee has completed a great deal of work for which he or she has not been paid. The claim in this case would be 'for so much as is deserved' for the work undertaken.

Quasi-Autonomous Governmental Organisation (QUANGO). An organisation set up and financed by the government but nominally capable of taking its own decisions. Examples include ACAS (qv) and the NCVQ (qv).

quasi-resolution of conflict model. A theory of managerial behaviour which asserts that managements typically seek to appease the conflicting demands of the various stakeholders (qv) in an organisation through making partial concessions to each of them, rather than conceding totally to some stakeholders but not at all to others.

queuing, psychological. A process by which the brain deals with information overload (qv) through storing items in a memory bank and processing them sequentially and in an orderly fashion.

quid pro quo. In a negotiation (qv), a reciprocal concession traded off in return for something given by the other side.

quittance. Legal discharge from an obligation (a debt for instance).

quorum. The minimum number of persons that must be present at a meeting before it can take decisions.

quoted (listed) companies. Public limited companies recognised by the Stock Exchange and having shares that are traded on its main market.

R

R phrase. A statement attached to the container of a hazardous substance (qv) warning that its contents are potentially harmful, e.g. the phrase 'Toxic by Inhalation'. *See* S - PHRASE.

race norming. Adjustment of the scores obtained from psychometric tests (qv) to take account of the (well-established) fact that certain ethnic groups consistently under-perform in such tests. Similar alterations can be imposed to accommodate social class considerations.

Race Relations Act 1976. A statute which outlaws unfair racial discrimination in recruitment and employment. Exemptions to the Act are similar to those which apply to the Sex Discrimination Act 1975 (qv).

Race Relations Employment Advisory Service. A branch of the Department of Employment established to advise and assist employers on the implementation of non-racially discriminatory employment policies.

racial discrimination. According to the United Nations, discrimination against persons via their exclusion, restriction or lack of preference in consequence of their race, colour, descent, or national or ethnic origin.

racism and xenophobia, EC declaration concerning. A joint declaration signed by the European Parliament, the Council of Ministers (qv) and the European Commission (qv) in 1986 to condemn racist sentiments and activities directed against non-EC nationals. It committed the Community to combat racism and xenophobia through the provision of information and education.

RADAR. The acronym for the Royal Society for Disability and Rehabilitation.

range statements. Specifications of the activities, processes, equipment and contexts to which NVQ elements of competence (qv) and performance standards (qv) apply.

ranking system. A non-analytical (qv) method of job evaluation (qv) in which management makes an overall assessment of each job taking into account all aspects of its duties. The method does not attempt to evaluate the individual demands of a position. A number of benchmark jobs (qv) are then identified at various points towards the top, middle and bottom of the job hierarchy. Each 'whole' job is compared against the benchmarks and slotted into the hierarchy at an appropriate level.

RAP. *See* RESEARCH ACTION PROGRAMME.

RAT. *See* ROLE ANALYSIS TECHNIQUE.

rate fixer. The person responsible for negotiating with shop stewards (qv) and for fixing wage rates per unit of output in a piece rate (qv) system.

ratification of a pay deal. The process whereby a wage agreement negotiated by national union officers is put to the union's membership for approval. Typically, the decision to accept or reject the deal is taken at the branch (qv) level of the union.

rating standard. A yardstick against which operatives' work effort may be assessed. The International Labour Office (qv) has published a commonly used standard based on a performance level of 100 to indicate brisk activity by an average experienced worker paid under a piece rate (qv) system and ranging from level 50 for slow and clumsy work to a maximum 150 for outstanding performance requiring intense effort and concentration. *See* STANDARD PERFORMANCE.

ratio analysis. Comparison of key ratios indicating a company's performance and profitability over time. Normal values for each ratio are established and acceptable deviations specified. Management by exception (qv) may then be applied.

ratio decidendi (reason for decision). A statement of the principles of law that a judge has applied to the legal problems raised by the facts of a particular case.

ratio delay study. *See* ACTIVITY SAMPLING.

rating, work study. A subjective assessment of the effort an operative puts into work. Normal working speed is rated at level 100 on the rating standard (qv) of the International Labour Office (qv). Ratings on workers suspected of going slow are adjusted downwards. *See* BASIC TIME.

rational decision making. A model which defines the steps a decision maker *ought* to follow when making rational decisions. The latter are decisions which achieve objectives as efficiently as possible in the context of the environment in which they are taken. Seven steps are involved: (i) identification of the problem; (ii) setting objectives; (iii) searching for alternative solutions; (iv) evaluating alternatives; (v) selecting a solution; (vi) implementation; and (vii) appraising the effectiveness of the solution chosen.

rational – emotional therapy. A training method intended to help people restructure their cognitions (qv). It presupposes that individuals disturb themselves by their own irrational beliefs, so that it is necessary to teach them how to think logically and objectively about certain issues. The technique has been used to assist the long-term unemployed to alter attitudes and self images which inhibit them from attempting to re-enter the workforce. *See* DISCOURAGED WORKER HYPOTHESIS.

rational expectations hypothesis. *See* ADAPTIVE EXPECTATIONS HYPOTHESIS.

rational legal authority. A term coined by sociologist Max Weber (qv) to describe the authority (qv) to control others granted to certain officeholders in a bureaucracy (qv). It involves the right of an officeholder to issue official directives and to impose sanctions based on the rules and procedures of the organisation.

rationalisation. Streamlining an organisation or function through eliminating redundant and duplicated activities, standardisation (qv) and variety reduction, and the rearrangement of resources to minimise waste. Fringe activities

with little growth potential will be removed. *See* REDUNDANCY.

rationalisation, psychological. An ego defence mechanism (qv) through which an individual mentally justifies an improper action about which he or she experiences guilty feelings.

rationalism. An approach to social analysis which regards individual behaviour as the outcome to logical thought and objective reasoning (rather than the consequence of past experience).

Raven's progressive matrices. Intelligence tests that present candidates with sets of patterns that have a piece missing from each pattern. The candidate must then select from a set of alternatives the pieces that fill the gaps. This is intended to measure an individual's speed of perception and response.

RCN. *See* ROYAL COLLEGE OF NURSES.

reaction formation. A Freudian ego defence mechanism (qv) whereby some individuals cope with emotions which are unacceptable to their conscious minds by expressing their commitment to the exact opposite. For example, an anti-pornography campaigner might, according to Freudian theory, simply be expressing his or her hidden sexual impulses.

real wage. The actual purchasing power of an employee's wage, i.e. money wages minus the current rate of inflation. An increase in the real wage means that prices rise by less than the increase in money wages received in a given period.

reality shock. Feelings of distress and personal inadequacy experienced by recently promoted individuals when confronted with large amounts of unpleasant work and numerous problems attached to their new positions.

reasonable behaviour, requirements for fair dismissal. The obligation imposed on employers by the Employment Protection (Consolidation) Act 1978 (qv) to behave in a reasonable manner before dismissing employees. Rules of natural justice (qv) must be applied, written warnings should be issued and the employee given help and sufficient time to remedy deficiencies.

reasonable care, obligations of employers. The common law requirement that employers take reasonable care not to subject their employees to unnecessary risk. This duty is personal and cannot be delegated to others. Failure to exercise reasonable care gives rise to the tort (qv) of negligence. In deciding whether an employer has exercised reasonable care a Court will consider whether the firm properly assessed (i) the likelihood of injury to its workers, (ii) the potential seriousness of accidents resulting from dangerous machines or processes and (iii) all the information available concerning the potential hazard. *See* INHERENT RISK.

reasonable management obligation. The implied contractual duty of an employer to behave reasonably and responsibly towards employees. Arbitrary and inconsiderate action can amount to a breach of a contract of employment.

reasonable skill and care, duty to exercise. The common law obligation of employees not to be unduly negligent and to be reasonably competent when performing their duties. Workers who fail to exercise reasonable skill and care may be regarded as having broken their contracts of employment (qv).

receiver. A person or organisation appointed by a Court to assume responsibility for the financial affairs of another person or organisation (the receiver of a bankrupt (qv) person for example).

recency effect. The opposite of a primacy effect (qv). It occurs when subsequent information has a stronger influence on cognitions, attitudes and perceptions than first impressions.

receptor processes. The means by which individuals sense cues and stimuli from the outside world. *See* PSYCHOMOTOR SKILL.

reciprocal determinism. A social theory which asserts that although a person's environment greatly affects his or her behaviour, the individual can equally influence and change the environment in which he or she exists.

reciprocal National Insurance agreements. Social Security agreements between the UK and certain other countries (including all EC and EFTA countries, Australia, New Zealand and

the United States) which protect entitlements to benefits and ensure equality of treatment for individuals who move from one country to another.

reckonable years. For state National Insurance retirement and widow's benefit purposes, a year in which at least 50 weekly Class I, II or III National Insurance (qv) contributions have been paid or credited to a person's account.

recognised trade union. An independent trade union (qv) with which an employing firm has at some time or other negotiated on *any* matter, which does not have to involve pay and conditions of employment.

recognition agreement. A document setting out the procedures to be followed in management/union relations within a firm. It will specify which agreements must be recorded formally and in writing; the duties and obligations of shop stewards (qv); the matters that shall be subject to negotiation; and rules concerning the channeling of grievances and the settlement of industrial disputes (qv).

recognition of craft and commercial competencies, EC Directives concerning. Systems for recognising the right to exercise certain craft and commercial occupations throughout the European Community. Individual workers must demonstrate that they have performed relevant work in a Community country for a set period of time. Details are contained in a series of Directives (qv) covering such occupations as hairdressing, forestry, various retail and wholesale activities, tax advisers, travel agents, etc.

recognition of trade unions, rule concerning. The consequence of the Employment Act 1980 (qv), that an employer's recognition of a union is purely voluntary and cannot be imposed through the law. This reversed the (complex) recognition provisions of the Employment Protection Act 1975 (qv) whereby a firm could have a union imposed upon it against its will.

recognition strategies. Management policies for dealing with claims for recognition by trade unions (qv). Initially, the firm might grant partial recognition (e.g. by allowing union officials to represent workers at grievance or disciplinary interviews while refusing to negotiate with the union over pay and conditions) and then gradually extend the range of topics discussed with the union until full collective bargaining (qv) is established.

record of achievement. A document issued to a school leaver that itemises his or her achievements and progress both within and outside the classroom, including achievements not tested by examinations.

recoupment of state benefits. Deductions of unemployment benefit and income support (qv) from the prescribed element (qv) of an Industrial Tribunal's (qv) award of compensation to an aggrieved worker.

recruitment. The administrative processes attached to staffing an enterprise; including the preparation of job (qv) and person specifications (qv), drafting job advertisements, selecting media to carry job advertisements, assessing appropriate salary levels for new employees, writing to candidates to invite them to attend interviews, etc. *See* SELECTION.

red circling. The practice in job evaluation (qv) of continuing to pay current salary levels to individuals whose jobs have been graded into lower wage categories, but paying a reduced wage rate to people who eventually take over these jobs.

Reddin, William. A leadership (qv) theorist who suggested the existence of four distinct management styles. The 'related' manager was defined as one who spends much time listening and talking to subordinates. 'Separated' managers prefer operating through formal rules. 'Dedicated' managers are task orientated and primarily concerned with productivity. 'Integrated' managers devote equal attention to personal relationships and to the needs of work. Each style is said to be appropriate for certain situations, but should not be universally applied.

reduced earnings allowance. A special disablement benefit (qv), payable in respect of certain accidents which occurred before 1 October 1990 and which resulted in the injured person not being able to follow his or her regular occupation, or one with equivalent earnings.

reductionism. In social analysis, the resolution of complex issues into simple constituent parts. It is sometimes used as a term of abuse against researchers who oversimplify complicated problems.

redundancy. A dismissal situation in which the firm's requirements for the employee to carry out work of a particular kind has ceased or diminished or is expected to do so. Employees covered by the Employment Protection (Consolidation) Act 1978 (qv) who are given notice of redundancy are entitled to (i) paid time off work to look for another job and (ii) a redundancy payment (qv).

redundancy, legal rights of trade unions. Legal rights conferred by the Employment Protection Act 1975 (qv) on recognised independent trade unions whereby employers must consult union representatives about proposed redundancies. Consultation must begin at least 30 days prior to the planned redundancy of between ten and 99 employees, or 90 days if 100 or more employees are to lose their jobs. Management must give reasons for the intended redundancies, specify selection criteria, and take into account union proposals for avoiding redundancies, giving reasons for rejecting these proposals where appropriate. *See* NOTIFICATION OF PLANNED REDUNDANCIES.

redundancy payments. Lump sum payments which firms are legally obliged to make to redundant employees who have completed at least two years' continuous service with the employing company. The worker receives one and a half week's pay for each year of employment (up to a maximum of 20 years) in which he or she was over 40 years of age, one week's pay for each year of service between 22 and 40, and half a week's pay for each year between 18 and 21. Redundancy payments are not taxable.

redundancy, presumption of. The explicit statement of the Employment Protection (Consolidation) Act 1978 (qv) that Courts will assume that dismissed employees are redundant (qv) (and thus entitled to redunancy payments (qv)) unless the employer can demonstrate that the dismissal was actually for another reason.

redundancy, relevant date of. For statutory purposes either the end of the employee's period of contractual or statutory notice, or if no notice need be given the date the termination takes effect. In the case of non-renewal of a fixed-term contract the date of redundancy is the day the contract expires.

redundancy rights, temporary protection of. The right under the Employment Protection (Consolidation) Act 1978 (qv) of a redundant worker to spend up to four weeks (or longer if a written agreement so provides) in an alternative job offered by the employer before deciding whether to accept it, without forfeiting his or her right to a redundancy payment if the alternative job turns out to be unsuitable.

redundancy, selection criteria for. Legal rules concerning an organisation's choice of the workers it makes redundant. These rules are contained in the Employment Protection Act 1975 (qv) and subsequent test cases, and must be 'fair and objective'. Among the fair criteria that could be applied are length of service, age, capability, qualifications, experience, past conduct and suitability for alternative employment.

re-engagement. A remedy for unfair dismissal (qv) through which the sacked worker is re-employed, but not in his or her previous job.

referee. Someone nominated by a job applicant to comment on his or her character, aptitude and general suitability for the vacant job.

reference. A statement provided by someone nominated by a job applicant to attest the latter's honesty, reliability and/or competence to undertake the duties attached to the vacant position.

reference group. An informal group against which an individual evaluates his or her beliefs, feelings, perceptions and behaviour. People use reference groups to justify their actions and to legitimise their attitudes.

reference, negligent. A carelessly written reference issued by an employer which misleads another employer about a worker's capabilities and which causes the new employer consequential loss.

Such references give rise to civil liability. If the negligent reference is defamatory the ex-employee may sue for compensation. However, liability for defamation does not arise provided defamatory comments were made 'in good faith'.

referent power. A person's power (qv) over a group resulting from his or her charisma, reputation and other personal qualities. A manager possessing referent power can inspire admiration and allegiance among subordinates.

reflation. Economic expansion resulting from government economic policies such as reduced taxes or interest rates or increased public spending.

reflexive conditioning. Another term for classical conditioning (qv).

reflexive response. In classical conditioning (qv), a response caused by the autonomic nervous system (qv).

Regional Development Grant. A cash subsidy once paid as of right to manufacturing firms investing in specified depressed areas. It was introduced by the Industry Act of 1972 and ran until 1988, when it was abolished and replaced by a system of discretionary subsidies.

Regional Employment Premium. A government subsidy once paid to all manufacturing businesses located in specified depressed areas. It operated between 1967 and 1976 and was based on the number of a firm's employees, with different amounts being paid for males, females and young people. The subsidy violated European Community rules on free competition and thus had to be abolished.

registered disabled person. Someone who is physically handicapped in consequence of injury, disease or congenital deformity and is registered as such with the Secretary of State for employment. In order to register the applicant must be certified as unable to undertake work for which he or she would be suited and qualified were it not for the disability. Firms requiring lift or car park attendants may only employ registered disabled people for these jobs, unless a special permit has been obtained from the Secretary of State for employment.

Registrar of Occupational and Personal Pension Schemes. A person appointed by the government under the 1990 Social Security Act to maintain a register of occupational and personal pension schemes in order that individuals may conveniently trace past preserved pension rights. Trustees of pension schemes are legally obliged to provide full details of them to the Registrar.

regression. A consequence of frustration (qv) or neurotic anxiety (qv) whereby the individual abandons all constructive attempts at solving problems and instead behaves in a childish way (e.g kicking a motor car because it will not start).

regressive bonus system. A wage incentive scheme in which bonus earnings increase by proportionately less than increases in performance. This contrasts with a 'progressive' system whereby bonuses increase relatively faster than efficiency improvements.

Regulations of the European Community. Laws imposed by the European Community that apply immediately and equally in all member states in the precise form in which they are specified. See DIRECTIVES, EUROPEAN COMMUNITY.

Rehabilitation of Offenders Act 1974. An Act of Parliament which determined that a job applicant with a criminal record does not have to reveal his or her criminal background to potential employers, provided the person has a spent conviction (qv). The Act does not apply to certain occupations, e.g. prison officers, lawyers or people who work with children.

reinforcement. Rewards (positive reinforcement) and punishments (negative reinforcement) that motivate people to behave in certain ways. See OPERANT CONDITIONING.

reinforcement contingencies. Relationships between behaviour and its reinforcing consequences, of which there are five major types: (i) *positive*, in which correct behaviour is followed by a reward; (ii) *negative*, whereby incorrect behaviour leads to an aversive stimulus (i.e. punishment); (iii) *escape*, whereby incorrect behaviour leads to an aversive stimulus that only ends when the incorrect behaviour is terminated; (iv) *avoidance*, in which punishment occurs unless the person actively attempts to mitigate adverse conse-

quences (e.g. getting wet after failing to take an umbrella on a journey on a rainy day); and (v) *extinction*, whereby correct behaviour has no identifiable consequences, so that it is eventually abandoned (for instance, a manager who continually ignores good work done by a subordinate, leading to loss of enthusiasm and lack of effort on the latter's part).

reinstatement. A remedy for unfair dismissal (qv) whereby the employer must treat the worker as if he or she had not been dismissed in the first instance. This requires that the firm make up to the worker any back pay, wage increases that should have been given, holiday entitlements or other benefits lost through the dismissal.

reinstatement following the birth of a child. The right conferred by the Employment Protection (Consolidation) Act 1978 (qv) on a female employee who has completed more than two years continuous employment (qv) (five years if she has worked between eight and 16 hours a week) to return to work up to 29 weeks after her confinement and to be reinstated in her old or an equivalent job. The woman must give notice of her intention to return. This notice must be in writing and submitted at least 21 days before taking maternity leave. If the employer writes to the employee within seven weeks of her confinement asking for confirmation of her intention to return to work she must reply within 14 days. The woman can resume work any time up to 29 weeks after the birth (with a possible four-week extension on medical grounds) provided she gives at least 21 days' notice of the date of her return. To qualify for the right to reinstatement the woman needs to have been continuously employed for at least two (five) years immediately prior to the eleventh week before the expected date of confinement. The right to reinstatement does not apply, however, if the woman's employing firm employed five or less workers (including the woman herself) when the woman took maternity leave and it is not reasonably practicable for the firm to re-engage the worker. This exemption is allowed under the Employment Act 1980 (qv).

relational database. A database (qv) with a facility for relating one file with others, e.g. employees' names and addresses might be related to the amounts of sick leave taken by each worker, bonus payments, etc. Searches of the database occur across several fields simultaneously.

relations analysis. A technique recommended by Peter Drucker for determining the best form of organisational structure for an enterprise. Key relations between managers at all levels within the organisation are identified and examined. These relationships may differ markedly from those indicated on a formal organisation chart (qv).

relationship chart (cross chart). A diagram showing patterns of inter-departmental movements of physical output within a firm's premises. The information gathered is used to plan the physical layout of production lines and plant and equipment (qv).

relationship orientated leader. According to F. E. Fiedler, a manager who recognises favourable characteristics in all his or her subordinates, even the subordinates with whom he or she least prefers working. See LEAST PREFERRED COWORKER (LPC) SCALE.

relative deprivation. Awareness by an individual that he or she is disadvantaged compared to others in the same category. This can lead to a collapse of morale and lack of effort.

relativism. The proposition that knowledge, beliefs and concepts (of right and wrong for instance) possess meaning only in the context of an individual's particular situation, so that it is not possible to define genuinely objective standards. Hence opinions and consequent decisions depend on personal circumstances, experience and the culture in which a person exists. 'Naive relativism' is the idea that since opinions are personal, their value can only be assessed against personal standards, i.e. that an individual is likely naively to assume that it is only his or her own opinion that has any importance.

relaxation allowance. An addition to the estimated time required by an operative to complete a task in order to allow the worker to recover from fatigue. Clerical work normally attracts an allowance of 15 per cent; heavy manual work is usually given 20 per cent.

reliable selection test. A selection test that provides consistent results when repeated on different groups of people. Thus, similar proportions of each sample of individuals should fall within certain score categories.

reliability of assessment. The extent to which assessment (qv) within a training programme is consistent over time and among assessors. Differences in grades awarded to trainees on different intakes to the programme should represent variations in participants' abilities rather than differences caused by the assessment process itself.

Relocation Agents, Association of. A national trade organisation formed to represent the interests of relocation agencies active in the industrial, commercial and private sectors. It publishes a code of practice (qv) and an annual directory of members.

relocation consultants. Human resources management consultants who assume responsibility for all the human problems resulting from a firm relocating its premises. They aim to ensure that the business runs smoothly immediately prior to the move, during it and in the subsequent settling down period. Services provided include property search, staff and union consultation, redundancy planning (including outplacement (qv) counselling), liaison with local authorities, removal of equipment and employees; and helping the latter to find suitable housing, new schools for children, jobs for spouses, etc.

remote damage. A loss or injury suffered by a worker in consequence of an employer's actions where the relationship between cause and effect is not 'reasonably foreseeable'. This is important in the law of negligence (qv) in that damages are only payable if an injury was caused by a direct breach of duty by the defendant. There has to be an identifiable chain of causation and no *novus actus interveniens* (new act intervening) that breaks the chain.

removal expenses. See FRINGE BENEFITS.

remuneration consultant. A personnel management consultant who specialises in the estimation of wage levels necessary to attract and retain good quality staff, in devising incentive schemes, assessing the tax efficiency of various remuneration systems and the implementation of salary structures.

remuneration policies. Employee reward systems which seek (i) to attract, retain and motivate high calibre workers and (ii) to provide attractive incentives for greater effort among employees.

repertory grid. A checklist of the key activities and modes of behaviour necessary for effective performance in a particular job. See KELLY'S REPERTORY GRID.

repetitive strain injury (RSI). Upper limb disorders (e.g. cramp, tenosynovitis, diffuse pain) resulting from prolonged work at a keyboard.

REPLAN. A government training programme intended to develop learning opportunities for unemployed adults. It is delivered by local education authorities, by the National Institute of Adult Continuing Education (NIACE) and by the Further Education Unit (FEU) of the Department of Education and Science. The FEU devises curricula for courses. NIACE has eight REPLAN field officers who liaise with local authorities to create training programmes for the unemployed.

reportable accident. Any accident resulting in death or which leads to an employee's absence from work of more than three days. Such accidents must be reported to the inspectorate of the Health and Safety Executive. 'Dangerous occurrences' which cause an interruption to work of 24 hours or more or are caused by the ignition of gas, vapour or celluloid substances are also reportable.

Reporting of Injuries, etc., Regulations 1985. Legally binding government regulations which compel employers to report to their local authority environmental health department all accidents that involve an employee being absent from work for three or more days. Accident report forms must be kept for at least three years. Self-employed people and trainees receiving instruction on a firm's premises are also covered by the regulations.

representational rights, granting of. An agreement between a management and a trade union or staff association whereby the trade union (qv) or staff association (qv) may represent employees in grievance and disciplinary procedures, may offer advice and suggestions, but cannot engage in collective bargaining (qv) over pay and other terms and conditions. Unions with representational rights automatically become recognised trade unions (qv). Typically the granting of representational rights is the first stage in a company's union recognition strategy (qv).

repression. An ego defence mechanism (qv) through which a person forces into his or her unconscious mind thoughts or memories of events the individual does not wish to accept ever happened.

repudiatory breach. A fundamental breach of a contract of employment whereby one of the parties to the contract indicates an unwillingness to abide by agreed terms and conditions. Examples are workers going on strike or firms cutting employees' wages. The injured party is entitled to withdraw from the contract.

Research Action Programme. An EC-funded scheme established to provide training support for transnational partnerships or business co-operation within the Community.

research and development (R&D). Acquisition of technical knowledge about products, processes, materials and working methods and the application of this knowledge to the solution of practical production problems.

reservation of title clause. A term in a contract of sale whereby the supplier retains ownership of goods delivered to customers until the goods have been fully paid for. If the customer defaults, having resold the items to third parties, the supplier may reclaim the goods from these third parties.

Reserve Forces (Safeguard of Employment) Act 1985. Legislation intended to guarantee the reinstatement in their previous jobs of reservists called up for military service. However, the employer need not pay wages or provide for the accrual of holiday entitlement during the worker's absence. Application for reinstatement must occur in writing within six weeks of the reservist's discharge, or as soon as possible thereafter if he or she is ill. On return, the reservist has the right not to be dismissed until the expiry of up to 52 weeks, the precise period depending on the length of military service.

resignation. A consequence of frustration (qv) that causes an individual to adopt apathetic attitudes and abandon all attempts at adapting to and coping with changed circumstances. An example is the unemployed person who after a long period of unemployment stays in bed most of the day instead of looking for work.

resignation while under notice of redundancy. An application by an employee under notice of redundancy to leave the firm without working out his or her notice. If the employer rejects the request and the worker still leaves early the employer can only claim damages through a special action in an Industrial Tribunal (qv), which will examine the reasonableness of the employer wanting the worker to stay on and why the latter wishes to leave early.

resource consultancy. Consultancy services which focus on the transfer of information from the consultant to the client in order to increase the latter's knowledge of a situation. *See* PROCESS CONSULTANCY.

respondent. The employer who defends an action in an Industrial Tribunal (qv). *See* PROCEDURE IN INDUSTRIAL TRIBUNALS.

respondent behaviour. Behaviour exhibited during classical conditioning (qv) whereby a stimulus automatically triggers a physical response, e.g. fear, excitement, hunger, sexual arousal, etc. *See* OPERANT BEHAVIOUR.

respondent conditioning. Another term for classical conditioning (qv).

response bias. A problem that sometimes arises in employee attitude and job satisfaction surveys whereby the people questioned tend to answer 'yes' to all questions or 'no' to all questions, regardless of the questions' contents. All the subject's responses are biased in the same direction.

responsibility accounting. Establishment of 'responsibility centres' akin to cost centres (qv) or profit centres within an organisation. The manager of each centre is held responsible for achieving preset objectives, controlling costs and explaining deviations of actual from target occurrences. *See* MANAGEMENT BY EXCEPTION.

responsibility, principle of. The proposition of the classical approach (qv) to management theory that a manager who delegates work to a subordinate should retain ultimate responsibility for its successful completion.

restart interviews. Counselling interviews given under the employment training (ET) (qv) scheme to people who have been unemployed for more than six months and are about to enter the ET programme.

restrictive covenant. A clause in an employee's contract of employment (qv) which seeks to prevent the employee (i) setting up in opposition to the employer, (ii) from making use of trade secrets or information acquired during the course of employment or (iii) otherwise damaging the employer's interests. Such covenants are only enforceable if they are reasonable in the interests of the parties and of the general public and do not prevent competition unduly. *See* OBJECTIVE KNOWLEDGE.

restrictive labour practices. Rules and working practices that lead to overmanning and/or the limitation of production in order to prevent redundancies or create jobs. *See* DEMARCATION DISPUTES.

restrictive trade practices. Arrangements between businesses that are intended to restrict competition and/or prevent the entry of new firms to a market or industry.

retail employees. According to the Wages Act 1986 (qv) anyone involved in the sale and supply of goods and services. This covers shop assistants plus any employee handling cash transactions with customers: bus conductors, milk deliverers, booking office clerks, bank counter staff, etc. *See* DEDUCTIONS FROM WAGES, LAWFUL.

Retail Prices Index (RPI). A measure of inflation compiled from a large sample of observations on price movements of goods and services entering a typical shopping basket. It is revised periodically to keep up with changes in the average pattern of consumer expenditure. The RPI is frequently used as a point of comparison in wage negotiations. *See* IMPLIED DEFLATOR FOR CONSUMERS' EXPENDITURE.

retained benefits. Retirement, death in service, or other benefits accumulated with an earlier employer under an occupational pension scheme and either carried forward into a new scheme or frozen until death or the age of retirement.

retainer. An annual fee paid to a professional adviser (a lawyer or firm of management consultants for example) which guarantee their immediate availability whenever the need arises.

retirement, avoidance of sex discrimination relating to. The legal requirement from 7 November 1987 that employers not impose different retirement ages for men and women or demote or dismiss a woman for reasons connected with retirement when a comparable male employee would not have been treated in this way.

retirement syndrome. A generic term covering all the psychological and physiological difficulties that some people experience after they retire. Symptoms include disorientation, apathy, failing physical health, financial problems and deteriorating social relationships.

retroactive inhibition. A problem that sometimes arises during employee training whereby the learning of new skills and/or information interferes with an individual's ability to use things he or she has previously learned. The opposite is 'proactive inhibition', where things learned in the past interfere with the capacity to learn new competencies (a two-finger typist learning to touch type for instance).

retrospective introspection. A counselling (qv) technique in which the counsellee is asked to recall his or her feelings in a past situation.

return on assets managed. The rate of financial return on the capital employed (qv) within a division, subsidiary or department.

revealing question. An interview question which indicates the preferences of the questionner, e.g. 'I like watching tennis, don't you?'

reverse buy out. A procedure whereby a private or unquoted public limited company takes over a quoted (qv) limited company and then itself becomes an integral part of the quoted firm.

reverse discrimination. *See* POSITIVE DISCRIMINATION.

reverse Oedipus complex. Middle aged managers' obsessive fears and resentments of managers younger than themselves whom they regard as presenting a threat to their status and security. The problem is especially severe when the younger managers have skills and knowledge of new management techniques that their supervisors do not possess. This envy of younger managers might then cause the older executives to seek to disrupt their young subordinates' careers.

revisionist school of organisational behaviour. An offshoot of the human relations approach (qv) to management. It is particularly critical of bureaucracies (qv) and pyramid (qv) organisation structures, alleging that bureaucracies cannot satisfy fundamental human needs and that flat organisations (qv) are generally superior to tall hierarchies.

reward power. Power (qv) derived from a manager's ability to reward subordinates, e.g. through giving pay rises, promotions, interesting work, opportunities for overtime, etc.

reward review. A periodic salary assessment to determine the extent (if any) of the increase in an employee's pay. Such reviews should normally occur *after* a performance appraisal (qv), and not at the same time. Otherwise, financial considerations may dominate an appraisal interview, at the expense of finding new ways to improve performance. Also, market forces can influence pay levels independent of the quality of individual performance.

rhocrematics. The study of the flow of production from the origin of raw materials through to their conversion into products and delivery to final consumers.

RICC. The acronym for the Retail Industry Capability Certificate.

RIDDO Regulations. *See* REPORTING OF INJURIES, ETC., REGULATIONS 1985.

right to manage clause. A clause inserted in a procedural agreement (qv) at management's insistence and stating that although management will endeavour to accommodate employee representatives' wishes, management reserves the ultimate right to implement changes without reference to the procedure. In a sense this is the opposite of a status quo agreement (qv).

ringi seido. A Japanese term for employee participation and bottom up management.

risk shift. The phenomenon observed within organisations that individuals are sometimes more ready to take risky decisions when acting as a member of a group than when taking decisions in isolation.

ROAM. *See* RETURN ON ASSETS MANAGED.

Robens Report. The report of a 1972 committee of enquiry into the causes and consequences of accidents at work. A major conclusion of the report was that workplace trade union representatives should be directly involved, via safety representatives (qv), in the enforcement of health and safety measures. The report led to the Health and Safety at Work Act 1974 (qv).

Robin Hood syndrome. A possible cause of theft (qv). The thief experiences a compelling desire to punish better-off colleagues by stealing from them. Other reasons for theft include hatred of an employing institution, low wages (inducing certain workers to 'top up' their incomes by stealing from the firm); the exhilaration that some people feel while committing crimes; and the potential for opportunistic theft (qv).

robotics. Use of reprogramable computers in automated machines to enable them to complete multiple functions such as grasping, lifting, machining, moving about, clearing up, etc.

role. A total and self contained pattern of behaviour typical of a person who occupies a particular social position. Role theory concerns how individuals behave, how they feel they ought to behave, and how they believe other people should respond to their actions.

role ambiguity. Feelings of uncertainty that arise when a person's role is not adequately defined. Role ambiguity causes stress (qv), insecurity and loss of self-confidence.

role analysis technique (RAT). An approach to organisational development (qv) that focuses on the precise definition of the roles (qv) and responsibilities of key workers, particularly their abilities to implement activity, approve or veto the actions of others, provide resources or control information.

role bargaining. An individual's attempt to redefine the boundaries of his or her role in consequence of not being able to fulfil all its obligations.

role categorisation. A form of stereotyping (qv) whereby an individual places into mental categories people undertaking various occupations. For example, a person might assume that all supervisors will behave in an authoritarian manner, regardless of their backgrounds or other personal circumstances. Such categorisations simplify interpersonal relationships because it is no longer necessary to analyse every situation the individual encounters. Rather, the person *assumes* that a certain mode of behaviour is to be expected from the other party and uses this preassumption to guide his or her reactions.

role conflict (role strain). The situation that occurs when an individual does not behave in accordance with the role expectations (qv) attached to a social position because to do so would impose too great a strain on that person. A personnel manager for example may be required to resist a union pay claim on behalf of the employing organisation, despite sympathising fundamentally with the employees' situation. Role conflict can lead to feelings of personal inadequacy, guilt and embarrassment. *See* ROLE BARGAINING.

role differentiation. The processes whereby the number of indepen-dent roles (qv) within an organisation increases and the roles themselves become more specialised.

role expectations. Standards and norms (qv) of conduct that the occupant of a role and others believe proper for holders for that position. For instance, the chief executive of a large organisation may be expected to speak and dress in a certain manner.

role modelling. The situation that occurs when a person behaves in a role (qv) in exactly the same way as he or she has observed other people behaving in a similar role. For example, managers sometimes treat their subordinates in a manner analogous to how they themselves are treated by their own superiors – who act as role models for the managers concerned.

role overload. The consequence of an individual not being able to cope with several roles (qv) simultaneously. This contrasts with 'role underload', which occurs when a person's employing organisation fails to require that person to fulfil as many roles as he or she can actually manage. Role underload leads to frustration (qv) and reduced performance.

role perception. A feeling concerning what constitutes correct behaviour in a certain role (qv).

role playing. A group training (qv) technique that requires each participant to act the part of a character in a certain business situation. Often, the character played is that of someone occupying a role opposite to the real life position of the participant. For example, a personnel manager might play the role of a trade union officer.

role set. All the people with whom an individual interacts in consequence of occupying a particular role. These other people are called the 'role partners' of the person concerned, who is referred to as the 'focal person' of the relationship.

roles of the personnel manager. *See* SERVICE ROLE; ADVISORY ROLE; FUNCTIONAL AUTHORITY.

rolling budget. A method for determining annual budgets whereby the amount allocated for the next 12 months is set at an amount just equal to actual expenditure over the last 12 months, updated on a month-by-month basis.

Rookes v. Barnard 1964. An important test case concerning the closed shop (qv). An employee (Rookes) was sacked for resigning from a trade union in a firm that operated a 100 per cent closed shop. Rookes sued some of the union's shop stewards (qv) and officials for damages. He succeeded on the grounds that union pressure on the employer to dismiss Rookes amounted to intimidation (qv)

and hence was not covered by the Trade Disputes Act 1906 (qv). The decision in Rookes v. Barnard was reversed by the 1965 Trade Disputes Act.

Rorschach ink-blot test. A projective technique for measuring personality. The subject is shown a series of figures (each made by folding a page over an ink blot) and then asked to state what they represent to that person. Figures are deliberately non-representational and roughly symmetrical. The test has proven useful for identifying people with severe mental disorders, but not for differentiating between psychologically 'normal' respondents.

ROSPA. *See* ROYAL SOCIETY FOR THE PREVENTION OF ACCIDENTS.

Rowan system. A wage incentive scheme introduced by James Rowan in the 1890s whereby bonuses accrue to workers who complete tasks in less time than expected. The system is progressive in that proportionally higher wages are offered as efficiency increases. *See* HALSEY SCHEME.

Royal College of Nurses (RCN). A certified trade union (qv) representing nurses and a professional body (qv) in its own right. It was founded in 1916, becoming a trade union in 1977.

Royal Society for the Prevention of Accidents (ROSPA). An organisation providing information and education on accident prevention. It publishes a monthly bulletin and arranges national safety campaigns.

Royal Society of Arts. An examining body offering qualifications in vocational subjects, notably in secretarial studies, clerical work and retail distribution.

RPI. *See* RETAIL PRICES INDEX.

RSA. *See* ROYAL SOCIETY OF ARTS.

Rucker plan. An added value (qv) group incentive scheme, popular in the 1950s, which gave collective bonuses according to the extent to which a firm's sales revenue exceeded the costs of raw materials and all other inputs during a certain period.

rudeness by employees. A reason for fair dismissal provided it amounts to an unambiguous rejection of the employer's authority. Whether such rejection has occurred depends on the words used although a single outburst would not normally justify dismissal. Employees may be fairly dismissed if they are rude to customers, so long as a proper disciplinary procedure is followed.

Rule 11. *See* TUC RULEBOOK.

rulebook. A pamphlet given to employees or a written statement pinned to a notice board explaining a firm's disciplinary procedures, rules and working methods. A rule book only forms part of a worker's contract of employment (qv) if this has been explicitly or implicitly agreed by the employee. Implicit agreement could follow from adherence to a certain set of rules which are well-established trade custom and practice in a particular industry.

Rural Development Commission Business Service. A government agency with 31 regional offices providing skills training to small businesses in rural areas. Courses are designed in such a way that they only take people away from their jobs for a short period.

S

S factor. *See* TWO FACTOR THEORY OF IN-
TELLIGENCE.

S phrase. A statement attached to the
container of a hazardous substance
(qv) indicating that its contents are
potentially harmful, and advising on
the precautions that need to be taken,
e.g. the phrase 'Avoid Contact with the
Skin!'. *See* R PHRASE.

safe conditions signs. *See* SAFETY SIGNS
REGULATIONS 1980.

**safe fellow employees, employer's obliga-
tion to provide.** The common law
duty of an employing organisation to
ensure that an employee's workmates
have the ability, knowledge and training necessary to complete their work
safely. This obligation extends to the
selection of persons who are to act as
company safety officers. Such individuals must be qualified and reasonably
capable of meeting the requirements
of the job.

safety committees. Bodies convened
under the Health and Safety at Work
Act 1974 (qv) to consider businesses'
health and safety policies and to investigate specific health and safety matters. A committee must be established
following the written request of any
two of a firm's safety representatives
(qv). The Health and Safety Commission (qv) recommends that safety
committees possess direct executive
authority and consist of equal numbers of management and trade union
representatives.

**Safety Equipment Distributors' Associ-
ation.** An organisation formed to
make representations to the Health
and Safety Executive (qv) and the British Standards Institution on behalf of
the safety equipment production industry. It maintains a list of approved
manufacturers of health and safety
equipment.

safety officer. A manager responsible
for a firm's health and safety policies.

It is important to distinguish between
safety officers (who represent management) and safety representatives (qv),
who act on behalf of recognised trade
unions (qv). Unlike union safety representatives, safety officers are not protected against criminal liability if they
fail to fulfil their duties.

safety policy, written statement of. A document which the Health and Safety at
Work Act 1974 (qv) requires all employers of five or more workers to draw
up in order to set out the firm's safety
policies, arrangements and procedures. It must itemise accident and
first aid arrangements, fire precautions, notes on hazards and dangerous
substances, safety training provisions,
and has to include a list of the people
responsible for the various aspects of
the firm's safety policies. The Health
and Safety Executive publishes a pro-
forma statement (available from
HMSO) with spaces into which a particular firm's safety policies may be inserted.

safety representatives. Employees selected by a recognised trade union
(qv) to deal with workplace health and
safety matters. Their authority derives
from the Health and Safety at Work
Act 1974 (qv), and are empowered to
conduct investigations into hazards,
accidents and dangerous occurrences.
Also they inspect workplaces and liaise
with external inspectors.

**Safety Representatives and Safety Com-
mittees Regulations 1977.** Detailed
rules concerning the rights and duties
of safety representatives (qv) appointed under the Health and Safety
at Work Act 1974 (qv). The latter enabled recognised unions (qv) to appoint safety representatives, rather
than their being elected by workplace
union members. Under the Regulations, appointed safety representatives
are legally entitled to paid time off to

attend safety training courses approved by the TUC or the safety representative's union. Complaints regarding employers' refusing to grant time off for safety training are heard by Industrial Tribunals (qv).

Safety Representatives, HSC Codes of Practice on. Two Codes of Practice (qv) issued by the Health and Safety Commission (qv) concerning safety representatives (qv) and the information and facilities to be provided to them by employers. The first code recommends that persons appointed as representatives should, if possible, have worked for their firms for at least two years. Representatives should cooperate with employers, take steps to become familiar with legal requirements and potential hazards in their workplaces, and promptly inform employers of any unhealthy or unsafe conditions or working practices. Employers should advise representatives of intended changes in production methods, and regularly update them with accident statistics and news of dangerous incidents. The second Code (entitled 'Time Off for the Training of Safety Representatives') suggests that representatives attend an approved safety training course as soon as possible following appointment, and that the course cover legal requirements and the nature of workplace hazards and possible measures for overcoming them.

safety representatives, TUC Code of Practice on. A voluntary Code of Practice (qv) drafted by the Trades Union Congress (qv) which specifies the facilities and assistance the TUC believes a company should give to safety representatives (qv). Recommended facilities include the use of a desk and filing cabinet, access to a telephone and photocopier, provision of a notice board, plus access to test equipment, relevant statutes, industry regulations, etc.

Safety Signs Regulations 1980. Legislation compelling employers to erect safety signs conforming to prespecified designs. 'Prohibition signs' must be circular with a red cross bar over a white background. 'Warning signs' need to be triangular with black words or symbols over a yellow background.

'Mandatory signs' giving instructions about certain courses of action have white words or symbols over a blue background on a circular sign. 'Safe conditions signs' are square on white words/symbols over a green background.

safety supervisors. Safety officers appointed by management and legally required under the statutory regulations governing certain dangerous industries.

sailing ship effect. The proposition that free and open competition is the primary cause of the implementation of change and the improvement of products and working methods. Advocates of this theory point to the fact that more progress was made in the technology of sailing ships during the 30 years following the introduction of competition from steam than had occurred in the previous five centuries.

SAINTA. The acronym for the Shipbuilding and Allied Industries National Training Association.

salary. Technically, a fixed annual amount, paid to an employee monthly in 12 equal instalments. In practice, however, the term is used interchangeably with 'wages', which used to refer only to weekly cash payments that were subject to fluctuation through overtime, piecework bonuses, etc.

salary administration. The design and maintenance of procedures for (i) determining appropriate salary levels for staff, (ii) establishing salary grades and (iii) deciding how quickly individuals should progress through the system.

salary attrition. See ATTRITION OF SALARY COSTS.

salary clubs. Combinations of employing organisations that collect and exchange information on pay movements in various industries and regions.

salary control systems. Measures for monitoring and constraining a firm's aggregate salary expenditures. Methods include salary surveys (qv), examination of compa-ratios (qv) and measurement of attrition of salary costs (qv).

salary progression curve. See MATURITY CURVE.

salary-related pension scheme. An occupational pension arrangement whereby the value of an individual's retirement pension is defined by a formula that relates to his or her earnings and length of membership of the scheme.

salary sacrifice. An arrangement whereby an employee formally agrees to give up part of his or her salary in favour of an equivalent amount being paid as an additional contribution to an occupational pension scheme.

salary surveys. Research into rates of pay in various industries, types of job and geographical areas, undertaken to enable companies to offer competitive salaries when recruiting new workers.

sale and leaseback. An agreement whereby a business sells its premises to an outsider for a modest price in return for the right to occupy these premises at a low rent for a predetermined period.

Salt, Titus (1803–1876). Philanthropist and owner of the (then) largest textile mill in Europe. Salt advocated the improvement of environmental conditions for workers. He built a model village ('Saltair' near Bradford) alongside his mill, with 850 houses and a wide range of social and cultural amenities. Provision of decent living conditions, Salt argued, would improve workers' morale, reduce absenteeism, encourage punctuality and increase productivity overall.

sandwich course. A vocationally orientated full-time degree and diploma course that combines periods at college with placements in industry. 'Thick' sandwich courses involve a single long period (up to a full year) with an employing organisation; 'thin' sandwich courses contain three or four brief periods of work experience, each lasting two or three months.

Sanitary Accommodation Regulations 1938. Government rules concerning the provision by employers of toilet facilities for employees. There has to be one private and clean water closet for every 25 workers (fewer if more than 100 workers are employed).

sapiential authority. Another term for the authority of a staff manager (qv), i.e. authority based on knowledge and expertise rather than on a line management (qv) position.

satisficing behaviour. Managerial behaviour which seeks to discover straightforward and easily applicable solutions to problems, without attempting to find optimum outcomes. It involves the use of simple 'rules of thumb', recognising thereby the impossibility of analysing huge amounts of complex information and examining every aspect of a complicated issue.

Seveso Directive. A name sometimes applied to the 1982 European Community Directive on measures that firms must implement to prevent industrial accidents. It followed an incident at Seveso in Italy when clouds of dioxin were released from drums being transported without any safety precautions. Under the Directive, manufacturers must inform the authorities of the locations of all substances, plant and machinery that could possibly cause major accidents.

scab. A term of abuse directed against workers who cross union picket (qv) lines.

Scad. *See* CELEX.

scaffolding, regulations concerning. Rules contained in the Construction (Working Places) Regulations 1966 requiring that scaffolding be assembled on safe and firm foundations and strictly perpendicular to the building it covers. All scaffolding work must be undertaken by skilled scaffolders and inspected according to procedures laid down in the Regulations. *See* LADDERS, REGULATIONS CONCERNING.

scalar chain. The hierarchy of managers having superior/subordinate relationships within an organisation (qv).

scalar principle. *See* CHAIN OF COMMAND.

Scanlon plan. A 1950s group incentive scheme which paid collective bonuses according to the value of the difference between a firm's sales revenues and its labour costs. If sales revenues fell, no bonuses were payable even though employees might have worked extremely hard. *See* RUCKER PLAN.

scapegoating. Blaming other people for one's own failures and misfortunes. It is a form of self-justification which enables the individual to cope with lack of success in a career. On the collective level, scapegoating can exert a positive influence through creating external 'enemies', hence increasing group cohesion.

Schedule D tax. Income tax paid by the self employed. It is collected in two instalments in January and July each year.

Schedule E tax. Income tax paid by employees via PAYE (qv).

scheduling of activities. Allocation of start and finish dates to the component jobs of a project, plus the determination of movements of raw material inputs, sub-assemblies, work-in-progress and finished goods between sections and departments.

schema (schemata). Organised patterns of thought and action that regulate a person's interactions with the environments in which he or she operates.

schema, analytical. A collection of definitions relating to a topic plus a series of analytical conclusions derived from the definitions.

schematic models. Decision models based on graphs, charts, rules and algorithms. These differ from 'mathematical models' which present analogues of the numerical relations between variables.

schizophrenic behaviour. Individual behaviour characterised by delusions, thought disorders, inappropriate emotionality and volatile actions.

school of thought. A collection of writers, thinkers and practitioners of a subject who all adhere to the same fundamental principles and doctrines concerning that subject. *See* SCIENTIFIC MANAGEMENT; CLASSICAL APPROACH; HUMAN RELATIONS APPROACH.

SCI. *See* STATUS CHARACTERISTICS INDEX.

science park. An area adjacent to an educational institution and providing low rent office and factory accommodation to firms that wish to make use of the educational institution's research facilities.

scientific management. An approach to management based on the work of F. W. Taylor. It emphasises the division of labour, work measurement, close supervision of operatives, piece rate (qv) wage systems and the careful selection of workers for jobs.

scored biographical data. *See* BIODATA.

SDI. *See* SELECTIVE DISSEMINATED INFORMATION SERVICE.

searching of employees. Examination of workers' clothing, bags and other possessions as they enter or leave an employer's premises. This is lawful only if the employee has previously agreed (explicitly or implicitly) to submit to a search. Otherwise the employer could be held liable for damages for assault and battery and/or breach of contract.

seasonal unemployment. Unemployment resulting from workers being laid off at certain times during the year. The building trade, the catering industry at holiday resorts and tourism are examples of industries prone to seasonal unemployment.

seating for employees, requirement to provide. The rule stated in s.13 of the Offices, Shops and Railway Premises Act 1963 (qv) that shops should provide at least one seat for every three shop assistants, provided sitting down does not interfere with their work.

secondary action. Industrial action (qv) directed against firms not directly involved in an industrial dispute (qv). It is only immune from civil legal liability when taken by (i) employees of suppliers or customers of the firm in dispute *and* when its primary purpose is to prevent or disrupt the supply of goods between the firm in dispute and its suppliers or customers or (ii) employees of an associated company and aimed at preventing the latter from taking over the work of the firm in dispute.

secondary group. *See* PRIMARY GROUP.

secondary picketing. Picketing by workers of a firm not directly involved in an industrial dispute.

secondary relationship. An impersonal and non-intimate relationship with other people.

secondary rewards. In classical (qv) and operant conditioning (qv), rewards connected with such things as social approval, money, recognition, job satisfaction, etc. Secondary rewards are learned and not innate to the individual.

secondary sector. That part of the economy concerned with manufacturing, processing raw materials, construction and energy production.

secondment. A temporary placing of an employee with another organisation or department.

secretarial trap. The situation that occurs when secretaries or personal assistants become so good at their jobs that they are indispensable to their bosses, who then refuse to promote them to higher positions.

Secretary of State for Employment. The Government Minister responsible for matters connected with employment and industrial relations. His or her main functions are (i) to issue, via ACAS (qv), Codes of Practice (qv) on the conduct of employee relations, (ii) to make legally binding regulations on a wide range of employment subjects and (iii) to review government expenditures in the employment field.

Section 21 orders. Annual statements issued under s.21 of the Social Security Pensions Act 1975 specifying the maximum amounts by which guaranteed minimum pensions (qv) and other benefits under contracted-out occupational pension schemes (qv) may be increased. Revaluations are based on an index of national annual earnings.

Section 32 annuity scheme. A device made available under the 1981 Finance Act whereby an employee who leaves an occupational pension scheme well before the age of retirement can still receive retirement benefits. The trustees of the scheme purchase an annuity (qv) in the ex-employee's name, the benefits of which are deferred until the date that he or she *would have* retired from employment.

secured creditors. Creditors with direct claims against a firm's assets, e.g. a bank which makes a loan against the security of a company's land and buildings.

SEDOC system. An EC programme for distributing information about unfilled job vacancies and special employment programmes throughout the Single Market.

seiri, seiton, seiso, seiketsu. The Japanese words for the 'four S's' said to underlie Japanese production philosophy. They stand for arrangement, order, cleaning and neatness, in that order. Cleaning and neatness on the factory floor is assumed essential for the maintenance of the quality of products.

selection. Assessment of candidates for vacant jobs and the choice of the most suitable people. It may involve interviewing, psychometric testing (qv) and the examination of biodata (qv).

selective disseminated information (SDI) service. A procedure whereby a database host (qv) sends to client companies regular printouts of updated information deemed relevant to the client's particular requirements.

self. A term used by certain psychologists to denote the conscious mind (roughly equivalent to the ego (qv) in Freudian analysis).

self-activation. Taking the initiative to control one's own destiny.

self-actualisation, need for. The highest level of need felt by a human being, i.e. to fulfil and extend his or her potential to the maximum.

self-administered pension scheme. An occupational pension scheme in which the trustees are personally and directly responsible for managing the scheme's investments and administration. This differs from an 'insured' pension scheme whereby the trustees pass members' contributions to an insurance company which then manages the scheme's investments. A 'small self-administered scheme' is one in which the directors of a company are the only or predominant members of the scheme and also its trustees. Such schemes (sometimes called 'captive schemes') are subject to special Superannuation Funds Office (qv) regulations.

self assessments. Performance appraisal (qv) reports that require employees to state how they themselves evaluate their own performances, quality of training and supervision received, effects of changes in job content, feasibility of their objectives, personal strengths and weaknesses, etc.

self-certification. *See* MEDICAL CERTIFICATES.

self-efficacy. The extent to which an individual believes he or she can successfully complete certain tasks in any given situation, e.g. a typist's self-confidence of being able to attain a particular typing speed in any office environment.

self-employed person. Someone conducting business on his or her own behalf as a sole trader (qv), rather than as an employee (qv) of an organisation or other person. The self-employed pay Schedule D (qv) income tax and Class II (qv) and Class IV National Insurance (qv) contributions.

self-employed persons, EC rules concerning. Freedoms established by Articles 52 to 66 of the Treaty of Rome (qv) and subsequent Community legislation whereby EC residents may set up businesses and provide services anywhere in the Community. Accordingly, self-employed EC nationals who move between countries are entitled to equal treatment with citizens of the host state, including equal treatment relating to sickness, invalidity, old age and other benefits.

self-employed persons with several sources of self employment, National Insurance and. The rule that a person with more than one source of self-employed income need only pay a single weekly Class II National Insurance contribution (qv).

self-estrangement. Feelings of loss of control over one's work and the environments in which it is undertaken. *See* ALIENATION.

self-fragmentation. Lack of coherence in a person's self-image, possibly resulting in bizarre attempts to re-establish an identity (frantic, ritualistic, but meaningless work activity for instance).

self-identity (self-image). The entire set of perceptions (qv) that an individual has about him or her self, deriving from experiences and personality (qv), and offering the person a means for interpreting his or her social role.

self-managed learning. A training method in which participants are responsible for managing their own learning, for deciding what they need to learn and (in conjunction with a facilitator) for choosing the learning methods appropriate for their requirements.

self-regulation. The situation that exists when an industry forms a quasi-independent body (i) to issue Codes of Practice (qv), (ii) to deal with complaints from the public and (iii) generally to 'police' the activities of firms in the industry. If self-regulation succeeds, governments are normally prepared to allow an industry to operate without legislative state intervention.

self supply. Using goods that have been produced or acquired by a firm for the internal purposes of that firm.

semantics. The science of 'meaning'. A meaning can be transmitted and perceived via gestures, spoken words, written words, symbols, tone of voice, appearance, etc.

semi-display advertisements. Job advertisements which appear in the same columns as linage (qv) advertisements but use a bold typeface to make them stand out on the printed page.

semi-skilled workers. Employees who perform work that requires dexterity, application of limited discretion, and which cannot be undertaken without basic training. However, significant decision making is not involved. *See* CRAFT WORKER; SKILLED WORKERS.

semi-variable cost. A cost of production that is partially fixed and partly variable. An example is the cost of electricity used for lighting a firm's premises which is switched on for longer spells during busy periods.

senser personality type. In the Jungian typology (qv), a person who is practical, patient, careful and systematic. Sensers are attentive to detail, but inclined to lose sight of the overall situation. They prefer concrete and structured tasks to having to work with vague ideas and concepts.

sensitivity analysis. The study of the key assumptions underlying intended actions. These assumptions are systematically altered, and 'what if' questions asked.

sensitivity training. Training intended to change attitudes and perceptions. *See* T-GROUP TRAINING.

sensory deprivation. A cause of boredom at work. It commonly results from monotonous jobs that deprive workers of the stimulations normally experienced in everyday life.

sensory motor activity. An activity that involves (i) the gathering of information via the senses (sight, hearing, etc.) and (ii) responding to the information through body movements.

sentence completion scale. A means for measuring employee motivation (qv) devised by J. Minor. It requires test subjects to complete 35 half finished sentences concerning their motivation to manage others. This motivation is assumed to involve the need to experience power and self-control; but low need for affiliation with colleagues.

sequential interviewing. A selection procedure in which a number of interviewers see a candidate separately one after another, rather than as a board. It is time consuming, but avoids many of the problems created by panel interviews (qv).

sequestration order. A Court order which places the property of a person or organisation (a trade union (qv) for instance) into the hands of a third party (the 'sequestrator') pending some action that has to be taken by the sequestrated organisation, or a successful appeal against the order.

serial learning. Absorption of instructional materials in a strict prespecified order.

SERPS. *See* STATE EARNINGS RELATED PENSION SCHEME.

service role of the personnel manager. That aspect of a personnel manager's work that involves mundane administrative duties such as drafting job advertisements, human resources planning (qv), implementation of the Health and Safety at Work Act, organising grievance procedures, etc. *See* ADVISORY ROLE.

714 Certificate. A document issued by the Inland Revenue to bona fide self-employed building workers, enabling them to claim exemption from the rule contained in the 1971 Finance Act that employers must deduct basic rate income tax, at source, from the wages of all building trade workers. *See* SUBCONTRACTORS IN THE CONSTRUCTION INDUSTRY, RULES ON THE TAXATION OF.

seven point plan. A standard format for conducting employment interviews devised by A. Rodger. Candidates are assessed under seven headings: physical make-up, attainments, general intelligence, specific aptitudes, personal interests, disposition and personal circumstances. *See* FIVE FOLD SYSTEM.

seven-S system. A technique for analysing an organisation's effectiveness under seven headings: strategy, structure, systems, style, staff, skills and shared values.

severance pay. Amounts paid to employees on their leaving a firm or being made redundant. Severance pay typically comprises accrued wages, impingement pay (qv) and other contractual items, plus an *ex gratia* (qv) payment.

Severe Disablement Allowance. State social security benefit paid to disabled people of working age who are unfit for employment but do not have enough National Insurance contributions to qualify for sickness or invalidity benefit.

sex discrimination. Treating an individual less favourably than persons of the opposite sex and/or unjustifiably requiring members of one of the sexes to comply with a rule which results in their receiving unfavourable treatment. *See* INDIRECT DISCRIMINATION.

Sex Discrimination Act 1975. A statute that makes it illegal to discriminate unfairly against either of the sexes or against married persons. Discrimination is forbidden in relation to recruitment, terms and conditions of employment, and access to training and promotion opportunities. There are a number of exceptions to the Act, notably where a person's employment concerns (i) work outside Great Britain, (ii) service in the armed forces, (iii) a religious organisation that operates a sex bar and (iv) duties for which sex is a genuine occupational qualification (qv). *See* INDIRECT DISCRIMINATION; VICTIMISATION.

Sex Discrimination Act 1986. An Act of Parliament that provided for common retirement ages for men and women entering employment from 7 November 1987. Women employed before that date must be allowed to continue working to the male retirement age in the employing organisation if they so wish. Pension ages under company superannuation (qv) schemes were not affected by the Act.

share option scheme. A fringe benefit (qv) established by the 1984 Finance Act under which the employee agrees to a monthly deduction from his or her wages in return for the right to purchase shares in the company at a (low) predetermined price a certain number of years in the future. If the option is not exercised the amount contributed is returned to the worker, plus interest.

shop floor. A factory workplace staffed by manual workers who undertake manufacturing activities.

shop steward. A workplace trade union representative. Shop stewards are not paid for their union work and are 'unofficial' in the sense that they do not determine union policy or take significant decisions on behalf of the union without its prior approval. Stewards recruit new union members, distribute information about the union, and communicate employee grievances to management.

shops. According to the Offices, Shops and Railway Premises Act 1963 (qv), places used for retail trade or business, including wholesale warehouses, catering establishments open to the public, retail auction sales and lending libraries.

Shops Act 1950. A statute that governs retail trading, general closing times, early closing days and Sunday employment (qv).

short interval scheduling. The division of routine work into sequences of individual tasks, each sequence lasting a short period (half an hour for instance) in order to apply Work measurement (qv) and operator rating (qv) to the performance of duties.

short time working. According to the Employment Protection (Consolidation) Act 1978 (qv) work that attracts less than half a normal week's pay. Employees on short time for four consecutive weeks (or any six weeks in 13) may claim they have been constructively dismissed (qv), provided normal work is not expected to resume within the next month and to last for at least three months. *See* NOTICE OF INTENTION TO CLAIM.

show of hands. A non-secret method of voting whereby each voter indicates his or her views by raising a hand. Under the Trade Union Act 1984 (qv), strike ballots (qv) should not be taken using an open show of hands.

SIC. *See* STANDARD INDUSTRIAL CLASSIFICATION.

sick building syndrome. The tendency of certain recently constructed office buildings that have air conditioning, sealed heating systems, sound-proofed rooms, etc., to create minor illnesses such as headaches, eye strain and lethargic depression among the people who work in them.

sick organisation. A management metaphor (qv) coined by M. Kets de Vries and D. Miller to describe organisations administered by neurotic managers who exhibit paranoid behaviour (qv),

the compulsive pursuit of perfection, desires to draw attention to themselves, depression (qv), and/or lack of energy and enthusiasm.

significant other. According to G. H. Mead, someone who reinforces the self-image of another individual and, in consequence, has an important relationship with that person.

Sikhs, rule concerning protective headgear. A special exemption to the Race Relations Act 1976 (qv) introduced via the Employment Act 1989 (qv) whereby Sikhs need not adhere to the statutory obligation to wear safety helmets while working on construction sites, provided they are wearing a turban. Firms are not allowed to require Sikh employees to wear helmets as a condition of their employment.

SILO. The acronym for School Industry Liaison Officer.

similar demands. Elements of jobs done by men and women that impose demands which are of equal value in terms of effort, skill, decision making, etc. The Equal Opportunities Commission gives the following examples of similar demands: responsibility for contacts with the public and responsibility for staff; lifting heavy weights occasionally and lifting small weights continuously; using a drilling machine and using a typewriter; diagnosing machine faults and analysing written reports. An example of dissimilar demands is driving a van compared with examining customer complaints. *See* UNEQUAL VALUE JOBS; BROADLY SIMILAR WORK.

similar value work. Work done by men and women in the same organisation which requires similar effort, skills, responsibility, decision taking, etc. Employees performing such work are legally entitled to equal pay. Complaints regarding this matter are heard by Industrial Tribunals (qv), which are empowered to institute independent job evaluations (qv) in complainants' companies. *See* EQUAL PAY (AMENDMENT) REGULATIONS (1983); SIMILAR DEMANDS.

similarity, principle of. *See* PRINCIPLE OF CLOSURE.

SIMO chart. *See* SIMULTANEOUS MOTION TIME CHART.

simplified occupational pension schemes. Company Superannuation schemes (qv) which adhere rigidly to rules specified by the Inland Revenue in order to guarantee their acceptance by the Superannuation Funds Office (qv) for contracting out purposes. Benefits must be exactly as laid down in specimen documents and must exclude payments to controlling directors. The scheme will then be approved automatically.

simulation analysis. A quantitative decision-making technique that systematically alters the parameters (limiting factors) and assumptions of a model and examines the consequences of the changes.

simultaneous motion time chart. A diagram used in motion study (qv) to record the times taken by each of a worker's hands to complete the motions necessary to undertake a task.

sinecure. A permanent and well paid job involving minimal effort or responsibility.

single door policy. A method for organising a personnel department whereby several personnel officers of equivalent rank assume equal responsibility for the firms personnel activities and deal with problems on a first-come first-served basis.

single industry union. A trade union (qv) that draws its members from just one industry. An example is the National Union of Mineworkers.

single loop learning. A term coined by Chris Argyris to describe the learning necessary for a worker to be able to apply existing methods to the completion of a job. This contrasted with 'double loop' learning that challenged and redefined the basic requirements of the job and how it should be undertaken.

single settlement date negotiations. An industrial relations pay bargaining situation in which all negotiations between management and the trade unions representing various groups of workers in a large organisation are scheduled for conclusion on the same date, rather than being spread throughout the year.

single stage assembly. A Japanese approach to assembly line production whereby each worker is held personally responsible for the successful operation of the *entire* assembly process. Em-

ployees might still have to complete single actions repetitively, but become involved in issues that affect the whole assembly line. This could enhance workers' interest and commitment.

single status. The practice of managers and all other grades of employee (including basic grade operatives) sharing the same canteen, using the same car park, wearing similar clothes, having equal access to company superannuation schemes and enjoying similar welfare and fringe benefits.

single-step day work system. A differential payment system (qv) containing two levels of payment: a basic rate and, for workers who exceed a certain level of performance, a higher rate set at a predetermined percentage above the basic amount. Thus, workers can select the pay band in which they operate, depending on their chosen level of performance. Schemes with several pay levels (each corresponding to a particular level of performance) are called 'multiple-step day work systems'.

single table bargaining. Industrial relations negotiations where the terms and conditions of an entire category of employee are settled at a single sitting. It is particularly appropriate in companies where several different unions cover the same type of worker (manual workers for example).

single union agreement. A deal whereby an employer will only recognise one union for the purpose of collective bargaining. Workers who wish to belong to a trade union must join this single union.

sister company. A foreign firm that supplies similar products and is of the same size and overall makeup as a UK business seeking a foreign partner. The sister company acts as a foreign agent and provides information on local business conditions. Reciprocal facilities are provided by the UK firm. Staff exchanges may occur as part of the arrangement. The European Commission has consistently encouraged sister company link-ups and has established a clearing system (the Business Co-operation Centre) for this purpose.

sit-in. A temporary occupation of an employer's premises by striking workers intended to interfere with the firm's capacity to continue operations. Technically, a sit-in is a form of trespass. However, workers may only be lawfully evicted after they have been served with notices to quit.

sitting next to Nellie. A phrase sometimes used to describe on-the-job training (qv) that involves sitting alongside and observing the work of an experienced person.

situational interviews. Employment interviews that ask candidates predetermined questions specifically related to critical tasks involved in a job, e.g. how the candidate would handle a particular assignment or cope with a certain situation.

situational management. A reactive management style (qv) whereby the manager adapts his or her leadership style to meet the needs of each specific situation, rather than applying a single approach regardless of circumstances. *See* CONTINGENCY THEORY; CLASSICAL APPROACH.

situational testing. The observation, recording and analysis of a test subject's responses and behaviour in a simulated real-life workplace situation.

16 PF test. *See* CATTELL's 16 PF TEST.

skill. A capacity to perform a task competently, normally involving a co-ordinated sequence of mental and/or physical activities.

skillcentres. Government training centres developed from training facilities first established to assist the rapid expansion of national output necessitated by the Second World War. Employers' demands for the services of skillcentres declined sharply during the 1980s. Skillcentre services are today provided only on a full cost basis.

skill ownership. A worker's ability to practise an occupational skill (qv) in a wide variety of situations, environments, contexts and conditions. Thus, a skill is 'owned' by an individual if its performance does not depend on the existence of predetermined conditions.

skilled workers. Employees whose experience and/or training enables them to complete a wide range of tasks and to determine and implement the best means for accomplishing task requirements. Skilled workers normally require less supervision than semi-skilled (qv) operatives.

skills analysis. An approach to training in which a skilled and experienced worker is observed on-the-job and his or her method of doing work broken down and analysed. This analysis provides a specification for the training of other workers, with detailed listings of all the tasks they must perform and the characteristics needed to complete them satisfactorily. Related techniques are 'task analysis (qv)', which examines the duties and behaviour patterns necessary to do a job, and 'faults analysis (qv)' which begins from a diagnosis of the faults that occur when performing certain duties.

skills exchange scheme. A system whereby a central body records all the skills and competencies possessed by each member of the scheme and makes this information available to all participants in order that members may approach each other with a view to learning skills already acquired by other members.

skills inventory. A detailed listing of all the competencies, work experiences, special abilities and qualifications possessed by current employees, including characteristics not strictly relevant to present occupations. The purpose is to inform management of all the jobs that existing staff might be capable of undertaking.

skills profiling. Comparison of the performance of a recently appointed employee with the standard expected of a fully competent worker in order to identify training requirements.

Skills Training Agency. A self-financing division of what used to be the Training Agency (qv) which offered skills training and staff development programmes. It was supported by a 'Mobile Training Service' capable of delivering training courses in STA 'Skillcentres' or on the client firm's premises.

skittle effect of training. Repercussions resulting from training a group of workers whereby the training given creates the need to train other groups. For example, training operatives to a new level of competence could then necessitate extra training for supervisors; better trained supervisors might require more extensively trained middle managers, and so on.

sleeping partner. A member of a partnership who contributes capital but takes no part in management. Sleeping partners can register with the Registrar of Companies and hence obtain limited liability in respect of the debts of the business. Also they are exempt from Class IV National Insurance (qv) contributions provided they take no part in the management of the business.

slowly developing diseases. Pneumoconiosis (including asbestosis and silicosis), byssinosis and certain other industrial diseases, the effects of which do not become apparent until many years after they are contracted. This creates difficulties in relation to claiming compensation from the past employers of affected workers. Special social security benefits are payable in such circumstances.

slush fund. A secret account established to enable a firm to make underhand payments (bribes for example) to customers, suppliers or other outsiders without recording the expenditure.

Small Employers' Relief. The ability of certain small businesses to reclaim 100 per cent of statutory sick pay (qv) from the DHSS, rather than the standard 80 per cent, after the sick worker has been absent for six weeks. To qualify for relief, the firm's gross National Insurance contribution payments to the DHSS (employer's *and* employee's) must have been less than £15,000 in the previous tax year.

Small Firms Merit Award for Research and Technology. A government-supported competition for small firms (employing less than 200 people) engaged in the development of high-risk projects, especially in the fields of biotechnology, information technology and advanced manufacturing. Prizewinners receive three quarters of the cost of a one year feasibility study for an intended new project.

SMART. *See* SMALL FIRMS MERIT AWARD FOR RESEARCH AND TECHNOLOGY.

SME. The acronym for 'Small- to Medium-sized Enterprises'.

Smith, Adam (1723–1790). Political economist whose book *The Wealth of Nations* (1775) analysed the economic effects of the (then) new approaches to factory organisation and labour management necessitated by recent technical innovations. Smith was especially interested in the consequences of the division of labour (qv).

smokestack industries. Traditional 'heavy' industries (e.g. steelmaking, ship-building, forging) based on labour-intensive (qv) production methods. Most of these industries went into severe decline in the 1970s.

social anthropology. The systematic analysis of social systems and cultures.

Social Charter of Fundamental Social Rights. *See* EUROPEAN SOCIAL CHARTER.

social cognition theory. The proposition that a person's ethical values are learned responses to his or her experiences of events and environments.

social contract (compact). An unsuccessful attempt during the 1970s to induce trade unions to accept pay restraint via incomes policies (qv) in return for the government (i) involving union leaders in economic policy making and (ii) helping unions achieve wide ranging social and political objectives.

Social Dialogue. *See* VAL DUCHESSE DIALOGUE.

social Darwinism. Application of Charles Darwin's concept of the survival of the fittest to social and economic matters. In a managerial context it implies that free and open competition among executives should naturally lead to the most able of them rising to senior positions.

social differentiation. The processes whereby a society differentiates into numerous occupations (qv), roles (qv) and groups fulfilling various functions.

Social Dimension Document, European Community. A working paper drafted by the European Commission in 1988 and updated annually. It contains recommendations on future EC policy *vis-a-vis* living and working conditions within the Community, employee training, the promotion of employment, work organisation and industrial relations. It was the precursor to the European Social Charter (qv).

social-emotional leader. An informal group leader to whom other group members voluntarily turn for emotional and social support. Such leaders typically exert much power (qv) within organisations.

social facilitation. The situation that occurs when the presence of others improves a person's capacity to perform simple tasks.

Social Fund of the European Community. *See* EUROPEAN SOCIAL FUND.

Social Fund scheme. A system of grants and loans made available by the DHSS to assist low-income families meet unexpected short term expenditure. Grants are available for funeral costs, maternity expenses and for individuals returning to the community after a period of residential care. Otherwise, interest-free loans are the only form of help available.

social learning theory. An approach to learning (qv) which asserts that everyone is born with an operational intellect that from the first day of life seeks to understand the outside environment. Hence, an individual's failure to learn results more from mismanagement of the learning process (e.g. bad schools and teachers) than from personal inadequacy.

social millieu. A person's immediate social environment.

social norm. A behavioural expectation common to all members of a society. Members of the society assess the appropriateness of their feelings, conduct and performance against these yardsticks.

social partners. *See* VAL DUCHESSE DIALOGUE.

social psychology. A mixture of sociology (qv) and psychology (qv) that examines individual behaviour in the context of social environments, focusing heavily on interpersonal relations.

social salon. An informal interest group with a high degree of interaction among its members.

social secretary. A nineteenth century term for a company industrial welfare officer.

Social Security Act 1975. A statute that created four types of benefit for victims of industrial injuries: accident, disablement, industrial disease and death. The first of these benefits was abolished in 1982, since when the victims of industrial accidents must claim statutory sick pay (qv) in the first instance.

Social Security and Housing Benefits Act 1982. The statute that made employers responsible for the administration of statutory sick pay (qv). If an employing firm refuses to pay statutory sick pay to a worker then the worker may demand a written justification of the decision, which is then referred to the DHSS for adjudication.

social self. Aspects of an individual's personality (qv) noticed by others during social intercourse.

social stratification. The grading of people into a socio-economic hierarchy of groups.

socialisation. The process whereby an individual acquires attitudes (qv), perspectives and opinions and adopts modes of behaviour acceptable to a society or organisation. Socialisation may be planned and structured or occur in informal and *ad hoc* ways.

Society of Graphical and Allied Trades (SOGAT). A trade union (qv) active in the printing, newsprint, cardboard, packaging and newspaper production and distribution industries.

sociobiology. Analysis of the biological foundations of certain categories of social behaviour.

sociodrama. A means for teaching interpersonal skills by requiring participants to assume roles in a problem situation and act out these roles in a group setting.

sociodynamics. The analysis of aggregate group structures, interrelations and behaviour.

sociogram. A chart showing patterns of attraction, dislike and indifference among members of a group.

sociogroup. A workgroup in which each member evaluates other members according to their levels of efficiency, their contributions to the smooth functioning of the group, and their conformity to group norms (qv).

sociologistic theorem. According to the sociologist T. Parsons the proposition that individual motivation (qv) tends to relate to and fit in with the value system of the society in which a person operates.

sociology. The study of patterns of interaction among individuals and within and between groups, focusing on the determinants of power (qv), status, influence and authority (qv), group values and norms, the effectiveness of interpersonal communications and social influences as a whole.

sociometric isolate. A group member who neither expresses social preferences for other group members nor has other members express a preference for involvement with that person.

sociometric relationship. A relationship between two members of a group that results from one member expressing a preference for involvement with the other, or rejection of the other, or indifference.

sociometric score. The extent to which a group member is selected for voluntary interaction by other group members.

sociometry. The systematic analysis of the causes and consequences of regularities in patterns of association between members of a group. A 'sociometric test' is an attempt to obtain quantitative data on the preferences of group members for associating with other members.

sociopathy. The disposition to act in an antisocial manner.

socio-technical sub-system (technical-human interface). The interrelation between an organisation's physical and technical resources and the people who utilise them.

Sod's law. A humorous term used to suggest that 'anything that can go wrong will go wrong at the most inconvenient moment'.

soft criteria. Subjective judgemental criteria used when selecting employees, as opposed to 'hard' criteria that involve factual information.

SOGAT. See SOCIETY OF GRAPHICAL AND ALLIED TRADES.

sogo sosha. A Japanese term denoting an organisation owned by a number of businesses to provide them with a wide range of integrated marketing, transport, financial and information services.

sole trader. A one person business operating without limited liability.

somatic disorders. Illnesses with physical rather than psychological causes. See PSYCHOSOMATIC DISORDERS.

sore thumbing. Identification of work that for some reason or other requires special consideration during job evaluation (qv) exercises, e.g. because the work contains unique duties that are impossible to compare with other activities. Separate evaluation procedures are applied to these special cases.

span of control. The number of direct subordinates reporting to a manager.

spare time activities, dismissal for. Sacking a worker because his or her activities undertaken out of working hours damage the employing firm's interests, e.g. by causing the employee to be too tired for work or because the activities directly compete with the employer's business. Contracts of employment restricting a worker's outside interests are legally binding only if they are reasonable in all the circumstances of the case.

SPEC. A special EC support programme for the creation of new jobs within Community states.

special award. A form of compensation for victims of unfair dismissal (qv) where the workers concerned were sacked for joining or refusing to join a trade union.

specific performance, order for. A Court order which requires the parties to a contract to honour their contracted obligations. However, English law does *not* permit orders for specific performance that relate to the fulfilment of contracts of employment (qv), unless an Industrial Tribunal (qv) has ordered the reinstatement (qv) or re-engagement (qv) of an unfairly dismissed (qv) worker. An employer's failure to obey one of the latter orders may result in the employee being awarded higher compensation.

speculative training. See TRAINING FOR STOCK.

spent conviction. A criminal conviction that the offending person is allowed to 'forget' after a certain period, e.g. three years following release from a prison sentence of up to six months. Sentences of imprisonment exceeding 30 months never become spent. Individuals with spent convictions are entitled to deny having been convicted, and it is unlawful to dismiss someone on these grounds if the conviction is subsequently discovered.

spider web organisation. An organisation structure (qv) based on the strict control of all functions by a single individual. Instead of having a conventional line and staff (qv) or matrix (qv) system, the organisation resembles a spider's web with one person at the centre. There is little communication or sharing of information among subordinates and an absence of standard rules and procedures. Employees' have vaguely defined job descriptions and their performances are appraised personally by the individual in control. Hence subordinates are kept in a state of confusion and dependence.

split brain psychology. A contentious and unproven hypothesis that the human brain possesses two 'hemispheres' each associated with various personality characteristics. The left hemisphere (supposedly located on the right hand side of the brain) is said to concern logic, analysis, planning and control of activities, the organisation of information, etc., whereas the right hemisphere is allegedly associated with intuition, spirituality, perception, creativity, conceptualisation, emotionality, and so on.

split-half reliability test. A method of aptitude testing (qv) whereby a test is given in two parts, with the second part assuming that the candidate has learnt from the first part and thus will repeat from memory some previous responses.

split shift system. A shift work arrangement involving the division of shifts into two or more time periods, with certain employees working part of each complete shift.

splot exercise. A method of outdoor management training (qv) in which participants are given a limited supply of ink pellets of a certain colour and a gun that fires them. They then spend the day trying to hit rivals with their own colour pellets while avoiding being hit by other colours.

sponsor, management development. *See* MENTOR.

sponsored mobility. The pattern of career (qv) development typically followed by the employees of large and bureaucratic organisations. There is a clearly defined career ladder and specific experience and qualification requirements for progression through the system. *See* CONTEST MOBILITY.

spontaneous recovery. In classical (qv) and operant conditioning (qv), the reappearance after a short period of a pattern of behaviour which, through conditioning, had been temporarily suppressed.

spreadsheets. A grid containing data and formulae which process the data. Modern spreadsheets are invariably computerised. They perform tedious and repetitious functions that are so extensive as to require enormous amounts of time were they to be completed manually, even with calculators.

SPRINT. An EC-funded programme intended to encourage technical innovation and technology transfer within the Community. It promotes employee exchanges among EC small- and medium-sized enterprises, supports certain trade fairs and professional advisory services, and helps with the communication of technical information between businesses.

SSP1(E). A form given by employers to sick workers excluded from statutory sick pay (qv) to enable them to claim State Sickness Benefit (qv). At the start of the 27th week of sickness the employer must issue a 'transfer form', SSP 1 (T), to such workers.

SSP1(L). *See* LEAVER'S STATEMENT.

SSP2. A record form drafted by the DHSS and approved by them for the purpose of showing how long a worker has been absent through sickness prior to the firm reclaiming statutory sick pay (qv).

staff association. An association of employees formed to represent workers in a particular company. Staff associations are not independent trade unions (qv), as they are not divorced from company management (which typically will have set up the association in the first instance). However, many staff associations negotiate with management on pay and conditions, and generally behave 'as if' they were trade unions.

staff development. *See* MANAGEMENT DEVELOPMENT.

staff manager. A manager who advises line (qv) executives but does not take or implement final decisions.

staff status. Special privileges sometimes given to office workers which distinguish them from production operatives. Examples include membership of supperannuation (qv) schemes, not having to clock in and out of the building, access to a staff restaurant rather than a works canteen, etc.

stage theory. The proposition that a manager's career (qv) comprises a series of clearly defined stages with critical turning points between phases. Each stage involves unique functions and patterns of behaviour, and conscious decisions have to be made to progress from one stage to the next.

stages and key points analysis. *See* TRAINING WITHIN INDUSTRY.

stagflation. The simultaneous occurrence of economic recession, increasing unemployment and rising inflation.

stairs in factories, regulations on. Rules specified in s.28 of the Factories Act 1961 (qv) requiring that handrails be provided on at least one side of factory (qv) staircases (both sides in particularly hazardous situations). *See* CONSTRUCTION (WORKING PLACES) REGULATIONS 1966.

stakeholder. A person or group with a vested interest in the behaviour of a company. Examples are shareholders, various categories of employee, customers, creditors, unions and possibly local and national government. Stakeholders may or may not hold formal authority (qv) although each will have invested something in the organisation, whether this be work, finance or other resources. Accordingly, every stakeholder will expect a reward from the enterprise and normally will wish to influence how this is determined.

standard costing. The computation of expected values for materials usages, input prices, labour needed for production, machine times and expenses, etc., followed by the comparison of these values with actual production costs.

standard hour. The amount of work (not time) that can be completed by an experienced operator working at rating standard (qv) 100 in one hour. A standard hour is divided into 60 standard minutes (qv).

Standard Industrial Classification (SIC). An internationally recognised system for categorising industries and sectors within industries.

standard minutes. A work study (qv) term used to describe the number of minutes needed for a competent worker on a piece rate (qv) wage system to complete a task in normal circumstances.

standard performance. The normal output in normal circumstances of an operative working at rating standard 100 (qv). It requires an effort broadly equivalent to that necessary to maintain a walking speed of four miles per hour.

standard time. The time needed by a competent, experienced and motivated worker to complete a task, allowing for contingencies and employee relaxation.

standardisation. Elimination of unnecessary variations in products, systems, designs or input materials.

standards of performance. Measures of the levels of performance required to achieve an element of competence (qv) in a National Vocational Qualification (NVQ), as stated in the appropriate performance criteria (qv).

standing committee. A committee that meets at regular predetermined intervals to consider matters relating to a certain subject (e.g. industrial relations or health and safety), which have arisen since the previous meeting.

standing orders. Rules and procedures governing the conduct of a meeting or committee.

State Earnings Related Pension Scheme (SERPS). The compulsory state pension scheme for non-contracted-out employees who do not belong to a private plan. Workers on SERPS pay approximately 2 per cent extra on their Class 1 National Insurance (qv) contributions. Employers pay an extra 3 per cent. SERPS pensions will comprise a basic amount plus a supplement dependent on the value of the individual's average lifetime earnings.

State Sickness Benefit. Sick pay for (i) employees excluded from statutory sick pay (qv), and (ii) the self-employed.

statement of affairs. A listing of all the assets and liabilities of a debtor following the initiation of bankruptcy proceedings against the person concerned.

status. The worth of a person as this is perceived by members of a group. It depends on the person's characteristics and contributions to the group and on his or her ability to satisfy the needs of other group members.

Status Characteristics Index (SCI). A scale to evaluate people's socio-economic status according to their occupations (qv), sources of income, house types and the areas in which they live.

status congruence. The situation prevailing when each member of an organisation regards his or her status (qv) as just and appropriate in relation to that person's contributions. An example of status incongruence might be the resentments felt by low-paid part time workers at being required to complete work identical to that of higher paid full time employees.

status quo agreement. A guarantee given by management to trade union representatives that none of a firm's existing workers will be made worse off in consequence of a work study (qv) or job evaluation (qv) exercise, and that major changes to working practices resulting from such exercises will not be implemented without union agreement.

statute law. Legislation enacted by Parliament. This overrides all other sources of law except for European Community Regulations, Directives (qv), and Decisions of the European Court of Justice. The meanings of words and phrases contained in statutes can themselves lead to legal disputes. Consequently, the civil courts may be called upon to determine the correct interpretation.

Statute of Artificers 1563. A law that made seven year apprenticeships compulsory for certain craft trades, thus restricting entry to many occupations. The Statute was rescinded in 1814.

statute of limitations. *See* LIMITATION ACT 1939.

statutory declaration. A written statement verifying certain facts or the occurrence of certain incidents made before a notary public (qv), Commissioner for Oaths, Justice of the Peace or a responsible Court official.

statutory instruments. Devices whereby government ministers are empowered to make laws on matters connected with the means for implementing specified Acts of Parliament. An example is the ability of the Secretary of State for Employment to alter compensation limits for unfair dismissal, redundancy, etc., at his or her discretion. This avoids Parliament having to debate these matters every time they arise.

statutory notice. *See* NOTICE PERIODS, STATUTORY.

statutory payments. Payments required by Act of Parliament, e.g. statutory sick pay (qv), maternity pay (qv) or redundancy (qv) payments.

statutory sick pay (SSP). State benefit payable to employees who cannot attend work in consequence of illness and who satisfy certain eligibility requirements. *See* STATUTORY SICK PAY, EMPLOYERS' LIABILITY TO ADMINISTER.

statutory sick pay, employers' liability to administer. The obligation under the 1982 Social Security and Housing Benefits Act of employers to pay sick workers their state sickness benefit for up to 28 weeks. The firm pays the worker his or her SSP and then deducts 80 per cent of the value of the remittance from its monthly cheque for tax and employer's National Insurance contributions sent to the Inland Revenue. Part time workers who earn more than a certain threshold are entitled to SSP, and there is no length of service qualification. Payment is only made for absences of more than three days and for whole days not parts. Small firms whose employees collectively pay less than a certain gross amount of Class I National Insurance (qv) contributions each year may claim 'Small Employers' Relief', which entitles them to recover from the Inland Revenue 100 per cent of the SSP paid to workers.

STEP. The acronym for Special Temporary Employment Programme.

stepped pay system. An approach to measured day work (qv) which defines several levels of performance with a rate of pay for each level. Employees may then choose the level at which they operate and are periodically checked to ensure their performance is at the appropriate level. Workers may ask to move up to a higher level if they feel they are capable of operating at that rate. Hence the method combines regular levels of pay with individual incentives.

stereotyping. The attribution (qv) to a person of a number of characteristics assumed typical of the group to which he or she belongs. Stereotypes are mental pictures of what certain types of people (e.g. ethnic minorities, religious groupings, doctors, accountants, trade unionists, army sergeants, etc.) are thought to be like. Thereby anyone belonging to one of these groups is instantly assumed to possess identical characteristics

stop-go cycle. The pattern of economic activity that characterised the UK economy for many periods during the post Second World War years. The government would stimulate the economy via increased public spending, tax cuts, etc., in order to create 'go' periods, which led to inflation and balance of payments deficits. To overcome these problems the government would then deflate the economy so as to terminate the economic expansions (the 'stop' phases of the cycle). Fresh 'go' periods could begin as soon as circumstances permitted. *See* DEMAND MANAGEMENT.

straight proportional bonus scheme. An employee wage incentive system through which workers begin to receive bonuses at rating standard 75 (qv). At level 100 the bonus is one third of the predetermined hourly rate for the job; before level 75 workers receive only the flat hourly rate. A ceiling on the bonus payable is imposed at level 125. Thus, performance at level 100 requires a one third increase in effort over performance at level 75, and is rewarded by a one third bonus on the standard hourly rate. Performance at the ceiling of level 125 attracts a bonus of two thirds of the hourly rate. Hence, effort and reward increase on a one- to-one basis.

stranger laboratory group. In T-group training (qv), a group exercise involving people who have not previously met and are unlikely ever again to encounter each other. This contrasts with a 'cousin group', which comprises persons of the same occupational rank but from different departments or companies; and with the 'diagonal slice', where group members come from different grades and occupations within the same company.

strategic business unit. A grouping of a company's activities where activity is (usually) taken from a different division or subsidiary. The SBU is then treated as a self-contained entity for the purposes of strategic planning and control.

strategic contingencies. Situations that arise wherein certain departments cannot complete their duties until other departments have already done their work, i.e. the performance of the functions of these department is contingent on activities undertaken elsewhere. Departments that are able to control critical contingencies can become extremely powerful within the organisation.

strategic management. The determination of where the organisation should be headed, the specification of general corporate objectives, and the overall selection of policies for guiding the firm.

strategic planning. Determination of the broad policies an enterprise is to follow and the actions necessary to achieve its overall goals.

stress. A syndrome comprising physiological and psychological reactions to mental tension. Stress is not a measurable entity; its existence is only apparent through its consequences.

stress interview. An employment interview that seeks to simulate the traumas and tensions attached to a highly stressful job in order to assess candidates' coping abilities.

stressor. An object or event that causes stress. Examples occur in the physical environment, in certain types of work, in organisational conflicts and in personal problems such as divorce or bereavement.

strike ballots. Secret ballots required by the Trade Union Act 1984 (qv) prior to a union taking industrial action (qv). The union calling the strike loses its immunity from legal action if the strike is not backed by a majority of those balloted. If no ballot is called then union members have the statutory right to have a Court declare the action unlawful.

strike indemnity fund. A pool of money, accumulated through annual contributions from members of an employers' association (qv), which can then be used to assist any of the Association's members whose workers go on strike.

strike pay. Financial support given to strikers by their trade unions (qv).

strike pay, Unemployment Benefit and. The rule whereby the DHSS assumes that striking workers are receiving certain amounts of strike pay from their trade unions when their dependants claim social security benefit during a strike. This reduces the benefit payable to the dependants of striking workers.

strikers. Employees (qv) who withdraw their labour during an industrial dispute (qv). Strikers cannot normally be sued for damages arising from their breaches of contracts of employment, but may be fairly dismissed. Workers dismissed while on strike are not entitled to redundancy payments (qv) even if a redundancy (qv) situation exists.

strikers, rule on the dismissal of. The requirement of the Employment Protection (Consolidation) Act 1978 (qv) that although it is generally fair (qv) to dismiss striking employees, the firm must sack *all* strikers and not just some of them – unless the people selected for dismissal were guilty of some special offence (violence on picket lines for instance). The Employmnet Act 1990 (qv) rescinded this rule in the case of workers who take unofficial action (qv). *See* STRIKERS UNDER NOTICE OF REDUNDANCY, DISMISSAL OF.

strikers under notice of redundancy, dismissal of. The rule embodied in the Employment Protection (Consolidation) Act 1978 (qv) that workers who go on strike *after* (but not before) being issued with notice of redundancy (qv) and are dismissed for having withdrawn their labour may still obtain their redundancy payments via an Industrial Tribunal (qv), which is empowered to award a 'just and equitable' amount.

strikes not immune from civil liability. Political, sympathy and demarcation strikes that render unions liable for damages to employers and other interested parties. A demarcation strike is not immune because it concerns a dispute between workers and an employer, so that it is not a trade dispute (qv) enjoying legal protection. 'Wildcat' strikes called out of spite and not connected to a bona fide trade dispute do not have immunity.

Strong–Campbell Vocational Interest Questionnaire. A device for measur-

ing an individual's preferences in relation to his or her activities, objects and personality types. Items are grouped into categories (e.g. adventure, service, relating to others) which are then combined into particular themes, such as 'scientific', 'social', etc.

structural authority. Another term for a line manager's (qv) authority.

structural forces. Influences on individual behaviour resulting from the structure of the social environment in which a person operates.

structural unemployment. Unemployment resulting from long-term changes in the supply and demand conditions of the labour market, e.g. the collapse of an industry, technological innovation leading to widespread redundancies, etc.

structuralist school. An offshoot of the human relations (qv) approach to management. It accepts the inevitability of conflict between individuals and their employing organisations, suggesting therefore that formal procedures based on pluralistic (qv) assumptions are necessary to resolve disagreements.

structured decisions. *See* PROGRAMMED DECISIONS.

structured interview. An interview that asks predetermined questions.

students employed during vacations. *See* P38(S).

sub-contractors in the construction industry, rules on the taxation of. Regulations contained in the Finance Acts of 1971 and 1980 whereby building firms are obliged to deduct, at source, basic rate income tax from payments made to uncertified sub-contractors. *See* 714 CERTIFICATE.

sub-culture. A culture (qv) within a culture. It retains the basic characteristics of the parent culture, but develops its own special features.

sub-cultures, organisational. The informal organisation, norms (qv) and social relationships within particular offices or departments. They result from shared experiences, the power of certain persons and the unofficial communication systems that sometimes arise within offices or departments.

subjective expectancy utility. According to H. J. Klein, the perceived attractiveness of a personal objective multiplied by the individual's expectation of achieving it.

subjective test. *See* OBJECTIVE TEST.

sublimation. An ego defence mechanism (qv) which causes people experiencing neurotic anxiety (qv) to divert their energies away from their difficulties and instead devote themselves totally to pursuits that do not create anxiety.

sub-optimisation. Satisficing behaviour (qv) where decision makers settle for a convenient solution achieved quickly and cheaply, rather than searching for the ideal outcome.

subsidiarity, principle of. In the European Community, the principle (agreed by all EC countries) that laws should be introduced at the Community level only if their desired outcomes cannot be achieved by national action in each member state.

subsistence theory of wages. An eighteenth century economic theory which asserted that wages would tend to settle at a level that provided workers with just a bare subsistence. Excessively high wages would lead to increases in the population and hence to competition among workers that could result in wage reductions. Wages below the subsistence level caused falls in the size of the population, leading to labour shortages and higher wages. *See* WAGE FUND THEORY OF WAGES.

sub-social behaviour. Patterns of personal behaviour that cannot be explained by social factors, e.g. behaviour resulting from genetic influences.

substantial reason for fair dismissal. A valid reason for fair dismissal not covered by the main provisions of the Employment Protection (Consolidation) Act 1978 (qv). Examples are workers who go on strike; and not being able to continue employing someone because to do so would cause the firm to break the law (e.g. using a van driver who has lost his or her driving licence).

substantive agreement. An agreement negotiated between management and trade union representatives that relates to pay, working hours, holiday entitlement or some other specific term or condition of employment. *See* PROCEDURAL AGREEMENT.

substantive motion. A motion that has been amended by resolution of a committee. It replaces entirely the original motion (qv) to which it relates.

suitability of alternative employment. *See* ALTERNATIVE EMPLOYMENT.

summary dismissal. Dismissal of an employee 'on-the-spot' without notice. This is not unfair or wrongful dismissal (qv) provided the worker's behaviour makes impossible the fulfilment of a contract of employment. Examples of behaviour possibly warranting summary dismissal are theft, abusiveness to customers or wilful disobedience.

summated attitude scale. *See* LIKERT SCALE.

summative assessment. Evaluation of a trainee's achievements on a component of a training programme in order to report his or her level of achievement to others. It is an end-record of performance (possibly used for certification of competence) rather than an aid to learning. *See* FORMATIVE ASSESSMENT.

Sunday employment of shop assistants, rules concerning. Regulations embodied in the Shops Act 1950 (qv) that require any shop assistant working more than four hours on a Sunday to be given a full day's holiday in lieu during the week before or the week after the Sunday in question. Sunday work of less than four hours must attract a half day's holiday on some other day. Off-licences and shops mainly selling refreshments are exempt from this ruling.

Sunday neurosis. Depression experienced by workaholics (qv) when they are not permitted to work (e.g. through an employing firm being closed on Sundays).

sunk cost. Expenditure on an activity or project that cannot be recovered if resources are switched to other activities or projects.

sunlighter. Someone who continues in full time employment beyond normal retirement age.

sunrise industry. A recently established and rapidly expanding industry, typically concerned with information technology (qv), microelectronics or computer applications.

sunset industry. A declining industry dependent on outdated technology.

Superannuation Funds Office (SFO). A branch of the Inland Revenue which decides whether private occupational pension schemes will be recognised for tax exemption purposes. The SFO sets conditions for such recognition, and generally regulates the pensions industry through the issue of guidance notes, by commenting on proposals for new schemes, and through a Code of Practice (qv) distributed to pension fund managers. See OCCUPATIONAL PENSIONS BOARD.

superannuation scheme. A company pension schemes that (normally) involves both the employer and employee contributing about 6 per cent of the employee's salary to a central fund. To qualify for contracted-out (qv) status the scheme must be established under an irrevokable trust and meet certain conditions, e.g. that the maximum (tax free) lump sum payable on retirement is no more than one and a half times the employee's final salary. See CLASS I NATIONAL INSURANCE.

SUPERCLASS. See NATIONAL DATABASE OF VOCATIONAL QUALIFICATIONS.

superego. See PERSONALITY, FREUDIAN THEORY OF.

supernumeraries. Workers who are surplus to an organisation's current requirements, e.g. in consequence of a work study (qv) exercise.

superordinate goals. High level broadly defined organisational objectives which all members of a work group (qv) or organisation should seek to accomplish. Examples are the maintenance and improvement of the quality of a firm's products and the provision of maximum customer care.

supervisor (first line manager). A manager who controls non-managerial employees but is controlled by other managers. Supervisors direct the day-to-day activities of operatives and other basic grade workers.

supervisory board. The upper level of a two-tier board of directors. Although they are currently uncommon in the UK, supervisory boards are mandatory for large companies in certain EC countries.

Supplementary Benefit. State benefit payable to unemployed workers in addition to their statutory unemployment pay. These benefits are not dependent on the values of the unemployed workers' previous national insurance contributions.

Supply of Goods and Services Act 1982. A statute requiring suppliers of goods that also have to be installed to install them within an acceptable time and with reasonable skill and care to ensure the goods satisfy the purpose for which they are intended.

supply side economics. Government economic policies that concentrate on directly improving industrial infrastructure, rather than on demand management (qv). Examples include national training programmes, regional development, and state assistance to exporters.

suprastructure of an organisation. The overall framework that governs the operation of an organisation, as shown (normally) in its organisation chart (qv). Instances of matters determined by an organisation's suprastructure are its degree of centralisation or decentralisation, authority systems and spans of control (qv). This differs from the infrastructure of an organisation, which involves its internal rules and procedures, information systems, job descriptions and so on.

surety. A promise evidenced by a legal document in order to guarantee settlement of a debt or the performance of a duty if the duty is not completed by another person. The document involved is called a surety bond.

surface bargaining. Negotiations in which there exist hidden agendas (qv), so that discussions relating to formal agenda items become superficial, meaningless and fail to achieve any tangible objective.

surrender value. In an occupational pension scheme (qv), the monetary value of its life assurance element if the member cashes in the policy on leaving the scheme in exchange for an immediately payable lump sum.

survival rate analysis. Computation of the percentages of a group of employees – all of whom were hired on the same date – that remain with the organisation after certain periods. For example, 10 per cent of a particular cohort might have left by the end of one year, 25 per cent after two years,

70 per cent after five, etc. Hence management can predict how long, on average, it takes for (say) half of all workers recruited on a certain date to leave the organisation.

suspension without pay. Laying an employee off without wages as a disciplinary measure or in consequence of shortage of work. This is lawful only if the suspended worker's contract of employment (qv) contains an express or implied term stating that suspension is permissible, or if unpaid layoffs are customary in a particular line of work. If it is impossible for a firm to provide work (e.g. because its premises have burned down) there is no common law obligation to pay employees' wages, although occasional shortages of work do not justify non-payment.

swearing, fair dismissal for. A sacking that is fair provided the language used was persistently or wilfully offensive to people who are not abnormally oversensitive. Dismissal for a single incident of swearing without giving the employee a chance to apologise would usually represent unfair dismissal (qv).

sweat shop. A derogatory term applied to a workplace where employees work long hours for low wages in poor physical working conditions that possibly contravene health and safety legislation.

swing shift. A team of employees which collectively moves from one shift to another to cover for labour shortfalls.

SWOT analysis. Detailed examination of a company's strengths and weaknesses and the opportunities and threats it confronts.

symbolic interaction, study of. Analysis of the roles of language and gestures in an individual's attempts to relate to his or her environments and in the formation of personality (qv) and self-image.

symbolic learning. Techniques of learning (qv) that cause learners to associate symbols such as pictures, mental images (of a green field or a certain type of animal for instance), particular words, etc., with specific topics, facts or actions.

sympathy strike. A strike (qv) called by workers in a firm or industry that is not related to another firm or industry in which industrial action (qv) is tak-

ing place. Its purpose is to encourage employers hit by sympathy strikes to bring pressure to bear on the employer(s) primarily involved in the industrial action to settle the dispute. Such secondary action (qv) is generally unlawful under the Employment Act 1980 (qv).

synchropay. The suggestion of the Confederation of British Industry and certain other bodies concerned with industrial relations that all the unions and employers in any given industry negotiate pay settlements on the same day each year, in order to avoid leap-frogging (qv).

syndicalism. A late nineteenth century political movement which advocated the nationalisation of all industries, accompanied by total workers' control. These aims were to be achieved through industrial action, including general strikes.

synectics. A problem-solving technique that involves narrowing down the number of possible solutions until the optimum solution is obtained.

synergy. The proposition that people working together are collectively more productive than the sum of their individual contributions, i.e. that 'two plus two makes five'.

synthesis, work study. A work measurement (qv) method whereby the time needed to complete a job is determined by totalling the times required by each of its elements (qv), where these elemental times are taken from published tables or from studies of other jobs.

synthetic times. Standard times (qv) for completing common tasks, taken from published tables. The latter are compiled from numerous timings of different workers doing the same job in similar circumstances.

system 4 managers. *See* LIKERT, RENSIS.

systematic training. The logical and analytical approach to the training function, involving (i) the identification of the training requirements implied by a company's business plan, (ii) planning and implementing a training programme and (iii) evaluating methodically the effectiveness of training. It requires close examination of the firm's product, production, organisation and other strategies and an assessment of their human resources implications.

systematics. Development of rules and procedures for the arrangement of things and people into categories.

systemantics. A term coined by John Gall in 1978 to describe the methodical analysis of business systems in order (i) to identify factors that could cause a system to collapse and (ii) to simplify systems.

Systeme Communautaire d'Acces a la Documentation. *See* CELEX.

systems analysis. Detailed examination of the methods, procedures, functions and activities used by organisations to achieve stated objectives.

systems approach to organisations. A theory that views organisations (qv) as conglomerations of inter-relating subsystems which collectively receive inputs of information, materials, human and other resources from the external environment and transform these into outputs of goods or services which are then returned to the outside world.

systems factors. Aspects of firms' environments that affect how they should behave. Examples are laws, customer attitudes, company structure and the stakeholders to whom the organisation is accountable.

systems man. A term sometimes used to describe a manager who consciously avoids personal association with other people; focusing instead on the mechanical completion of tasks and the operation of bureaucratic procedures. Such managers are generally efficient, committed to their employing organisations and occasionally ruthless. However, they lack empathy and tend to resist changes in working practices.

LEARNING RESOURCE CENTRE
THOMAS ROTHERHAM COLLEGE
MOORGATE ROAD
ROTHERHAM S60 2BE
TEL. 0709 828606

T

tachograph. A device for recording the movements of a commercial vehicle and the number of hours worked by its driver. Tachographs are legally required for all commercial vehicles weighing more than 3.5 tonnes or carrying more than nine people on journeys within the European Community.

tacit collusion. In negotiation (qv), implicit agreements entered into without any outward indications of their existence being suggested by either party, but which clearly benefit both sides.

tactics. The practical methods for implementing strategic decisions. *See* STRATEGIC MANAGEMENT.

Taff Vale case. An important test case concerning trade unions (qv) heard by the House of Lords in 1901. Following the Trade Union Act 1871 (qv) and the Employers and Workmen Act 1875 (qv) unions had assumed they could not be sued for the damages they inflicted on employers during industrial disputes. In the Taff Vale case, however, the Law Lords ruled that this was not the situation, and awarded an employing company substantial damages against a union for loss of profit resulting from a strike. The Trade Disputes Act 1906 (qv) overturned this decision.

Taguchi methods. Quality management systems which emphasise the need to minimise variability in production rather than to check and measure output.

tall organisation. An organisation structure with narrow spans of control (qv), thus creating many levels of authority between the apex of the organisation and its base. This facilitates specialisation of functions, co-ordination and communication within the system. Employees have a career ladder and can expect regular promotions.

tangible assets. Physical assets such as land and buildings, stocks, equipment, etc., as opposed to intangible assets (qv), e.g. goodwill (qv) or intellectual property (qv).

Tannenbaum, R., and Schmidt, W. H. Leadership theorists who in 1958 published a highly influential article in the *Harvard Business Review* arguing that managers should consider three sets of factors when choosing a leadership style. The first set relates to the background, attitudes and experience of the leader; the second to the characteristics of subordinates (their competence, interests, ambitions, etc.); and the third to the nature of the situation involved (type of task, culture of the organisation, extent of group cohesion, and so on).

TAPs. *See* TRAINING ACCESS POINTS.

Tariff 1. A list of charges imposed by the Performing Rights Society Ltd for licences to play gramophone records, cassette tapes, compact discs, radio or television sets in factories, offices or canteens. Fees vary according to the number of workers employed on the firm's premises.

task abilities scale. A job analysis (qv) measurement device through which a job's contents are studied and the traits necessary for its successful completion identified. Trait factors include limb co-ordination, reaction time and verbal comprehension.

task analysis. The detailed examination of the skills and behaviour needed to undertake a job.

task and bonus system. A differential payments (qv) scheme devised by H. L. Gantt (qv). A guaranteed minimum wage was paid for performance below a certain standard, with a 20 per cent bonus for performance above this level.

task and finish system. A wage payment system whereby the employee receives a set wage but is entitled to leave work as soon as an agreed task has been completed. Local authority refuse collectors are an example of workers paid in this manner.

task-based appraisal. An approach to performance appraisal (qv) involving the assessment of an employee's efforts solely in terms of his or her success in completing certain prespecified tasks.

Task Force for Human Resources, Education, Training and Youth. A part of the European Commission's (qv) Directorate-General V (Employment, Industrial Relations and Social Affairs) that is particularly concerned with education, ERASMUS, university–industry co-operation in vocational training, COMETT, training for technological change, and vocational qualifications.

task identity. The extent to which a job requires the completion of natural work units (qv).

task management abilities. Employee competencies associated with (i) the organisation of duties, (ii) establishing priorities and time management, and (iii) the capacity to respond to unpredicted events.

Tavistock Institute of Human Relations. A social science research, consulting and publishing organisation highly influential in the 1950s and early 1960s.

tax code. A number issued to an employer to indicate how much tax to deduct from an employee's wages. The number shows the taxpayer's total allowances, and is followed by a letter relating to his or her age or marital status.

taxation of tangible items lent to workers. The rule contained in the 1976 Finance Act that items other than motor cars provided to employees (e.g. video recorders, boats, television sets) are subject to annual tax of 20 per cent of their market values at the times they were first provided.

Taylor, F. W. (1856–1917). Founder of the scientific (qv) approach to management. His ideas were explained in a highly influential book, *Scientific Management*, published in 1911.

Taylor–Russell method. A technique of utility analysis (qv) that uses the same steps as the Brogden–Hunter method (qv) but which assumes that a certain proportion of recruits will *never* be competent in their jobs, no matter

how much training they receive or experience they acquire. Hence the costs of having such employees are incorporated into the utility calculations.

teachers working in the European Community, rules concerning. EC regulations allowing qualified teachers in publicly funded schools in one member state to become members of the teaching professions of other Community countries without having to requalify. If teacher training differs markedly between two member states, the host country is entitled to require immigrant teachers to take an aptitude test or undergo three years' supervised practice.

teaching company. The application of the concept of the 'teaching hospital' to industrial training. A company and an academic institution join forces to provide trainees with 'hands on' experience of business problems in real life situations. Schemes are set up through the government's 'Enterprise and Education Initiative'.

teaching machine. A means for presenting programmed learning (qv) materials in the absence of a human instructor. The machine will modify its own behaviour in the light of a user's responses to questions.

team. A working group whose members voluntarily co-operate and co-ordinate their activities and enthusiastically work to achieve the group's aims.

team building. In organisational development (qv), the improvement of interpersonal communications, decision making, target setting and group interactions in order to enhance group cohesion (qv).

team rate. An hourly rate for consultancy services charged by consultancy organisations which assume that a senior person will be engaged on a project for a certain proportion of its duration; that a junior consultant will undertake a certain share of the work; and that a certain amount of secretarial/administrative support will be necessary.

team spirit. High motivation within a work group (qv) resulting from group cohesion (qv), feelings of attachment to a team (qv), interaction among group members, effective leadership (qv) and perceptions that the distribution of duties and responsibility within the group is fair.

Technical and Vocational Education Initiative (TVEI). A government scheme set up in 1983 whereby local education authorities submitted to the Manpower Services Commission (qv) proposed curricula for training courses intended to equip 14- to 18-year-olds with nationally recognised vocational qualifications (qv). Each TVEI programme had to last for four years and to include work experience, written assessment, counselling and instruction in technical and problem-solving skills.

technical efficiency. A term used by economists to denote the most efficient use of scarce resources for the production (qv) of goods or the provision of services.

technical savings. Unit cost reductions obtained from the intensification of production (continuous shift working for example), improved maintenance of equipment (leading to less frequent equipment failure) and greater overall production efficiency.

technical sub-system. Those aspects of an organisation (qv) that are concerned with the selection of techniques of production and the knowledge required to implement production systems.

technology. The utilisation of the materials and processes necessary to transform inputs into outputs.

Technology-Aided Home Based Work. *See* NETWORKING.

technology transfer. The application to one firm or industry of new working methods, materials, equipment or means for converting inputs into outputs developed in another firm or industry.

technostructure. The totality of an organisation's methods and procedures for standardising, controlling and regulating work processes.

TECs. *See* TRAINING AND ENTERPRISE COUNCILS.

TEED. *See* TRAINING, ENTERPRISE AND EDUCATION DIVISION OF THE DEPARTMENT OF EMPLOYMENT.

telework. *See* NETWORKING.

temperature, legal minimum working. The minimum temperature that, under the Offices, Shops and Railways Premises Act 1963 (qv) a firm's premises must attain within the first hour of the working day. This is 16 degrees Centigrade (60.8 degrees Fahrenheit) in normal circumstances. The Fuel and Electricity (Heating and Control) Amendment Order 1980 imposed the condition that businesses must not use energy to raise the temperature of their premises above 19 degrees Centigrade (66.2 degrees Fahrenheit) unless industrial processes or customer comfort require more heating.

temperatures needed for comfortable work. Normally 15°–20°C (60°–70°F) for light work, 12°–15°C (55°–60°F) for heavy work and 19°–23°C (67°–73°F) in offices.

temporary replacements, fair dismissal of. The dismissal of workers who were taken on temporarily as replacements for permanent employees (qv) absent through medical suspension (qv) or pregnancy. Such a dismissal is not unfair provided the temporary worker was informed in writing at the outset that he or she would be sacked following the return of the permanent employee, even if the temporary replacement is covered by employment protection legislation.

temporary workers, Draft EC Directive concerning. A proposal of the European Commission similar in content to the Draft Directive on part time workers (qv), but concerning temporary and fixed contract employment. Individuals engaged under temporary contracts would have to be informed by their employers of the reasons for not being employed on a permanent basis, and would be entitled to social security benefits identical to those of permanent workers. Employers would be obliged to tell temporary workers of the existence of permanent vacancies within their firms.

TEMSUS. *See* TRANS EUROPEAN MOBILITY SCHEME FOR UNIVERSITY STUDENTS.

tenure, security of. The situation that exists when a person's future employment within an organisation is assured.

terminal assessment. Appraisal of a trainee's competence at the end of a course, as opposed to continuous assessment (qv) throughout the programme.

terms and conditions of employment. Rights, duties and obligations specified in a worker's contract of employment (qv). Examples include wages, holiday entitlements, meal breaks and rest periods, hours of work, fringe benefits, etc.

terotechnology. A holistic approach to the appraisal of new investments. It considers all the costs, benefits and implications of an intended project.

tertiary sector. Economic activities concerned with the distribution of goods and the provision of services.

TFE deflator. *See* TOTAL FINAL EXPENDITURE DEFLATOR.

T-group training. A group training method in which the instructor takes a back seat and encourages group members to help and learn from each other while completing group tasks.

TGWU. *See* TRANSPORT AND GENERAL WORKERS' UNION.

theft. The dishonest appropriation of someone else's property with the intention of permanently depriving the other person of that property. It is not theft if a worker takes property genuinely believing that it belongs to him or her, or believes the owner would give consent to its removal. Theft is a valid reason for fair dismissal (including summary dismissal (qv)) provided a proper investigation has been conducted.

theft, motives for. *See* ROBIN HOOD SYNDROME.

thematic apperception test. A personality test that presents the candidate with a set of ambiguous pictures, leaving him or her to write out what they mean to that person. The written interpretations are then analysed to identify the implications of the use by the test subject of certain words and his or her projection of various mental images.

theory X and theory Y. Assumptions about human nature supposedly held by managers. Theory X assumptions are that workers are naturally lazy and require close supervision and control; theory Y assumptions assert that employees are inherently hard working and may therefore be relied upon to devote their full energies to completing their duties.

theory Z. A term coined by W. Ouchi to describe the Japanese approach to management, which he regarded as comprising three essential strategies: commitment by companies to the long-term employment of their workers; the projection of the philosophy of the organisation to the individual employee; and intense socialisation of recruits into a firm's existing value system. A number of 'techniques' were said to be associated with these strategies: seniority based promotion; continuous training and appraisal; group-centred working methods; employee participation in decision making; and a production-centred approach containing, nevertheless, a great concern for employees' welfare.

therblings. An anagram of the surname of the Gilbreths (qv) and the title given by them to the 17 basic movements in the Gilbreth system (qv).

think tank. A committee of experts from different functional backgrounds who come together to combine their knowledge, exchange opinions and think innovatively about difficult problems.

thinking. The manipulation of messages received from the outside world. Messages are examined, combined and/or compared with each other. The processes involved in thinking are called the cognitive processes. *See* COGNITION.

thinking personality type. In the Jungian typology (qv), a person who is logical, analytical and objective. However, such individuals may be insensitive and misunderstand other people's values.

Thorndike's law of effect. A theory of learning (qv) which asserts that if a trainee's response to a stimulus is immediately reinforced via praise, financial reward, etc., then the response is likely to be repeated.

3-D organisational effectiveness programme. An extension to Blake and Mouton's managerial grid (qv) suggested by W. J. Reddin in order to include a third dimension, 'managerial effectiveness'. Managers are tested to establish their management styles.

threshold agreement. A negotiated pay deal whereby employee wages automatically increase by a predetermined amount as soon as the rate of inflation reaches a certain level.

threshold traits analysis system. A technique of job analysis (qv) that analyses the attributes needed by a worker to perform a job under five main headings. The headings are: physical, mental, learned behaviour, motivation and ability to work in a group.

Thurstone scale. A scale for measuring 'primary mental abilities', i.e. verbal, numerical, spatial, reasoning, memory, word fluency and perceptual speed.

time and a half. An hourly pay rate 50 per cent higher than the normal level. Similarly, rates may be quoted at 'time and a quarter', 'time and three-quarters', double time (qv), etc.

time and lime contract. A sub-contracting arrangement whereby the contract price is based on the direct costs (qv) of materials, labour and other prespecified expenses, plus an agreed profit markup based on a fixed percentage of these outlays. The name derives from the method's origins in the building trade. A major problem with time and lime contracting is its inbuilt incentive for sub-contractors to overspend on materials and labour.

time card. A record of a worker's times of attendance at an employer's premises. It may be handwritten or, more usually, attested mechanically through inserting time cards into a time clock that punches holes in the cards to indicate the times a worker entered and left the firm.

time limits on applications to Industrial Tribunals. Statutory periods within which claims must be presented to Industrial Tribunals (qv). Examples are three months for cases of alleged unfair dismissal (qv), six months for a demand for a redundancy payment (qv), three months for a request for a protective award (qv), or six months for a complaint of unfair discrimination if lodged by the Equal Opportunities Commission (qv). An application must be lodged strictly within such periods or the case will not be considered.

time off for job hunting by workers facing redundancy. Entitlements under the Employmnet Protection Act 1975 (qv) whereby employees under notice of redundancy must be given reasonable amounts of paid leave in order to look for other jobs or to arrange training. Complaints about employers refusing requests for such leave are heard by Industrial Tribunals (qv),

which can award workers up to two fifths of a week's pay as compensation.

time off for union duties, Code of Practice regarding. A Code of Practice (qv) issued by ACAS in 1977 which provides employers with practical guidance on how much paid time off work they should allow union representatives for union duties as specified by the Employment Protection Act 1975 (qv). Under the Code, union representatives' requests for time off should be scheduled so as not to disrupt production or endanger workers' health and safety. Employers should allow representatives paid time off to consult with union members, to undertake collective bargaining, handle employee grievances, represent workers at disciplinary interviews and to inform union members of the outcomes to negotiations.

time off work, entitlement to. The right under the Employment Protection (Consolidation) Act 1978 (qv) of an employee (qv) to take reasonable paid time off work to (i) perform union duties (qv), (ii) undertake certain public duties (qv), (iii) look for other work while under notice of redundancy (qv), (iv) act as a safety representative (qv) and (v) receive ante-natal care.

time rate (flat wage rate). A wage payment system which gives the worker a constant predetermined wage each week or month regardless of his or her effort or output.

time span of discretion. An approach to work analysis and payment that relates employee remuneration to 'responsibility', as measured by the time periods that elapse between checks or appraisals of the employee's work. The longer the time spans between checks the greater the degree of responsibility assumed to be associated with the job.

time study. Measurement of the times taken to complete particular tasks under specified conditions and the determination of the time necessary to finish a task at a defined level of performance.

toilet facilities. *See* SANITARY ACCOMMODATION REGULATIONS 1938.

token strike. A temporary withdrawal of labour (e.g. for half a day) by employees who wish to display their displeasure at the employing firm's behaviour or to demonstrate their ability to organise a total stoppage.

top down planning. An approach to corporate planning (qv) whereby senior management hands down specific objectives to subordinates, without the latters' participation in the planning process.

top hat pension schemes. Superannuation (qv) systems for senior managers in which benefits available under the main fund are supplemented by additional non-contributory payments. Employers' contributions to top hat systems are normally tax free.

topping out. A ceremony to celebrate the successful completion of a project.

TOPS. *See* TRAINING OPPORTUNITIES SCHEME.

torch lusspanik. A German term used to describe a hyperactive management style. *See* MANAGEMENT STYLE, COMPULSIVE.

tort. A 'civil wrong' which causes damage to other people. Examples are negligence, libel and trespass on property. Anyone who suffers as a result of a tortious act may seek compensation through the legal system.

Total final expenditure deflator. An index of the prices charged for all goods produced in the British economy.

total loss control. A holistic approach to (i) accident prevention and (ii) the minimisation of losses to a business caused by pollution. It involves the analysis and measurement of potential hazards, safety training, safety audits, spot checks and reporting procedures.

total quality control. An approach to quality management (qv) that requires genuine and enthusiastic commitment to quality improvement from all levels within an organisation – from the lowest grade of worker to the senior management of the firm. Various incentive and employee participation systems are applied to attain this commitment (e.g. quality circles (qv)).

total systems approach. An approach to organisation design (qv) and development that regards organisations as conglomerations of interrelating subsystems that need to be integrated to form a larger overall business system. *See* SYSTEMS APPROACH TO ORGANISATIONS.

Towne plan. A group bonus system that pays to group members a bonus of 50 per cent of the labour costs saved through increased group efficiency. It is named after Henry R. Towne, an American engineer who in 1886 published an influential paper advocating scientific management (qv).

trade credit. The short-term funds made available to a business through delaying the payment of suppliers' invoices.

trade cycle (business cycle). Long-term regularities in the pattern of economic activities within an industrial nation, alternating between several years of recession and several years of economic growth.

trade dispute. A dispute between workers and their employers to which legal immunity (qv) applies. Immunity is only available for disputes concerning terms and conditions of employment, dismissal, discipline (qv), negotiation and consultation procedures, or other matters strictly related to workers' jobs. Secondary actions (qv), political disputes, sympathy strikes, actions concerning the recognition of trade unions and actions not supported by a ballot of union members do not qualify for immunity.

Trade Disputes Act 1906. A statute enacted to overturn the decision of the House of Lords in the Taff Vale case of 1901 (qv). The Taff Vale decision had the effect of making unions liable to be sued for civil damages arising from industrial disputes (qv). Unions became legally immune from tort (qv) actions of this kind.

Trade Disputes Act 1960. A statute which liberalised existing rules on lawful picketing (qv).

Trade Disputes Act 1965. *See* ROOKES V. BARNARD 1964.

trade marks. Names, symbols, logos or other distinguishing features placed on articles by manufacturers or distributors to distinguish them from items supplied by other businesses.

trade off. In negotiations (qv), the sacrifice of a demand in return for an equivalent concession by the other side.

trade union. An association of workers formed to protect their interests in employment situations. The 1974 Trade

Union and Labour Relations Act (qv) defines an 'independent' trade union as one that is free from control or interference by an employer, and which registers as such with the government Certification Officer (qv). *See* STAFF ASSOCIATION; IMMUNITY OF TRADE UNIONS.

trade union accounts, right of inspection. The right, conferred by the Employment Act 1988 (qv), of individual members of trade unions (qv) to inspect their unions' accounting records.

Trade Union Act 1871. A statute that removed legal restrictions on trade unions (qv) and protected their funds (by granting immunity from civil liability arising from trade disputes (qv)).

Trade Union Act 1913. *See* POLITICAL FUNDS.

Trade Union Act 1984. A statute that placed trade unions (qv) under the obligation to ensure that all voting members of their principal executive committees (qv) have been elected by the union's membership, and that all such elected committee members are re-elected every five years. Additionally, the Act removed immunity from unions and their officials in cases where they induce a breach of contract or interfere with a contract without having balloted their members in advance.

Trade Union Advisory Committee. A part of the Organisation of Economic Co-operation and Development (OECD) comprising representatives of national trade unions in OECD member countries. Its purpose is to advise the OECD on employment protection and industrial relations matters.

Trade Union Amalgamations Act 1917. *See* TRADE UNION AMENDMENT ACT 1876.

Trade Union (Amalgamations) Act 1964. *See* TRADE UNION AMENDMENT ACT 1876.

Trade Union Amendment Act 1876. Legislation specifying procedures for the amalgamation of trade unions. A two thirds majority of members voting on the issue in each union was required before a merger could take place. This was changed by the 1917 Trade Union Amalgamation Act to at least 50 per cent of those entitled to vote, with a minimum excess of 20 per cent of those in favour (e.g. 30 per cent for the amalgamation, 20 per cent against). Today's position is as speci-

fied in the Trade Union (Amalgamations) Act 1964 whereby a simple majority vote in each union is all that is required.

Trade Union and Labour Relations Acts 1974 and 1976. Statutes which restored to workers complete immunity from civil action in relation to industrial disputes (qv), effectively reversing legislation that in 1971 had removed certain immunities. The Acts confirmed the right of employees (qv) not to be unfairly dismissed (qv); defined what is meant by an independent trade union (qv); and established the position of a government Certification Officer (qv). The extent of immunity has been altered by subsequent legislation. *See* EMPLOYMENT ACT 1982.

Trade Union and Trade Disputes Act 1927. Legislation introduced in the wake of the British General Strike of 1926. It made illegal any political strike aimed at coercing the government into taking political action. Additionally, the Act compelled 'contracting-in' in relation to political funds (qv). *See* CONTRACTING OUT OF POLITICAL CONTRIBUTIONS.

trade union ballots. Secret ballots held by independent trade unions (qv) under the 1984 Trade Union Act concerning industrial action (qv), elections of union officers (qv) or amendments to the rules of the union. The costs of holding union ballots may be reimbursed by the Secretary of State for Employment.

trade union compliance with Acts of Parliament. The strict duty of an independent trade union (qv) to comply with the technical requirements of all statutes concerning employment, trade union behaviour and industrial relations – on pain of losing their immunity from civil actions brought by employers and other interested parties. If union members do not adhere to statutory requirements the union must immediately, publicly and genuinely dissociate itself from members' unlawful actions.

trade union, legal status of. The situation determined by the Trade Union and Labour Relations Act 1974 (qv), and the Employment Act 1982 (qv), whereby trade unions do not possess their own legal identities (i.e. they are not 'corporate bodies') but, provided they register with the Certification Officer (qv), can enter into contracts, own and transfer property, sue and be sued in their own name, and are exempt from civil liability in relation to genuine trade disputes (qv).

trade union liability for torts. The liability for damages of independent trade unions (qv) for unlawful industrial actions committed 'on their behalf' (i.e. endorsed by one of the union's executive committees or by a 'responsible' union officer). Liability could arise from secondary action (qv), from seeking to bring about a closed shop (qv), from actions not in furtherance of a trade dispute (qv) or from certain strikes not supported by a secret ballot. There is an upper limit on the maximum damages payable, dependent on the size of the union.

Trades Council. A regional grouping of trade unions which meets periodically to discuss issues and developments in industrial relations occurring in the area concerned. Trades Councils represent trade union interests at the local level, and might co-ordinate industrial actions (qv) in disputes where several unions are involved. Councils are voluntary organisations and rarely employ full time officials. The Trades Council movement is affiliated to the Trades Union Congress (qv), to which it sends a delegate each year.

Trades Union Congress (TUC). The national association of British Trade unions, formed in 1868. It exists to (i) promote the interests of the trade union movement, (ii) conduct research into industrial relations, (iii) act as a mouthpiece for organised labour at the national level, (iv) promote international labour solidarity and (v) settle inter-union disputes. It is a federation of independent bodies and not a 'union of unions'. Trade unions (qv) registered with the Certification Officer (qv) do not have to belong to the TUC. *See* BRIDLINGTON AGREEMENT.

trading account. The account in which a business computes its gross profit (qv).

traditional authority. Authority (qv) possessed by a person regarded by subordinates as having rightfully inherited a high status position.

trainability tests. Selection tests intended to establish whether job applicants have the potential to learn a new skill within a certain period. A small part of the job is taught to the applicant, who is then examined to establish whether he or she has learnt the material satisfactorily.

trainee-centred learning. An approach to training that requires trainees to undertake independent research and to complete assignments (individually or in groups) rather than attend lectures.

Trainer Training (TT). A government scheme for the training of employment training (ET) (qv) and youth training (YT) (qv) instructors. It is administered by Training and Enterprise Councils (TECs) (qv) and delivered through a national network of 'accredited training centres' (ACTs) contracted by TECs to provide the training.

training. Instruction on how to use knowledge; as opposed to 'education', which concerns the intrinsic value of knowledge itself. Training is utilitarian and instrumental, and has direct practical objectives.

Training Access Points (TAPs). A national system of computerised data bases from which information on UK training programmes may be obtained. Access points are situated in job centres and certain libraries, and in mobile TAP units which visit employers' premises.

Training Agency. An arm of the Employment Department Group (qv) that sought to help the unemployed, (especially the long-term unemployed) find jobs through improving their skills, enterprise and employability. It was also concerned with assisting young people to make the transition from school to work via the provision of various training programmes. The Training Agency's responsibilities were taken over by the Training Enterprise and Education Division (qv) of the Department of Employment.

Training Agents. Government appointed or approved organisations responsible for placing unemployed workers with local firms under the Employment Training Scheme (qv). Employers did not have to pay wages to or

National Insurance for the trainees they received, but were expected to contribute a small amount (subject to individual negotiation) towards the overall costs of the system. The maximum training period was 12 months.

Training and Enterprise Councils (TECs). Groups of local company managing directors and senior business executives which in 1990 took over the Training Agency's (qv) local offices. There are about 80 TECs in England and Wales, formed as independent companies. Each TEC liaises with a government appointed regional official. TECs are intended to provide Britain with a skilled workforce. To achieve this goal they contract training providers (e.g. local colleges or employment training (qv) managers) to deliver courses and other training that correspond to specifications laid down by the area TEC. The aim is to match the training provided to the needs of local businesses. TECs do not themselves provide training or training assistance.

Training Commission. The precursor of the Training Agency (qv), to which all the Training Commission's functions were transferred in 1988.

training credit scheme. A system introduced in 1991 for financing the training of school leavers. Young people in certain areas receive 'vouchers' worth £1,500 which they then present to either (i) an employer who offers suitable training or (ii) a training institution if they are unemployed.

training cycle. Four sequential stages in the training process: identification and specification of training needs; design of a training programme; implementation; and evaluation.

Training, Enterprise and Education Division (TEED) of the Department of Employment. The successor to the Training Agency (qv), which itself succeeded the Training Commission (qv). It exists primarily to liaise with Training and Enterprise Councils (TECs) (qv). It does not specify and control training and enterprise programmes in its own right.

Training for Enterprise Programme. A collection of schemes for training people to start new businesses or improve the performances of existing firms.

training for stock (speculative/countercyclical training). Training undertaken in anticipation of new skill requirements and/or a cyclical upturn in the national economy.

training levies. Special charges that Industrial Training Boards (qv) were statutorily permitted to impose on all firms deemed to fall within a particular industry. Proceeds were then used to finance industry training programmes. Nearly all the Training Boards which possessed this right have now been abolished.

training needs analysis. The systematic examination of the gap between the skills, knowledge and attitudes necessary to perform a job well and those possessed by the current incumbent of the position. This exercise can also be undertaken for an entire organisation. *See* SYSTEMATIC TRAINING.

Training Opportunities Scheme (TOPS). A government scheme introduced in 1972 in order to provide unemployed people with the opportunity to acquire skills and occupational qualifications. It involved a system of grants towards the living expenses of those in training, retraining or undertaking professional courses intended to further a trainee's overall career. TOPS grants were subsequently taken over by alternative government training programmes.

training, quality of. A collection of attributes of a training programme including (i) bringing the trainee to a prespecified level of ability within a maximum period, (ii) satisfying the skill requirements of employing firms and (iii) meeting the individual trainee's career development needs.

Training Resource Centres. Units established in further education colleges for the purpose of helping students manage their own training. Tutors do not 'teach' the students as such; rather they help learners identify their training needs and advise on where to find suitable training materials.

training simulator. A training situation in which (i) real life working conditions are replicated, (ii) the trainee can control the working environment and (iii) no damage occurs when mistakes are made.

Training Within Industry (TWI). A training technique devised in the United

States during the Second World War and used extensively in British industry in the 1950s and 1960s. TWI schemes were government sponsored and survived until 1987. The method involved breaking jobs into separate units and analysing how each part should be completed. Segmented job components were then taught separately.

trait based appraisal. Elements of performance appraisal (qv) exercises that seek to assess the personal characteristics of appraisees in relation to criteria such as initiative, dependability, co-operation, etc.

trait theory. A theory of leadership (qv) which asserts that certain people are born with or otherwise acquire personal qualities (e.g. assertiveness, self-confidence, reliability) that make them effective leaders.

Trans European Mobility Scheme for University Students (TEMSUS). A companion to the COMETT (qv) and ERASMUS (qv) initiatives intended to facilitate education and training exchanges between the EC and central and eastern Europe.

transactional analysis. A means for understanding and changing interpersonal behaviour, based on the work of the psychologist E. Berne. It assumes that all grown up individuals possess three 'ego states': the parent (concerning attitudes towards right and wrong); the child (associated with wanting, manipulating and playfulness); and the adult (involving logic, rationality and objective thinking). All three exist simultaneously within the person, though any one of them may dominate at any particular moment. *See* LIFE POSITION.

transactional interaction. A communication between persons of unequal status which sets out mutual rights and obligations.

transactional leadership. Leadership that focuses on (i) providing subordinates with the resources necessary to complete their duties, and (ii) helping subordinates undertake tasks. The approach does not attempt to motivate subordinates into transcending immediate operational requirements.

transcendental leadership. *See* TRANSFORMATIONAL LEADERSHIP.

transfer of learning. The situation that occurs when having learned one thing makes it easier to learn something else. For example, a person who has learnt word-processing using a certain package (Wordstar for instance) will quickly be able to operate a different system (e.g. Locoscript). This is 'positive' transfer. However, negative transfer is also possible. Here, learning a new task is more difficult in consequence of previous training. Consider for instance a 'two finger' typist who then tries to learn touch typing. *See* IDENTICAL ELEMENTS; TRANSFER THROUGH PRINCIPLES.

Transfer of Undertakings Directive 1977. An EC Directive that requires employers to consult with workers with a view to (i) avoiding dismissals and (ii) guaranteeing workers' accumulated employment rights, on the transfer of ownership of enterprises. In the UK this led to the Transfer of Undertakings (Protection of Employment) Regulations 1981 (qv).

Transfer of Undertakings (Protection of Employment) Regulations 1981. A law that requires the purchaser of a business to take over all the accumulated employment rights of workers who were employed in the business immediately before the transfer.

transfer payments. A term used by economists to denote social security benefits such as state retirement pensions, statutory sick pay, unemployment benefit, etc., which do not represent the creation of wealth and as such do not form part of the country's gross domestic product (qv).

transfer payment between pension schemes. A payment made by the trustees of one occupational pension scheme to the trustees of another in order to transfer an employee's benefits when he or she changes jobs. The payment may be made in cash, or through the purchase from an insurance company of the employee's choice of a Section 32 Annuity (qv) in favour of that person.

transfer through principles. A theory regarding the transfer of learning (qv) which asserts that transfer is facilitated not only through identical elements (qv) in jobs but also because learners can often apply to new tasks general principles derived from experience acquired in previous employment.

transformational leadership. Charismatic leadership which inspires subordinates to levels of motivation considerably higher than are objectively required to complete their duties.

transitional unemployment. Unemployment resulting from workers changing their jobs and hence being temporarily out of work between the end of one job and the start of another.

Transport and General Workers' Union (TGWU). One of Britain's largest trade unions. It is a general union open to all types of worker.

Transport Salaried Staff Association (TSSA). A white collar trade union (qv) that recruits employees in British Rail, the docks, road haulage, freight forwarding and the travel and hotel industries.

travel to and from work, rule on liability for accidents. The legal rule that employers are responsible for damage suffered by employees when travelling between places of work (e.g. to collect materials or equipment), but not for damages resulting from journeys between home and work unless the employer provides the transport or controls the journey, e.g. by requiring one employee to give a lift to another.

Treasury model. An economic forecasting model used by HM Treasury to predict the state of the economy for the next 12 to 15 months. It has over 1,000 equations intended to identify the links between wages, prices, output and employment.

Treaty of Rome. The original 1956 agreement which established the European Economic Community. *See* ARTICLES 117 AND 118.

trespass. Illegal entry to someone else's property or an infringement of an individual's safety and freedom. The latter is known as 'trespass to the person' and includes assault, unlawful arrest and false imprisonment.

tripartism. A philosophy of social organisation and industrial relations which advocates bringing together the government, the TUC (qv) and the CBI (qv) in order to determine economic policy making and to involve unions and employers' associations in the operation of statutory bodies (ACAS (qv) and the Health and Safety Commission (qv) for example).

Trist, E. L., and Bamforth, K. W. Industrial sociologists who in the 1940s studied the effects of the introduction of new mechanised methods on working groups in the British coal mining industry, concluding that social and technical factors inter-relate to affect job performance via a socio-technical system within which various working methods can be imposed, with differing social and psychological consequences. This implied the need for job design (qv) and a systems approach to organisations (qv).

Truck Acts. Legislation of 1831, 1896 and 1940 which prohibited the payment of employees' wages in any form other than legal tender. The aim was to prevent employers paying their workers in goods and/or vouchers that could only be used in shops owned by the employing company. These Acts were replaced by the Wages Act of 1986 (qv).

trust. Money or property held for the benefit of others by persons ('trustees') specially appointed for this purpose. Trustees may not themselves profit from the situation.

trust and confidence, obligations of employers and employees. The common law duty of each party to a contract of employment (qv) to treat the other with trust and confidence. Employers must be considerate to their employees; while the latter are required to behave in a discreet and trustworthy manner.

trustees. Individuals or organisations responsible for administering the resources of other people or organisations. Examples are trust companies such as investment trusts or unit trusts, and trustees of bankrupt persons.

TSSA. *See* TRANSPORT SALARIED STAFF ASSOCIATION.

TT. *See* TRAINER TRAINING.

TTTA. The acronym for the Timber Trade Training Association.

TUC. *See* TRADES UNION CONGRESS.

TUC Rulebook. A document listing the objectives of the Trades Union Congress (qv) and the obligations it imposes on member unions. Among the most important rules are Rule 11, which requires affiliated unions to inform the TUC of the details of inter-union disputes; Rule 12, which allows the TUC to resolve inter-union conflicts; and Rule 13, that enables the TUC to expel any member whose activities are detrimental to the interests of the trade union movement.

turkey farm. A department to which an organisation's incompetent managers are assigned in order to group them together in one place. The department involved will usually be responsible for functions the mismanagement of which cause minimal damage to the organisation's work.

TVEI. *See* TECHNICAL AND VOCATIONAL EDUCATION INITIATIVE.

20 per cent director. A director (qv) who controls directly or through beneficiaries at least 20 per cent of the ordinary share capital of a company. Special rules apply to the occupational pension benefits available to such directors, e.g. limits on the minimum age of retirement, maximum cash payouts, restrictions on the range of persons allowed to benefit from the insured director's death in service, etc.

TWI. *See* TRAINING WITHIN INDUSTRY.

twilight shift. A working period in the early/late evening, e.g. 6.00 to 10.00 pm.

two factor theory of intelligence. A theory advanced by C. Spearman in 1927 which suggested the existence of a general factor ('G') underlying human intelligence and applicable to all fields of human endeavour. The 'G-factor' was independent of factors (referred to as 'S-factors') specific to particular situations.

two factor theory of motivation. A motivation (qv) theory that distinguishes between 'motivators' (e.g. interesting work, responsibility assumed, promotion prospects) which actively encourage employees to work harder, and 'hygiene' or 'maintenance' factors the absence or inadequacy of which causes dissatisfaction – but which do not of themselves induce additional effort. Examples of maintenance factors are low pay, poor supervision, unpleasant working conditions and the absence of fringe benefits.

two handed process chart. A diagram consisting of two columns each showing the movements of one of a worker's hands while completing a task.

two-monday mornings syndrome. The problem that sometimes arises with job sharing (qv) schemes whereby two people each require time to set up their operations and to become acclimatised to work within the same week; rather than just one person experiencing the 'Monday morning' feeling.

two tier boards of directors. The situation common in Continental European companies whereby large firms have two boards of directors: an 'executive board' comprising managerial employees responsible for tactics (qv) and operational management and, above that, a supervisory board (qv) which takes strategic decisions. This arrangement is legally compulsory in some EC nations, with elected worker directors having to sit on the supervisory board.

two way communication. Communication (qv) that involves a response (e.g. the expression of an opinion) from the message recipient. This contrasts with 'one way communication' whereby the recipient merely sees or hears messages (via notice boards or public address announcements for instance).

type A people. High activity individuals with 'fast track' existences who constantly seek to accomplish too much in too short a period. Such people tend to be assertive, restless and are more prone to heart disease than the alternative type B people, who are able to relax easily, are unassertive and conciliatory.

type theories of personality. Analyses of personality (qv) characteristics that seek to classify individuals into a handful of personality categories. The approach has a long history. For instance, in 400 BC the Greek physician Hippocrates postulated the existence of just four types of temperament: optimistic, melancholic, irritable, and apathetic. Modern type theories are embedded in the Myers–Briggs (qv) indicator and the Cattell 16PF test (qv).

U

UCATT. *See* UNION OF CONSTRUCTION, AL-LIED TRADES AND TECHNICIANS.

UCW. *See* UNION OF COMMUNICATION WORKERS.

U-form organisation. Another term for functional organisation (qv). The name derives from the fact that within a functional structure, authority can be traced upwards through the chain of command (qv) to a single 'unitary source'.

ultra vires contract. A contract that is not legally enforceable because the person or organisation making it had no legal power to enter the contract in the first instance.

umpire. In the context of arbitration (qv) of an industrial dispute, an independent person appointed to settle an issue when the arbitration procedure involves more than one arbitrator and the arbitrators themselves are unable to agree.

uncertainty avoidance theory. A model of managerial behaviour which asserts that managements typically attempt to gain control over their environments, even if the measures needed for this result in lower profits. For example, a management may choose to involve trade unions in decision making in order to create stable industrial relations (qv), despite the unions' consequent ability to interfere with the profitable administration of the firm.

unconditioned response. *See* CONDITIONED RESPONSE.

unconditioned stimulus. In classical conditioning (qv), a stimulus that naturally evokes a reflexive response (qv). The association of an unconditioned stimulus (e.g. presentation of food to a hungry dog) with another stimulus (ringing a bell for instance) can cause the second stimulus itself to elicit the reflexive response (e.g. the dog salivating).

unconscious mind. That part of the psyche to which the individual assigns drives and yearnings, the possession of which he or she is not prepared to admit consciously. However, the contents of the unconscious mind may surface occasionally, and psychological attempts to repress or inhibit these thoughts can result in irrational and disturbed behaviour.

underachiever. *See* OVERACHIEVER.

understudying. A technique of mangement development (qv) in which an executive (qv) temporarily acts as an assistant to a more senior manager in order to gain an appreciation of the content and difficulties of the senior manager's job.

unearned income. *See* EARNED INCOME.

unemployability supplement. A special form of disablement benefit (qv) payable in certain cases to victims of industrial accidents or diseases occurring prior to 6 April 1987 (when the scheme was abolished).

unemployment, definition of. According to UK government statistics, all people who are registered unemployed *and* claiming benefit. Hence the definition excludes unemployed people who choose not to claim benefit or are not entitled to benefit. Also it does not take account of people who are on government training and community employment schemes who would otherwise be unemployed.

unemployment pay. State benefit paid to unemployed workers who are above school-leaving age and have been 'employed earners' (i.e. not self-employed). To qualify for benefit, claimants need to have paid Class I National Insurance contributions on earnings of at least 25 times the weekly lower earnings limit. Maximum benefit is only available on earnings of at least 50 times the lower weekly limit in the preceding tax year. Income support (qv) is available to people with insufficient Class I contributions.

unemployment trap. A possible consequence of the poverty trap (qv) in the sense that being in the poverty trap may dissuade a person from accepting an offer of employment.

unequal value jobs. Jobs done by men and women that vary not only in their content but also with respect to the effort, skill and decision-making abilities needed to perform them. The relevant yardstick is the demands made on the employee while doing the work, rather than the value of the work to the firm as perceived by the employing company. See EQUAL PAY (AMENDMENT) REGULATIONS 1983; SIMILAR DEMANDS.

Unfair Contract Terms Act 1977. A statute restricting to certain specified circumstances the use of disclaimers and exemption clauses in contracts. Thus for example a notice on a factory gate declaring that 'anyone entering these premises does so at their own risk' has no legal validity because this statement seeks to avoid responsibility for injuries to employees or others that might arise through the firm's negligence or failure to implement a statutory (qv) requirement.

unfair dismissal. The sacking of an employee who is not excluded from the 1978 Employment Protection (Consolidation) Act (qv) for anything other than incapability (qv), gross misconduct (qv), genuine redundancy (qv), or some other substantial reason (qv). Cases concerning alleged unfair dismissal are heard by Industrial Tribunals (qv). See REASONABLE BEHAVIOUR.

unfair dismissal, excluded persons. Workers who cannot claim unfair dismissal under the Employment Protection (Consolidation) Act 1978 (qv); namely, employees who (i) have completed less than two years' continuous employment (qv) working at least 16 hours per week (five years for workers who do between eight and 16 hours a week), (ii) ordinarily work outside Great Britain, (iii) are employed under a fixed-term contract of one year or more and have signed an agreement not to bring an action for unfair dismissal on expiry of the contract, or (iv) are above the normal retirement age.

unfair dismissal, remedies for. Options potentially available to unfairly dismissed workers whose Industrial Tribunal (qv) actions have succeeded; namely, reinstatement (qv), re-engagement (qv) and compensation. Employers are not legally obliged to take back workers they have unfairly dismissed, but will have to pay increased amounts of compensation if they fail to do so. There are four types of compensation: the basic award (qv), the compensatory award (qv), the additional award (qv), and the special award (qv). The basic and compensatory awards are reduced if the Industrial Tribunal (qv) hearing the case believes the employee contributed to the dismissal. Compensatory awards can also be cut where dismissed workers fail to attempt to find alternative jobs within a reasonable period.

UNICE. See UNION DES INDUSTRIES DE LA COMMUNAUTE EUROPEENNE.

Unified Vocational Preparation Programme. A precursor to the Youth Training Scheme (qv).

uniform costing. Application of standard rules for the allocation of overheads and other costs within the various divisions or subsidiaries of the same enterprise.

unincorporated associations. Associations that have no legal existence independent of their members. Common examples are partnerships (qv) and trade unions (qv). See INCORPORATED ASSOCIATIONS.

union density. The proportion of employees who belong to a trade union in a particular workplace, firm or industry.

Union des Industries de la Communaute Europeenne (UNICE). An international organisation formed to represent the views of the central employers' associations (qv) (the CBI for example) of 22 European states. It co-ordinates members' opinions and presents them to bodies such as the European Commission (qv), the European Parliament and the EC Council of Ministers (qv). UNICE has a full time secretariat and operates through five policy committees: economic affairs; external relations; company affairs; industrial affairs; and social affairs.

union duties, time off for. The right conferred on employees by the

Employment Protection (Consolidation) Act 1978 (qv) to receive paid time off during working hours for the completion of union duties. To be eligible for paid time off an employee must be an official of a recognised (qv) and independent trade union (qv). Periods taken must be 'reasonable' and the duties performed need to relate to relations between workers and the employing organisation.

union membership agreements. Contracts established under the Trade Union and Labour Relations Acts of 1974 and 1976 (qv) for the purpose of forming and/or maintaining a closed shop (qv). The Employment Act 1988 (qv) (which makes the dismissal of a worker for non-union membership automatically unfair (qv)) and the Employment Act 1990 (qv) (which outlaws the pre-entry closed shop) have rendered such agreements unenforceable.

Union of Communication Workers (UCW). A UK trade union (qv) that recruits manual workers in the Post Office, plus certain types of employee in British Telecom and Girobank.

Union of Construction, Allied Trades, and Technicians (UCATT). A trade union (qv) active in the shipbuilding, construction engineering and furniture making industries, in local authorities and the NHS. It is particularly strong in the house and office building industry.

Union of Shop, Distribution and Allied Workers (USDAW). A trade union (qv) active in the retail distribution and hairdressing industries. It recruits white collar workers and shop assistants.

unit costing. A technique of overhead allocation involving the division of a firm's fixed costs by the number of units of output. The method is suitable for continuously manufactured products where each unit of output is identical.

unit linked annuity. A retirement annuity (qv) which relates the annuitant's pension to the current market value of a unit trust, equity fund, property fund, gilt edged or similar investment fund.

unit of competence. A combination of elements of competence (qv) specified by the NCVQ (qv) and collectively ac-

cepted by employers and an industry lead body (qv) as relevant for the award of an NCVQ qualification. The latter will comprise a number of related units of competence, each concerned with competence in a different activity within a job. Units of competence reflect the skill, knowledge and understanding necessary for successful completion of appropriate duties and specify the performance required to demonstrate competence.

unitarism. The belief that both sides of industry (management and employees) have identical interests and hence may be expected to pull together towards a common objective and to work as a team (qv). Co-operation is taken for granted; dissent cannot be understood.

United Road Transport Union (URTU). A trade union (qv) that organises and represents road haulage drivers. It was originally formed as the 'United Carters' Association in 1890.

unity of command. A principle of organisation which asserts that each employee should only be accountable to one boss.

unity of direction. The proposition of the classical approach (qv) to management that all divisions, departments and sections of an enterprise should share common perspectives, work towards common objectives and have the same superordinate goals (qv).

universalisability principle. The idea that all business decisions that require an ethical judgement should be taken in the same way, according to a predetermined set of strict moral principles.

unofficial industrial action. Strikes and other actions against employers initiated without the knowledge and/or consent of an independent trade union (qv). Sometimes unofficial actions are led by workplace shop stewards (qv).

unofficial sanctions. Measures taken by employers in retaliation against a union which has ordered its members to work to rule (qv). Actions could include the strict enforcement of petty rules, withdrawal of employee privileges (refusing requests for time off for example) and generally attempting to make employees' lives disagreeable. If excessive, such behaviour could lead to employees resigning their jobs and then claiming unfair constructive dismissal (qv).

unsocial hours. Working periods outside those normally worked, e.g. twilight (qv) or night shift periods, or the early morning hours.

up front payments. Remuneration paid on settlement of a contract (usually a contract for services (qv) rather than a contract of employment) prior to work being commenced.

Urban Development Corporations. Government bodies established in 1988 to improve the physical environments of inner city areas. They have access to public funds which are then used to stimulate private sector investment.

Urban Programme. A government regional development scheme intended to promote co-operation between local authorities and local commercial enterprises, without significant amounts of additional state funding.

URTU. See UNITED ROAD TRANSPORT UNION.

Urwick, Lyndall F. (1891–1983). Management consultant and advocate of scientific management (qv) and the classical approach (qv) to organisation.

Urwick-Orr profile method. A job evaluation method (qv) which categorises jobs into 'families' prior to comparing them using points (qv) and grading systems (qv). The technique relies heavily on employee participation during the evaluation process.

USDAW. See UNION OF SHOP, DISTRIBUTION, AND ALLIED WORKERS.

utility analysis. Calculation of the monetary costs and benefits of various means of selecting job applicants in order to compare alternative recruitment strategies. The costs and benefits of each method are related to those expected if candidates are selected at random. Costs include job advertisement expenses, the effects of underperformance by a poorly selected employee, replacement costs of unsatisfactory workers who resign or are fired, etc. Benefits relate to the ability to promote satisfactory recruits after a short period, improved organisational performance, harmonious group relations, etc. See BROGDEN–HUNTER METHOD; TAYLOR–RUSSELL METHOD.

utmost good faith, principle of. The legal duty of a party to a contract to disclose all material facts relevant to the agreement, even if the other party has not asked for specific details. This is particularly important for insurance contracts.

V

Val Duchesse dialogue. Meetings between European Community employers' organisations, employee organisations (trade union bodies for example) and public enterprises (the three sides being collectively referred to as the 'social partners' of the European Community) initiated by the European Commission (qv) to discuss EC social policy. The dialogue resulted in a 1988 EC paper on the need for cooperation between the social partners on social issues. *See* DEGIMBE REPORT.

valence. The strength of a person's desire for an outcome or the occurrence of a particular event. Valence is a critical element of Vroom's (qv) theory of motivation (qv), which can be stated by the formula:

$$\text{Motivation} = \text{Valence} \times \text{Expectation}.$$

See EXPECTANCY THEORY.

validation of training courses. Assessment of whether the objectives of training courses have been attained and, if so, whether this has actually helped employees improve their job performances.

validity of selection tests. The desirable property of a selection test that it measure precisely what it is intended to measure. For instance, an intelligence test (qv) should evaluate the test subject's intelligence and not general knowledge obtained from past schooling. *See* CONTENT VALIDITY; PREDICTIVE VALIDITY; CONSTRUCT VALIDITY; and CONCURRENT VALIDITY.

value added evaluation of training. An approach to the assessment of the efficiency of training courses. Trainees' competencies are measured on entry to a course and when the course is completed, and a value is assigned to the difference. This value is then compared with tables of expected values for trainees possessing various backgrounds and prior levels of education.

These tables are computed from observations on large nationwide samples of trainees completing similar courses. Thus, a course which improves trainees' competencies by the national average value in less than the national average period will be rated as highly effective.

value added statement. An analysis of the sources of extra value added to a firm's purchases of raw materials and input components, e.g. via manufacturing, assembly, warehousing and distribution.

value added tax (VAT). A tax levied at each stage in the production and distribution process. A business charges VAT to its customers but may reclaim the VAT it pays when purchasing its own supplies. In consequence the business pays tax only on 'value added' to inputs.

value analysis. The critical examination of the functions of a product to establish whether these functions could be fulfilled by an item with a lower cost of production.

value system. A set of interrelated attitudes, ideas and perspectives on issues that determine an individual's or a society's views on right and wrong and what constitutes correct behaviour.

vandalism. Violence against property, ranging from graffiti to the actual destruction of physical items. A wide ranging research study into the causes of vandalism conducted by the Home Office in 1978 concluded that most vandalism is directed against communal parts of institutions rather than against personal property. *See* CRIMINAL DAMAGE; ACQUISITIVE VANDALISM.

variable costs. Costs which vary according to the volume of output. Examples include raw materials used in production, piece rate (qv) wages, electricity used to power a machine, etc. *See* OVERHEADS.

variable factor programming (VFP). A technique of work measurement (qv) containing the following steps: (i) evaluating the content of the work to be completed; (ii) timing the jobs undertaken by workers and averaging these (including the average times needed for interruptions) over a four week period; (iii) establishing target times for various activities; and (iv) drafting 'variable staffing tables' that specify the number of labour hours required for different volumes of work, thus enabling the prediction of the number of employees needed.

ventilation requirements. Obligations imposed on employers by the Factories Act 1961 (qv), requiring them (i) to ventilate rooms so as to carry away dust and fumes, (ii) to take all reasonable measures to prevent employees from inhaling injurious or offensive dust and fumes and (iii) to stop substantial amounts of dust accumulating in any room.

venture capital. A minority shareholding in a young and rapidly expanding business taken by an outside body (e.g. a merchant bank) in order to inject capital into the company in return for a high rate of return. Typically, the venture capital agreement provides for (i) the resale of the shares to the company on a prespecified future date at a (high) predetermined price and (ii) some involvement of the venture capital provider in the management of the firm.

verification of training. The process of monitoring a training course and checking the reliability of assessment (qv) of the programme.

versatility. See ADAPTABILITY.

vertical communication. Formal exchanges of information up and down the hierarchical chain of command (qv) of an organisation.

vertical integration. Mergers or takeovers of businesses at different stages in the chain of production, distribution or supply. 'Backward integration' involves taking over a firm at a previous stage in the chain (e.g. a producer of raw materials). 'Forward integration' occurs when a business takes over an organisation at a later stage in the chain (a retailer for instance). See HORIZONTAL INTEGRATION.

vertical loading. Job enrichment (qv)

via the allocation to workers of higher level responsibilities (administration or supervisory work for example) in order to increase their job satisfaction.

vested benefits. Benefits attached to an occupational pension scheme and to which an employee is unconditionally entitled, as of right.

vested rights. Rights transferred to a person or organisation by another person or organisation. An example is the assignment of the benefits from an endowment insurance policy to a bank as security against a loan.

vestibule training. Training that occurs in a room set up to reproduce the actual conditions of the workplace, with exactly the same machines and equipment, materials, environmental circumstances, etc., as exist in the workshops or offices where trainees will eventually be employed.

VET. See VOCATIONAL EDUCATIONAL TRAINING.

VFP. See VARIABLE FACTOR PROGRAMMING.

vibration white finger (VWI). An industrial injury involving loss of blood circulation in the hands in consequence of prolonged exposure to high levels of vibration. VWF may result from operating pneumatic hammers, chain saws, portable grinders or other mechanically driven vibrating tools.

vicarious (imitative) learning. Learning (qv) via the observation of others. The learner watches how other people behave and notes the consequences of their behaviour.

vicarious liability. The legal doctrine which ensures that responsibility for an employee's (qv) breach of a statute or common law duty lies with the employing organisation and not with the employee him or her self, provided the latter was acting 'in the course of employment' (i.e. undertaking duties authorised by the employer or incidental to the employee's work). Vicarious liability does *not* extend to criminal actions or to certain aspects of the Health and Safety at Work Act 1974 (qv) which states that any person acting in a managerial capacity may be held personally liable for offences committed against the Act if that person agreed, actively or passively, to the commission of the offence or if it was attributable to his or her neglect.

vicarious liability of a trade union. The liability of a certified trade union (qv) for civil damages arising from acts authorised or endorsed by a 'responsible union official' (e.g. a member of one of the union's principal executive committees (qv). The Employment Act 1982 (qv) limits the amount of damages payable, according to the size of the union's membership.

victimisation. Treating an employee less favourably than others because he or she complains of not receiving a statutory right or helps someone else complain of unfair treatment. *See* SEX DISCRIMINATION ACT 1975.

videotex. The international term for information systems through which databases (qv) are accessed from users' computer terminals and the desired information displayed on the user's VDU (where it can be read, added to and manipulated).

view data. *See* VIDEOTEX.

viscidity. Solidarity within a group.

visual display units, EC Directive on. A directive (qv) of the European Community specifying minimum health and safety requirements for employees who work with display screen equipment. Employers must analyse VDU workstations in order to identify potential hazards, train employees in the proper use of VDU equipment, schedule employees' workloads to avoid protracted screen contact periods, and provide VDU workers with eyetests and special spectacles if their normal spectacles are not suitable for VDU jobs. The Directive also imposes technical standards for screen sizes, luminosity, keyboard design, etc.

Vocational Educational Training (VET). Education and training intended to prepare people for social, economic and technical (skills related) aspects of work.

vocational interest inventories. Standardised inventories (qv) intended to measure personal interests for the purpose of providing career (qv) guidance. Individuals indicate their hobbies and recreational and other non-job related activities, and complete a questionnaire which confronts them with a list of pairs of activities from which they must indicate which of each pair they most enjoy doing and which they like least. The premise underlying such exercises is that people are more suitable for certain occupations if they possess interests similar to individuals who have already succeeded in those occupations. *See* KUDER PREFERENCE RECORD.

vocational qualification. A statement attesting a person's competence in relation to an occupation. *See* NCVQ.

vocational training. Training that leads to the possession of an occupational skill.

volenti non fit injuria. A defence against an employer's liability for an industrial injury sustained by a worker. It is available when the injured person *obviously* consented to accept the risk of the injury, e.g. a professional boxer hurt by an opponent's punch during a boxing match.

voluntarism. A philosophy of industrial relations which asserts that employers and unions should be left to resolve disputes and reach collective agreements voluntarily, without the existence of laws governing industrial relations or the ability of one of the parties to a dispute to take the other to Court. *See* NORMATIVE APPROACH TO INDUSTRIAL RELATIONS.

Vredeling proposal. A draft Directive of the European Commission (qv) intended to compel large companies to inform and consult with workers on strategic and other policy matters.

Vroom, V. H. A motivation (qv) theorist who asserted that an individual's behaviour is affected by (i) what the person wants to happen, (ii) that person's estimate of the probabilities of various events occurring, including the desired outcome and (iii) the strength of a person's belief that a certain outcome will satisfy his or her needs. *See* EXPECTANCY THEORY; VALENCE.

VTP. An EC supported partnership between an industry and a university. The VTP scheme is intended to facilitate advanced training for new technologies within Community countries.

Vroom–Yetton leadership model. *See* NORMATIVE DECISION-MAKING MODEL.

W

wage. *See* SALARY.

wage controls. Laws and government regulations forbidding the payment of wage increases that exceed certain predefined limits to workers in particular industries and occupations.

wage drift. The tendency of locally negotiated wage rates to rise ('drift') above national minima agreed between panels of unions and employers' associations. It results from astute bargaining by plant level union representatives.

wage effort bargain. The amount of work to be done for an agreed wage, including the effort put into the job as well as how many hours are worked.

wage fund theory of wages. A nineteenth century economic theory which asserted that wage levels depended on the magnitude of accumulated capital investment within an economy.

wage–price spiral. The proposition that inflation is substantially attributable to wage increases obtained by unions via collective bargaining. Higher wages mean higher costs for firms which are assumed automatically to pass these on to consumers in the form of higher prices. This increases the cost of living, leading to employee demands for still higher wages to compensate for the consequent fall in their living standards. *See* WAGE PUSH INFLATION.

wage push inflation. Price rises caused by firms passing on to customers higher wage costs resulting from employees obtaining pay increases in excess of increases in productivity. *See* WAGE–PRICE SPIRAL.

wage restraint, appeals for. Government exhortations to trade unions (qv) and other employee representative groups not to demand wage increases exceeding certain prespecified levels. *See* INCOMES POLICIES.

Wage Statistics in the European Community, Guide to Current Sources. A publication of the Statistical Office of the European Community, available in Britain from HMSO.

Wages Act 1986. A statute that removed all previous restrictions on employers paying workers by means other than cash (or cheque or credit transfer). It also specified the circumstances in which deductions from wages are allowable. The Act covers self-employed contractors as well as employees. If an employer makes an unauthorised deduction the worker or sub-contractor may apply to an Industrial Tribunal (qv) for compensation.

Wages Arrestment Limitation (Scotland) Act 1870. The statute which governs the issue of attachment of earnings (qv) orders in Scotland. It specifies limits on the amount of money that can be 'arrested' from an individual's wages each week.

Wages Councils. Statutory bodies set up to fix basic pay in certain industry groupings where individual places of employment are too small and scattered for trade unions to become established. Currently, Councils exist for 11 industry groupings. Councils comprise equal numbers of employer and employee representatives, plus three independent members. They set a minimum hourly rate for the first 39 or 40 hours of work (depending on the industry) and a minimum overtime rate for hours worked thereafter. Prior to 1986, Councils could set minimum periods for paid holidays, but this is no longer possible. Workers under 21 years of age are not covered by Council orders. *See* WAGES INSPECTOR.

wages in lieu of notice. Wages paid to workers under notice of dismissal in order to pay them up to the ends of their notice periods without their having to turn up for work.

wages inspector. An official attached to a Wages Council (qv) who possesses the legal power to enter, search and interrogate employees of businesses in the industry covered by the Council. The inspector's role is to ensure that employers pay wages at least equal to the minimum specified by a Council order, and may prosecute employers who fail to do so. Guilty employers might then be fined and ordered to pay compensation to their workers.

waiting days. Days when an employee is sick but not entitled to statutory sick pay (qv). Three waiting days are necessary prior to entitlement. However, if two or more periods of incapacity (qv) to work fall within a period not exceeding eight weeks they become 'linked', so that waiting days occur only within the *first* period of incapacity. Statutory sick pay is paid for each day of following periods.

waiting time. Losses in working time caused by interruptions that are beyond a worker's control, e.g. through machine breakdowns, shortages of raw materials, power failures, etc. See CONTINGENCY ALLOWANCE.

waiver of breach of contract. The situation that arises when an employer summarily dismisses an employee an unreasonably long time after the worker committed the offence for which he or she is dismissed. A long delay prior to dismissal will normally be regarded by an Industrial Tribunal (qv) as a decision by the employer to ignore the misconduct, hence causing the dismissal to be unfair (qv).

warning signs. See SAFETY SIGNS REGULATIONS 1980.

warnings to employees. See FAIR PROCEDURES PRIOR TO DISMISSAL; ACAS CODE ON DISCIPLINARY AND OTHER PROCEDURES IN EMPLOYMENT.

warrant of execution. A Court order against a debtor enabling a Court bailiff to seize the debtor's goods to the value necessary to clear his or her outstanding balances.

washing facilities, obligations to provide. Requirements incorporated into the Factories Act 1961 (qv) and the Offices, Shops and Railway Premises Act 1963 (qv) whereby employers must provide washing facilities with clear and running hot and cold water, plus soap and towels or hot air hand driers.

wastage curve. A graph showing the per-

centages of a firm's workers that resign in various age categories (e.g. 16–20 years; 21–25, 26–30; etc.). Normally the highest wastage rates are among young workers and those approaching the normal age of retirement. The lowest rates occur among middle aged people.

WEA. See WORKERS' EDUCATIONAL ASSOCIATION.

Weber, Max (1864 – 1920). A sociologist noted for his analysis of the theory of bureaucracy (qv). Weber distinguished three basic types of organisation: the 'charismatic' (members of which unquestioningly accept the leader's wishes and rules); the 'traditional', which is based on precedent and custom; and the 'rational–legal' i.e. the bureaucracy.

Wechsler Adult Intelligence Test. An intelligence test devised in the 1940s and intended to overcome the biases introduced by IQ tests through the requirement of such tests that test subjects be able to read (which means that tests necessarily assess linguistic ability to some extent). Hence the tests included picture arrangement tasks, block design, object assembly and similar non-linguistic assignments.

week of employment. For the purposes of UK employment legislation, Sunday until the following Saturday. Thus, a period of employment from (say) Wednesday until the Tuesday of next week does not count as a full week of employment.

week's pay. The *gross* weekly pay of an employee that applies to the computation of a redundancy payment (qv) or a basic award (qv) following a worker's successful unfair dismissal (qv) action. A week's pay comprises the employee's basic wage plus normal bonus and merit payments and compulsory (but not voluntary) overtime.

WEEP. See WORK EXPERIENCE ON EMPLOYERS' PREMISES PROGRAMME.

weighted application blank. A form used to collect biodata (qv). The questions asked are designed to gather information relevant to what is already known about workers who exhibit low labour turnover and high productivity, e.g. that they live locally, have a telephone, are married with no children, are over 30, have more than 12 years' education, etc.

Weiner hypothesis. Martin Weiner's proposition that from the 1850s onwards, British families that benefited from industry consciously chose to have their children educated in the arts, the humanities, the traditional professions such as law and medicine, and not in technology. This, he asserts, created a social climate hostile to industrial management which led to the emergence of an education system fundamentally opposed to the teaching of technical and vocational subjects.

welfare services. *Ex gratia* assistance provided by firms to employees as a fringe benefit. Examples include bereavement and retirement counselling, recreational facilities, help with housing or transport, legal advice, occupational health screening, benevolent funds and rehabilitation schemes for injured workers.

white collar crime. Crime conducted by business men and women (often people with good jobs carrying high salaries). Examples are fraudulent misrepresentation, embezzlement (qv), and insider dealing.

white collar workers. Clerical, technical and administrative employees, as opposed to 'blue collar' manual workers.

white collar unionism. Membership of independent trade unions (qv) by white collar workers (qv). Bank employees', teachers' and civil servants' unions are examples of white collar trade unions.

white knight. A third party approached by the target of an attempted hostile takeover and invited to purchase a majority shareholding in the target company to enable it to avoid falling into the hands of an unwelcome predator.

Whitley committee. A government-sponsored committee which in 1917 advocated industry wide (rather than plant level) collective bargaining and the establishment of 'Joint Industrial Councils'. 'Whitley Councils' were set up for the Civil Service in 1919 and for a handful of public sector service industries thereafter. However, they failed to achieve popularity in the private sector.

whiz kid, organisational. A term of abuse occasionally used to describe a recently appointed junior manager who attracts the favourable attention of senior executives and then ruthlessly pursues his or her own career without considering the consequences of his or her actions for other people.

whole learning. A learning (qv) experience in which all aspects of a topic or procedure are learned jointly at the same time. This enables the learner to see the relevance and overall context of the materials to be learned, but is not suitable for voluminous and/or complex topics. *See* LEARNING IN PARTS; WHOLE TRAINING METHOD.

whole training method. A training technique whereby the trainee attempts to absorb all aspects of a job simultaneously. This contrasts with the majority of alternative approaches to training, which utilise step-by-step instruction that transmits information in small and independent units. *See* WHOLE LEARNING.

Wider Opportunities Training Programme. An MSC (qv) sponsored scheme intended to help unemployed adults improve their basic skills. It was eventually incorporated into the employment training (qv) programme.

widowed mother's allowance. State benefit payable to a widow whose deceased husband satisfied certain National Insurance (qv) contribution conditions and (i) has children under 19 years of age for whom child benefit is payable or (ii) is expecting the late husband's child.

widow's allowance. *See* WIDOW'S PAYMENT.

widow's benefits, termination of. The rule that all widow's benefits cease on the death of the widow, on her remarriage or her living with a man as his wife.

widows, National Insurance and. *See* CERTIFICATE OF REDUCED LIABILITY.

widow's payment. A single lump sum social security payment to widows bereaved after 11 April 1988. This replaced 'Widow's Allowance', which was a weekly payment for the first 26 weeks of widowhood. Claimants must be under 60, or over 60 provided the late husband was (i) under 65 when he died or (ii) over 65 but not entitled to a retirement pension.

widow's pension. State benefit payable to widows who are aged 45 or more when their husband die, provided (i) their husbands satisfied certain National Insurance contribution conditions, and (ii) they do not receive widowed mother's allowance (qv). The weekly amount depends on the widow's age at the time of her bereavement.

wild cat strike. An unofficial (qv) strike called vexatiously and without notice or any serious attempt to negotiate a settlement to the dispute.

WIPO. See MADRID PROTOCOL.

WIS. See WOMEN'S INFORMATION SERVICE.

WITA. The acronym for the Water Industries Training Association.

withdrawal. Excessive introspection caused by a person's rejection of the culture, norms (qv) and internal structures of the organisation in which he or she operates.

without prejudice communication. A means for making a written offer of compensation in a legal dispute without the offer being taken to represent an admission of guilt by the person initiating the communication. The words 'without prejudice' are prominently displayed across the letter head. Thereafter the letter cannot normally be produced as evidence in a Court action connected with the dispute. See WITHOUT PREJUDICE OFFER.

without prejudice offer. An offer to pay compensation to a legal adversary (e.g. an employee claiming unfair dismissal) without accepting any legal liability for the events leading up to the offer. Without prejudice payments are sometimes made to avoid the costs and inconveniences of litigation, even though the party making the payment does not believe it was in the wrong. See WITHOUT PREJUDICE COMMUNICATION.

Women's Information Service (WIS). An EC organisation established to promote the equality of women within Community states. It produces a multilingual newsletter with information and comment on EC employment policies of special interest to female workers.

wonder woman syndrome. Health and emotional problems resulting from stress (qv) and overwork by women managers who attempt simultaneously to run a home and family *and* pursue a demanding career.

Woodward, Joan (1916–1971). A management theorist who argued that the type of technology used in production was a major determinant of the suitabilities of various forms of organisation structure for manufacturing firms. According to Woodward, rigid and formal hierarchies with specialisation of functions and the division of labour were best for assembly line mass production, whereas participative and human relations approaches (qv) were appropriate for small batch production (qv) or production in a continuous flow (qv).

work. The expenditure of energy in order to attain a goal. It involves the completion of tasks and the assumption of responsibilities.

work-based learning, assessment of. Evaluation of a trainee's competencies as they relate to workplace situations. This needs to be criterion referenced (qv), performance based, and outcome led (qv). See WORKPLACE ASSESSMENT.

work ecology. The study of the effects of the spatial distribution of workers on their productivity, efficiency and ability to relate to their surroundings.

work estimation. Prediction of the times needed to complete tasks in situations where precise work measurement (qv) is not possible.

work ethic. The belief that work is a moral obligation and that work should occupy a central position in a person's life.

Work Experience on Employers' Premises (WEEP) Programme. A precursor to the Youth Training Scheme (qv).

work factor method. A technique of motion study (qv) which identified four basic variables affecting the time needed to perform an operation, namely: body member used, distance travelled, amount of manual control necessary and weight or resistance encountered.

work group. A collection of two or more people at work with a common purpose. Work groups may be created by management to perform specific functions, or can emerge naturally by themselves. See PRIMARY GROUP; FORMAL GROUP.

work inhibition, Freudian theory of. According to the psychologist Sigmund Freud, impaired work performance caused by a sense of personal inadequacy rooted in neurotic disorders. It results in fatigue, job dissatisfaction, giddiness and somatic illness. Freud and his followers suggested that work inhibition commonly results from the failure of an individual's family adequately to prepare the person for the childhood transition into school. This leads to disappointments and problems at school to which the individual reacts in certain (inhibited) ways. Confronted with disappointments and difficulties at work the same adult individual may respond in a similar manner.

work measurement. The assessment of times taken when completing tasks in order to reduce operating costs (especially labour costs) and improve management control. It seeks to ascertain how long jobs should take in normal circumstances. *See* RATING STANDARD; MOTION STUDY.

work overload. A source of stress (qv) arising from having to complete too much work, or work that is too difficult. The latter situation is called 'qualitative overload'. Work underload, conversely, occurs when an employee is not sufficiently challenged by his or her job.

work permits. Documents that need to be obtained from the Department of Employment by employers for named non-EC foreign and Commonwealth nationals for specific identified jobs in order that these individuals may work in the United Kingdom. Permits must be issued prior to the worker entering the country, and last for 12 months in the first instance. Normally, only workers between 23 and 54 are entitled to permits. Immigrants with at least one UK grandparent do not require a permit. Extensions of permits beyond 12 months are possible. After four years the worker can stay indefinitely and take any form of employment in any company. The prospective employer must demonstrate the need for the foreign worker, that no EC resident labour is available, and that attempts have been made to fill the vacancy locally.

work profiling system. A method of job analysis (qv) based on questionnaires issued to job occupants. The system analyses jobs according to: time spent on various tasks, importance of each task, work environment, organisational involvement and job autonomy. This information is used to generate person specifications (qv) describing the ideal candidates for different types of job.

work psychology. According to the British Psychological Society, those areas of psychology (qv) particularly concerned with industrial/vocational issues. Examples of relevant issues are employee selection, training and appraisal, ergonomics (qv), career choice and counselling (qv), job design (qv), employee attitudes and related matters.

Work Related Further Education (WRFE). Vocationally orientated courses offered by local authority further education colleges following the approval by a local Training and Enterprise Council (qv) (TEC) of a three-year plan for providing such courses submitted by the colleges' local education authority to the Training, Enterprise and Education Directorate (TEED) (qv).

work sample test. *See* ANALOGOUS TEST.

work station. A physical area consciously arranged to facilitate the completion of tasks, particularly tasks relating to word processing, computing, technical drawing, assembly of components, etc.

work study. The systematic and detailed analysis of work and the factors that cause and prevent increased efficiency. *See* WORK MEASUREMENT; METHOD STUDY; INDUSTRIAL ENGINEERING.

work to rule. A technique of industrial action (qv) in which employees refuse to undertake any duties not strictly covered by their contracts of employment. *See* GO SLOW.

work underload. *See* WORK OVERLOAD.

workaholics. Individuals who are addicted to work and who experience uncontrollable desires to work incessantly. Workaholism often results from anxiety (qv) or problems experienced in non-work related dimensions of a person's life, so that the affected individual turns to work in order to obtain feelings of security, usefulness, self confidence and personal worth. Workaholicism can be unhealthy, leading to excessive tiredness, isolation from society and family problems.

worker director. An employee elected by fellow workers to sit on the board of directors of a company. Worker directors are legally required on the supervisory boards (qv) of large businesses in several Continental European countries. *See* COMPANY LAW, FIFTH EC DRAFT DIRECTIVE ON.

Workers' Educational Association (WEA). A voluntary educational organisation which offers evening courses (usually in non-vocational subjects) for people in employment who do not possess academic qualifications.

working capital. Current assets (qv) less current liabilities (qv).

Workmen's Compensation Acts 1925–1945. Legislation which compelled employers to pay compensation to workers killed or disabled by industrial accidents or certain industrial diseases. The Acts were replaced by the National Insurance (Industrial Injuries) Act 1946 (qv) but continued to apply in relation to all claims where the accident or disease occurred prior to 5 July 1948.

Workmen's Compensation (Supplementation) Scheme 1982. A statute which increased the benefits payable to workers injured by industrial accidents or diseases occurring prior to 5 July 1948.

workplace agreements. *See* LOCAL COLLECTIVE BARGAINING.

workplace assessment. Assessment (qv) of an employee's performance at the place of work. This is not the same as work based assessment, which means the evaluation of a person's competencies 'relating to' work rather than actually at the workplace.

Works Councils. A means for involving employees in management decision making via regular meetings between management and employee representatives.

Works Councils, European Community proposals concerning. The European Commission's 1991 suggestions concerning compulsory management consultation with employees in large EC firms. Under the proposals, any business with more than a total of 1,000 workers and which employs at least 100 people in any two or more EC states would be obliged to establish Works Councils at the request of management or employee representatives.

Councils would meet at least once a year, and would have to be consulted about any management proposal with serious implications for workers' interests.

works manager. An executive responsible for the efficient running of the manufacturing activities of a business.

works of engineering construction. Notional factories (qv) concerned with railway construction, work on docks, harbours and canals, tunnelling, bridge-building, sewage work, road building and similar engineering works.

workspace premises. Units of floorspace in large open plan buildings that serve as premises for small businesses. Overheads and common services (telephone switchboard, conference rooms, photocopiers, etc.) are shared by the various occupants.

World Confederation of Labour. An international organisation formed in 1920 to represent the interests of trade unions in about 80 member countries. It is based in Brussels and came to be associated with unionism in non-communist states. *See* WORLD FEDERATION OF TRADE UNIONS.

World Federation of Trade Unions. An international organisation formed in 1945 to represent the interests of trade unions in about 50 member countries. It is based in Prague and came to be associated with unionism in communist states. *See* WORLD CONFEDERATION OF LABOUR.

WORM (Write Once Read Many Times). *See* CD-ROM.

WRFE. *See* WORK-RELATED FURTHER EDUCATION.

writing down allowances. *See* DEPRECIATION.

written statement of reasons for dismissal, employee's right to receive. The right conferred by the Employment Act 1989 (qv) of an employee with at least two years' continuous service to be given a written statement of the reasons for his or her dismissal. The statement must be supplied within 14 days of a formal request.

WRNAFE. The acronym for work-related non-advanced further education.

wrongful dismissal. Dismissal without sufficient notice or in breach of a clause in a worker's contract of employment (qv). Anyone may be wrongfully dismissed; there is no length of service requirement as is the case with unfair dismissal (qv). The aggrieved worker sues for damages to compensate for the loss incurred. Cases are heard by the conventional Courts and not by Industrial Tribunals (qv). A person wrongfully sacked has a duty to try to mitigate his or her loss, i.e. to look for another job.

wrongful dismissal, deductions from damages. Amounts deducted by Courts from the compensation payable to workers who win wrongful dismissal (qv) cases. Deductions apply to earnings from other employment during the period of notice the sacked employee was not given, tax and National Insurance contributions that would have been paid on worker's wages, plus unemployment benefit received while the person was out of work. *See* MITIGATION OF LOSS.

wrongful trading. Continuing to run a failing company when there is no reasonable chance of it not becoming insolvent. Members of a company guilty of wrongful trading can be held personally liable for its debts. Wrongful trading results from 'poor judgement', it is not fraud. *See* FRAUDULENT TRADING.

X

X-chart. A matrix diagram indicating the functional structure of a department. A list of all the duties performed within the department is written down the left-hand side of the diagram and a row of all department employees is written across the top. Crosses are then placed in the boxes that relate people to duties, hence showing who does what and the individuals who contribute most of the work to the department.

xenocentrism. The compulsive desire to become a member of reference groups (qv) to which one does not currently belong.

X-inefficiency. A term coined by H. Leibenstein to describe sub-optimal business performance caused by bad management and poor organisation.

Y

Yearbook of Labour Statistics. An annual publication of the International Labour Organisation (ILO) containing labour force statistics for the last ten years on more than 180 countries and regions.

yellow dog contracts. An abusive description of contracts of employment which require employees to promise not to join trade unions (qv). Nowadays such contracts have no legal effect.

Yes for Europe programme. An EC-funded project that provides for young people between the ages of 15 and 25 obtaining work experience of up to 18 months' duration in other EC countries.

YOP. *See* YOUTH OPPORTUNITIES PROGRAMME.

young person. For statutory employment purposes, someone between 16 and 18 years of age.

Youth Opportunities Programme (YOP). The precursor to the Youth Training Scheme. It provided work experience with an element of training for school leavers, and was financed by the European Community's Social Fund. YOP was superseded by the Youth Training Scheme (YTS) (qv) in 1982.

Youth Training (YT). The successor to the Youth Training Scheme (YTS). It is administered by Training and Enterprise Councils (TECs) (qv) and intended to equip trainees with a level II NCVQ qualification. There is no standard model for the delivery of YT; local TECs may modify the scheme to suit local requirements.

Youth Training Scheme (YTS). A national training scheme introduced in 1982 to find work for unemployed school-leavers. The latter were engaged by employers on an organised training programme which included a minimum amount of off-the-job training (qv) that was provided either by the employer or a college of further education. Trainees received a small weekly wage paid for by the government and financed partially from the European Social Fund. The scheme offered two years' training to 16-year-olds and one year's training to 17-year-olds.

YT. *See* YOUTH TRAINING.

YTS. *See* YOUTH TRAINING SCHEME.

Z

zero base budgeting. A budgeting method which assumes that no money whatsoever will be allocated to any given departmental budget at the start of each year. Hence, department heads must fully justify each and every annual demand for resources.

zero based management. An approach to business and administration that emphasises the need for straightforward policies, simple organisational systems and the elimination of all superfluous activities.

zero defects quality control. An approach to quality management (qv) which attempts to eliminate entirely all production errors and defective output, in contrast to specifying an acceptable proportion of defective items. Usually, zero defect production is feasible, but only at an extremely high financial cost.

zero sum bargaining. An industrial relations negotiating situation in which each party trades concessions to the extent that their total gains and losses add up to zero.

zero sum game. A situation in which one person's gain is another's loss, so that nobody 'wins' in the long term. Distributive negotiation (qv) is an example.

Ziegarnik effect. The proposition advanced by the psychologist B. Zeigarnik that individuals are more likely to remember the details of work that has been interrupted than work which was completed without incident and on time. Also, Ziegarnik alleged, employees experience greater job satisfaction (qv) if they are able to see and control an entire operational work cycle from start to finish.

zone of indifference. Psychological limits that individuals sometimes set in relation to the amount of authority they will accept from a superior. These limits might depend on a person's rank in an organisation, length of service, and the nature of the personal relationship between subordinate and boss.

zone of stability. According to A. Toffler, a personal relationship or organisational or institutional affiliation that provides an individual with relief from stress (qv).